macOS Monterey™

for
dummies®
A Wiley Brand

macOS Monterey™

by Bob LeVitus
Houston Chronicle "Dr. Mac" columnist

macOS Monterey™ For Dummies®

Published by: **John Wiley & Sons, Inc.,** 111 River Street, Hoboken, NJ 07030-5774, www.wiley.com

Copyright © 2022 by John Wiley & Sons, Inc., Hoboken, New Jersey

Published simultaneously in Canada

For general information on our other products and services, please contact our Customer Care Department within the U.S. at 877-762-2974, outside the U.S. at 317-572-3993, or fax 317-572-4002. For technical support, please visit https://hub.wiley.com/community/support/dummies.

Wiley publishes in a variety of print and electronic formats and by print-on-demand. Some material included with standard print versions of this book may not be included in e-books or in print-on-demand. If this book refers to media such as a CD or DVD that is not included in the version you purchased, you may download this material at http://booksupport.wiley.com. For more information about Wiley products, visit www.wiley.com.

Library of Congress Control Number: 2021946369

ISBN 978-1-119-83696-4 (pbk); ISBN 978-1-119-83713-8 (ebk); ISBN 978-1-119-83714-5 (ebk)

SKY10030786_102221

Contents at a Glance

Introduction 1

Part 1: macOS Basics 5
CHAPTER 1: macOS Monterey 101 (Prerequisites: None) 7
CHAPTER 2: Desktop and Windows and Menus (Oh My!) 23
CHAPTER 3: What's Up, Dock? 45
CHAPTER 4: Getting to Know Finder and Its Desktop 65
CHAPTER 5: Delving Even Deeper into Monterey's Desktop and Finder 97

Part 2: How Stuff Works 111
CHAPTER 6: Having It Your Way 113
CHAPTER 7: Opening and Saving Files 131
CHAPTER 8: File and Folder Management Made Easy 157
CHAPTER 9: Comprehending the macOS Clipboard 171

Part 3: Getting Things Done 177
CHAPTER 10: Five Terrific Time-Saving Tools 179
CHAPTER 11: Organizing Your Life 197
CHAPTER 12: Are You Siri-ous? 217
CHAPTER 13: Maps Are Where It's At 223
CHAPTER 14: Apps Born in iOS 235

Part 4: Getting Along with Others 247
CHAPTER 15: (Inter)Networking 249
CHAPTER 16: Dealing with People 261
CHAPTER 17: Communicating with Mail and Messages 271
CHAPTER 18: Sharing Your Mac and Liking It 293

Part 5: Getting Creative 323
CHAPTER 19: The Musical Mac 325
CHAPTER 20: The Multimedia Mac 341
CHAPTER 21: Words and Letters 353
CHAPTER 22: Publish or Perish: The Fail-Safe Guide to Printing 363

Part 6: Care and Feeding 377

CHAPTER 23: Features for the Way You Work 379

CHAPTER 24: Safety First: Backups and Other Security Issues 405

CHAPTER 25: Utility Chest 419

CHAPTER 26: Troubleshooting macOS 435

Part 7: The Part of Tens 445

CHAPTER 27: Ten Ways to Speed Up Your Mac Experience 447

CHAPTER 28: Ten Great Websites for Mac Freaks....................... 455

Index 461

Table of Contents

INTRODUCTION 1
    About This Book. 1
    Foolish Assumptions. 3
    Icons Used in This Book 3
    Beyond the Book 4
    Where to Go from Here 4

PART 1: MACOS BASICS 5

CHAPTER 1: macOS Monterey 101 (Prerequisites: None) 7
    Gnawing to the Core of macOS 8
    A Safety Net for the Absolute Beginner (or Any User) 10
        Turning the dang thing on 10
        What you should see on startup 11
        Shutting down properly 14
        A few things you should definitely not do with your Mac 15
        Point-and-click 101 16
    Not Just a Beatles Movie: Help and the Help Menu 18

CHAPTER 2: Desktop and Windows and Menus (Oh My!) 23
    Touring Finder and Its Desktop 24
    Anatomy of a Window 25
        Top o' the window to ya! 27
        A scroll new world 29
        (Hyper)active windows 30
    Dialog Dealie-Boppers 32
    Working with Windows 34
        Opening and closing windows 34
        Resizing windows and window panes 35
        Moving windows 35
        Shuffling windows 36
    Menu Basics 38
        The ever-changing menu bar 39
        Contextual (shortcut) menus: They're sooo contextual! 39
        Recognizing disabled options 41
        Navigating submenus 42
        Under the Apple menu tree 43
        Using keyboard shortcut commands 44

CHAPTER 3: What's Up, Dock? 45

A Quick Introduction to Your Dock 46
  The default icons of the dock 47
  Trash talkin' 49
  Opening application menus on the dock 51
  Reading dock icon body language 53
  Opening files from the dock 54
Customizing Your Dock 54
  Adding dock icons 54
  Removing an icon from the dock 57
  Resizing the dock 58
  What should you put on your dock? 58
  Setting your dock preferences 60

CHAPTER 4: Getting to Know Finder and Its Desktop 65

Introducing Finder and Its Minions: The Desktop and Icons 66
  Introducing the desktop 66
  Bellying up to the toolbar 68
  Figuring out what an icon is 71
  Identifying your Finder icons in the wild 72
Aliases Are Awesome! 73
  Creating aliases 75
  Deleting aliases 76
  Hunting down an alias's parent 76
The View(s) from a Window 76
  Moving through folders fast in Column view 77
  Perusing in Icon view 79
  Listless? Try viewing folders as a list 79
  Hangin' in the Gallery (view) 81
  What's next on the (View) menu? 82
Finder on the Menu 84
  The actual Finder menu 84
  Like a road map: The current folder's pop-up menu 87
  Going places with the Go menu 88
Customizing Finder Windows 90
  Adding folders to the sidebar 90
  Setting Finder preferences 90
Digging for Icon Data in the Info Window 93

CHAPTER 5: Delving Even Deeper into Monterey's Desktop and Finder 97

Cleaning Up Your Desktop Automatically with Stacks 97
  Managing your Stacks 100

Quick Actions: Now Playing All Over Monterey. 101
    Getting the most out of Markup 101
    Trimming video without launching an app 104
Do It Quicker with Finder Quick Actions .105
    Creating PDFs without launching an app. 105
    Creating custom Finder Quick Actions 106
Four More Cool Monterey Tricks. 107
    Shooting screens. 107
    Dynamic desktop images 109

PART 2: HOW STUFF WORKS 111

CHAPTER 6: **Having It Your Way** 113
Introducing System Preferences. 113
The Desktop & Screen Saver System Preferences Pane 115
    The Desktop tab. 116
    The Screen Saver tab 117
The General System Preferences Pane 118
Adjusting the Keyboard, Mouse, Trackpad, and Other
Hardware 121
    The Keyboard System Preferences pane. 122
    The Mouse System Preferences pane 126
    The Bluetooth System Preferences pane. 127
    The Trackpad System Preferences pane 127
The Sound System Preferences Pane. 129
    Changing sound effects 129
    Choosing output and input options 130

CHAPTER 7: **Opening and Saving Files** 131
A Quick Primer on Finding Files. 132
Understanding the macOS Folder Structure. 132
    Understanding nested folders. 134
    From the top: The Computer folder 135
    Peeking into the Applications folder. .136
    Visiting the Library folders 136
    Let it be: The System folder 137
    There's no place like Home 137
    Your personal library card 139
Saving Your Document Before It's Too Late 141
    Stepping through a basic save. 142
    Save As versus Duplicate: Different names for the
    same result. 148
Open, Sez Me 150
    With drag-and-drop. 152
    With a Quick Look 152

When your Mac can't open a file. 153
With the application of your choice 154

CHAPTER 8: **File and Folder Management Made Easy** 157
Organizing Your Stuff in Folders 157
Files versus folders 158
Organizing your stuff with subfolders 158
Creating new folders. 160
Navigating with spring-loaded folders 161
Smart folders 162
Shuffling Files and Folders 164
Moving files and folders 165
Selecting multiple icons 166
Playing the icon name game: Renaming icons 167
Renaming multiple icons at once 168
Compressing files 168
Getting rid of icons 168
The Incredible iCloud+ (and iCloud Drive) 169

CHAPTER 9: **Comprehending the macOS Clipboard** 171
Introducing the Clipboard 171
Copying Files and Folders. 173
Pasting from the Clipboard 175
Monterey's Universal Clipboard 175

PART 3: GETTING THINGS DONE 177
CHAPTER 10: **Five Terrific Time-Saving Tools** 179
With a Quick Look 180
Share and share alike with the Share menu 181
Slide into Slideshow (full-screen) mode 182
Spotlight on Finding Files and Folders Faster 183
Using the Find command 184
Using the Spotlight menu and its keyboard shortcut 186
Blast Off with Mission Control. 187
The Mission Control pane: It's painless 187
Hot corners are hot stuff!. 189
Mission Control's Spaces from 30,000 feet (an overview). 190
Getting around in space(s). 192
Taking Control of Essential Settings 193
Launchpad: The Place for Applications 194

CHAPTER 11: **Organizing Your Life** 197
Keeping Track with Calendar. 198
Navigating Calendar views. 198
Creating calendars. 199

Deleting a calendar 200
Creating and managing events 201
Reminders: Protection Against Forgetting. 203
Getting started with Reminders 204
To do or not to do: Setting reminders .205
Sharing lists and assigning reminders .206
Everything You Need to Know about Notification Center 207
Tweaking Notification settings. 207
Widget management 101 209
Using Notification Center 210
Getting focused 210
Use Notes for Making Notes 211
Take a Quick Note with Quick Note 215
Tracking Productivity with Screen Time 215

CHAPTER 12: **Are You Siri-ous?** 217
What Siri Can Do for You 217
Working with Siri 219
Making Siri Your Own 220

CHAPTER 13: **Maps Are Where It's At** 223
Finding Your Current Location with Maps. .223
Finding a Person, Place, or Thing 224
Views, Zooms, and Pans. 225
Maps and Contacts 227
Time-saving Map Tools: Favorites, Guides, and Recents. 228
Favorites 228
Guides 229
Recents 230
Smart Map Tricks. 230
Get route maps and driving directions. 230
Get walking directions 231
Get directions for public transportation 232
Get traffic info in real time. 232
Flyovers and look arounds. 232
Do more on the Info sheet. 233

CHAPTER 14: **Apps Born in iOS** 235
Taking Stock of the Market with Stocks 236
Adding and deleting stocks, funds, and indexes. 237
Details, details, details 237
Charting a course 238
Read All about It in News 239
What are your interests? 239
How News works. 240
Managing your news. 240

Recording Memos with Voice Memos 241

Recording a voice memo 241

Listening to a voice memo 242

Naming a voice memo 243

Trimming a voice memo. 243

Automating Repetitive Tasks with Shortcuts. 244

Controlling Lights, Locks, and More with Home 245

PART 4: GETTING ALONG WITH OTHERS .247

CHAPTER 15: **(Inter)Networking** 249

Getting Connected to the Internet 250

Your internet service provider and you 251

Plugging in your internet-connection settings 251

Browsing the Web with Safari 253

Owning your toolbar. 254

Using the Safari sidebar 255

Checking out Help Center 260

CHAPTER 16: **Dealing with People** 261

Collecting Your Contacts 261

Adding contacts. 262

Importing contacts from other programs .263

Creating a basic group 264

Setting up a smart group (based on contact criteria). 266

Deleting a group or smart group 266

Sync + Contacts = your contacts everywhere 267

Audio and Video Calls with FaceTime. 268

About SharePlay 269

CHAPTER 17: **Communicating with Mail and Messages** 271

Sending and Receiving Email with Mail 271

Setting Up Mail. 272

A quick overview of the toolbar. 272

Composing a new message 274

Sending email from the Contacts app 276

Checking your mail 278

Dealing with spam. 279

Mailboxes smart and plain. 280

Changing your preferences 282

Sign here, please 283

Mail rules rule 284

Take a (Quick) look and (Slide) show me some photos 286

Markup and Mail Drop 286

Finding and Listening to Podcasts with the Podcasts App 348
You're the Star with Photo Booth 349
Viewing and Converting Images and PDFs in Preview. 351

CHAPTER 21: Words and Letters 353
Processing Words with TextEdit 354
Creating and composing a document 354
Working with text 355
Adding graphics to documents 358
Font Mania 359
Types of fonts. 360
Managing your fonts with Font Book 360

**CHAPTER 22: Publish or Perish: The Fail-Safe Guide
to Printing** 363
Before Diving In 364
Ready: Connecting and Adding Your Printer. 364
Connecting your printer 365
Setting up a printer for the first time 365
One last thing: Printer sharing. 368
Set: Setting Up Your Document with Page Setup 368
Print: Printing with the Print Sheet. 370
Printing a document 370
Choosing among different printers 371
Choosing custom settings 371
Saving custom settings. 374
Preview and PDF Options. 374

PART 6: CARE AND FEEDING 377
CHAPTER 23: Features for the Way You Work. 379
Finally, a Dark Mode 380
App Shopping, Improved 381
Using Your iPhone as Your Mac's Camera or Scanner. 383
Talking and Listening to Your Mac 386
Keyboard System Preferences pane: You talk and
your Mac types. 386
Commanding your Mac by voice. 388
Listening to your Mac read your screen. .389
Automatic Automation 392
Script Editor app: Write and edit AppleScripts 392
Automator app: Automate almost anything 394
A Few More Useful Goodies. 396
Accessibility System Preferences pane: Make your Mac
more accessible. 396

Communicating with Messages. 288
    What the heck is an iMessage? 289
    Chit-chatting with Messages 289

CHAPTER 18: Sharing Your Mac and Liking It. 293

Introducing Networks and File Sharing 294
    Portrait of home office networking. 295
    Three ways to build a network 297
Setting Up File Sharing 299
Access and Permissions: Who Can Do What. 300
    Users and groups and guests 300
    Creating users 302
    macOS knows best: Folders shared by default. 306
    Sharing a folder or disk by setting permissions 307
    Useful settings for permissions. 311
    Unsharing a folder. 314
Connecting to a Shared Disk or Folder on a Remote Mac. 314
Changing Your Password 318
    Changing your account password on your Mac 319
    Changing the password of any account but your own
    on your Mac 319
More Types of Sharing 320
    Sharing a screen 320
    Sharing the internet 321
    And yet more ways to share 322

PART 5: GETTING CREATIVE 323

CHAPTER 19: The Musical Mac 325

Apple Music and iTunes Match Rock!. 326
Introducing Music (the App Formerly Known as iTunes). 327
Working with Media 330
    Adding songs 330
    Listening to Radio 332
All about Playlists. 334
    Creating a regular playlist 334
    Working with smart playlists 336
    Working with the Genius playlist. 337
    Burning a playlist to CD 338

CHAPTER 20: The Multimedia Mac 341

Playing Movies and Music in QuickTime Player 342
Watching TV 343
Using the Books App. 344
    Buying an e-book or audiobook 345
    Shopping for e-books without Apple 347

Battery and Energy Saver System Preferences panes: For energy conservation and sleep..........................398

Bluetooth System Preferences pane: Where Bluetooth lives 399

Ink System Preferences pane: Visible to pen-input tablet users only 400

Automatic Login in the Users & Groups System Preferences pane: Don't bother with the login screen 400

Allow your Apple Watch to unlock your Mac...................401

Boot Camp Assistant app: Run Windows on your Mac . . . really 401

AirPlay and AirPlay to Mac 402

Handoff..403

Universal Control..404

CHAPTER 24: Safety First: Backups and Other Security Issues
....405

Backing Up Is (Not) Hard to Do 406

Backing up with Monterey's excellent Time Machine 406

Backing up by using the manual, brute-force method 409

Backing up by using commercial backup software 410

Why You Need Two Sets of Backups 411

Non-Backup Security Concerns.................................412

About viruses and other malware.............................412

Install recommended software updates 414

Protecting Your Data from Prying Eyes 415

Blocking or limiting connections............................416

Locking down files with FileVault 416

Setting other options for security 417

CHAPTER 25: Utility Chest
.................................419

In the Applications and Utilities Folders........................419

Calculator 419

Activity Monitor 421

Disk Utility..422

Keychain Access...427

Passwords System Preferences pane.........................429

Migration Assistant 429

System Information...430

Terminal 430

Screenshot 431

The best keyboard shortcut to memorize 432

Monterey screen-shooting options...........................433

Monterey screen recording 434

CHAPTER 26: **Troubleshooting macOS** 435

About Startup Disks and Booting 435
Finding or creating a startup disk 436
They call it a prohibitory sign for a reason 436
Recovering with Recovery HD 438
Step 1: Run First Aid 438
Step 2: Safe boot into Safe mode 439
Step 3: Zapping the PRAM/NVRAM 440
Step 4: Reinstalling macOS. 441
Step 5: Things to try before taking your Mac in for repair 441
If Your Mac Crashes at Startup 442
Managing Storage 442

PART 7: THE PART OF TENS. 445

CHAPTER 27: **Ten Ways to Speed Up Your Mac Experience** 447

Use Those Keyboard Shortcuts. 447
Improve Your Typing Skills. 448
Try a Different Keyboard 449
Change Your Resolution 450
Purchase a Faster Mac 450
Add RAM 451
Add a Second Display 451
Use Your iPad as a Second Display. 452
Upgrade to a Solid-State Drive (SSD) 452
Get More Storage 453

CHAPTER 28: **Ten Great Websites for Mac Freaks** 455

The Mac Observer 456
Macworld 456
TidBITS 456
iMore. 457
AppleWorld.Today. 457
The Wirecutter 457
Apple Support 458
Other World Computing. 458
Apple's Refurbished and Clearance Store 459
Six Colors 459

INDEX. 461

Introduction

You made the right choice twice: macOS Monterey (version 12.0) and this book. Take a deep breath and get ready to have a rollicking good time. That's right. This is a computer book, but it's fun. What a concept! Whether you're brand-spanking new to the Mac or a grizzled Mac vet, I guarantee that reading this book to discover the ins and outs of macOS Monterey will make learning easy. If it weren't true, I couldn't say it right on the cover!

About This Book

This book's roots lie with my international best seller *Macintosh System 7.5 For Dummies,* an award-winning book so good that long-deceased Mac clone-maker Power Computing gave away a copy with every Mac clone it sold in the '90s (back when clones were a thing).

macOS Monterey For Dummies is the latest revision and has been, once again, completely updated for macOS Monterey. In other words, this edition combines all the old, familiar features of literally dozens of previous editions — but, as always, I've lovingly updated every word to reflect the latest from Apple and feedback from my readers. Speaking of which, if you have comments — good or bad — please email me at Monterey4Dummies@boblevitus.com!

Why write a *For Dummies* book about Monterey? Well, Monterey is a big, somewhat complicated personal-computer operating system. So, *macOS Monterey For Dummies,* a not-so-big, not-too-complicated book, shows you what Monterey is all about without boring you to tears or poking you with sharp objects.

In fact, I think you'll be so darned comfortable that I wanted the title to be *macOS Monterey Made Easy,* but the publishers wouldn't let me. Apparently, my publisher has rules, and using *Dummies* in this book's title is one of them.

And speaking of dummies — remember, that's just a word. I don't think you're a dummy at all — quite the opposite! My second choice for this book's title was *macOS Monterey For People Smart Enough to Know They Need This Book,* but you can just imagine what Wiley thought of that.

The book is chock-full of information and advice, explaining everything you need to know about macOS Monterey in language you can understand — along with time-saving tips, tricks, techniques, and step-by-step instructions, all served up in generous quantities.

Another rule we *Dummies* authors must follow is that our books cannot exceed a certain number of pages. (Brevity is the soul of wit, and all that.) So, while I wish I could have included some things that didn't fit, I feel confident you'll find what you need to know about using macOS Monterey in this book.

Still, a few things bear further looking into, such as these:

>> **Information about many of the applications (programs) that come with macOS Monterey:** An installation of macOS Monterey includes nearly 60 applications, mostly located in the Applications and Utilities folders. I'd love to walk you through each one of them, but that would have required a book a whole lot bigger, heavier, and more expensive than this one.

I brief you on the handful of bundled applications essential to using macOS Monterey — namely, Calendar, Contacts, Messages, Mail, Safari, Siri, TextEdit, and the like — as well as several important utilities you may need to know how to use someday.

>> **Information about Microsoft Office, Apple lifestyle and productivity apps (iMovie, Numbers, Pages, GarageBand, and so on), Adobe Photoshop, Quicken, and other third-party applications:** Okay, if all the gory details of all the bundled (read: *free)* macOS Monterey applications don't fit here, I think you'll understand why digging into third-party applications that cost extra was out of the question.

>> **Information about programming for the Mac:** This book is about *using* macOS Monterey, not writing code for it. Dozens of books — most of which are two or three times the size of this one — cover programming on the Mac.

Within this book, you may note that some web addresses break across two lines of text. If you're reading this book in print and want to visit one of these web pages, simply key in the web address exactly as it's noted in the text, pretending as though the line break doesn't exist. If you're reading this as an e-book, you've got it easy — just click the web address to be taken directly to the web page.

Foolish Assumptions

Although I know what happens when you make assumptions, I've made a few anyway.

First, I assume that you, gentle reader, know nothing about using macOS — beyond knowing what a Mac is, that you want to use macOS, that you want to understand macOS without having to digest an incomprehensible technical manual, and that you made the right choice by selecting this particular book. And so I do my best to explain each new concept in full and loving detail. Maybe that's foolish, but . . . that's how I roll.

Oh, and I also assume that you can read. If you can't, ignore this paragraph.

Icons Used in This Book

Little pictures (icons) appear off to the left side of the text throughout this book. Consider these icons miniature road signs, telling you a little something extra about the topic at hand. Here's what the different icons look like and what they all mean.

TIP

Look for Tip icons to find the juiciest morsels: shortcuts, tips, and undocumented secrets about Monterey. Try them all; impress your friends!

REMEMBER

When you see this icon, it means that this particular morsel is something that I think you should memorize (or at least write on your shirt cuff).

TECHNICAL STUFF

Put on your propeller-beanie hat and pocket protector; these parts include the truly geeky stuff. It's certainly not required reading, but it must be interesting or informative, or I wouldn't have wasted your time with it.

WARNING

Read these notes very, very, very carefully. (Did I say *very?*) Warning icons flag important cautionary information. The author and publisher won't be responsible if your Mac explodes or spews flaming parts because you ignored a Warning icon. Just kidding. Macs don't explode or spew these days. But I got your attention, didn't I?

NEW

Well, now, what could this icon possibly be about? Named by famous editorial consultant Mr. Obvious, this icon highlights things new and different in macOS Monterey.

Beyond the Book

In addition to what you're reading right now, this product also comes with a free access-anywhere cheat sheet that provides handy shortcuts for use with macOS Monterey, offers my backup recommendations, and more. To get this cheat sheet, simply go to www.dummies.com and type **macOS Monterey For Dummies Cheat Sheet** in the Search box.

Where to Go from Here

The first few chapters of this book are where I describe the basic things that you need to understand to operate your Mac effectively. If you're new to Macs and macOS Monterey, start there.

Although macOS Monterey looks slightly different from previous versions, it works the same as always (for the most part). So, the first part of the book presents concepts so basic that if you've been using a Mac for long, you might think you know it all — and okay, you might know some (or most) of it. But remember that not-so-old-timers need a solid foundation, too. So here's my advice: Skim through stuff you already know and you'll get to the better stuff sooner.

I would love to hear how this book worked for you. As mentioned, sending me your thoughts, platitudes, likes, dislikes, and comments will make me a happy author. Did this book work for you? What did you like? What didn't you like? What questions were unanswered? Did you want to know more (or less) about something?

I have received more than 100 suggestions about previous editions, many of which are incorporated here. So please (please!) keep the tradition alive and email me at Monterey4Dummies@boblevitus.com with your suggestions.

I appreciate your feedback, and I *try* to respond to all reasonably polite email within a few days.

So what are you waiting for? Go on and enjoy the book!

1
macOS Basics

IN THIS PART . . .

Find the most basic of basics, including how to turn on your Mac.

Make the dock work harder for you.

Get a gentle introduction to Finder and its desktop.

Find everything you need to know about Monterey's windows, icons, and menus (oh my)!

Get all the bad puns and wisecracks you've come to expect.

Discover a plethora of Finder tips and tricks to make life with Monterey even easier (and more fulfilling).

» **Turning your Mac on and off**

» **Getting to know the start-up process**

» **Avoiding major Mac mistakes**

» **Pointing, clicking, dragging, and other uses for your mouse**

» **Getting help from your Mac**

Chapter **1**

macOS Monterey 101 (Prerequisites: None)

C ongratulate yourself on choosing macOS Monterey version 12.0, also known as the 18th release of the venerable operating system formerly known as OS X (which was pronounced "oh-ess-ten"). Now, congratulate yourself again for making your Mac even easier to use, with hundreds of tweaks to help you do more work in less time, plus a user interface overhaul that once again affects almost every pixel on the screen.

In this chapter, I start at the very beginning and talk about macOS in mostly abstract terms; then I move on to explain what you need to know to use macOS Monterey successfully. A number of features I describe haven't changed in years (other than adopting the updated Monterey graphic look), so if you've been using macOS for a while, much of the information in this chapter may seem hauntingly familiar.

But if you decide to skip this chapter because you think you have all the new stuff figured out, I assure you that you'll miss at least a couple of things that Apple didn't bother to tell you.

Tantalized? Let's rock.

Gnawing to the Core of macOS

The operating system (that is, the *OS* part of *macOS*) is what makes your Mac a Mac. Without it, your Mac is nothing but a pile of silicon and circuits — no smarter than a toaster.

"So what does an operating system do?" you ask. Good question. The simple answer is that an OS controls the basic and most important functions of your computer. In the case of macOS and your Mac, the operating system

» Manages memory

» Controls how windows, icons, and menus work

» Keeps track of files

» Manages networking and security

» Does housekeeping (No kidding!)

Other forms of software, such as word processors and web browsers, rely on the OS to create and maintain the environment in which they work their magic. When you create a memo, for example, the word processor provides the tools for you to type and format the information and save it in a file. In the background, the OS is the muscle for the word processor, performing the following crucial functions:

» Providing the mechanism for drawing and moving the onscreen window in which you write the memo

» Keeping track of the file when you save it

» Helping the word processor create drop-down menus and dialogs for you to interact with

» Communicating with other programs

» And much, much more (stuff that only geeks could care about)

So, armed with a little background in operating systems, take a gander at the next section before you do anything else with your Mac.

One last thing: As I mention in this book's Introduction (I'm repeating it here in case you normally don't read introductions), macOS Monterey comes with nearly 60 applications in its Applications and Utilities folders. Although I'd love to tell you all about each and every one, I have only so many pages at my disposal.

THE MAC ADVANTAGE

As someone once told me, "Claiming that macOS is inferior to Windows because more people use Windows is like saying that all other restaurants serve food that's inferior to McDonald's."

We might be a minority, but Mac users have the best, most stable, most modern all-purpose operating system in the world, and here's why: Unix, on which macOS is based, is widely regarded as the best industrial-strength operating system on the planet. For now, just know that being based on Unix means that a Mac running macOS benefits from nearly four decades of continuous Unix development, which means less downtime. Being Unix-based also means getting far fewer viruses and encounters with malicious software. But perhaps the biggest advantage macOS has is that when an application crashes, it doesn't crash your entire computer, and you don't usually have to restart the computer to continue working.

By the way, since the advent of Intel-powered Macs more than a decade ago, you can run Windows natively also on any Mac powered by an Intel processor, as I describe in Chapter 23. Note that the opposite isn't true: You can run Windows on your Intel-based Mac if you care to, but you *cannot* run macOS on a Dell or HP or any other computer not made by Apple (at least not without serious hacking, which is probably illegal anyway).

In June 2020, Apple announced that the Mac will transition from Intel processors to Apple's custom silicon processors "to deliver industry-leading performance and powerful new technologies." The bad news is that Macs with Apple processors can't run Windows (or most other operating systems) natively. The good news is that Windows 10 on ARM Preview and Windows 11 (when released) already run on Macs with Apple processors under third-party virtualization software such as Parallels Desktop (www.parallels.com), and virtualization support will only get better in the future.

Please don't let that Unix or Windows stuff scare you. It's there if you want it, but if you don't want it or don't care (like most users, including yours truly), you'll rarely even know it's there. In fact, you'll rarely (if ever) see the word *Unix* or *Windows* again in this book. As far as you're concerned, Unix under the hood means your Mac will just run and run and run without crashing and crashing and crashing. As for Windows, your Mac can probably run it if you need it; otherwise, it's just another checklist item on the list of reasons Macs are better than PCs.

A Safety Net for the Absolute Beginner (or Any User)

In the following sections, I deal with the stuff that macOS Help doesn't cover — or doesn't cover in nearly enough detail. If you're a first-time Mac user, please, *please* read this section of the book carefully; it could save your life. Okay, okay, perhaps I'm being overly dramatic. What I mean to say is that reading this section could save your Mac or your sanity. Even if you're an experienced Mac user, you may want to read this section. Chances are you'll see at least a few things you've forgotten that will come in handy now that you've been reminded of them.

Turning the dang thing on

Okay. This is the big moment — turning on your Mac! Gaze at it longingly first, and say something cheesy, such as, "You're the most awesome computer I've ever known." If that doesn't turn on your Mac (and it probably won't), keep reading.

Apple, in its infinite wisdom, has manufactured Macs with power buttons on every conceivable surface: on the front, side, and back of the computer itself, and even on the keyboard and monitor.

So if you don't know how to turn on your Mac, don't feel bad; just look in the manual or booklet that came with your Mac. It's at least one thing that the documentation *always* covers.

You don't have that little booklet? Most Macs have the power button in the upper-right corner of the keyboard (notebooks), the back of the screen (iMacs), or the back of the enclosure (Mac Mini); it usually looks like the little circle thingy you see in the margin.

Don't bother choosing Help ⇨ macOS Help, which opens the Help Viewer program. It can't tell you where the switch is. Although the Help program is good for finding out a lot of things, the location of the power button isn't among them. If you haven't found the switch and turned on the Mac, of course, you can't access Help anyway. (D'oh!)

TIP

Launch the Books (formerly iBooks) app and click the Book Store icon (top left) to search its built-in store for the name of your Mac plus the word *Essentials* (for example, "MacBook Essentials," "iMac Essentials," or "MacBook Pro Essentials"). Click the Only Show Free Titles check box near the upper-right corner of the Books window, and grab the free Essentials e-book with your Mac's name, by Apple. At around 150 pages each, these booklets aren't in any way comprehensive, but they do include information you won't find elsewhere, including where to find the power button on your particular Mac.

What you should see on startup

When you finally do turn on your Mac, you set in motion a sophisticated and complex series of events that culminates in the loading of macOS and the appearance of the macOS desktop. After a small bit of whirring, buzzing, and flashing (meaning that the OS is loading), macOS first tests all your hardware — slots, ports, disks, random access memory (RAM), and so on. If everything passes, you'll see a tasteful whitish Apple logo in the middle of your screen, as shown in Figure 1-1.

FIGURE 1-1:
This is what you'll see if everything is fine and dandy when you turn on your Mac.

Here are the things that you might see when you power-up your Mac:

TIP

WARNING

>> **Login screen:** You might or might not see the macOS login screen. Here, you choose your user account, enter your name and password, and press Return or Enter (or click the little right-arrow-in-a-circle in the password field), and away you go.

If you don't want to type your name and password every time you start or restart your Mac (or even if you do), check out Chapter 23 for the scoop on how to turn the login screen on or off.

You should turn off the login screen only if you're confident you'll be the only one touching the machine. With the login screen disabled, your Mac and everything in it is completely available to anyone who turns it on, which is usually *not* a good thing. So I don't recommend turning off the login screen if your Mac is a laptop. And even desktop Mac users should think twice before turning it off.

Either way, the desktop soon materializes before your eyes. If you haven't customized, configured, or tinkered with your desktop, it should look pretty much like Figure 1-2. Now is a good time to take a moment for positive thoughts about the person who convinced you that you wanted a Mac. That person was right!

FIGURE 1-2:
The desktop after a brand-spanking-new installation of macOS Monterey.

REMEMBER

TIP

>> **Blue/black/gray screen of death:** If any of your hardware fails when it's tested, you may see a blue, black, or gray screen.

Some older Macs played the sound of a horrible car wreck instead of the chimes, complete with crying tires and busting glass. It was exceptionally unnerving, which might be why Apple doesn't use it anymore.

The fact that something went wrong is no reflection on your prowess as a Mac user. Something is broken, and your Mac may need repairs. If this is happening to you right now, check out Chapter 26 to try to get your Mac well again.

If your computer is under warranty, set up a Genius Bar appointment at your nearest Apple Store or dial 1-800-SOS-APPL, and a customer service person can tell you what to do. Before you do anything, though, skip ahead to Chapter 26. It's entirely possible that one of the suggestions there will get you back on track without your having to spend even a moment on hold.

>> **Prohibitory sign or flashing question mark in a folder:** Most users eventually encounter the prohibitory sign or flashing question mark in a folder (as shown in the margin). These icons mean that your Mac can't find a startup disk, hard drive, network server, or DVD-ROM containing a valid Mac operating system. See Chapter 26 for ways to ease your Mac's ills.

>> **Kernel panic:** You may occasionally see a block of text in several languages, including English, as shown in Figure 1-3. This means that your Mac has experienced a *kernel panic,* the most severe type of system crash. If you restart your Mac and see either message again, look in Chapter 26 for a myriad of possible cures for all kinds of ailments, including this one.

FIGURE 1-3:
If you're seeing
something like
this, things are
definitely not fine
and dandy.

How do you know which version of the macOS your computer has? Simple:

1. **Choose About This Mac from the menu (the menu with the symbol in the top-left corner of the menu bar).**

   A window pops up on your screen, as shown in Figure 1-4. The version you're running appears just below *macOS* near the top of the window. Version 12.0 is the release we know as *Monterey*.

   TECHNICAL STUFF

   If you're curious or just want to impress your friends, you might want to know that version 11 was Big Sur; version 10.15 was Catalina; 10.14 was Mojave; 10.13 was High Sierra; 10.12 was Sierra; 10.11 was El Capitan; 10.10 was Yosemite; 10.9 was Mavericks; 10.8 was Mountain Lion; 10.7 was Lion; 10.6 was Snow Leopard; 10.5 was Leopard; 10.4 was Tiger; 10.3 was Panther; 10.2 was Jaguar; 10.1 was Puma; and 10.0 was Cheetah.

2. **(Optional) Click the Overview, Displays, Storage, Support, or Resources tabs to see additional details about your Mac.**

3. **Click the System Report button to launch the System Information application and see even more details.**

   The System Information app shows you even more about your Mac, including bus speed, number of processors, caches, installed memory, networking, storage devices, and much more. You can find more about this useful program in Chapter 25.

FIGURE 1-4:
See which version
of macOS you're
running.

Shutting down properly

Turning off the power without shutting down your Mac properly is one of the worst things you can do to your poor Mac. Shutting down your Mac improperly can really screw up your hard or solid-state drive, scramble the contents of your most important files, or both.

WARNING

If a thunderstorm is rumbling nearby, or you're unfortunate enough to have rolling blackouts where you live, you may really want to shut down your Mac and unplug it from the wall. (See the next section, where I briefly discuss lightning and your Mac.) If it's a laptop, you can just disconnect it from its charging cable and continue using it if you like.

To turn off your Mac, always use the Shut Down command from the (Apple) menu and then click the Shut Down button in the Are You Sure You Want to Shut Down Your Computer Now? dialog.

TIP

When the Shut Down button (or any button, for that matter) is highlighted, you can activate it by pressing the Return or Enter key rather than clicking it.

ETERNALLY YOURS . . . *NOW*

macOS is designed so that you never have to shut it down. You can configure it to sleep after a specified period of inactivity. (See Chapter 23 for more info on the Energy Saver and Battery System Preferences panes.) If you do so, your Mac will consume very little electricity when it's sleeping and will usually be ready to use (when you press any key or click the mouse) in a few seconds. On the other hand, if you're not going to be using your Mac for a few days, you might want to shut it down anyway.

Note: If you leave your Mac on constantly, and you're gone when a lightning storm or rolling blackout hits, your Mac might get hit by a power surge or worse. So be sure you have adequate protection — say, a decent surge protector designed for computers — if you decide to leave your Mac on and unattended for long periods. See the section "A few things you should definitely not do with your Mac," elsewhere in this chapter, for more info on lightning and your Mac.

One last thing: If your Mac is a laptop and will be enclosed in a bag or briefcase for more than a few hours, turn it off. Otherwise, it could overheat — even in Sleep mode.

The Are You Sure You Want to Shut Down Your Computer Now? dialog sports a check box option: Reopen Windows When Logging Back In. If you select this check box, your Mac will start back up with the same windows (and applications) that were open when you shut down (or restarted). I think that's pretty darn sweet, but you can clear the check box and disable this option if that's not what you want!

Most Mac users have been forced to shut down improperly more than once without anything horrible happening, of course — but don't be lulled into a false sense of security. Break the rules one time too many (or under the wrong circumstances), and your most important files could be toast. The *only* time you should turn off your Mac without shutting down properly is when your screen is completely frozen or when your system crashed due to a kernel panic and you've already tried everything else. (See Chapter 26 for a list of those "everything elses.") A stubborn crash doesn't happen often — and less often under macOS than ever before — but when it does, forcing your Mac to turn off and then back on might be the only solution.

A few things you should definitely not do with your Mac

In this section, I cover the bad stuff that can happen to your computer if you do the wrong things with it. If something bad has already happened to you . . . . I know, I'm beginning to sound like a broken record, but see Chapter 26.

>> **Don't unplug your desktop Mac when it's turned on.** Very bad things can happen, such as having your OS break. See the preceding section, where I discuss shutting down your system properly.

Note that this warning doesn't apply to laptops as long as their battery is at least partially charged. As long as there's enough juice in the battery to power your Mac, you can connect and disconnect its power adapter to your heart's content.

>> **Don't use your Mac when lightning is near.** Here's a simple life equation for you: Mac + lightning = dead Mac. 'Nuff said. Oh, and don't place much faith in inexpensive surge protectors. A good jolt of lightning will fry the surge protector and everything plugged into it, including computers, modems, printers, and hubs. Some surge protectors can withstand some lightning strikes, but those warriors aren't the cheapies that you buy at your local computer emporium. Unplugging your Mac from the wall during electrical storms is safer and less expensive. (Don't forget to unplug your external routers, network hubs, printers, and other hardware that plugs into the wall as well; lightning can fry them, too.)

For laptops, disconnect the power adapter and all other cables because whatever those cables are connected to could fry — and fry your laptop right along with it. After you do that, you can use your laptop during a storm if you care to. Just make sure that it's 100 percent wireless and cableless when you do.

>> **Don't jostle, bump, shake, kick, throw, dribble, or punt your Mac, especially while it's running.** Older Macs contain a hard drive that spins at 5,200 revolutions per minute (rpm) or more. A jolt to a hard drive while it's reading or writing a file can cause the head to crash into the disk, which can render many — or all — files on it unrecoverable. Ouch!

TIP

Don't think you're exempt if your Mac uses a solid-state drive with no moving parts. A good bump to your Mac could damage other components. Treat your Mac like it's a carton of eggs, and you'll never be sorry.

>> **Don't forget to back up your data!** If the files on your hard drive mean anything to you, you must back up. Not maybe. *Must.* Even if your most important file is your last saved game of Bejeweled, you still need to back up your files. Fortunately, macOS includes an awesome backup utility called Time Machine. (Unfortunately, you need an external hard drive to take advantage of it.) So I beg you: Please read Chapter 24 now, and find out how to back up before something horrible happens to your valuable data!

TIP

I *strongly* recommend that you read Chapter 24 sooner rather than later — preferably before you do any significant work on your Mac. Dr. Mac says, "There are only two kinds of Mac users: Those who have lost data and those who will." Which kind do you want to be?

>> **Don't kiss your monitor while wearing stuff on your lips.** For obvious reasons!

WARNING

Definitely do not use household window cleaners or paper towels on your screen. Either one can harm it. Instead, use a soft clean cloth (preferably microfiber), and if you're going to use a liquid or spray, make sure it's specifically designed not to harm computer displays. Finally, only spray the cleaner onto a *cloth;* never spray anything directly onto the screen.

Point-and-click 101

Are you new to the Mac? Just figuring out how to move the mouse around? Now is a good time to go over some fundamental stuff that you need to know for just about everything you'll be doing on the Mac. Spend a few minutes reading this section, and soon you'll be clicking, double-clicking, pressing, and pointing all over the place. If you think you have the whole mousing thing pretty much figured out, feel free to skip this section. I'll catch you on the other side.

Still with me? Good. Now for some basic terminology:

>> **Point:** Before you can click or press anything, you have to *point* to it. Place your hand on your mouse, and move it so that the cursor arrow is over the object you want — such as on top of an icon or a button.

If you're using a trackpad, slide your finger lightly across the pad until the cursor arrow is over the object you want.

>> **Click:** Also called *single click.* Use your index finger to push the mouse button (or the left mouse button if your mouse has more than one) all the way down and then let go so that the button (usually) produces a satisfying clicking sound. (If you have one of the optical Apple mice, you push the whole thing down to click.) Use a single click to highlight an icon, press a button, or activate a check box or window.

In other words, first you point and then you click — *point and click,* in computer lingo.

If you're using a trackpad, press down on it to click.

>> **Double-click:** *Click twice* in rapid succession. With a little practice, you can perfect this technique in no time. Use a double-click to open a folder or to launch a file or application.

Trackpad users: Press down on the pad two times in rapid succession.

>> **Secondary-click:** Hold down the Control key while single-clicking. (Also called *Control-click* or *right-click*.)

Trackpad users can either hold down the Control key while pressing down on the trackpad with one finger, or tap the trackpad with two fingers without holding down the Control key.

If tapping your trackpad with two fingers didn't bring up a little menu, check your Trackpad System Preferences pane (see Chapter 6).

Control-clicking displays a *contextual* menu (also known as a *shortcut menu)*. In fact, if you're blessed with a two-or-more-button mouse (such as the Apple Magic Mouse), you can right-click and avoid having to hold down the Control key. If it doesn't work, you can enable this feature in the Mouse System Preferences pane.)

>> **Drag:** *Dragging* something usually means you have to click it first and hold down the mouse or trackpad button. Then you move the mouse on your desk or mouse pad (or your finger on the trackpad) so that the cursor and whatever you select moves across the screen. The combination of holding down the button and dragging the mouse is usually referred to as *clicking and dragging.*

>> **Wiggle (or jiggle):** This welcome improvement is awesome when you lose track of the pointer on your screen. Just wiggle your mouse back and forth (or jiggle your finger back and forth on the trackpad) for a few seconds and the pointer will magically get much bigger, making it easier to see on the screen. And, of course, when you stop wiggling or jiggling, the pointer returns to its normal size.

>> **Choosing an item from a menu:** To get to macOS menu commands, you must first open a menu and then choose the option you want. Point at the name of the menu you want with your cursor, press the mouse button, and then drag downward until you select the command you want. When the command is highlighted, finish selecting by letting go of the mouse button.

TIP

If you're a longtime Mac user, you probably hold down the mouse button the whole time between clicking the name of the menu and selecting the command you want. You can still do it that way, but you can also click the menu name to open it, release the mouse button, point at the item you want to select, *and then click again.* In other words, macOS menus stay open after you click their names, even if you're not holding down the mouse button. After you click a menu's name to open it, you can even type the first letter (or letters) of the item to select it and then execute that item by pressing the spacebar or the Return key. Furthermore, menus remain open until you click something else.

Go ahead and give it a try . . . I'll wait.

REMEMBER

The terms given in the preceding list apply to all Mac laptop, desktop, and pro systems. If you use a trackpad with your Mac, you'll want to add a few more terms — such as *tap, swipe, rotate, pinch,* and *spread* — to your lexicon. You can read all about them in Chapters 2 and 13.

Not Just a Beatles Movie: Help and the Help Menu

One of the best features of all Macs is the excellent built-in help, and macOS Monterey doesn't cheat you on that legacy: This system has online help in abundance. When you have a question about how to do something, Help Center is the first place you should visit (after this book, of course).

Clicking the Help menu reveals the Search field at the top of the menu and the macOS Help item. Choosing macOS Help opens the window shown in Figure 1-5.

Table of contents icon

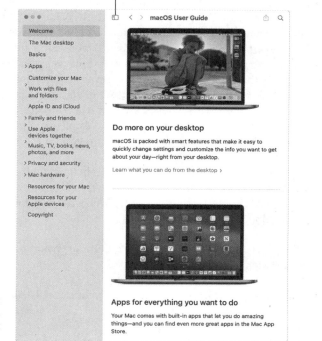

FIGURE 1-5:
Mac Help is
nothing if not
helpful.

TIP

Although the keyboard shortcut for Help no longer appears on the Help menu, the same shortcut as always, Shift+⌘+?, still opens Help.

You can browse Help by clicking a topic in the table of contents and then clicking a subtopic. If you don't see the table of contents, click the Table of contents icon, labeled in Figure 1-5.

To search Mac Help, simply type a word or phrase in either Search field — the one in the Help menu itself or the one near the top of the Help window on the right side — and then press Return. In a few seconds, your Mac provides one or more articles to read, which (theoretically) are related to your question. As long as your Mac is connected to the internet, search results include articles from the Apple online support database.

Although you don't have to be connected to the internet to use Mac Help, you do need an internet connection to get the most out of it. (Chapter 15 can help you set up an internet connection, if you don't have one.) That's because macOS installs only certain help articles on your hard drive. If you ask a question that those articles don't answer, Mac Help connects to the Apple website and downloads the answer (assuming that you have an active internet connection). These answers appear when you click Show All near the bottom of some article lists. Click one of these entries, and Help Viewer retrieves the text over the internet. This is sometimes inconvenient but also quite smart, because Apple can update the Help system at any time without requiring any action from you.

Furthermore, after you ask a question and Mac Help has grabbed the answer from the Apple website, the answer remains on your hard drive forever. If you ask for it again — even at a later date — your computer won't have to download it from the Apple website again.

If you see a See More Results on the Web link, you can click it to launch Safari and perform a web search for the phrase you typed.

macOS also has a cool feature I like to call *automatic visual help cues.* Here's how they work:

1. **In the Help menu's Search field, type a word or phrase.**

2. **Select any item that has a menu icon to its left (such as the items with *Trash* in their names in Figure 1-6).**

   The automatic visual cue — an arrow — appears, pointing at that command in the appropriate menu.

Finally, don't forget that most apps have their own Help systems, so if you want general help with your Mac, you need to first click the Finder icon in the dock, click the desktop, or use the app-switching shortcut ⌘+Tab to activate Finder. Only then can you choose Mac Help from Finder's Help menu.

| Finder | File | Edit | View | Go | Windo | Help |

New Finder Window ⌘N
New Folder ⇧⌘N
New Folder with "Move to Trash" ⌃⌘N
New Smart Folder
New Tab ⌘T
Open ⌘O
Open With >
Close Window ⌘W

Get Info ⌘I
Rename
Compress
Duplicate ⌘D
Make Alias ⌃⌘A
Quick Look ⌘Y
Print ⌘P

Share >

Show Original ⌘R
Add to Dock ⌃⇧⌘T

Move to Trash ⌘⌫
Eject ⌘E

○ ○ ○ ○ ○ ○ ○

Tags...

Find ⌘F

trash ⊗

Menu Items
▣ Empty Trash...
▣ Move to Trash

Help Topics
⑦ If the Trash contains recovered files on Mac
⑦ Change Finder preferences on Mac
⑦ Use the Dock on Mac
⑦ How Apple helps protect the environment
⑦ Delete files and folders on Mac
⑦ What's it called on my Mac?
⑦ If your Mac restarts and a message appears
⑦ Change the alert sounds on Mac
⑦ Create and use your own input source on Mac
⑦ What is malware on Mac?
⑦ Show All Help Topics

Chapter **2**

Desktop and Windows and Menus (Oh My!)

This chapter introduces important features of macOS, starting with the first things you see when you log in: Finder and its desktop. After a quick look around the desktop, you get a look into two of its most useful features: windows and menus.

Windows are (and have always been) an integral part of using your Mac. In fact, Macs had windows before Microsoft Windows was invented.

Windows in Finder (or, as a Windows user might say, "on the desktop") show you the contents of the hard drive, optical drive, flash (thumb) drive, network drive, disk image, and folder icons. Windows in applications do many things. The point is that windows are part of what makes your Mac a Mac; knowing how they work — and how to use them — is essential.

Menus are another quintessential part of the Mac experience. The latter part of this chapter starts you out with a few menu basics. As needed, I direct you to other parts of the book for greater detail. So relax and don't worry. By the end of this chapter, you'll be ready to work with windows and menus in any application that uses them (and most applications, games excluded, do).

Touring Finder and Its Desktop

Finder is the program that creates the desktop, keeps track of your files and folders, and is always running. Just about everything you do on your Mac begins and ends with Finder. It's where you manage files, store documents, launch programs, and much more. If you ever expect to master your Mac, the first step is to master Finder and desktop.

Finder is the center of your macOS experience, so before I go any further, here's a quick description of its most prominent features:

>> **Desktop:** The *desktop* is the area behind the windows and the dock. In macOS 12.0 the default desktop picture is a colorful abstract graphic.

It's also where your startup disk icon (ordinarily) lives.

TIP

If you don't see a disk icon on the desktop, never fear — you learn how to enable this behavior in Chapter 4.

The desktop isn't a window, yet it acts like one. Like a folder or disk window, the desktop can contain icons. But unlike most windows, which require a bit of navigation to get to, the desktop is always there behind any open windows, making it a great place for icons you use a lot, such as oft-used folders, applications, or documents.

TECHNICAL STUFF

Some folks use the terms *desktop* and *Finder* interchangeably to refer to the total Mac environment you see after you log in — the icons, windows, menus, and all that other cool stuff. Just to make things confusing, the background you see on your screen — the picture behind your hard drive icon and your open windows — is *also* called the desktop. In this book, I refer to the application you use when the desktop is showing as *Finder*. When I say *desktop,* I'm talking about the picture background behind your windows and the dock, which you can use as a storage place for icons if you like.

Don't panic. The desktop metaphor used by Monterey will become crystal clear in upcoming pages and chapters.

>> **Dock:** The dock is Finder's main navigation shortcut tool. It makes getting to frequently used icons easy, even when you have a screen full of windows. Plus, it's extremely customizable, as you find out in Chapter 3.

>> **Icons:** Icons are the little pictures you see in folder and disk windows and on your desktop. Icons represent the things you work with on your Mac, such as applications (programs), documents, folders, utilities, and more.

>> **Windows:** Opening most icons (by double-clicking them) makes a window appear. Windows in Finder show you the contents of disk drive and folder icons; windows in applications usually show the contents of documents. In the sections that follow, you can find the full scoop on Monterey windows.

>> **Menus:** Menus let you choose to do things, such as create new folders; duplicate files; and cut, copy, or paste text. I introduce menu basics later in this chapter in the "Menu Basics" section; you find details about working with menus for specific tasks throughout this book.

Whereas this chapter offers a basic introduction to Finder and desktop, Chapter 8 explains in detail how to navigate and manage your files in Finder. But before you start using Finder, it helps to know the basics of working with windows and menus; if these Mac features are new to you, I suggest that you read this entire chapter now and pay special attention to Chapter 8 later.

Anatomy of a Window

Windows are a ubiquitous part of using a Mac. When you open a folder, you see a window. When you write a letter, the document that you're working on appears in a window. When you browse the internet, web pages appear in a window . . . and so on.

For the most part, windows are windows from program to program. You'll probably notice that some programs (Adobe Photoshop or Microsoft Word, for example) take liberties with windows by adding features such as custom toolbars or textual information (such as zoom percentage or file size) around the edges of the document window and in toolbars.

Don't let it bug you; that extra fluff is just window dressing (pun intended). Maintaining the window metaphor, many information windows display different kinds of information in different *panes,* or discrete sections within the window.

When you finish this chapter, which focuses exclusively on macOS Finder windows, you'll know how to use most windows in most applications. And so, without further ado, the following list gives you a look at the main features of a typical Finder window (as shown in Figure 2-1). I discuss these features in greater detail in later sections of this chapter.

TIP

If your windows don't look exactly like Figure 2-1, don't be concerned. You can make your windows look and feel any way you like. As I explain later in the "Working with Windows" section, moving and resizing windows are easy tasks.

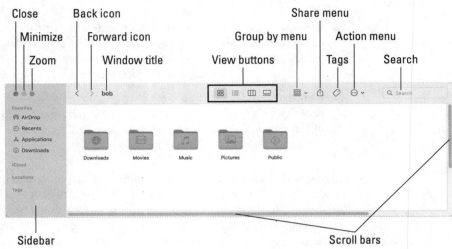

Close
Minimize
Zoom
Back icon
Forward icon
Window title
Share menu
Group by menu
View buttons
Action menu
Tags
Search

FIGURE 2-1:
A typical Finder
window in macOS
Monterey.

Sidebar

Scroll bars

Meanwhile, here's what you see on the toolbar:

» **Close, Minimize, and Zoom buttons:** Shut 'em, shrink 'em, and grow 'em.

» **View icons:** Choose among four exciting views of your window: Icon, List, Column, and Gallery. Find out more about views in Chapter 4.

» **Group By menu:** Click this little doohickey to group this window's icons by Name, Kind, Application, Date Modified, Date Created, Date Last Opened, Date Added, Size, or Tags. Or, of course, by None, which is the default.

» **Action menu:** This icon is really a pop-up menu of commands you can apply to currently selected items in the Finder window or on the desktop. It's nearly the same list of commands you'll find in the contextual (shortcut) menu when you right-click or Control-click that item or items.

TIP

Note that some menu icons and items in these menus aren't available (appear dimmed) until you select one or more icons in the Finder window. If nothing happens when you click a toolbar icon, click a file or folder icon to select it and try again.

» **Window title:** Shows the name of the window (*bob* in Figure 2-1).

TIP

⌘-click (or Control-click) the window title to see a pop-up menu with the complete path to this folder. (Try it now.) This tip applies to most windows you'll encounter, not just Finder windows. So ⌘- or Control-click a window's title (a right-click or two-fingered tap on a trackpad will work, too), and you'll (usually) see the path to its enclosing folder on your disk, though some third-party apps don't follow this convention.

To see the path from your hard or solid-state drive to the active window, choose View ⇨ Show Path Bar. The path will appear at the bottom of all Finder windows until you choose View ⇨ Hide Path Bar.

>> **Share menu:** Another icon that's a menu. Click it to share selected files or folders via Mail, Messages, AirDrop, or Notes. Or click More to add other commands to your Share menu, such as Add (the selected item) to Photos or Reminders.

>> **Tags menu:** Yet another menu; click it to assign a tag to the selected files or folders.

>> **Search:** Click the magnifying glass icon and then type a string of characters in the field that appears. Monterey's Spotlight search feature digs into your system to find items that match by filename or document contents (yes, it will find words within most documents).

>> **Scroll bars:** Use the scroll bars for moving around a window.

>> **Sidebar:** Frequently used items live here.

>> **Forward and Back icons:** These icons take you to the next or previous folder, respectively, displayed in this particular window. The first time you open a window, neither icon is active; in Figure 2-1, only the Back icon is active.

As you navigate from folder to folder, these icons remember your breadcrumb trail so you can quickly traverse backward or forward, window by window. You can also navigate backward or forward from the keyboard by using the shortcuts ⌘ +[for Back and ⌘ +] for Forward.

The Forward and Back icons remember only the other folders you've visited in *that* tab. If you've set a Finder preference so that folders always open in a new window — or if you forced a folder to open in a new window, which I describe in a bit — the Forward and Back icons won't work.

Top o' the window to ya!

Take a gander at the top of a window — any window. You see three buttons in the top-left corner and the name of the window to the right of the Back and Forward icons. The three buttons (called *gumdrop buttons* by some folks because they look like, well, gumdrops) are officially known as Close, Minimize, and Zoom, and their colors (red, yellow, and green, respectively) are designed to pop off the screen.

Here's what they do:

>> **Close (red):** Click this button to close the window.

>> **Minimize (yellow):** Click this button to minimize the window. Clicking Minimize appears to close the window, but instead of making it disappear, Minimize adds an icon for the window to the right side of the dock.

TIP

See the section about minimizing windows into application icons in Chapter 3 if a document icon doesn't appear in your dock when you minimize the document's window.

To view the window again, click the dock icon for the window that you minimized. If the window happens to be a QuickTime movie, the movie audio continues to play and a tiny still image from the video appears as its icon in the dock. (I discuss the dock in detail in Chapter 3.)

>> **Zoom (green):** Click a window's green Zoom button, and the window expands to cover the whole screen, including the menu bar.

TIP

If you prefer the old behavior, where a window zoomed to the largest size it could but didn't cover the full screen, hold down the Option key when you click the green button.

To shrink the window back to its previous dimensions, slide the cursor up to the very top of the screen, wait for the menu bar to appear, and then click the green Zoom button.

Another way to escape from a full-screen window, at least in Finder, is to press the Esc key on your keyboard. Sadly, this trick doesn't work with all apps, though it's quite useful in apps that support it (most Apple apps and many others) as well as in Finder.

Split View is semi-hidden beneath the green Zoom button. To see Split View in action, first click the green button for a moment — that is, perform the first half of a click without releasing the button. Or *hover* the cursor over the Zoom button for a moment (without clicking).

Either way, a pop-up menu with three (or more) options appears; select Enter Full Screen, Tile Window to Left of Screen, or Tile Window to Right of Screen.

NEW

You may see additional options to move the window to a different device (such as an iPad) via Sidecar if a suitable device is close enough to your Mac (see Chapter 27).

After assigning a window to the left or right half of the screen, the other half displays miniature versions of all open windows. Hover the cursor over a miniature window to see its name; click a miniature window and it fills that half of the screen.

To work in Split View, click either window to activate it and do what you have to do. To activate the other window, click it. To exit Split View, do one of the following:

- Press Esc.

- Move the pointer to the top of the screen; when the buttons (for both windows) reappear, click any button.

- Quit either application.

A scroll new world

Yet another way to see more of what's in a window or pane is to scroll through it. Scroll bars appear at the bottom and right sides of any window or pane that contains more stuff — icons, text, pixels, or whatever — than you can see in the window. Figure 2-2, for example, shows two instances of the same window: Dragging the scroll bar on the right side of the smaller window would reveal the icons above and below the six (whole) icons that are currently visible. Dragging the scroll bar on the bottom of the smaller window would reveal items to the left and right of the six that are currently visible.

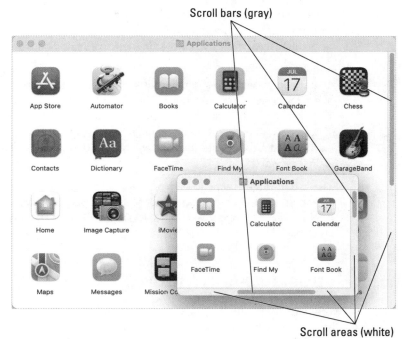

Scroll bars (gray)

Scroll areas (white)

FIGURE 2-2:
The same window twice. Use the scroll bars in the front window to see the icons above, below, to the left, or to the right.

Simply click and drag a scroll bar to move it up or down or side to side.

If your scroll bars don't look exactly like the ones in Figure 2-2 or work as described in the following list, don't worry. These are System Preferences you can configure to your heart's desire, as you discover in Chapter 6.

Here are some ways you can scroll in a window:

>> **Click a scroll bar and drag.** The content of the window scrolls proportionally to how far you drag the scroll bar.

>> **Click in the scroll bar area but don't click the scroll bar itself.** The window scrolls either one page up (if you click above the scroll bar) or down (if you click below the scroll bar). You can change a setting in your General System Preferences pane to cause the window to scroll proportionally to where you click.

TIP

For what it's worth, the Page Up and Page Down keys on your keyboard function the same way as clicking the white scroll area (the vertical scroll bar only) in Finder and many applications. These keys don't work in every program, though, so don't become too dependent on them. Also, if you purchased a mouse, a trackball, or another pointing device that has a scroll wheel, you can scroll vertically in the active (front) window with the scroll wheel or press and hold down the Shift key to scroll horizontally. Alas, this horizontal scrolling-with-the-Shift-key works in Finder windows but not in all applications. For example, it works in the Apple TextEdit application, but not in Microsoft Word.

>> **Use the keyboard.** In Finder, first click an icon in the window and then use the arrow keys to move up, down, left, or right. Using an arrow key selects the next icon in the direction it indicates — and automatically scrolls the window, if necessary. In other programs, you might or might not be able to use the keyboard to scroll. The best advice I can give you is to try it — either it will work or it won't.

>> **Use a two-finger swipe (on a trackpad).** If you have a notebook with a trackpad or use a Magic Trackpad or Magic Mouse, just move the arrow cursor over the window and then swipe the trackpad with two fingers to scroll.

(Hyper)active windows

To work within a window, the window must be active. The *active* window is always the frontmost window, and *inactive* windows always appear behind the active window. You might not see an inactive window if it's behind a bigger window, active or not.

Only one window can be active at a time. To make a window active, click it anywhere — in the middle, on the title bar, or on a scroll bar. It doesn't matter where; just click anywhere to activate it.

TIP

The exceptions are the Close, Minimize, and Zoom buttons on inactive windows, which always do what they do, regardless of whether a window is active or inactive.

Look at Figure 2-3 for an example of an active window in front of an inactive window (the Applications window and the Utilities window, respectively).

Inactive window

FIGURE 2-3:
An active window in front of an inactive window.

Active window

The following is a list of the major visual cues that distinguish active from inactive windows:

>> **The active window's title bar:** By default, the Close, Minimize, and Zoom buttons are bright red, yellow, and green, respectively, and the inactive windows' buttons are light gray.

TIP

This is a nice visual cue. Colored items are active, and gray ones are inactive. Better still, if you move your mouse cursor over an inactive window's gumdrop buttons, they light up in their usual colors so you can close, minimize, or zoom an inactive window without first clicking it to making it active. Neat!

>> **The active window's toolbar:** Toolbar icons are darker and more distinctive; the inactive window's toolbar icons are light gray and more subdued.

>> **The active window's drop shadow:** Notice how the active window has a more prominent shadow? This tricks your eye into thinking the active window is in front of the inactive one.

One last thing: If you're wondering how to resize a window, just hover the cursor over a window's edge or corner or over the dividing line between two panes in the same window (such as the sidebar and the main area of Finder windows). A helpful little arrow appears as a visual cue that you can now drag the edge, corner, or dividing line to resize the window or pane.

Dialog Dealie-Boppers

Dialogs are special windows that pop up over the active window. You generally see them when you select a menu item that ends in an ellipsis (. . .).

Dialogs can contain a number of standard Mac features (I call them *dealie-boppers*), such as radio buttons, pop-up menus, tabs, text-entry fields, and check boxes. You see these features again and again in dialogs. Take a moment to look at each of these dealie-boppers in Figure 2-4.

>> **Radio buttons:** *Radio buttons* are so named because, like the buttons on your car radio (if you have a very old car), only one at a time can be active. (When they're active, they appear to be pushed in, just like the old radio buttons.) Radio buttons always appear in a group of two or more; when you select one, all the others are automatically deselected.

TIP

Here's a nifty and undocumented shortcut: You can usually select check boxes and radio buttons by clicking their names (instead of the buttons or boxes).

>> **Tabs:** When a dialog contains more information than can fit in a single window, the info may be divided among panes denoted by tabs. In Figure 2-4, the New Document tab is selected on the left, and the Open and Save tab is selected on the right.

>> **Pop-up menus:** These menus are appropriately named because they pop up when you click them. In Figure 2-4, right, all five pop-up menus (Opening Files, Saving Files, Document Type, Styling, and Encoding) are unclicked and unpopped.

You can always recognize a pop-up menu because it appears in a slightly rounded rectangle and has a double-ended arrow symbol (or a pair of arrows, if you like) on the right.

Have you figured out yet what radio buttons, tabs, and pop-up menus have in common? *Hint:* All three enable you to make a single selection from a group of options. (Well, okay, that was more of an answer than a hint.)

>> **Text-entry fields:** In text-entry fields, you type text (including numbers) from the keyboard. In Figure 2-4, left, the Width, Height, Author, Organization, and Copyright options are text-entry fields.

>> **Check boxes:** The last dealie-bopper that you see frequently is the check box. In a group of check boxes, you can select as many options as you like. Check boxes are selected when they contain a check mark and deselected when they're empty, as shown in Figure 2-4.

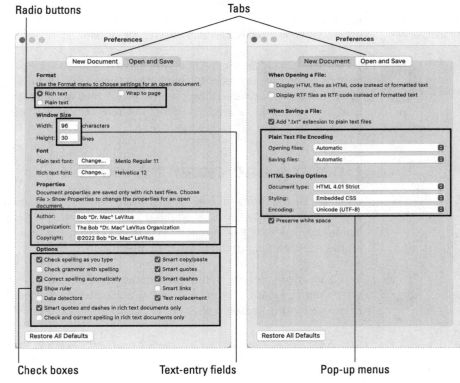

FIGURE 2-4:
This Preferences window offers most of the dealie-boppers you're ever likely to encounter.

I couldn't find a dialog or window that included all the aforementioned dealie-boppers as well as the one other dealie-bopper you should become familiar with, the disclosure triangle. If you see a triangle in a dialog or sheet, try clicking it. If it's a disclosure triangle, it will reveal additional options (or its contents if it's a folder in Finder's List view, as you see in Chapter 8).

TECHNICAL
STUFF

Some applications have *tri-state* check boxes (and no, I'm not talking geography here). These special check boxes are empty when nothing in the group is selected, sport an X when everything in the group is selected, and sport a minus sign (−) when some items in the group are selected and some are not.

Working with Windows

In the following sections, I give you a closer look at windows themselves: how you move them, size them, and use them. And although Monterey windows are similar to windows you've used in other versions of macOS (and even, dare I say it, Windows), you may just discover a new wrinkle or two.

TIP

If you're relatively new to the Mac, you may want to read this section while sitting at your computer, trying the techniques as you read them. Most people find it easier to remember something they've read if they actually do it. If you've been using your Mac for a while, you've probably figured out how windows work by now.

Opening and closing windows

To start peering into windows on your Mac, first you need to know how to open and close them. When you're working in Finder, you can choose the following commands from the File menu. Note that you'll probably find similar commands on the File menu of programs other than Finder.

TIP

You'll use many of these commands frequently, so it would behoove you to memorize their keyboard shortcuts. If you're not sure how keyboard shortcuts work, check out "Using keyboard shortcut commands," later in this chapter.

>> **New Finder Window (⌘+N):** Opens a new Finder window. In other programs, ⌘+N might open a new document, project, or whatever that program helps you create.

>> **Open (⌘+O):** Opens the selected item, be it an icon, a window, or a folder.

>> **Close Window (⌘ +W):** Closes the active window. If no windows are open or if no window is selected, the Close Window command appears dimmed and can't be chosen. Or if you prefer, you can close a window by clicking the red Close button in the top-left corner.

If you hold down the Option key with the File menu open, the Close Window command changes to Close All. This useful command enables you to close all open Finder windows. But it shows up only when you press the Option key or use its keyboard shortcut (⌘+Option+W); otherwise, it remains hidden.

Note that several other commands in the File menu transmogrify when you press the Option key. It would be off topic to get into them here, but here's a tip: Press the Option key, and browse all Finder menus. At least a dozen useful commands appear only when the Option key is pressed. Press it early and often for hidden (often time-saving) commands.

Resizing windows and window panes

If you want to see more (or less) of what's in a window, just hover the pointer over any edge or corner and drag. When the cursor turns into a little double-headed arrow, click and drag to resize the window.

Display windows, like those in Finder, frequently consist of multiple panes. For example, in a Finder window, note the thin line that divides the sidebar pane on the left from the contents pane on the right. When your mouse pointer hovers over the thin line, the cursor changes to a vertical bar (or it could be horizontal if the panes are one above the other) with little arrows pointing out of both sides, as shown in the margin.

When you see this cursor, you can click and drag anywhere in the dividing line that separates the sidebar from the rest of the window. Doing so resizes the two panes relative to each other; one gets larger and one gets smaller.

Moving windows

To move a window, click anywhere in a window's gray title bar or toolbar (except on a button, an icon, a menu, or a Search field) and drag the window to wherever you want it. The window moves wherever you move the mouse, stopping dead in its tracks when you release the mouse button.

If you can't find the cursor on the screen, wiggle your finger on the trackpad or jiggle the mouse. In Monterey, these movements magnify the pointer to make it easier to find onscreen.

Shuffling windows

I've already spent plenty of pages giving you the scoop on how to work with windows. But wait. There's more! The commands on the Window menu provide tools you can use to manage your windows.

Here is a brief look at each of the items on the Window menu. (And if you're unfamiliar with menus and keyboard shortcuts, you find out how they work later in this chapter.)

>> **Minimize (⌘+M):** Use this command to minimize the active Finder window to the dock and unclutter your desktop. It's the same as clicking the yellow gumdrop button.

>> **Zoom:** This command does the same thing as the green gumdrop button. If you've forgotten what the green gumdrop does already, just turn back a few pages to the "Top o' the window to ya!" section and read it again.

>> **Tile Window to Left Side of Screen:** Invokes Split Screen mode and moves the active window to the left half of the screen.

>> **Tile Window to Right Side of Screen:** Invokes Split Screen mode and moves the active window to the right half of the screen.

   You may see additional options to move the window to a different device (such as an iPad) via Sidecar when a suitable device is close enough to your Mac (see Chapter 27).

>> **Cycle through Windows (⌘+`):** Each time you choose this command or use the keyboard shortcut for it, a different window becomes active. So if you have three windows — call 'em Window 1, Window 2, and Window 3 — and you're using Window 1, this command deactivates Window 1 and activates Window 2. If you choose it again, the command deactivates Window 2 and activates Window 3. Choose it one more time, and it deactivates Window 3 and reactivates Window 1.

The next four commands in the Window menu help you manage Monterey Finder window tabs. If you're a fan of tabbed browsing (*à la* Safari), you'll love tabs in a Finder window.

Tabs let you view multiple folders or disks or both in a single window, with each folder or disk in its own tab, as shown in Figure 2-5.

Tabbed windows are an ingenious way to cram a lot of information into a little space. I've tried a number of third-party utilities that purported to provide tabbed Finder windows, but I've never found one that's reliable and robust enough to continue using. This one, on the other hand, just works.

Monterey, like its last few predecessors, includes system-wide tabbed windows, which should work in almost every application that uses windows. The cool part is the app doesn't have to be updated in any way — Monterey grafts tabbed windows onto almost every app that displays multiple windows.

The remaining commands in the Window menu are as follows:

» **Show Previous Tab (Control+Shift+Tab):** Each time you choose this command or use its keyboard shortcut, the previous tab — the one to its left, unless it's the leftmost tab — becomes active. For example, in Figure 2-5, Documents is the active tab. Use this command, and Applications becomes the active tab. Use it a third time, and Downloads becomes active. Because Downloads is the leftmost tab, if you use this command yet again, it wraps around and Documents becomes the active tab again.

» **Show Next Tab (Control+Tab):** Same as Show Previous Tab except in reverse. Instead of showing the previous tab (the one to the left), this command shows the next tab (the one to the right). Use this command three times in a row (refer to the order shown in Figure 2-5), and you see the Downloads tab, then the Applications tab, and finally the Documents tab again.

» **Move Tab to New Window (no keyboard shortcut):** Does just what it says; it moves the active tab into a new window of its own.

» **Merge All Windows (no keyboard shortcut):** Combines all open windows and tabs in one window.

TIP

You can click a tab and drag it left or right to change the order. You can also drag and drop a tab from one Finder window to another. The trick is to click directly on a tab and drag it *onto the tabs in the target window*. If you release it anywhere else, the tab will be displayed in a new window.

One more thing: In Monterey, all these commands and keyboard shortcuts appear in most apps that display windows.

» **Bring All to Front (no keyboard shortcut):** Windows from different applications can interleave. For example, you can have (from front to back) a Finder window, a Microsoft Word window, an Adobe Photoshop window, another Microsoft Word window, and another Finder window. In this example, choosing Bring All to Front while Finder is the active application enables you to have both Finder windows move in front of those belonging to Word and Photoshop.

TIP

If you want to bring all the windows belonging to Finder (or any other program, for that matter) to the front at the same time, you can also click the appropriate dock icon (Finder, in this case).

If you hold down the Option key when you click the Window menu, Minimize Window changes to Minimize All, and the Zoom command changes to Zoom All.

» **Other items:** The remaining items on the Window menu — if any — are the names of all currently open Finder windows. Click a window's name to bring it to the front.

Menu Basics

Mac menus are often referred to as *pull-down menus.* To check out the macOS menus, click the Finder button on the dock to activate Finder and then look at the top of your screen. From left to right, you see the Apple menu, the Finder menu, and six other menus. To use an macOS menu, click its name to make the menu appear and then click (or drag down) to select a menu item. Piece of cake!

Note that menus stay down after you click their names, and stay open until you either select an item or click outside the menu's boundaries.

The ever-changing menu bar

Before you start working with macOS menus, you really, really should know this: *Menu items can change unexpectedly.* Why? Well, the menus you see on the menu bar at the top of the screen always reflect the program that's *active* at the time. When you switch from Finder to a particular program — or from one program to another — the menus change immediately to match whatever program you switched to.

Figure 2-6 shows the menu bars for Finder, Preview, and TextEdit applications.

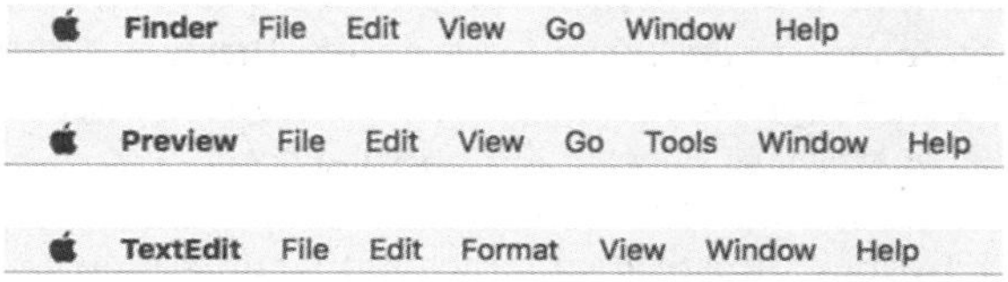

FIGURE 2-6:
Menu bars change to reflect the active application.

🍎	**Finder**	File	Edit	View	Go	Window	Help

🍎	**Preview**	File	Edit	View	Go	Tools	Window	Help

🍎	**TextEdit**	File	Edit	Format	View	Window	Help

An easy way to tell which program is active is to look at the application menu — it's the leftmost menu with a name, just to the right of the Apple menu. When you're in Finder, of course, the application menu reads *Finder.* But if you switch to another program (by clicking its icon on the dock or by clicking any window associated with the program) or launch a new program, that menu changes to the name of the active program.

When you have an application open, the commands on the menu change, too — but just a little bit. What makes this cool is that you have access to some standard application menu items whether you're running Mail, Safari, or almost any other app. For example, most (but not all) applications have Cut, Copy, and Paste commands in their Edit menus, and Open, Save, and Print commands in their File menus. You can find much more about commands for applications in Part 3, which explains how applications that come with macOS Monterey can help you get things done.

Contextual (shortcut) menus: They're sooo contextual!

Contextual menus (also called *shortcut menus*) list commands that apply only to the item that is currently selected. Contextual menus might be available in windows, on icons, and in most places on the desktop.

To see whether a contextual menu is available, either hold down the Control key and click — which you can call a *Control-click* to sound cool to your Mac friends — or, for those with two or more buttons on their mice, *right-click.* Finally, most Mac laptops (as well as the Magic Trackpad and the Magic Mouse) let you click the trackpad using two fingers to simulate a right-click or a Control-click.

TIP

If this doesn't work for you, launch System Preferences and click the Trackpad icon. Click the Point & Click tab and make sure that Click with Two Fingers is selected as your Secondary Click and (of course), the Secondary Click check box is enabled.

Another reason the contextual menu might not appear is that it is available only if any of its commands make sense for the item that you Control-click or right-click. That's why people call 'em *contextual!* They're specific to the current context, which is whatever is selected or Control-clicked.

Figure 2-7, left, shows the contextual menu that appears when you Control-click (or right-click) a document icon. Figure 2-7, right, shows the contextual menu you see when you Control-click the desktop.

| Open |
| Open With ⟩ |
| Move to Trash |
| Get Info |
| Rename |
| Compress "I am a document!" |
| Duplicate |
| Make Alias |
| Quick Look "I am a document!" |
| Share ⟩ |
| Quick Actions ⟩ |
| Copy "I am a document!" |
| Import from iPhone ⟩ |
| Use Stacks |
| Sort By ⟩ |
| Clean Up Selection |
| Show View Options |
| ○ ○ ○ ○ ○ ○ ○ |
| Tags... |
| Set Desktop Picture |

| New Folder |
| Get Info |
| Import from iPhone ⟩ |
| Change Desktop Background... |
| Use Stacks |
| Sort By ⟩ |
| Clean Up |
| Clean Up By ⟩ |
| Show View Options |

| ✓ None |
| Snap to Grid |
| Name |
| Kind |
| Date Last Opened |
| Date Added |
| Date Modified |
| Date Created |
| Size |
| Tags |

FIGURE 2-7:
Only relevant items appear in a contextual menu.

Contextual menus are also available in most applications. Open your favorite app and try Control-clicking to find out whether those menus are there. In most cases, using a contextual menu is a quick way to avoid going to the menu bar to choose a command. In some programs — such as iMovie and Music — contextual menus are the *only* way to access some commands.

To make the Finder-related contextual menus available to users who didn't have the foresight to purchase this book, Apple added the Action icon (shown in the margin) to the toolbar. As a result, people who don't know about Control-clicking or right-clicking (or have only one free hand) can access most contextual menu commands by clicking the Action button and displaying its context-sensitive menu of shortcuts. You, on the other hand, gentle reader, know how to get at these commands without having to run your mouse all the way up to the Action icon in the toolbar. Plus, a handful of commands appear in the Control-click/right-click contextual menu but don't appear in the Action icon/menu.

REMEMBER

Get in the habit of Control-clicking (or right-clicking or two-finger clicking) items on your screen. Before you know it, using contextual menus will become second nature to you.

Recognizing disabled options

Menu items that appear in black on a menu are currently available. Menu items that aren't currently available are grayed out, to indicate that they're disabled for the time being. You can't select a disabled menu item.

In Figure 2-8, the File menu on the left is pulled down while nothing is selected in Finder; this is why many of the menu items are disabled (in gray). These items are disabled because an item (such as a window or an icon) must be selected for you to use one of these menu items. For example, the Show Original command is grayed out because it works only if the selected item is an alias. On the right side of Figure 2-8, I selected a document before I pulled down the menu; note that many of the formerly disabled commands are enabled when an icon is selected. (The Show Original command is still grayed out because the selected icon is not an alias.)

Finally, note that items that end in an ellipsis (. . .), such as the Tags command in Figure 2-8, will open a dialog with additional options.

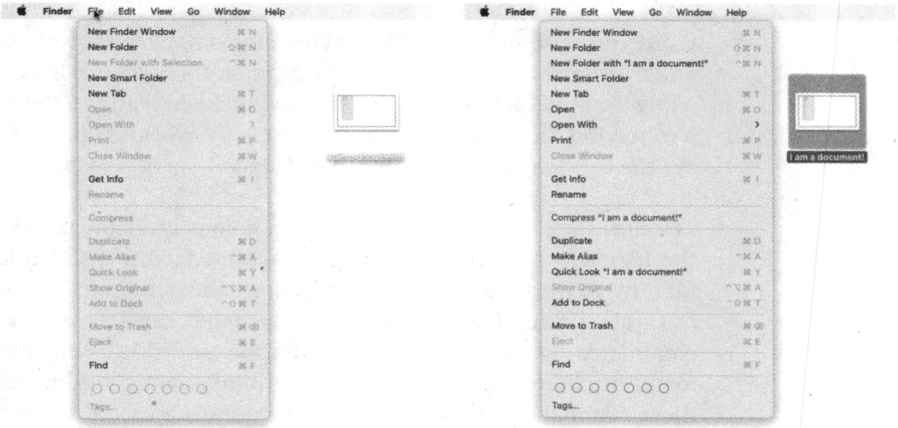

FIGURE 2-8:
File menu with
nothing selected
(left) and with a
document icon
selected (right);
the disabled
items appear
grayed out.

Navigating submenus

Some menu items have more menus attached to them, and these are called *submenus,* which are menus that are subordinate to a menu item. If a menu has a black arrow to the right of its name, it has a submenu.

To use a submenu, click a menu name once (to drop the menu down) and then slide your cursor down to any item with a black arrow. When the item is highlighted, move your mouse to the right just slightly. The submenu should pop out of the original menu's item, as shown in Figure 2-9.

FIGURE 2-9:
The Apple menu's
Recent Items
selection, with its
submenu
popped out.

Under the Apple menu tree

On the far-left side of the menu bar sits a little , which displays a menu when clicked. No matter what application is active, the menu is always available in the top-left corner of your menu bar.

TIP

The menu bar is always available, even with apps that hide it in full-screen mode. To make it reappear, move the pointer to the top of the screen, wait a second or two, and watch the menu bar magically reappear.

From top to bottom, the menu gives you a number of options, including the following:

» **About This Mac:** Choose this item to see what version of macOS you're running, what kind of Mac and processor you're using, how much memory your Mac has, the name of your startup disk, and much more. The window sports multiple tabs across the top of the window — Overview, Displays, Storage, and so on.

Click the System Report button on the Overview tab to launch the Apple System Information utility; there, you can find out more than you'll probably ever want or need to know about your Mac's hardware and software.

Click the Software Update button on the Overview tab to have your Mac check with the mothership (Apple) to see whether any updates are available for macOS, its included applications, third-party applications purchased at the Mac App Store, other Apple-branded applications (such as GarageBand, Final Cut Pro, Pages), or even Apple-branded peripheral devices, such as the iPod or iPhone.

» **System Preferences:** Choose this item to open the System Preferences app (which I discuss further in Chapter 6 and elsewhere).

» **App Store:** Choose this item to launch the Mac App Store app.

» **Recent Items:** This option lets you quickly access applications, documents, and servers you've used recently, as shown previously in Figure 2-9.

» **Force Quit:** Use this option only in emergencies. What's an emergency? Use it when an application becomes recalcitrant or otherwise misbehaves or refuses to quit when you say Quit.

TIP

Memorize the keyboard shortcut for Force Quit (⌘+Option+Esc). Sometimes a program gets so badly hosed that you can't click anywhere and other keyboard shortcuts won't do anything at all. It doesn't happen often, nor does it happen to everyone. If it should happen to you, calmly press the magic key combo you memorized (⌘+Option+Esc), and the Force Quit Applications dialog (usually) appears. Click the name of the program that's acting up and then click the Force Quit button or press the Return key to make the balky application stop balking.

WARNING

The reason Force Quit should be used only in an emergency is that if you use it on an application that's working fine and have any unsaved documents, your work since the last time you saved the file will be blown away.

Or not. The Auto Save and Versions features are *still* the default for Apple's own applications. You read more about these features in Chapter 7; if the app you're using supports Auto Save features, you shouldn't lose much (if any) work regardless of when you last saved.

» **Shut Down options:** These five commands do exactly what their names imply:

- *Sleep:* Puts your Mac into an energy-efficient state of suspended animation. See the section about Energy Saver in Chapter 23 for details on the Energy Saver System Preferences pane and sleeping.

- *Restart:* Quits all open programs and restarts your Mac. It's quite polite about this task, asking if you want to save any unsaved changes in open documents before complying.

- *Shut Down:* Turns off your Mac. Refer to Chapter 1 for details.

- *Lock Screen (⌘+Control+Q):* Locks your screen instantly, and then requires your account password to unlock it.

- *Log Out <your account name> (⌘+Shift+Q):* Quits all open programs and logs you out. Again, your Mac will be ever so polite, asking if you want to save unsaved changes in open documents before complying. When it's done, the login screen appears.

Using keyboard shortcut commands

Most menu items, or at least the most common ones, have *keyboard shortcuts* to help you quickly navigate your Mac without having to haggle so much with the mouse. Using these key combinations activates menu items without using the mouse; to use them, you press the Command (⌘) key and then press another key (or keys) without releasing the ⌘ key. Memorize the shortcuts that you use often.

Learn how to change keyboard shortcuts and even how to create ones of your own in Chapter 6.

REMEMBER

Some people refer to the Command key as the *Apple key.* That's because on many keyboards that key has both the pretzel–like Command key symbol (⌘) and an Apple logo (🍎) on it. To avoid confusion, I always refer to ⌘ as the Command key.

» Discovering the default dock icons

» Talkin' trash

» Checking out dock icons and their menus

» Delving into dock customization

Chapter **3**

What's Up, Dock?

T he dock appears at the bottom of your screen by default, providing quick access to your most often-used applications, documents, and folders.

TIP

Some users prefer to have the dock located on the left or right side of the screen instead of at the bottom. You see how to relocate your dock (and more) in the coming pages.

Folder icons on the dock are called *stacks*, which display their contents as your choice of a fan, a grid, or a list when clicked.

Other icons on the dock open an application or document with one click.

The dock is your friend. It's a great place to put files, folders, and apps you use a lot so that they're always just one click away.

REMEMBER

A dock icon is merely a pointer (also known as an *alias* or a *shortcut*) to applications, documents, and folders stored on your hard drive. So, you can add and remove icons from your dock (as you discover shortly) without affecting the actual applications, documents, and folders. Don't be shy about adding items you use often as well as removing items you don't use.

A Quick Introduction to Your Dock

Take a minute to look at the row of icons at the bottom of your display. That row, gentle reader, is the *dock* (shown in Figure 3-1), and those individual pictures are known as *icons* (which I discuss in greater detail momentarily). Note that I chopped the dock in Figure 3-1 into two pieces (with the left half on top) to make the icons bigger and easier to see.

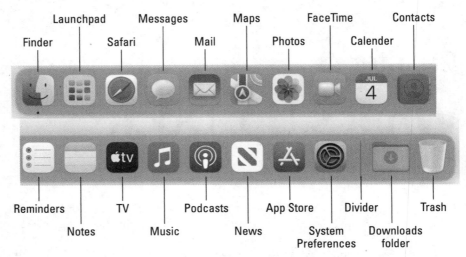

FIGURE 3-1:
The dock and all its default icons.

Launchpad   Messages   Maps   FaceTime   Contacts

Finder   Safari   Mail   Photos   Calender

Reminders   TV   Podcasts   App Store   Divider   Trash

Notes   Music   News   System Preferences   Downloads folder

REMEMBER

Icons in the dock and Launchpad (see Chapter 10) are odd ducks; you activate them with a single click. Just remember that almost all other Finder icons are selected (highlighted) when you single-click them and opened only when you double-click them.

Here's the rundown on what happens when you click dock icons:

» If it's an **application icon,** the application opens and becomes active. If the application is already open, it becomes active, which brings its menu and all its windows to the front.

» If it's a **document icon,** that document opens in its appropriate application, which becomes the active application. If that application is already open, it becomes the active application with this document in the front.

REMEMBER

If the item is an application or document and is already open when you click its dock icon, the app or document becomes active.

>> If it's a **folder icon or disk icon,** a stack, fan, or grid with its contents appears so you can choose an item. If you choose Show in Finder from this menu, the folder's window opens in Finder.

The default icons of the dock

By default, the dock contains a number of commonly used macOS applications, and you can also store your own applications, files, or folders there. (I show you how to do that in the "Adding dock icons" section, later in this chapter.)

But first, look at the items you find in a standard macOS Monterey dock. If they aren't familiar to you, they certainly will be as you get to know Monterey.

I admit that I can't do justice to all the programs that come with macOS Monterey that aren't, strictly speaking, part of the operating system (OS). Alas, some of the programs in the default dock are ones you won't be seeing much more of. But I'd hate to leave you wondering what all those icons in the dock are, so the following list gives you a brief description of each default dock icon (moving from left to right onscreen). If additional coverage of an item appears elsewhere in the book, the list tells you where:

>> **Finder:** The always running application that manages the desktop, files, folders, disks, and more (this chapter and Chapters 4-8)

>> **Launchpad:** A display of all your applications on a grid that looks suspiciously like an iPad or iPhone (Chapter 10)

>> **Safari:** A web browser (Chapter 15)

>> **Messages:** A program for sending and receiving text and multimedia messages as well as transferring files to and from and remotely controlling other Macs (Chapter 17)

>> **Mail:** An email program (Chapter 17)

>> **Maps:** A program with maps and driving directions (Chapter 13)

>> **FaceTime:** A video chat program (Chapter 15)

>> **Photos:** A program for managing and editing photographs (Chapter 20)

>> **FaceTime:** A program for making and receiving audio and video calls (Chapter 15)

>> **Calendar:** A calendar program for managing appointments and events (Chapter 11)

>> **Contacts:** A contact manager application (Chapter 16)

- >> **Reminders:** A to-do list and reminder application (Chapter 11)

- >> **Notes:** A program for making notes (Chapter 11)

- >> **TV:** A video player and store (Chapter 20)

- >> **Music:** An audio player and store (Chapter 19)

- >> **Podcasts:** A podcast player (Chapter 20)

- >> **News:** A news reader (Chapter 14)

- >> **Mac App Store:** Where you buy Mac apps from Apple (Chapter 23)

- >> **System Preferences:** An application to configure the way many aspects of your Mac work (Chapters 6, 18, and 23)

- >> **Divider:** The line that separates apps on the left and documents or folders on the right (this chapter)

- >> **Downloads folder:** A folder that contains files downloaded by Safari or Mail (Chapter 4)

- >> **Trash:** Where you drag files and folders to delete them, or drag removable media to eject it (this chapter)

To get a quick look at the name of a dock icon, just move (hover) your pointer over any item in the dock. Like magic, that item's name appears above it (like *Safari* on the left side of Figure 3-4, later in this chapter).

It's likely that your dock won't look *exactly* like the one shown in Figure 3-1. If you added icons to your dock before you upgraded to Monterey, for example, you'll see those icons. If you have Apple apps such as iMovie, GarageBand, Pages, Numbers, or Keynote installed, or you get a new Mac with Monterey preinstalled, you may see their icons in your dock. And if you've deleted one of the default icons shown in Figure 3-1 from your dock under a previous version of macOS, it won't come back when you upgrade to Monterey.

If you don't understand what I just said or want to make your dock look exactly like the one shown in Figure 3-1, I have good news: You find out how to do that and much more before the end of this chapter.

Also, if you see a question mark instead of an icon in the dock, the file (application, document, or folder) it represents has been deleted.

Trash talkin'

The *Trash* is a special container where you put the items you no longer want to hang around on your hard drive(s). Got four copies of a document named *Letter to the Editor re: Bird Waste Issue* on your hard drive? Drag three of them to the Trash. Tired of tripping over old PDF and DMG files you've downloaded but no longer need? Drag them to the Trash, too.

To put something in the Trash, just drag its icon onto the Trash icon in the dock and it will move into the Trash. As with other icons, when the Trash icon is highlighted you know that you've connected with the Trash while dragging. And as with other dock icons, the Trash icon's name appears when you move the cursor over the icon.

Two other ways to put items into the Trash are to select the items you want to dispose of and then choose File ➪ Move to Trash or press ⌘+Delete (⌘+Backspace on some keyboards).

TIP

If you accidentally move something to the Trash and want it back right now, you can magically put it back where it came from in two ways.

Way #1

Choose Edit ➪ Undo or press ⌘+Z.

Finder usually remembers more than one action for Undo and can often undo the last *few* things you did in Finder. That's the good news. The bad news is that it redoes things in reverse order, so don't wait too long. If you perform several other file-related activities in Finder, you'll have to Undo all those actions before you can Undo your accidental Move to Trash.

In other words, as soon as you create or rename a folder, move a file from one place to another, drag a different file to the Trash, create an alias, or almost anything that affects a file or folder, choosing Edit ➪ Undo or pressing ⌘+Z will undo *that* action first.

You'll find that some Finder actions — most of the items in the View menu, for example — don't affect Undo. So if you drag a file to the Trash and then switch views (see Chapter 4), Undo will still un-trash the file.

Even if you do something and can't use Undo, files you drag to the Trash aren't deleted immediately. You know how the garbage in the can on the street curb sits there until the sanitation engineers come by and pick it up each Thursday? Monterey's Trash works the same way, but without the smell. Items sit in the Trash, waiting for a sanitation engineer (you) to come along and empty it.

Way #2

So, if you miss the window of opportunity to use the Undo command, don't worry; you can still retrieve the file from the Trash:

TIP

>> **To open the Trash and see what's in there,** just click its icon on the dock. A Finder window called Trash opens, showing you the files it contains (namely, files and folders put in the Trash since the last time it was emptied).

>> **To retrieve an item that's already in the Trash,** drag it back out, either onto the desktop or back into the folder where it belongs.

Or use the secret keyboard shortcut: Select the item(s) in the Trash that you want to retrieve and press ⌘+Delete. This technique has the added benefit of magically transporting the files or folders you select from the Trash back into the folder from which they came. And, unlike Undo, the secret keyboard shortcut will work on a file or folder at any time, or at least until the next time you empty the Trash. Try it — it's sweet.

And if that doesn't work, you can right-click or Control-click a file and choose Put Back from the contextual menu.

>> **To empty the Trash,** choose Finder ⇨ Empty Trash or press Shift+⌘+Delete. If the Trash window is open and files are in the Trash, you see an Empty button just below its toolbar on the right. Clicking the button, of course, also empties the Trash.

You can also empty the Trash from the dock by positioning the pointer on the Trash icon and right-clicking (or Control-clicking) the Trash icon. The Empty Trash menu item pops up like magic. Move the pointer over Empty Trash to select it and then release the mouse button.

WARNING

Think twice before you invoke the Empty Trash command. After you empty the Trash, the files that it contained are pretty much gone forever, or at least gone from your hard drive. There is no Undo for Empty Trash. So my advice is: Before you get too bold, read Chapter 24, and back up your hard drive at least once (several times is better). After you get proficient at backups, chances improve greatly that even though the files are technically gone forever from your hard drive, you can get them back if you really want to (from your backups).

The Trash icon shows you when it has files waiting for you there; as in real life, Trash that contains files or folders looks like it's full of crumpled paper (look ahead to Figure 3-2). Conversely, when your Trash is empty, the Trash icon looks, well, empty.

Finally, although you can't open a file that's in the Trash, you can select it and use Quick Look (shortcut: ⌘+Y) to see its contents before you decide to use Empty Trash and permanently delete it.

And that's pretty much all there is to know about the Trash.

Opening application menus on the dock

Single-clicking an application icon on the dock launches that application — or, if the application is already open, switches you to that application and brings forward all open windows in that application.

But some application icons on the dock — such as Calendar, Safari, and Music — also hide menus containing some handy commands. (Folder icons in the dock have a different but no less handy menu, which I discuss in a moment.)

You can make menus for applications on the dock appear in two ways:

>> Press and continue to hold down the mouse button.

>> Right-click or Control-click.

TIP

If you use a trackpad or a Magic Mouse, a two-finger tap should do the trick. (If it doesn't do the trick, check out the Mouse and Trackpad System Preferences sections in Chapter 6.)

Do any of the preceding and you'll see a menu for that dock icon, as shown in Figure 3-2 for the App Store icon.

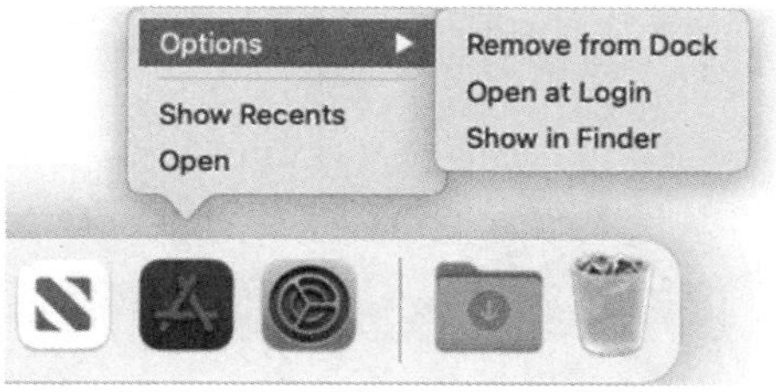

FIGURE 3-2:
The Options submenu for an application icon (Mac App Store) on the dock.

The Options submenu offers three choices:

>> **Keep in (or Remove from) Dock:** Adds the application's icon to the dock (or removes it from the dock), waiting until after you quit the application if it's running.

>> **Open at Login:** Launches this application automatically every time you log in to this user account. This is handy for apps you want to keep running all the time, such as Mail or Safari.

>> **Show in Finder:** Opens the enclosing folder (in this instance, that would be the Applications folder) and selects the application's icon.

The other options in the menu follow:

>> **Show Recents (if available):** Displays recently used windows for this app if there are any.

>> **Open/Quit:** Opens the app, or quits the app if it's already open.

So there you have it: The default Options menu for applications, which is what you'll see for most applications when they aren't open.

One last thing: When you right-click/Control-click the dock icon for an application that's currently running (look for the little dot below its icon), you may see different menus, like the ones shown in Figure 3-3 (clockwise from top left: Safari, Preview, System Preferences, TextEdit, and Music).

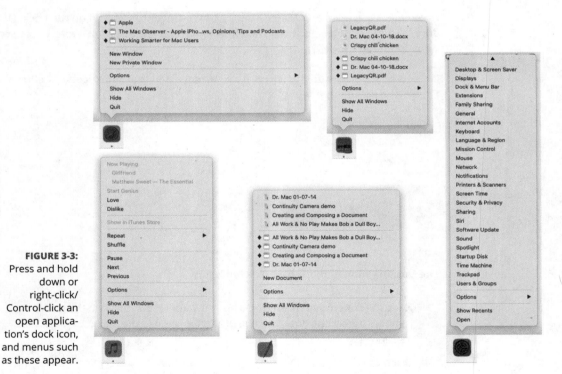

FIGURE 3-3: Press and hold down or right-click/ Control-click an open application's dock icon, and menus such as these appear.

As you can see, some open applications provide useful program-specific commands or options.

TIP

Music has one of my favorite dock menus, letting me control my music from the dock with options such as Play/Pause, Next or Previous Track, Repeat, and Shuffle.

Other programs, including Preview and Safari in Figure 3-3, offer you a list of open windows with a check mark to indicate the active window or diamonds (as shown) to indicate windows minimized to the dock.

Finally, the items above the list of open windows for TextEdit are recently used documents.

Reading dock icon body language

As you use the dock or when you're just doing regular stuff on your Mac, the dock icons like to communicate with you. They can't talk, so they have a few moves and symbols that indicate things you might want to know. Table 3-1 should make those moves and symbols crystal clear.

TABLE 3-1 **What Dock Icons Are Telling You**

Icon Movement or Symbol	What It Means
The icon moves up and out of its place in the dock for a moment.	You single-clicked a dock icon, and it's letting you know that you activated it.
The icon does a little bouncy dance when that program is open but isn't *active* (that is, the menu bar isn't showing, and it isn't the frontmost program).	The program desires your attention; give its icon a click to find out what it wants.
A dot appears below its dock icon.	This application is open.
An icon that isn't ordinarily in the dock magically appears.	You see a temporary dock icon for every program that's currently open until you quit that application. The icon appears because you've opened something or something has opened itself automatically. When you quit, its icon magically disappears.

Opening files from the dock

REMEMBER

One useful function of the dock is that you can use it to open an application quickly and easily. The following tips explain several handy ways to open what you need from the dock:

>> **You can drag a document icon onto an application's dock icon.** If the application knows how to handle that type of document, its dock icon is highlighted, and the document opens in that application. If the application can't handle that particular type of document, the dock icon isn't highlighted, and you can't drop the document onto it.

TIP

I'm getting ahead of myself here, but if the application can't handle a document, try opening the document this way: Select the document icon and choose File ⇨ Open With, or right-click/Control-click the document icon and use the Open With menu to choose the application you want to open the document with. And if you hold down the Option key, the Open With command changes to Always Open With, which enables you to change the default application that opens this document permanently.

>> **You can find the original icon of any item you see in the dock by choosing Show in Finder from its dock menu.** This trick opens the window containing the item's actual icon and thoughtfully selects that icon for you.

Customizing Your Dock

The dock is a convenient way to get at oft-used icons. By default, the dock comes stocked with icons that Apple thinks you'll need most frequently (refer to Table 3-1), but you can customize it to contain any icons that you choose, as you discover in the following sections. You also find out how to resize the dock to fit your new set of icons and how to tell dock icons what your preferences are.

Adding dock icons

REMEMBER

You can customize your dock with favorite applications, a document you update daily, or maybe a folder containing your favorite recipes. Use the dock for anything you need quick access to.

Adding an application, file, or folder to the dock is as easy as 1-2-3:

1. **Open a Finder window that contains an application, a document file, or a folder you use frequently.**

   You can also drag an icon — including a hard drive icon — from the desktop or any Finder window.

2. **Click the item you want to add to the dock.**

   As shown in Figure 3-4, I chose the TextEdit application. (It's highlighted.)

3. **Drag the icon out of the Finder window and onto the dock.**

   The icons to the left and right of the new icon magically part to make room for it. Note that the dock icon isn't the actual item. That item remains wherever it was — in a window or on the desktop. The icon you see in the dock is a shortcut that opens the item. I briefly mentioned aliases (known as *shortcuts* in the Windows world) earlier, but the icon on the dock is actually an alias of the icon you dragged onto the dock.

   Furthermore, when you remove an icon from the dock, as you find out how to do in a moment, you aren't removing the actual application, document, or folder. You're removing *only its shortcut* from the dock.

FIGURE 3-4: Adding an icon to the dock is as easy as 1-2-3. Just drag the icon onto the dock.

Folder, disk, document, and URL icons must sit on the right side of the divider line in the dock; application icons must sit on the left side of it. Why does the dock force these rules upon you? I suppose that someone at Apple thinks this is what's best for you. Who knows? But that's the rule: apps on the left; folders, disks, documents, and URLs on the right.

As long as you follow the rule, you can add several items to either side of the divider line at the same time by selecting them all and dragging the group to that side of the dock. You can delete only one icon at a time from the dock, however.

Adding a URL to the dock works slightly differently. Here's a quick way to add a URL to the dock:

1. **Open Safari, and go to the page with a URL that you want to save in the dock.**

2. **Click the small icon that you find to the left of the URL in the address bar and drag it to the right side of the dividing line in the dock.**

3. **Release the mouse button when the icon is right where you want it in the dock.**

   The icons in the dock slide over and make room, as shown in Figure 3-5, and the URL appears as a dock icon. From now on, when you click the URL icon that you moved to your dock, Safari opens to that page.

Drag from here...

FIGURE 3-5:
Drag the icon from Safari's address bar to the right side of the dock.

...to here

TIP

If you open an item whose icon that normally doesn't appear in the dock, and you want to keep its temporary icon in the dock permanently, you have two ways to tell it to stick around after you quit the program:

>> Control-click (or click and hold down) and choose Options ⇨ Keep in Dock from the menu that pops up.

>> Drag the icon (for an application that's currently open) off and then back to the dock (or to a different position in the dock) without letting go of the mouse button.

Removing an icon from the dock

Removing an item from the dock is as easy as 1-2-3 but without the 3:

1. **Drag its icon off the dock and onto the desktop.**

2. **When you see the Remove bubble, release the icon (mouse button).**

3. **There is no Step 3.**

You can also choose Remove from Dock in the item's dock menu to get it out of your dock, but this way is way more fun.

REMEMBER

You can't remove the icon of a program that's currently running from the dock by dragging it. Either wait until you quit the program or Control-click (or click and hold down) and deselect Options ⇨ Keep in Dock.

Also, note that by moving an icon off the dock, you aren't moving, deleting, or copying the item itself; you're just removing its icon from the dock. The item is unchanged. The icon is sort of like a library catalog card: Just because you remove the card from the card catalog doesn't mean that the book is gone from the library.

TIP

The dock used to come with your Documents and Applications folders installed by default. Ever since Mountain Lion, the dock does not include those folders, at least not by default. I mention this only because having those folders on the dock is convenient, and you should consider adding them to your dock if they aren't already there.

On the other hand, for those with Macs that once ran OS X 10.7 (Lion) or earlier versions and have since been upgraded to Monterey, your Documents and Applications folders should still be on your Monterey dock unless you removed them at some point.

Resizing the dock

If the default size of the dock bugs you, you can make the dock smaller and save yourself a lot of screen real estate. This space comes in especially handy when you add your own stuff to the dock.

To shrink or enlarge the dock (and its icons) without opening the Dock Preferences window, follow these steps:

1. **Make the Sizer appear by moving your cursor over the divider line that you find between apps and documents near the right side of the dock.**

2. **Drag the Sizer down to make the dock smaller, holding down the mouse button until you find the size you like.**

   The more you drag this control down, the smaller the dock gets.

3. **To enlarge the dock again, just drag the Sizer back up.**

   Bam! Big dock! You can enlarge the dock until it fills your screen from side to side.

What should you put on your dock?

Put things on the dock that you need quick access to and that you use often, or add items that aren't quickly available from menus or a Finder window's sidebar. If you like using the dock better than the Finder window's sidebar (for example), add your Documents, Movies, Pictures, Music, or even your Home folder or hard drive to the dock.

I suggest adding these items to your dock:

>> **A word-processing application:** Most people use word-processing software more than any other applications. Just drag the icon for yours to the left side of the dock, and you're good to go.

TIP

If you don't have a word processor such as Microsoft Word or Apple Pages already, give TextEdit a try. It's in every macOS Applications folder, and it's more powerful than you expect from a freebie.

>> **A project folder:** You know — the folder that contains all the documents for your thesis, or all the notes for the biggest project you have at work, or your massive recipe collection . . . whatever. If you add that folder to the dock, you can access it more quickly than if you have to open several folders to find it.

>> **A special utility or application:** The Preview application is an essential part of my work because I receive a lot of different image files every day. You may also want to add internet-enabled programs you use (such as Skype, Spotify, and Twitter), your favorite graphics applications (such as Adobe Photoshop or Photoshop Elements), or the game you play every afternoon when you think the boss isn't watching.

>> **Your favorite URLs:** Save links to sites that you visit every day — the ones you use in your job, your favorite Mac news sites, or your personalized page from an internet service provider (ISP). Sure, you can make one of these pages your browser's start page or bookmark it, but the dock lets you add one or more additional URLs. (Refer to the "Adding dock icons" section, earlier in this chapter, for details.)

TIP

You can add several URL icons to the dock, but bear in mind that the dock and its icons shrink to accommodate added icons, which makes them harder to see. Perhaps the best idea — if you want easy access to several URLs — is to create a folder full of URLs and put that folder on the dock. Then you can just press and hold your cursor on the folder (or Control-click the folder) to pop up a menu with all your URLs.

REMEMBER

Even though you can make the dock smaller, you're still limited to one row of icons. The smaller you make the dock, the larger the crowd of icons you can amass. You have to determine for yourself what's best for you: having lots of icons available in the dock (even though they might be difficult to see because they're so tiny) or having less clutter but fewer icons on your dock.

Figure 3-6 shows my dock, customized to my liking. Note that it's been split in half for this figure, to make it easier for you to discern the individual icons.

FIGURE 3-6:
I keep icons for the apps I use most in my dock, which is split into two parts for this illustration.

Left side of my dock:

Right side of my dock:

TIP

After you figure out which programs you use and don't use, it's a good idea to relieve overcrowding by removing the ones you never (or rarely) use from the dock.

Setting your dock preferences

You can change a few things about the dock to make it look and behave just the way you want it to. First, I cover global preferences that apply to the dock itself. After that, I discuss some preferences that apply only to folder and disk icons in the dock.

Global dock preferences

To change global dock preferences, choose ➪ System Preferences and then click the Dock & Menu Bar icon. The System Preferences application opens to the Dock & Menu Bar pane (see Figure 3-7).

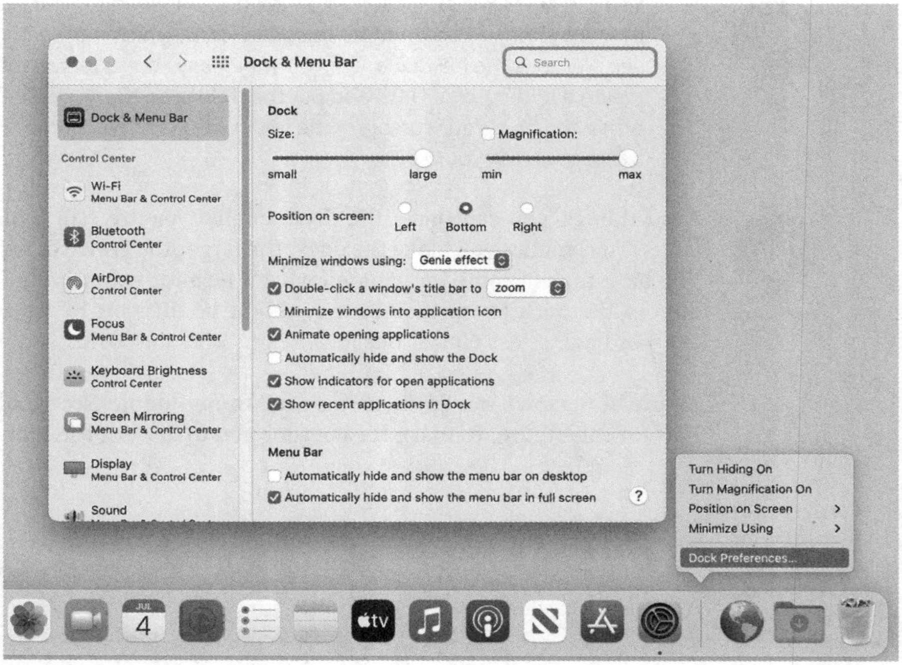

FIGURE 3-7: The Dock & Menu Bar System Preferences pane (left) and the dock resizer shortcut menu (right).

You can open the Dock & Menu Bar System Preferences pane also by right-clicking or Control-clicking the dock resizer and choosing Dock Preferences from the shortcut menu.

TIP

Now you can adjust your dock with the following preferences:

>> **Size:** Note the slider bar here. Move this slider to the right (larger) or left (smaller) to adjust the size of the dock in your Finder. As you move the slider, watch the dock change size. (Now, *there's* a fun way to spend a Saturday afternoon!)

As you add items to the dock, the icons — and the dock itself — shrink to accommodate the new ones.

>> **Magnification:** This slider controls how big icons grow when you pass the arrow cursor over them. Or you can deselect this check box to turn off magnification entirely.

>> **Position on Screen:** Choose one of these three radio buttons to attach the dock to the left side, the right side, or the bottom of your screen (the default). I prefer it on the bottom, but you should probably try all three before you decide.

>> **Double-Click a Window's Title Bar to Minimize (or Zoom):** If you select this option, double-clicking anywhere in a window's title bar minimizes (or zooms) the window.

This option achieves the same result as clicking the (usually) yellow Minimize button in a window's upper-left corner. The difference is that the Minimize button is a tiny target and way over on the upper-left side of the window, whereas the title bar — the area to the right of the three gumdrops, which include the window's title (*Dock* & Menu Bar in Figure 3-7) — is a much easier target.

>> **Minimize Windows Using:** From this handy pop-up menu (PC users would call it a *drop-down list,* but what the heck; there's no gravity in a computer screen anyway), choose the animation that you see when you click a window's Minimize (yellow by default) button. The Genie Effect is the default, but the Scale Effect seems a bit faster to me.

>> **Minimize Windows into Application Icon:** If you select this option, when you minimize a window by clicking its yellow Minimize button, you won't see a separate dock icon for that window. If this option isn't selected, each window you minimize gets its own personal icon on the right side of your dock.

>> **Animate Opening Applications:** macOS animates *(bounces)* dock icons when you click them to open an item. If you don't like the animation, deselect (that is, uncheck) this check box, and the bouncing ceases evermore.

>> **Automatically Hide and Show the Dock:** Don't like the dock? Maybe you want to free the screen real estate on your monitor? Then choose the Automatically Hide and Show the Dock check box; after that, the dock displays itself only when you move the cursor to the bottom of the screen where the

dock would ordinarily appear. It's like magic! (Okay, it's like Windows that way, but I hate to admit it.)

If the dock isn't visible, deselect the Automatically Hide and Show the Dock check box to bring back the dock. The option remains turned off unless you change it by selecting the Automatically Hide and Show the Dock check box. Choose ➪ Dock ➪ Turn Hiding On (or use its keyboard shortcut ⌘+Option+D).

The keyboard shortcut ⌘+Option+D is a toggle, so it reverses the state of this option each time you use it.

TIP

>> **Show Indicators for Open Applications:** Select this option if you want all open applications to display a little black indicator dot below their icon on the dock, like the Finder icon in Figure 3-1. This program is open, whereas the others — the ones without black dots — are not. If you disable this option (although I can't imagine why you'd ever want to), none of your dock icons will ever display an indicator dot.

>> **Show Recent Applications in Dock:** This setting automatically adds icons for apps that you've used recently but that aren't kept in the dock. They then appear in a special Recent Applications section of the dock between your application icons on the left and the folder and Trash icons on the right, as shown in Figure 3-8.

Notice the dividing lines, which represent the left and right edges of the Recent Applications section.

FIGURE 3-8:
The three apps I used most recently are in the Recent Applications section of the dock.

Folder and disk dock icon menu preferences

If you click a folder or disk icon in the dock, its contents are displayed in a fan, grid, or list menu, as shown in Figure 3-9.

If you right-click or Control-click a folder or disk icon in the dock, its Options menu appears, as shown in Figure 3-10.

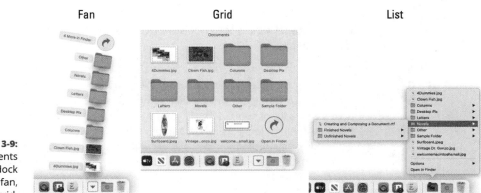

Fan   Grid   List

FIGURE 3-9:
My Documents folder's dock menu as a fan, list, and grid.

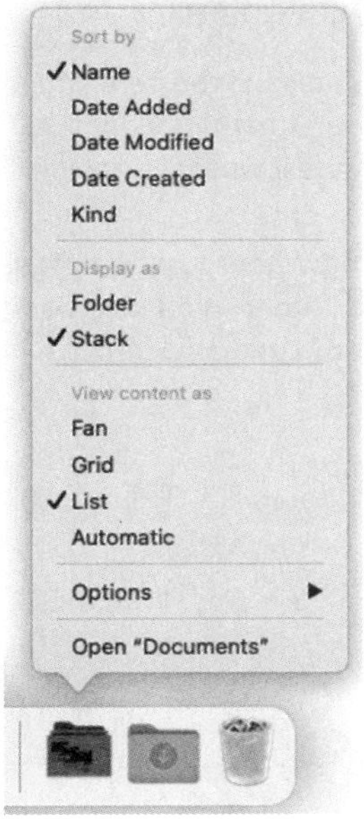

FIGURE 3-10:
The Options menu for my Documents folder.

Here are the choices on the Options menu:

>> **Sort By** determines the order in which items in the folder or drive appear when you click its dock icon.

>> **Display As** determines what the dock icon for a folder or drive looks like. If you choose Stack, the icon takes on the appearance of the last item moved into the folder or drive. If you choose Folder, the dock icon looks like a folder, as does the Documents folder icon in Figure 3-9.

» **View Contents As** lets you choose Fan, Grid, or List as the menu type for the folder or drive.

TIP

The default is Automatic, which is to say that the dock tries to choose the menu for you. I much prefer choosing the menu I consider most appropriate for a particular folder or drive. I like list menus best, especially for folders or drives with a lot of subfolders. As you can see in Figure 3-9, the list menu is the only one that lets you see and access folders inside folders (and subfolders inside other subfolders). For folders with images, I like the grid menu because it displays easily discernible icons for the folder or drive's contents. The fan menu is fantastic (ha!) when the folder or drive contains only a few items.

» **The Options submenu** contains the following items:

- *Remove from Dock* removes the icon from the dock.

- *Show in Finder* opens the window containing the item and selects the item. So, for example, in Figures 3-9 and 3-10, my Home (or iCloud) folder would open, and the Documents folder inside it would be selected.

The dock is your friend. Now that you know how it works, make it work the way you want it to. Put those programs and folders you use most in the dock, and you'll save yourself a significant amount of time and effort.

» Getting to Know Finder

» **Using aliases: The greatest things since sliced bread**

» **Viewing windows four ways**

» **Navigating Finder**

» **Customizing Finder windows**

» **Setting Finder preferences**

» **Getting information on icons**

Chapter **4**

Getting to Know Finder and Its Desktop

O n your Mac, Finder is your starting point — the centerpiece of your Mac experience, if you will — and it's always available. In Finder windows or the desktop, you can double-click your way to your favorite application, your documents, or your folders. So, in this chapter, I show you how to get the most from Finder and its desktop.

By the way, Finder has so many features that I divided them into two chapters — this one and Chapter 5, in which you discover additional Monterey desktop and Finder features to save you time and effort.

I suggest reading (or at least skimming) this chapter first. That's not just because this is Chapter 4 and 4 comes before 5. Rather, this chapter covers basic Finder and desktop features you need to grok before the features in Chapter 5 will make sense.

Introducing Finder and Its Minions: The Desktop and Icons

Finder is a special application unlike any other. Its most significant difference from other applications is that it launches automatically when you log in, is always running in the background, and doesn't include a Quit command. Put another way, Finder is omnipresent.

The desktop is a special part of Finder unlike any other.

Finally, icons and windows are the units of currency used by Finder and the desktop.

Before I tackle any deep thoughts — such as what Finder does or what the desktop is — I start with a quick overview of some of the icons you're likely to encounter as you get to know Finder and the desktop.

Introducing the desktop

The *desktop* is the backdrop for Finder — everything you see behind the dock and any open windows. The desktop is always available and is where you can usually find your hard drive icon(s).

TIP

If your desktop doesn't display hard drive icons and you wish it did, stay tuned.

Explaining Finder and its desktop will be a whole lot easier with a picture for reference, so take a gander at Figure 4-1, which is a glorious depiction of a typical macOS Monterey Finder.

If you're not familiar with Finder and its desktop, here are a few tips that will come in handy as you become familiar with the icons that hang out there:

>> **Icons on the desktop behave the same as icons in a window.** You move them and copy them just as you would icons in a window. The only difference is that icons on the desktop aren't in a window. Because they're on the desktop, they're more convenient to use.

>> **The first icon you need to get to know is the icon for your startup disk (a hard drive or SSD; see Figure 4-2).** You used to be able to find it on the top-right side of the desktop, as mine is in Figure 4-1. Yours probably has the name Macintosh HD unless you've renamed it. (I renamed mine *Monterey* SSD; see the section on renaming icons in Chapter 8 if you'd like to rename your own drive.)

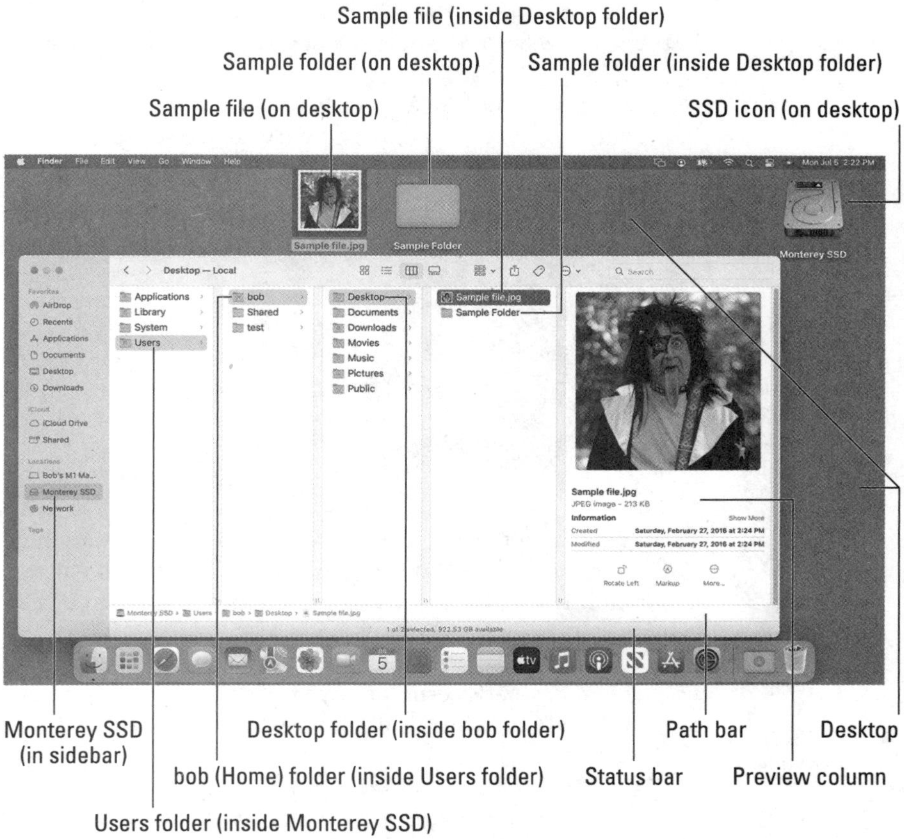

Sample file (inside Desktop folder)

Sample folder (on desktop)   Sample folder (inside Desktop folder)

Sample file (on desktop)   SSD icon (on desktop)

FIGURE 4-1:
A typical Finder
and desktop.

Monterey SSD   Desktop folder (inside bob folder)   Path bar   Desktop
(in sidebar)

bob (Home) folder (inside Users folder)   Status bar   Preview column

Users folder (inside Monterey SSD)

You can see how selected and deselected hard or solid-state drive icons look in Figure 4-2, too.

Monterey doesn't display the startup disk's icon on the desktop by default. So, if you don't see your startup (boot) disk's icon on the desktop but you'd like to (as I do), select the check box for hard drives in Finder Preferences as described in the "Setting Finder preferences" section, later in this chapter.

>> **Other disc or hard drive icons appear on the desktop by default.** When you insert a CD or DVD or connect an external hard drive or a thumb drive, the disc or drive icon does appear on the desktop near the top-right corner. This feature *is* enabled by default; if yours isn't enabled, just open Finder Preferences and select its check box as described later in the chapter.

>> **You can move an item to the desktop to make it easier to find.** Simply click any icon in any window and then, without releasing the mouse button, drag it out of the window and onto the desktop. Then release the mouse button. This will move the icon from wherever it was to the desktop. You can now drag the icon elsewhere on the desktop if necessary.

FIGURE 4-2:
Selected (left) and unselected (right) solid-state disk icons.

WARNING

If you drag an item from an external volume to any location on your startup disk (including the desktop), the item is copied, not moved. Put another way, the item is moved if it's on the same disk or volume, and copied if it's on another disk or volume.

TECHNICAL
STUFF

Volume is the generic term for any storage container — a hard drive, solid-state drive, CD, DVD, disk image, or remote disk — that appears in the sidebar's Locations section.

TIP

At the bottom of the Finder window in Figure 4-1 are two optional bars. The lower of the two is called the *status bar;* it tells you how many items are in each window and, if any are selected, how many you've selected out of the total, as well as how much space is available on the hard drive containing this window. And just above the status bar is the *path bar,* which shows the path from the top level of your hard drive to the selected file (which is Sample File.jpg in Figure 4-1). You can show or hide the status bar by choosing View ⇨ Hide/Show Status Bar and show or hide the path bar by choosing View ⇨ Hide/Show Path Bar. Finally, when the toolbar is hidden (see the next section, "Bellying up to the toolbar"), the status bar moves to the top of the window (the path bar remains at the bottom of the window no matter what).

Bellying up to the toolbar

In addition to the sidebar (introduced in Chapter 2) and some good old-fashioned double-clicking, the macOS Finder window offers additional navigation aids on the toolbar — namely, the Back and Forward icons, as well as the extra-helpful View icons. You can find other handy features on the Go menu, discussed a little later in this chapter.

In case you didn't know, the toolbar (see Figure 4-3) is the area at the top of all Finder windows, which (among other things) displays the window's name. On the toolbar you'll find icons to navigate quickly and act on selected icons.

FIGURE 4-3:
A Finder window's default toolbar.

To activate a toolbar icon, click it once.

You say you don't want to see the toolbar at the top of the window? Okay! Just choose View ⇨ Hide Toolbar or use its keyboard shortcut (⌘+Option+T), and it's gone. (If only life were always so easy!) Want it back? Choose View ⇨ Show Toolbar or use the same keyboard shortcut: ⌘+Option+T.

Alas, hiding the toolbar also hides the useful sidebar. If only you could choose to hide them independently. . .. I find this fact annoying because I use the sidebar a lot but don't use the toolbar much. To make matters worse, View ⇨ Hide Sidebar (shortcut: ⌘+Option+S) lets you hide the sidebar without hiding the toolbar. It's been like this for a long time, and for whatever reason, you *still* can't hide the toolbar while keeping the sidebar visible! Boo. Hiss.

REMEMBER

When you hide the toolbar, opening a folder spawns a *new* Finder window. The default, which is probably what you're used to, is for folders to open in place, displaying their contents in a tab in the current window.

The toolbar's default icons are shown in Figure 4-3. So if you customized your toolbar by choosing View ⇨ Customize Toolbar, yours won't look exactly like Figure 4-3.

TIP

To see text labels for your toolbar icons (as shown in Figure 4-3), choose View ⇨ Customize Toolbar and then choose Icon and Text from the pop-up Show menu in the lower-left corner of the Customize Toolbar sheet.

Here is the lowdown on the toolbar's default icons, from left to right:

>> **Forward and Back icons:** Clicking the Forward and Back icons displays the folders that you've viewed in this window in sequential order. It's a lot like using a web browser.

Here's an example of how the Back icon works. Say you're in your Home folder; you click the Favorites icon, and a split-second later, you realize that you actually need something in the Home folder. Just a quick click of the Back icon and — *poof!* — you're back Home. As for the Forward icon, well, it moves

TIP

you in the opposite direction, through folders that you've visited in this window. Play around with them both; you'll find them invaluable. The keyboard shortcuts ⌘+[for Back and ⌘+] for Forward are even more useful (in my opinion) than the icons.

>> **View icons:** The four View icons change the way that the window displays its contents.

You have four ways to view a window: Icon, List, Column, and Gallery. Some people like columns, some like icons, and others love lists or galleries. To each their own. Play with the four Finder views to see which one works best for you. For what it's worth, I usually prefer Column view with a dash of List view thrown in when I need a folder's contents sorted by creation date or size. And the Gallery view is great for folders with documents because you can see the contents of many document types right in the window, as I explain shortly.

TIP

Don't forget that each view also has a handy keyboard shortcut: ⌘+1 for Icon view, ⌘ +2 for List view, ⌘+3 for Column view, and ⌘+4 for Gallery view. (Views are so useful you'll find an entire section devoted to them later in this chapter.)

>> **Group By/Sort By:** Click this icon to see a pop-up menu with options for grouping this window's contents. Hold down the Option key to change the sort order (within the selected group). Note that the Group By/Sort By menu works in all four views. Read more about Group By/Sort By in "What's next on the (View) menu?" later in this chapter.

>> **Share:** Click here to share the selected items with others. A pop-up menu lets you choose to share via Mail, Messages, AirDrop, or Notes.

Monterey's extensible architecture lets you add other services (such as Vimeo or LinkedIn) and apps (such as Photos and Aperture) to your Share menu. To manage these extensions, choose More from the Share pop-up menu. Alternatively, you can launch the System Preferences application, click the Extensions icon, and then click the Share Menu item on the left side of the window.

>> **Add Tags:** Click here to assign one or more colored tags to selected items. You find out more about tags and tagging in the "Customizing Finder Windows" section, later in this chapter.

>> **Action:** Click this icon to see a pop-up menu of all the context-sensitive actions you can perform on selected icons, as shown in Figure 4-4.

TIP

If you see angle brackets (>>) at the right edge of the toolbar, as shown in Figure 4-4, at least one toolbar item is not visible. Click the angle brackets and a menu displays all hidden items (Group By, Share, Add Tags, and Action in Figure 4-4). Or expand the window so it's wide enough to display all the items in the toolbar.

>> **Search:** Click the little magnifying glass and the Search box appears. This is a nifty way to quickly search for files or folders. Just type a word (or even just a few letters), and in a few seconds, the window fills with a list of files that match. You can also start a search by choosing File ⇨ Find (shortcut: ⌘+F). You find out all about searching in Chapter 10.

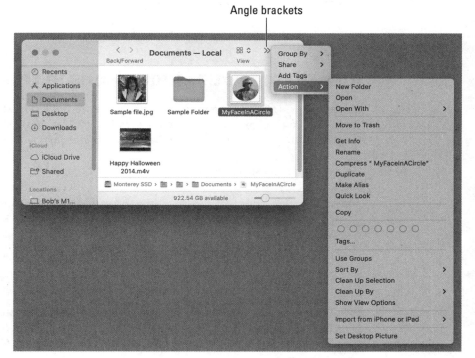

FIGURE 4-4:
Use the Action pop-up menu to perform common actions on selected items.

Figuring out what an icon is

What's an icon? Glad you asked. Each Finder icon represents an item or a container on your hard drive. *Containers* — hard drives, USB thumb drives, folders, CDs, DVDs, shared network volumes, and so on — can contain a virtually unlimited number of application files, document files, and folders (which can contain an unlimited number of application files, document files, and folders).

Icons on the dock and the sidebar of Finder windows are not the same as the Finder icons I describe in this chapter. They're simply convenient pointers to actual Finder icons. Technically, dock and sidebar icons are aliases. (If you don't yet know what an alias is, you're going to find out long before the thrilling conclusion of this chapter.)

Anyway, working with icons is easy:

>> Single-click to select.

>> Double-click to open.

>> Click and drag to move.

>> Release mouse button to drop.

But enough talk. It's time to see what these puppies look like.

Identifying your Finder icons in the wild

Although icons all work the same, they come in different kinds, shapes, and sizes. When you've been around the Mac for a while, you develop a sixth sense about icons and can guess what an unfamiliar icon contains just by looking at it.

Here are the major icon types:

>> **Application icons** are *programs* — the software you use to accomplish tasks on your Mac. Mail, Safari, and Calendar are applications. So are Microsoft Word and Adobe Photoshop.

Application icons come in a variety of shapes. For example, application icons are often square-ish, diamond-shaped, rectangular, or just oddly shaped. The first row of icons in Figure 4-5 displays application icons of various shapes.

>> **Document icons** are files created by applications. Letters created with TextEdit are documents. This chapter began life as a document created in Microsoft Word. And spreadsheet, PDF, video, image, and song files are all documents.

Document icons are often reminiscent of a piece of paper, as shown in the second row of icons in Figure 4-5.

TIP

If your document icons are generic (like the first four icons in the second row of Figure 4-5) but you'd prefer icons that reflect their contents (like the last two icons in the second row of Figure 4-5), open View Options or use the ⌘+J shortcut, and then select the Show Icon Preview check box (see Chapter 23 for additional details about View Options).

>> **Folder and disk icons** are the Mac's organizational containers. You can put icons — and the applications or documents they stand for — in folders or disks. You can put folders in disks or in other folders, but you can't put a disk inside another disk.

WARNING

Folders look like, well, manila folders (what a concept) and can contain just about any other icon. You use folders to organize your files and applications on your hard drive. You can have as many folders as you want, so don't be afraid to create new ones. The thought behind the whole folders thing is pretty obvious: If your hard drive is a filing cabinet, folders are its drawers and folders (duh!). The third row in Figure 4-5 shows some typical folder icons.

And while disks behave pretty much like folders, their icons often look like disks, as shown in the last row in Figure 4-5.

>> **Alias icons** are wonderful — no, make that *fabulous* — organizational tools. I like aliases so much that they get an entire section to themselves.

Find My	Font Book	GarageBand	Home	Image Capture	iMovie

| an archive document.zip | a PDF document.pdf | a Word document.doc | another Word document.docx | a picture document.png | a GarageBand document.band |

| Desktop | Documents | Downloads | Movies | Music | Pictures | Public |

| disk icon | another disk icon | backup disk icon | USB disk icon | DVD disk icon |

FIGURE 4-5:
Icons come in many shapes and designs.

TIP

If you're looking for details about how to organize your icons in folders, move them around, delete them, and so on, hang in there. Chapter 8 is about organizing and managing files and folders.

Aliases Are Awesome!

An *alias* is a tiny file that automatically opens the file, folder, disk, or network volume that it represents. Although an alias is technically an icon, it's different from other icons; it actually does nothing but open a different icon when you double-click. Put another way, aliases are organizational tools that let you store an icon in more than one place without creating multiple copies of the file.

An alias is very different than a duplicated file. For example, the Preview application uses around 12 megabytes (MB) of disk space. If I were to *duplicate* Preview, I'd have two files on my hard drive, requiring around 12MB of disk space apiece.

An *alias* of Preview, on the other hand, looks just like the original Preview icon and opens Preview when you double-click it — but it uses a mere 4 kilobytes (K) of disk space — a tiny fraction of its parent icon's size. So try placing aliases of programs and files you use most often in convenient places such as the desktop or a folder in your Home folder.

Why else do I think that aliases are so great? Well, they open any file or folder (or application) on any hard drive from anywhere else on any hard drive — which is a very good trick. But there are other reasons why I think aliases are awesome:

TIP

>> **Convenience:** Aliases enable you to make items appear to be in more than one place, which on many occasions is exactly what you want to do. For example, keep an alias of your word-processing program on your desktop and another in your Documents folder for quick access. Aliases enable you to open your word processor right away without having to navigate into the depths of your Applications folder every time you need it.

While you're at it, you might want to put an icon for your word processor in both the dock and the sidebar to make it even easier to open your word processor without a lot of clicking.

>> **Flexibility and organization:** You can create aliases and store them anywhere on your hard drive to represent the same document in several different folders.

>> **Integrity:** Some programs must remain in the same folder as their supporting files and folders. These programs won't function properly unless they're in the same folder as their dictionaries, thesauruses, data files (for games), templates, and so on. Thus, you can't put the actual icons for such programs on the desktop without impairing their functionality. An alias lets you access a program like that from anywhere on your hard drive. (And it's probably best to leave all your apps in the Applications folder, where they belong.)

I admit I'm somewhat old-school when it comes to organizing my files in the proper folders (see Chapter 8), but Monterey's speedy Spotlight search mechanism along with tools such as Launchpad and Mission Control (all, not coincidentally, discussed in Chapter 10), as well as the sidebar's Recents item, let you find pretty much any file on your disk in seconds.

Creating aliases

When you create an alias, its icon looks the same as the original icon it represents, but the suffix *alias* is tacked onto its name, and a tiny arrow called a *badge* (as shown in the margin) appears in the bottom-left corner of its icon. Figure 4-6 shows an alias and its *parent* icon — the icon that opens if you double-click the alias.

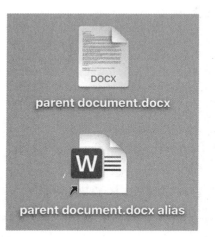

FIGURE 4-6:
An alias (bottom) and its parent.

To create an alias for an icon, do one of the following:

>> Click the parent icon and choose File ⇨ Make Alias.

>> Click the parent icon and press ⌘+Control+A.

>> Click the parent icon and use the Action menu's Make Alias command (in the toolbar of all Finder windows).

>> Click an icon while holding down the Control key (or right-click it or tap it with two fingers on a trackpad) and then choose the Make Alias command from the contextual menu that appears. (You can explore contextual shortcut menus — which are very cool — in Chapter 2.)

>> Click any file or folder, press and hold down ⌘+Option, and then drag the file or folder while continuing to hold down ⌘+Option. Presto! An alias appears where you release the mouse button. As a bonus, when you create an alias this way it doesn't inherit the *alias* suffix in its name.

TIP

When I first create a file, I save it in its proper folder inside the Documents folder in my Home folder. If it's a document that I plan to work on for more than a day or two (such as a magazine article or book chapter), I make an alias of the document (or folder) and plop it on my desktop. After I finish the article or chapter and submit it to an editor, I trash the alias, leaving the original file safe and sound, filed away in its proper folder, and leaving my desktop clean and uncluttered.

Deleting aliases

This is a short section because deleting an alias is such an easy chore. To delete an alias, simply drag it onto the Trash icon on the dock. That's it! You can also Control-click it and choose Move to Trash from the contextual menu that appears (right-click or Control-click or two-finger tap), or select the icon and press ⌘+Delete.

Deleting an alias does *not* delete the parent item. (If you want to delete the parent item, you have to go hunt it down and kill it yourself.)

Hunting down an alias's parent

Suppose that you create an alias of a file, and later you want to delete both the alias and its parent file, but you can't find the parent file. What do you do? Well, you can use Finder's Find function to find it (try saying that three times real fast), but here are faster ways to find the parent icon of an alias:

» Select the alias icon and choose File ➪ Show Original.

» Use the keyboard shortcut ⌘+R.

» Select the alias icon and use the Action menu's Show Original command.

» Control-click (or right-click or two-fingered tap on a trackpad) the alias icon and choose Show Original from the contextual menu.

Any of these methods opens the window containing the parent document with its icon preselected for your convenience.

The View(s) from a Window

Views are part of what makes your Mac feel like *your* Mac. Monterey offers four views so you can select the best one for any occasion. Some people like one view so much that they rarely (or never) use others. Other people, like me, memorize the keyboard shortcuts to switch views instantly without reaching for the mouse. Try 'em all, and use the one(s) you prefer.

Moving through folders fast in Column view

Column view is a darn handy way to quickly look through a lot of folders at once, and it's especially useful when those folders are filled with graphics files. The Column view is my favorite way to display windows in Finder.

To display a window in Column view, shown in Figure 4-7, click the Column view icon on the toolbar (as shown in the margin), choose View ⇨ As Columns from Finder's menu bar, or press ⌘+3.

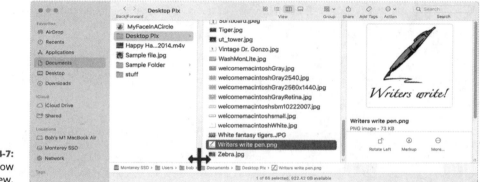

Here's how I clicked around in Column view to see the list of folders and files you see in Figure 4-7:

1. When I clicked the Documents icon in the sidebar, its contents appeared in the column to the right.

2. When I clicked the folder titled Desktop PIx (note that I accidentally capitalized the *l*) in this column, its contents appeared in the second column.

3. When I clicked Writers write pen.png in the second column, the contents of that file appeared in the third column along with information about the file, such as its size (10 KB) and the date and time it was created, modified, and last opened.

The third column is displaying a preview, a feature available in all views by choosing View ⇨ Show/Hide Preview. You can modify the information you see in the preview by choosing View ⇨ Show Preview Options and enabling the items you want displayed in the preview column.

Here are some helpful tips when you're poking around Column view:

TIP

WARNING

>> **You can have as many columns in a Column view window as your screen can handle.** Just drag any edge or corner of the window to enlarge it so new columns have room to open. You can also click the green Zoom (Maximize) button to make the window fill the screen. (**Hint:** To get out of full-screen mode, press Esc or move your cursor to the top of the screen and click the green Zoom button that appears near the top-left corner.)

If you Option-click the green Zoom button, the window will expand just enough to display all columns with content in them.

>> **You can use the little column divider lines at the bottom of every column to resize the column width.**

You'll see the resizer cursor when your mouse pointer is directly over the two tiny lines at the bottom of the column divider line, as shown in Figure 4-7.

To be specific:

- If you drag the resizer left or right, the column to its left resizes.

- If you hold down the Option key when you drag a divider line, *all* columns resize at the same time.

- If you double-click a divider line, the column to its left expands to the Right Size, which is the width of the widest item in the column.

- If you press Option before you double-click a divider line, all columns expand individually to their Right Size.

- If you right- or Control-click a divider line, you see a pop-up menu with three sizing options: Right Size This Column, Right Size All Columns Individually, and Right Size All Columns Equally. You'll also see Import from iPhone or iPad if an iPhone or iPad is near (or connected to) your Mac.

>> **The preview column displays information about the highlighted item to its left, but only if that item isn't a folder or disk.** Why? Well, if it were a folder or disk, its contents would be in this column.

For many items, the picture you see in the preview column is an enlarged view of the file's icon. You only see a preview (as shown in Figure 4-7) when the selected item is saved in a format that Quick Look (which you discover in Chapter 10) can interpret (which is to say, most image file formats, including TIFF, JPEG, PNG, GIF, and PDF to name a few, as well as many other file formats, including Microsoft Word and Pages).

TIP

If you don't like having the preview displayed in Column view (but want it to remain in all other views), choose View ⇨ Show View Options and deselect the check box for Show Preview Column. You can do the same for any other view, or turn the preview off in all views by choosing View ⇨ Hide Preview.

Perusing in Icon view

Icon view is a free-form view that allows you to move your icons around within a window to your heart's content. Refer to Figure 4-4 to see icons in my Documents folder displayed in Icon view.

To display a window in Icon view, click the Icon view icon in the toolbar (shown in the margin), choose View ➪ As Icons from Finder's menu bar, or press ⌘+1.

TIP

The best part of Icon view, at least in my humble opinion, is the Icon Size slider in the lower-right corner of the status bar in Icon view windows. Note that the status bar and Icon Size slider move to the top of the window if the window's sidebar and toolbar are hidden.

Listless? Try viewing folders as a list

Now I come to my second-favorite view, List view (shown in Figure 4-8). I like it so much because of the little angle bracket to the left of each folder. These angle brackets, which were called *disclosure triangles* in earlier macOS releases, let you see the contents of a folder without actually opening it. This view also allows you to select items from multiple folders at once and move or copy items between folders in a single window. Finally, it's the view used to present Spotlight search results.

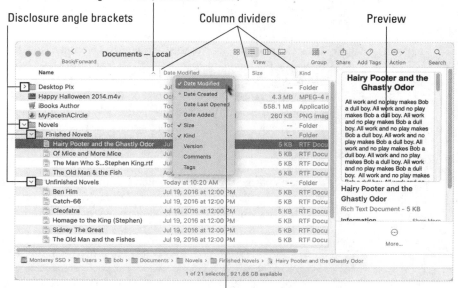

FIGURE 4-8:
A window
in List view.

To display a window in List view, click the List view icon on the toolbar (shown in the margin), choose View ➪ As List from the Finder menu bar, or press ⌘+2.

When you're in List view, the following tips can help you breeze through your folders to find what you're looking for:

TIP

WARNING

>> **To disclose a folder's contents, click the angle bracket to its left or, if it's selected, press the right-arrow key.** Figure 4-8 shows the result of either clicking the angle bracket to the left of the Novels folder or selecting (highlighting) the Novels folder and pressing the right-arrow key.

I pressed Option+→ in Figure 4-8, so all the Novels folder's subfolders (the Finished Novels and Unfinished Novels folders in this case) also expanded. And if either of these subfolders (or any other subfolder in the Novels folder) had subfolders, they too would have been expanded when I pressed Option+→.

To close an open folder, click the angle bracket again or select the folder and press left-arrow. To close all open folders in a List view window, choose Edit ➪ Select All (or press ⌘+A) and then press Option+←.

The angle brackets don't appear if you're using groups. To see the angle brackets, choose View ➪ Use Groups or use its keyboard shortcut, ⌘+Control+0 (zero). These are toggles, and will turn groups off if they're enabled or on if they're disabled. You could also choose None from the Group icon/menu in the toolbar.

Disclosure angle brackets and groups are an either/or situation — you either have disclosure angle brackets or groups but not both at the same time (in the same window or tab).

>> **Click the column header to sort items in List view.** Note the little upside-down *v* at the right edge of the selected column (the Name column in Figure 4-8). That's the column's sorting indicator. If the *v* points upward, as it does in Figure 4-8, the items in the corresponding column are sorted in alphabetical order; if you click the header (Name) again, the triangle will flip upside down and point downward and the items will be listed in the opposite (reverse alphabetical) order. This behavior is true for all columns in List view windows.

>> **You can change the order in which columns appear in a window.** To do so, press and hold down on a column's name, and then drag it to the left or right until it's where you want it. Release the mouse button, and the column moves.

The exception (isn't there always an exception?) is that the Name column always appears first in List view windows; you can move all other columns about at will. In fact, you can even hide and show columns other than Name if you like using the View Options window.

TIP

TIP

It's even easier to hide or maximize columns by right- or Control-clicking anywhere on any column header (as shown below the Date Modified column in Figure 4-8). Column names with check marks are displayed; column names that are unchecked are hidden.

You can fine-tune all four views and the desktop by using the View Options window. Just choose View ➪ Show View Options or press ⌘+J. The options you see apply to the active window or the desktop. Click the Use as Defaults button to apply these options to all windows in that view (that is, Icon, List, Column, or Gallery).

>> **To widen or shrink a column, hover the cursor over the dividing line between that column and drag left or right.** When your cursor is over the dividing line in the header, it changes to a double-headed resizer, as shown in the margin.

Hangin' in the Gallery (view)

Gallery view is the latest iteration of what used to be called the Cover Flow view. To display a window in Gallery view, click the Gallery view icon on the toolbar (shown in the margin), choose View ➪ As Gallery from Finder's menu bar, or press ⌘+4. Figure 4-9 shows Gallery view.

FIGURE 4-9:
A window in Gallery view.

Although Gallery view is useful only for folders with documents or images, it does offer at least three cool features:

>> The selected item (Writers write pen.png in Figure 4-9) appears in a preview in the top part of the window.

>> The preview column displays additional information about the selected item.

>> You can quickly flip through the previews by clicking the images to the left or right of the current preview image or by pressing the left- or right-arrow key.

What's next on the (View) menu?

The Finder View menu offers several commands in addition to the four views. These commands might help you peruse your icons more easily:

>> **Use Groups:** Active window only. When enabled, it subdivides the items in the active window into groups, as shown in Figure 4-10, which is grouped by Date Last Opened.

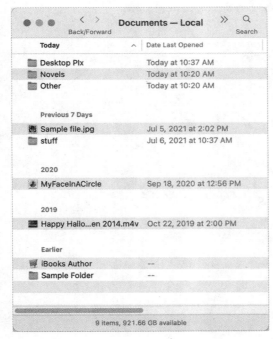

FIGURE 4-10: The items in this window are grouped by Date Last Opened.

>> **Sort By:** This submenu offers the following options for sorting items in the active window:

- None (shortcut: ⌘+ Option+Control+0)
- Snap to Grid
- Name (shortcut: ⌘+ Option+Control+1)
- Kind (shortcut: ⌘+ Option+Control+2)
- Date Last Opened (shortcut: ⌘+ Option+Control+3)
- Date Added (shortcut: ⌘+ Option+Control+4)
- Date Modified (⌘+ Option+Control+5)
- Date Created (strangely, there's no shortcut for this command)
- Size (shortcut: ⌘+ Option+Control+6)
- Tags (shortcut: ⌘+ Option+Control+7)

Note that the Sort By command becomes Group By when Groups are enabled.

>> **Clean Up:** Clean Up is available only in Icon view or on the desktop when no windows are active. Choose this command to align icons to an invisible grid; you use it to keep your windows and desktop neat and tidy. (If you like this invisible grid, don't forget that you can turn it on or off for the desktop and individual windows by using View Options.) If no windows are active, the command instead cleans up your desktop. (To deactivate all open windows, just click anywhere on the desktop or close all open windows.)

TIP

If any icons are selected (highlighted) when you pull down the View menu, you see Clean Up Selection rather than Clean Up. If you choose this command, it moves only the icons that are currently selected.

>> **Clean Up By:** This command combines the tidiness of the Clean Up command with the organizational yumminess of the Sort By command, which I mention earlier in this chapter and discuss in more detail shortly.

This command sorts the icons by your choice of criteria, namely:

- Name (shortcut: ⌘+Option+1)
- Kind (shortcut: ⌘+Option+2)
- Date Modified (shortcut: ⌘+Option+5)
- Date Created (no shortcut)
- Size (shortcut: ⌘+Option+6)
- Tags (shortcut: ⌘+Option+7)

TIP

Clean Up By is similar to the Sort By command, but unlike Sort By, Clean Up By is a one-time affair. After you've used it, you can once again move icons around and reorganize them any way you like.

Unlike Clean Up By, which is a one-shot command, Sort By is persistent and will continue to reorganize your icons automatically. In other words, you can't move icons around manually in an arranged window.

One last thing: The Clean Up and Clean Up By commands are available only for windows viewed as icons. The Sort By command is available in all four views and remains in effect if you switch to a different view or close the window. To stop Finder from arranging icons in a window, choose None from the View ⇨ Sort By submenu or Option + click the toolbar's Group pop-up menu and choose None.

WARNING

If you're like me, you've taken great pains to place icons carefully in specific places on your desktop. If so, the Clean Up By and Sort By commands will mess up your perfectly arranged desktop icons. And alas, cleaning up your desktop is still not something macOS lets you undo.

Finder on the Menu

Finder's menu bar is packed with useful goodies; in the following sections, I look at those that pertain specifically to using Finder.

The actual Finder menu

Here are a few of the main items you can find on the Finder menu:

>> **About Finder:** Choose this command to find out which version of Finder is running on your Mac. This menu item isn't particularly useful — or at least not for very long. But when a different application is running, the About Finder item becomes About application name and usually gives information about the program's version number, the developers, and any other tidbits that those developers decide to throw in. Sometimes these tidbits are useful, sometimes they're interesting, and sometimes they're both.

>> **Preferences:** Use the choices here to control how Finder looks and acts. Find out the details in the "Setting Finder preferences" section, later in this chapter.

>> **Services:** One of the cool features of macOS applications is the accessibility of Services. If nothing is selected in Finder, the Services menu is empty, as shown in the top panel of Figure 4-11. When a Finder icon or icons are selected, you

can choose from four Services, as shown in the middle panel of Figure 4-11. Finally, if a word or words are selected in an application (TextEdit is shown in Figure 4-11), you have five different options, as shown in bottom pane of Figure 4-11.

In other words, the items you see in the Services menu are context-sensitive, so what you see in yours will depend on what you have selected. If you look in the Services menu and don't find anything interesting, try selecting something else and looking again; you might be pleasantly surprised.

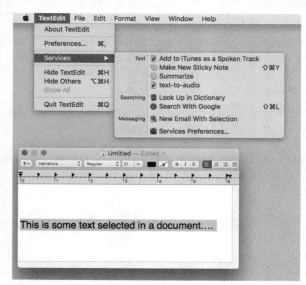

FIGURE 4-11: Services available with nothing selected (top), an icon selected (middle), and some text selected in a TextEdit document (bottom).

Finally, if you'd like to add even more services to this menu, choose the last item in the menu, Services Preferences. You can then enable dozens of useful services that aren't available by default.

» **Hide Finder (⌘+H):** Use this command when Finder windows are open and are distracting you. Choosing it makes Finder inactive (another program becomes active) and hides any open Finder windows. To make Finder visible again, either choose Show All from the application's self-named menu (the one that bears the name of the active application, such as Finder, TextEdit, or System Preferences) or click the Finder icon, shown in the margin here, on the dock.

TIP

The advantage to hiding Finder — rather than closing or minimizing all your windows to get a clean screen — is that you don't have to open them all again when you're ready to get the windows back. Instead, just choose Show All (to see all windows in all apps) or click the Finder icon on the dock to see all Finder windows.

» **Hide Others (Option+⌘+H):** This command hides all windows associated with all running programs except the active program. It appears in most applications' self-named menus and is good for hiding distractions so you can focus on one thing: the unhidden application.

TIP

Another easy way to hide all open applications and windows while activating Finder is to hold down the ⌘ and Option keys and click the Finder icon on the dock. This technique works with whatever application is active, not just Finder. So if you're surfing the web and decide you want to see only Safari's windows on your screen, ⌘+Option-click the Safari icon on the dock, and it will happen instantly.

» **Show All:** Use this command as the antidote to both of the Hide commands. Choose this, and nothing is hidden anymore.

Note that all three of these commands require that at least one application be running and not hidden (in addition to Finder). Put another way, when Finder is the only app running or not hidden, these three commands are grayed out and unavailable.

TIP

You can achieve much the same effect as all this hide-and-show jazz with Mission Control, which I discuss in Chapter 10.

Finally, if you noticed that Finder menu's Empty Trash command isn't mentioned here, that's because it gets detailed coverage in Chapter 8.

Like a road map: The current folder's pop-up menu

On every window's title bar is the name of the folder (or disk) that you're viewing in this window: the highlighted folder. You know that already. What you might not know is that it offers a hidden road map to this folder from the top level. The following steps explain how it works:

1. ⌘-**click or Control-click the folder's name in the title bar.**

A pop-up menu appears, with the current folder (Desktop in Figure 4-12) at the top.

2. **Select any folder in the menu, and release the mouse button to display that folder's contents.**

As shown in Figure 4-12, the contents of the Desktop folder — three screen shot files — are displayed in the window. If I highlight the bob folder (as I have in Figure 4-12) and release the mouse button, the contents of the bob folder would replace the contents of the Desktop folder in this window.

3. **After jumping to a new folder, you can click the Back button.**

Hey, you're right back where you were before you touched that pop-up menu!

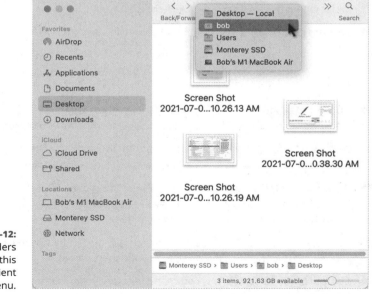

FIGURE 4-12:
Traverse folders from this convenient pop-up menu.

TIP

Don't forget that you can display the path bar near the bottom of the window (it's displayed in Figure 4-12) by choosing View ➪ Show Path Bar. Then you can double-click any folder displayed in the path bar to open it. This last trick works not only on Finder windows but also with the title bar of most document windows (Word, Photoshop, and so on), showing you the path to the folder containing the document you're working on.

Going places with the Go menu

The Go menu is chock-full of shortcuts. The items on this menu take you to places on your Mac — many of the same places you can go with the Finder window's toolbar — and a few other places.

The following list gives you a brief look at the items on the Go menu:

>> **Back (⌘ +[):** Use this menu option to return to the last open Finder window. It's equivalent to the Back button on the Finder toolbar, in case you have the toolbar hidden.

>> **Forward (⌘ +]):** This command is the opposite of using the Back command, moving you forward through every folder you open. Remember that if you haven't gone back, you can't go forward.

>> **Enclosing Folder (⌘ +↑):** This command tells the Finder window to display the folder where the currently selected item is located.

>> **Recents (Shift+⌘ +F):** This command shows you all your document files at once.

TIP

This is a good time to choose View ➪ Sort By (or View ➪ Group By) to put these files into a semblance of order.

>> **Documents (Shift+⌘ +O):** You'll probably use this command often because the Documents folder is a great place to save documents you create.

>> **Desktop (Shift+⌘ +D):** Use this command to display the Desktop folder, which contains the same icons as the desktop you see behind open windows.

>> **Downloads (Option+⌘ +L):** This opens your Downloads folder, which is where files you download in Safari, save as attachments in Mail, or receive via AirDrop (explained shortly) are saved by default.

>> **Home (Shift+⌘ +H):** Use this command to have the Finder window display your Home folder (which is named with your short name).

>> **Computer (Shift+⌘ +C):** This command tells the Finder window to display the Computer level, showing your network and all your disks.

>> **AirDrop (Shift+⌘+R):** AirDrop lets you share files wirelessly with anyone around you. No setup or special settings are required. Just click the AirDrop icon in the Finder sidebar, use this menu item, or use the keyboard shortcut, and your Mac automatically discovers other people nearby who are using AirDrop.

AirDrop works between Macs and most iDevices running iOS 8 or later.

>> **Network (Shift+⌘+K):** This command displays whatever is accessible on your network in the Finder window.

>> **iCloud Drive (Shift+⌘+I):** This command opens a window that displays the contents of your iCloud drive (which you read more about in Chapter 8).

>> **Applications (Shift+⌘+A):** This command displays your Applications folder, the usual storehouse for all the programs that came with your Mac (and the most likely place to find the programs you install).

>> **Utilities (Shift+⌘+U):** This command gets you to the Utilities folder inside the Applications folder in one fell swoop. The Utilities folder is the repository of such useful items as Disk Utility (which lets you erase, format, verify, and repair disks) and Disk Copy (which you use to create and mount disk-image files).

>> **Recent Folders:** Use this submenu to quickly go back to a folder that you recently visited. Every time you open a folder, macOS creates an alias to it and stores it in the Recent Folders folder. You can open any of these aliases from the Recent Folders command on the Go menu.

>> **Go to Folder (Shift+⌘+G):** This command summons the Go to the Folder window. Look at your desktop. Maybe it's cluttered with lots of windows, or maybe it's empty. Either way, suppose you're several clicks away from a folder that you want to open. If you know the path from your hard drive to that folder, you can type the path to the folder in the Go to the Folder text box — separating folder names with forward slashes (/) — and then click Go to move (relatively) quickly to the folder you need.

TIP

The first character you type must also be a forward slash.

This particular dialog is a tad clairvoyant in that it tries to guess which folder you mean by the first letter or two that you type after a forward slash. If the folder you seek isn't in the list of suggestions, just keep typing.

>> **Connect to Server (⌘+K):** If your Mac is connected to a network or to the internet, use this command to reach those remote resources.

One last thing: If you're looking for the Library folder inside your Home folder, which used to appear in the Go menu (before OS X 10.7 Lion), it's now hidden for your protection (as I explain in Chapter 7). To reveal it, hold down the Option key before you open the Go menu.

Customizing Finder Windows

Finder is outrageously handy. It not only gives you convenient access to multiple windows but also offers ways to tweak what you see until you get what works best for you. So whereas earlier sections in this chapter explain what Finder is and how it works, the following sections ask, "How would you like it to be?"

Adding folders to the sidebar

Adding any file or folder you like to the sidebar is easy. All you need to do is select the file or folder you want to add and choose File ⇨ Add to Sidebar from the menu bar (or use its shortcut ⌘+Control+T). You can now use the item anytime you like by clicking it in the sidebar of any Finder window. Better still, you can move files or folders into folders in the sidebar by dragging them onto the folder's sidebar icon.

TIP

You can add folders (but not files) to the sidebar by dragging them onto the sidebar.

WARNING

Be careful not to drag a folder *onto* another folder or it will be moved into that folder instead of being added to the sidebar. You'll see a little line above or below existing folders in the sidebar; that shows you where this folder will appear if you release the mouse button. If a folder in the sidebar is highlighted and you don't see the little line, releasing the mouse button will not add the folder to the sidebar, but will move it into the highlighted folder.

To remove an item from the sidebar, right- or Control-click the item and choose Remove from Sidebar. Or drag the item off the sidebar and release the mouse button when the little x-in-a-circle appears.

Setting Finder preferences

You can find Finder and Desktop preferences by choosing Finder ⇨ Preferences. In the Finder Preferences window that appears, click the icons in the toolbar to select one of the four Finder Preferences panes: General, Tags, Sidebar, and Advanced.

General pane

In the General pane, you find the following options:

>> **Show These Items on the Desktop check boxes:** Select or deselect these check boxes to choose whether icons for hard drives; external disks; CDs,

DVDs, and iPods; and connected servers appear on the desktop. macOS Monterey deselects all four options by default. If you don't want disk icons cluttering your beautiful desktop, deselect (clear) these check boxes. When they're deselected, you can still work with hard drives, CDs, DVDs, and other types of disks. You just have to open a Finder window and select the disk or disc you want in the sidebar.

>> **New Finder Windows Show:** Here, you can choose whether opening a new Finder window displays Recents, your Home folder (which is my preference), the Documents or Desktop folders, or any other disk or folder. (Recents is the default.)

>> **Open Folders in Tabs Instead of New Windows check box:** Selecting this check box spawns a new tab in the current window when you press ⌘ and double-click a folder or disk.

TIP

If you don't enable it, ⌘+double-clicking a folder or disk icon opens it in a new window.

The default behavior is for folders to open in place when you double-click (open) them, which prevents window clutter. If you want a new window or tab instead, press ⌘ before you double-click. This forces the folder to open in a new window or tab (depending on whether the box is checked or not). Between this feature and Column view, I rarely need more than two windows onscreen, and I get by most of the time with a single window with multiple tabs.

Tags pane

The Tags pane is where you manage your tags, which appear in Finder's File menu, the right- or Control-click shortcut menu, the sidebar, and the toolbar. You can see a file or folder's tags in Finder windows, Get Info windows and inspectors, and applications' Open and Save dialogs and sheets, and you can use them as criteria for searches and smart folders.

TECHNICAL STUFF

A sheet is nothing more than a dialog that is attached to a document window's title bar and can't be moved. Some apps use sheets, other apps use dialogs, but either way you'll see the same options.

>> To rename a tag, click its name and type a new one.

>> To change a tag's color, click the colored circle to the left of its name and choose a different color.

>> Select the boxes for tags that you want to appear in the sidebar and toolbar.

TIP

To see your deselected tags in the sidebar or toolbar, click All Tags in (Sidebar) or Show All (toolbar).

Now, here's how to use 'em. To assign tags to icons, first select the icon(s) and then follow these steps:

1. **Choose File ⇨ Tags and click one or more of the colored dots in the Tags section.**

2. **Right- or Control-click and click one or more of the colored dots in the Tags section of the shortcut menu.**

3. **Click the Tags icon on the toolbar and click one or more tags.**

Here are a few more handy tricks with tags:

>> **To create a custom tag on the fly:** Right- or Control-click an item, choose Tags, type a label for the new tag, and then press Return.

>> **To untag an item:** Right- or Control-click the item, choose Tags, select the tag you want to remove, and then press Delete.

>> **To remove every instance of a tag from every file and folder on your disk:** Right- or Control-click the tag in the Tags pane of Finder Preferences, and then choose Delete Tag. Don't worry. Deleting a tag won't delete the items; it just removes that tag from every item.

TIP

Click the tags in your sidebar to see every file on all connected hard drives with that tag.

Sidebar pane

The Sidebar pane lets you choose which items are displayed in the sidebar. Select the check box to display the item; deselect the check box to not display it.

Advanced pane

The Advanced pane is just big enough to offer the following check boxes and a pop-up menu:

>> **Show All Filename Extensions check box (off by default):** Tells Finder to display the little two-, three-, four-, or more character filename suffixes (such as .doc in summary.doc) that make your Mac's file lists look more like those of a Linux (or Windows) user. The Finder hides those from you by default, but if you want to be able to see them in Finder when you open or save files, you need to turn on this option.

>> **Show Warning Before Changing an Extension check box (on by default):** Allows you to turn off the nagging dialog that appears if you attempt to change the two-, three-, four-, or more character file extension.

>> **Show Warning Before Removing from iCloud Drive (on by default):** Does what it says — warns you before you remove a file or folder from your iCloud drive.

>> **Show Warning Before Emptying the Trash check box (on by default):** Allows you to turn off the nagging dialog telling you how many items are in the Trash and asking whether you really want to delete them.

>> **Remove Items from the Trash After 30 Days check box (off by default):** This option does exactly what it says: It automatically deletes any item in the Trash for more than 30 days. Think of it as automatic emptying of the Trash for items that have been there 30 days or longer.

>> **Keep Folders on Top (two check boxes, both off by default):** These two options sort folders first, then files:

- **In Windows when Sorting by Name:** Enable this one to sort folders before files in all windows sorted by name.

- **On Desktop:** Enable this check box to sort folders before files on the desktop.

>> **When Performing a Search drop-down menu:** Lets you choose the default search location when you initiate a search as described earlier in this chapter. Your choices are Search This Mac (the default), Search the Current Folder, and Use the Previous Search Scope.

Digging for Icon Data in the Info Window

Every icon has an Info window that provides information about that icon and enables you to choose which other users (if any) you want to have the privilege of using this icon. (I discuss sharing files and privileges in detail in Chapter 18.) The Info window is also where you can lock an icon so that it can't be renamed or dragged to the Trash.

To see an icon's Info window, click the icon and choose File⇨Get Info (or press ⌘+I). The Info window for that icon appears. Figure 4-13 shows the Info window for an image (a .jpg file named Kiss).

Documents, folders, and disks each have slightly different Info windows. In this section, I give you highlights on the type of information and options that you can find.

The gray triangles reveal what information for an icon is available in this particular Info window. The sections that you see for most icons include the following:

» **Add Tags:** Click in this field to add tags to this item.

» **General:** For information of the general kind, such as

- *Kind:* What kind of file this is — an application, document, disk, folder, and so on

- *Size:* How much hard drive space this file uses

- *Where:* The path to the folder that contains this file

- *Created:* The date and time this file was created

- *Modified:* The date and time this file was last modified (that is, saved)

Six other check boxes may or may not appear in the General section of a particular Info window. Here's the scoop on this sextet of optional options:

- *Version:* Copyright information and the file's version number.

- *Shared Folder* (check box): Designates the folder as Shared, so other users are allowed to see and use its contents. You find out all about sharing in Chapter 18.

- *Stationery Pad* (check box): This one appears only in the Info window of document icons. If you select it, the file becomes a template. When you open a Stationery Pad document, a copy of its contents appears in a new Untitled document that you would typically save with a descriptive name.

- *Locked* (check box): If this box is selected, you receive the following warning if you try to put the item in the Trash: *This Item Is Locked. Do You Want to Move It to the Trash Anyway?* Your options are Stop and Continue. If you continue, the item goes into the Trash as usual. Then, when you try to empty the Trash, you receive another warning: *There Are Some Locked Items in the Trash. Do You Want to Remove All the Items, Including the Locked Ones, or Just the Unlocked Ones?* Your choices this time are Cancel, Remove Unlocked Items, and Remove All Items. If you choose to Remove All Items, the locked item(s) is/are deleted. If you choose Remove Unlocked Items, the locked item(s) remain(s) in the Trash, and you receive the *There Are Some Locked Items* warning again the next time you try to empty it.

  To remove the locked item from the Trash, click the Trash icon in the dock and drag the locked item out of the Trash and into a folder or onto the desktop.

- *Prevent App Nap* (check box): macOS can tell when an app is completely hidden behind other windows. If an app isn't currently doing something — playing music, downloading files, or checking your email, for example — App Nap conserves valuable battery life on laptops by slowing the app down. As soon as you activate the app again, it shifts back to full speed instantly.

  While App Nap can reduce CPU energy use by up to 23 percent, it may interfere with some programs' operation. If it does, try enabling this check box.

» **More Info:** When the file was created, modified, and last opened (documents only).

» **Name & Extension:** Tells the full name, including the (possibly hidden) extension.

» **Comments:** Provides a field in which you can type your own comments about this icon for Spotlight to use in its searches.

I talk about searching a little earlier in this chapter and discuss Spotlight searches in greater detail in Chapter 10.

» **Preview:** When you select a document icon, the menu offers a Preview option that you use to see a glimpse of what's in that document. You can also see this preview when you select a document icon in Column view; it magically appears in the rightmost column. If you select a QuickTime movie or sound, you can play your selection right there in the preview pane without launching a separate application. And when you select most pictures, you see a preview of the actual picture (me in Kiss makeup on Halloween in Figure 4-13).

» **Sharing & Permissions:** Governs which users have access to this icon and how much access they are allowed. (See Chapter 18 for more about access privileges.)

TIP

If you press the Option key before you pull down Finder's File menu, the Get Info command changes to Show Inspector (alternatively, press ⌘+Option+I). The Get Info Inspector window looks and acts almost exactly like Get Info windows with two whopping exceptions:

» **Inspector displays info for only the currently selected icon.** If you click a different icon, Inspector instantly displays the info for the icon you clicked. That means you can Get Info on lots of icons in a row using the arrow keys or by pressing Tab or Shift+Tab. Try it — it's cool.

» **Cumulative info is displayed if multiple icons are selected.** In other words, if more than one icon is selected, Inspector displays the total size for all the selected files or folders or both.

And that's about it for icons, which are among the most fundamental parts of what makes your Mac a Mac (and not a toaster or an Xbox).

Chapter 5

Delving Even Deeper into Monterey's Desktop and Finder

In this chapter, you discover cool features you may not be familiar with — such as Stacks and Quick Actions — as well as features you (should) already know and love, such as Quick Look and the Preview pane. Along the way I also point out a handful of useful interface features that make Finder better.

And now, without further ado, let's dive into the power and magic of Stacks on your desktop.

Cleaning Up Your Desktop Automatically with Stacks

I've seen a lot of users' Mac desktops over the years, and many of them look something like Figure 5-1.

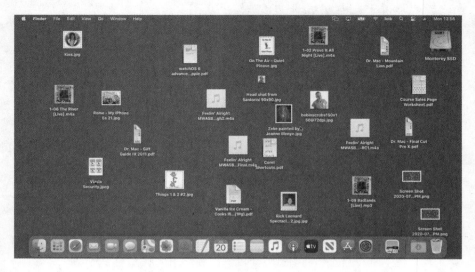

FIGURE 5-1:
A messy,
disorganized
desktop.

In the past, my advice to people with messy desktops was to select all the icons on the desktop, put them in one folder, and then rename the folder something like Former Desktop icons. It worked but using Monterey's Stacks is better and easier.

You can organize your desktop using Stacks in three ways:

>> Choose View ➪ Use Stacks.

>> Use the keyboard shortcut ⌘+Control+0 (that's a zero).

>> Right- or Control-click anywhere on the desktop, and then choose Use Stacks from the shortcut menu.

REMEMBER

The Use Stacks command is available only when the desktop is active, so if an active window is on your screen, you'll see Use Groups rather than Use Stacks.

When you choose Use Stacks, your desktop transforms instantly from the mess shown in Figure 5-1 to the four nicely organized stacks shown in Figure 5-2. Folders on the desktop are not affected by using Stacks; all other icons on the desktop are organized automatically into stacks (Images, PDF Documents, Music, and Screen Shots in Figure 5-2).

Single-click a stack to see its contents, as shown in Figure 5-3 for the Images stack.

Note that the expanded stack (Images, directly below the Monterey disk icon) now displays a down-facing arrow (or a triangle, depending on how you look at it) in Figure 5-3. That indicates that the stack is expanded. Click the stack again to close it. Finally, note that stacks ignore your disk icons (if any).

FIGURE 5-2:
Stacks create
order out of
chaos.

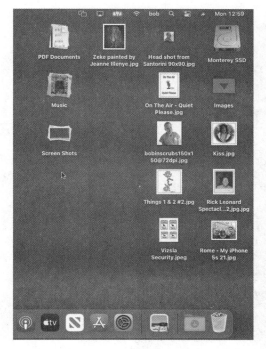

FIGURE 5-3:
Single-click a
stack (Images) to
see its contents.

Managing your Stacks

Choosing Use Stacks is just the start of things. When you're using Stacks, you can group items by choosing View ⇨ Group Stacks By, which offers the following choices:

>> None (no keyboard shortcut)

>> Kind (Control+⌘+2)

>> Date Last Opened (Control+⌘+3)

>> Date Added (Control+⌘+4)

>> Date Modified (Control+⌘+5)

>> Date Created (no keyboard shortcut)

>> Tags (Control+⌘+7)

All figures in this chapter so far have their stacks grouped by Kind, but it may be easier to find what you're looking for if you use one of the other options. For example, if you know when you added, modified, or last opened the file, you can choose one of the date-based options, such as Date Created, which is shown in Figure 5-4.

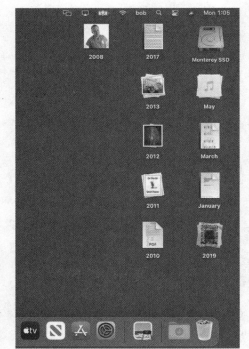

FIGURE 5-4:
Grouping stacks by Date Created gives you a different perspective than grouping them by Kind.

You can also right- or Control-click and choose Group Stacks By, which offers all the same commands except None.

Finally, if you're not already using Tags (discussed in Chapter 4) to organize your files, Stacks may be just the incentive you need to start.

Quick Actions: Now Playing All Over Monterey

Quick Actions are mini-apps that let you perform certain tasks without launching a real application. You'll find them in the Preview pane of Finder windows, in Quick Look windows, and in shortcut menus. They're super useful and can save you the time and effort of opening a program to perform a simple task, such as adding circles and arrows to an image (and much more), trimming video, and rotating pictures.

Getting the most out of Markup

In Monterey, the Markup icon (shown in the margin) and the Rotate icon (see Figure 5-5) are available in Quick Look windows and the Preview pane of Finder windows, and the commands are in Finder's shortcut menu (right- or Control-click).

FIGURE 5-5:
Click the Markup icon to see the Markup toolbar; click the Rotate icon to rotate your image in 90° increments.

TIP

When you click the Rotate icon, the default is to rotate your document counter-clockwise by 90°. If you'd rather rotate clockwise, press Option before you click.

When you have an image selected and you click the Markup icon in a Quick Look overlay, in a Preview pane in a Finder window, or in a Finder shortcut menu, an overlay appears displaying the image below the Markup toolbar, as shown in Figure 5-6.

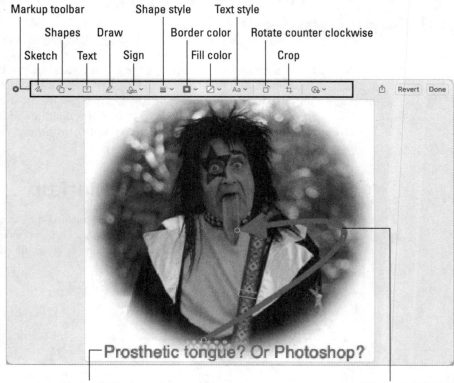

Markup toolbar   Shape style   Text style

Shapes   Draw   Border color   Rotate counter clockwise

Sketch   Text   Sign   Fill color   Crop

Prosthetic tongue? Or Photoshop?

text added with Markup   arrow added with Markup

FIGURE 5-6:
The Markup toolbar above an image to which I added text and an arrow by using Markup.

And here's how the tools work:

>> **Sketch:** Sketch a shape with a single stroke. Here's the cool part: If your drawing is recognized as a standard shape — a circle, a rectangle, an arrow, or such — it's replace d by a perfectly drawn rendition of the shape. If you don't like it perfect, you can use what you drew instead by choosing it from the palette that appears after you use the tool.

>> **Shapes:** Click a shape to place it on the image, and then drag the shape where you want. To resize a shape, use its blue handles. If the shape has green handles, you can use them to alter the shape.

You can also zoom in or out and highlight specific shapes using the pair of tools at the bottom of the Shapes drop-down (and shown in Figure 5-7):

- *Highlight:* Drag the highlight where you want. To resize it, use the blue handles.

- *Loupe:* Drag the loupe over the area you want to magnify. To increase or decrease the magnification level, drag the green handle; to increase or decrease the size of the loupe, drag the blue handle. To further magnify an area, you can create additional loupes and stack them, using the yellow guides that appear to align them.

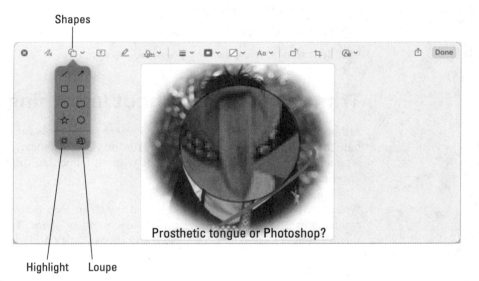

FIGURE 5-7:
The shapes
drop-down (left)
and the loupe in
action (right).

Shapes

Prosthetic tongue or Photoshop?

Highlight   Loupe

>> **Text:** Type your text, and then drag the text box where you want.

>> **Draw:** Use your finger to draw a shape with a single stroke. Press more firmly on the trackpad to draw thicker, heavier lines. Note that this tool is available only on computers with a Force Touch trackpad.

>> **Sign:** If signatures are listed, click one and drag it where you want. To resize it, use the blue handles.

To create a signature:

- *Using your trackpad:* Click the Sign tool, click Create Signature if shown, and then click Trackpad. Click the text as prompted, sign your name on the trackpad using your finger, and then click Done. If you don't like the results, click Clear and try again. If your trackpad supports it, press your finger more firmly on the trackpad to sign with a heavier, darker line.

- *Using a camera:* Click the Sign tool, click Create Signature if shown, and then click Camera (Mac camera) or iPhone or iPad (camera). Hold your signature (on white paper) facing the camera so that your signature is level with the blue line in the window. When your signature appears in the window, click Done. If you don't like the results, click Clear and try again.

» **Shape style:** Change the thickness and type of lines used in a shape or add a shadow to a shape.

» **Border color:** Change the color of a shape's border.

» **Fill color:** Change the color of a shape's fill.

» **Text style:** Change the font type, style, and color.

Trimming video without launching an app

Although QuickTime Player has allowed you to trim videos for years, you have to launch it and usually wait a few seconds for the video to appear. Monterey includes a faster, easier way to trim your videos without launching QuickTime Player (or another app).

 When a video file is selected, you'll find the Trim icon (shown in the margin) available in Quick Look windows, in Finder preview panes, and in the shortcut menu (right- or Control-click a video and choose Quick Actions ➪ Trim).

Click the Trim icon and a filmstrip appears below the video with handles for setting the beginning and end of the video, as shown in Figure 5-8.

Drag the left handle to where you want the video to begin, and then drag the right handle to where you want the video to end. Click Done and you're done. Your video has been trimmed of excess footage without launching an app.

One more thing: All tools discussed in this section are part of a Monterey feature called Quick Actions.

Video to be deleted

FIGURE 5-8:
Drag the handles
to set the start
and end points.

Start of Video   End of Video

Do It Quicker with Finder Quick Actions

You've already seen several of Monterey's Finder Quick Actions — Rotate, Markup, and Trim, to be precise — but there are a couple of actions that can help you get more out of your Quick Actions.

The first is the Create PDF Quick Action, which does what its name implies and more; the second is creating your own Quick Actions with Automator (discussed in Chapter 23), which may be the coolest thing about Quick Actions.

Creating PDFs without launching an app

In most applications, you can create a PDF from the Print sheet (see Chapter 22). But wouldn't it be nice if you could create PDFs without launching an application and choosing Print?

In Monterey it's no problem. Just use the Create PDF Quick Action, which you'll find in Quick Look windows, in the Preview pane of Finder windows, and in the shortcut menu (right- or Control-click).

Actually, it is a problem if you want to use the Create PDF Quick Action on files other than images. It won't work with a Word, Pages, Excel, or TextEdit document, or other document types. But, if your files are images — JPEG, TIFF, PNG, and such — you can turn them into PDFs with a click.

You can tell if the file can be converted because the Create PDF command or icon appears only when suitable files are selected, as shown in Figure 5-9.

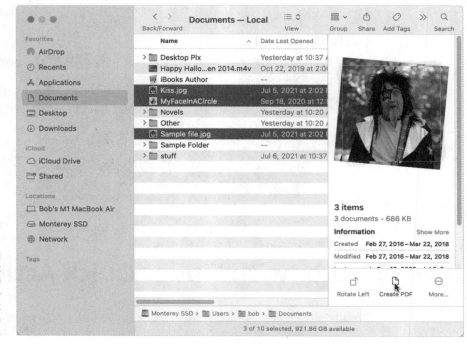

TIP

If the Create PDF Quick Action icon doesn't appear in the Preview pane when you select an image or images, try clicking the More icon (three dots in a circle) since the Create PDF Quick Action occasionally hides there.

Here's a cool feature: If you select multiple image files, as I did in Figure 5-9 before using Create PDF, the result is a multipage PDF file with one image on each page — a kind of virtual contact sheet. Neat!

Creating custom Finder Quick Actions

The Markup, Rotate, Trim, and Create PDF Quick Actions are useful and a welcome addition to Finder, but wouldn't you love to be able to create your own Quick Actions to appear in Quick Look windows, in the Preview pane of Finder windows, and in the shortcut menu (right- or Control-click)?

You'll be happy to know that you can, and doing so is relatively easy using Automator, which comes with Monterey. That's all I have to say here. See near the end of Chapter 23 for a nice tutorial on building Quick Actions with Automator.

Four More Cool Monterey Tricks

In addition to Stacks and Quick Actions, Monterey includes several other enhancements, such as a nifty mechanism for capturing still and video images from your Mac screen, desktop pictures that change to reflect the time of day, the recently used apps section of the dock, and using Gallery view as a photo browser.

Shooting screens

If you've used a Mac for long, you probably know that you can grab a picture of what's on your screen by using the shortcuts ⌘+Shift+3 for the whole screen or ⌘+Shift+4 to select a window or part of the screen. Those shortcuts and features have been around since time immemorial.

When you take a screenshot using your old-school shortcuts — ⌘+Shift+3 or ⌘+Shift+4 — a thumbnail of the screenshot appears in the lower-right corner of the screen.

If you do nothing, the thumbnail disappears after about 5 seconds, and then the screenshot is saved on your desktop. To see additional options, right- or Control-click the thumbnail and choose from the shortcut menu, as shown in Figure 5-10.

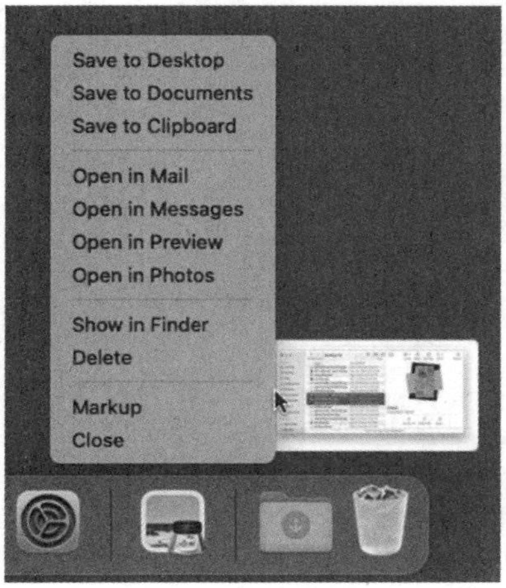

FIGURE 5-10:
After you take a screenshot, a thumbnail appears in the lower-right corner of the screen; right- or Control-click for additional options.

Or just single-click the thumbnail before it disappears and the image opens in a window with Markup tools so you can annotate the image before you save it.

When you have finished annotating, click Done to save the screenshot and annotations to the desktop, or click Revert to close the overlay without saving your annotations.

TIP

If you don't want to save a file at all, add the Control key to the keyboard shortcut (⌘+Shift+Control+3 or ⌘+Shift+Control+3). Instead of saving the screenshot to a file, it will be sent to the clipboard, so you can paste it into any document that will accept an image from the clipboard.

But it gets even better with one more fabulous screen-shooting shortcut that provides even more control over screenshots and adds the capability to record screen movies. This magical shortcut is ⌘+Shift+5, and it's the only shortcut you really have to memorize because its floating toolbar, shown in Figure 5-11, includes all the functionality of the ⌘+Shift+3 and ⌘+Shift+4 shortcuts and more.

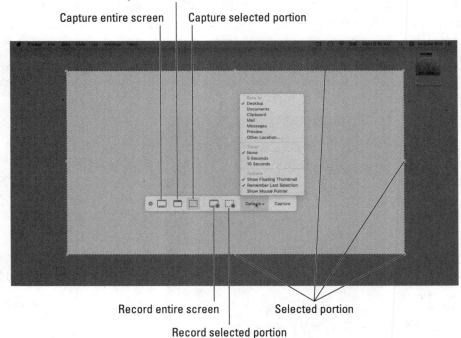

Capture selected window

Capture entire screen   Capture selected portion

FIGURE 5-11:
The screenshot toolbar appears when you press ⌘+Shift+5.

Record entire screen   Selected portion

Record selected portion

Notice the Options pop-up menu, which lets you do the following:

>> Change the destination for screenshots from Desktop (the default) to Documents, Clipboard, Mail, Messages, Preview, or Other Location.

>> Set a timer for shots.

>> Turn on and off the floating thumbnail.

>> Remember the last selection you made (or not).

>> Show or hide the mouse pointer.

 After configuring the options, you capture screenshots by clicking the Capture button. If you've chosen a movie option — Record Entire Screen or Record Selected Portion — the Capture button turns into the Record button; click it to begin recording. When you do, the Stop Recording icon appears in the menu bar (and shown in the margin). Click it to end your recording.

Bottom line: Memorize Monterey's one keyboard shortcut to rule them all — ⌘+Shift+5 — and use it for all your screen-capturing needs.

Dynamic desktop images

Although I cover using desktop pictures in Chapter 6, I'd like to highlight a feature here: dynamic desktops.

When you choose your desktop picture, you'll find a pair of dynamic desktop options above all the normal desktop pictures in the Desktop & Screen Saver System Preferences pane.

Because a picture is worth a thousand words, take a gander at Figure 5-12, which explains it all.

That's all.

And that retires the side, at least as far as features in Monterey's Finder are concerned. Onward!

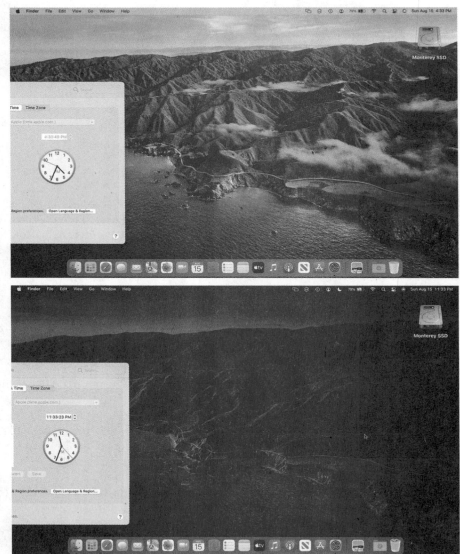

FIGURE 5-12:
A dynamic desktop at 4:33 PM (top) and 11:33 PM (bottom).

2

How Stuff Works

Customize and organize macOS Monterey to suit your style.

Understand what goes where, and why.

Save and open files.

Get the secret to finding anything, anywhere, on any disk.

Mastering Mission Control — try saying that three times real fast.

Find time-saving secrets of Quick Look and Launchpad.

Master the Monterey Clipboard.

» **Beautifying your Monterey with a desktop background and screen saver**

» **Working with those wonderful dashboard widgets**

» **Customizing hardware and keyboard shortcuts**

» **Setting up for superb sound**

Chapter **6**

Having It Your Way

E veryone works a bit differently, and everyone likes to use the Mac in a particular way. In this chapter, you find out how to tweak various options so everything is just the way you like it. The first things many people like to do are set their background and screen saver to something more interesting. You can begin with that stuff, but keep in mind that you can do much more.

You can change the colors in windows, the standard font, and more if you like. Your Mac lets you choose how onscreen elements behave and how your hardware — such as the keyboard, mouse, and wireless Bluetooth gadgets — interact with your Mac.

Introducing System Preferences

You should start by becoming familiar with System Preferences, which lives in the Applications folder and appears on the menu and in the dock.

The following steps explain how to move around the System Preferences window, no matter what you're trying to tweak:

1. **Open the System Preferences window, shown in Figure 6-1.**

You can open System Preferences in at least four ways:

- Double-click the System Preferences icon in your Applications folder.
- Choose ⇨ System Preferences.
- Click the System Preferences icon in Launchpad.
- Click the System Preferences icon on your dock.

2. **Click any of the icons in the System Preferences window.**

The contents of the window change to reflect the options for whichever icon you click. When this happens, I call the window a *pane*. So, for example, when you click the General icon in the System Preferences window, the icons disappear and are replaced by the General System preferences pane.

When you finish working with System Preferences panes, you should (of course) quit by choosing System Preferences ⇨ Quit System Preferences (shortcut: ⌘+Q) or clicking the red gumdrop (close) button.

REMEMBER

Although System Preferences quits when you close its window, *many other apps DON'T quit when you close their last open window.* Worse, there's no easy way to know if an app will or won't quit when you close its last window (so pay attention).

3. **Click the Show All icon in the toolbar to exit the pane and return to the icons in the System Preferences window.**

You can accomplish the same thing by choosing View ⇨ Show All Preferences, or by pressing ⌘+L; both return you to the window with icons for all your System Preferences panes.

Alternatively, you can choose a different preference pane right from the View menu or the dock icon menu, both shown in Figure 6-1.

TIP

If you right- or Control-click the System Preferences icon on the dock (or just press and hold down for a couple of seconds), a menu pops up listing all available preference panes. The cool part is that this works only when the System Preferences app isn't running. When you know which pane you need, this shortcut is often the fastest way to get to it.

Last but not least, note that you can navigate to the next or previous pane you've viewed with the Back and Forward icons beside the red and yellow gumdrops (shortcuts ⌘+[and ⌘+], respectively). Back and Forward commands also appear on the View menu.

FIGURE 6-1:
The View menu (left), the System Preferences window organized alphabetically (center), and the dock icon menu (right).

TIP

You can get rid of the categories (shown in Figure 6-1) and display the icons in alphabetical order, which I find convenient. To switch to alphabetical view, choose View⇨Organize Alphabetically. The categories disappear, the window shrinks, and the icons are alphabetized. To switch from alphabetical view back to category view, choose View⇨Organize by Categories.

TIP

Monterey lets you hide little-used System Preferences pane icons. To manage icons, choose View⇨Customize, and a little check box appears next to each icon. Deselect the box if you want to hide the icon; select the box to make the icon reappear.

Click Done in the toolbar or choose View⇨Customize again to exit selecting mode.

The Desktop & Screen Saver System Preferences Pane

Figure 6-2 shows my desktop with a portrait of my dog Zeke painted by talented artist Jeanne Illenye. (Refer to the default Monterey desktop background in Chapter 1.)

Image well

FIGURE 6-2:
My beautified
desktop.

The Desktop tab

Here's how you can change your desktop picture:

1. From the desktop, choose ⌘ System Preferences.

TIP

Or right- or Control-click the desktop, choose Change Desktop Background from the contextual menu, and skip to Step 3.

The System Preferences window appears.

2. Click the Desktop & Screen Saver icon.

When the Desktop & Screen Saver pane appears, click the Desktop tab (if it's not selected already, as it is in Figure 6-2).

3. Click a folder in the column on the left, and then click a picture in the area on the right.

In Figure 6-2, I clicked a picture called *Zeke painted by Jeanne Illenye*, one of the items in the Desktop Pictures folder you see in the column on the left.

TIP

You have at least three other ways to change your desktop picture:

» Drag a picture file from the Finder onto the *image well* (the little rectangular picture to the left of the picture's name, labeled in Figure 6-2).

>> Click the Desktop tab in the Desktop & Screen Saver System Preferences pane and then click the + icon at the bottom of the list on the left. Choose a folder in the standard Open File sheet and that folder appears in the list; you can use any picture files it contains for your desktop picture.

>> Click the disclosure triangle next to Photos in the column on the left side of the Desktop & Screen Saver Preferences pane and choose from pictures stored in your Photos library.

Although I love having a beautiful desktop picture, I use a gray desktop (click Solid Colors in the list, and then click the gray color swatch) for most figures in this book to make it easier to discern fine details.

TIP

If you need a color other than the 16 hues displayed in the Desktop & Screen Saver System Preferences pane, click the Custom Color button. When the Color Picker window appears, either click a color to choose it or click the eyedropper icon and then click any color displayed on your screen to select and use that color.

The Screen Saver tab

macOS Monterey comes with several screen-saver modules, and many more are available for free (search the internet for *macOS Screen Saver*). To set up your screen saver, follow these steps:

1. **Open System Preferences, click the Desktop & Screen Saver icon, and then click the Screen Saver.**

2. **In the Screen Savers column on the left side of the pane, choose a screen saver that interests you.**

Scroll down to see all the available Slideshows and Screen Savers.

TIP

If you can't decide, enable the Use Random Screen Saver check box (bottom left) and your Mac will choose a different screen saver at random each time the screen saver kicks in.

3. **(Optional) To see what the chosen module looks like in action, click the preview image on the right.**

A little Preview button appears on the image when you hover your cursor over it to remind you how to see a preview. Nice touch!

Press any key or click anywhere to end the test.

4. **After you choose a screen saver, select the number of minutes you want the Mac to wait before activating the screen saver from the Start After pop-up menu.**

5. **Select the Show with Clock check box to display a digital clock along with the screen saver.**

6. **(Optional) Click the Hot Corners button to choose which corner of your screen activates the screen saver and which disables it.**

   If you enable this option, when you move your cursor to the chosen corner of the screen, you activate or disable the screen saver until you move the cursor elsewhere. Note that hot corners are optional and are turned off by default.

7. **When you're done, close the Desktop & Screen Saver pane.**

TIP

You can require a password to wake your Mac from a screen saver (or sleep). To do so, follow these steps:

1. **From the main System Preferences screen, click the Security & Privacy icon.**

   The Security & Privacy System Preferences pane appears.

2. **Click the General tab.**

3. **Select the Require Password after Sleep or Screen Saver Begins check box.**

4. **Choose a length of time from the pop-up menu between the words Password and After.**

   Your options range from Immediately to 8 hours, with six other options between. If you wouldn't want someone to sit down at your computer and have access to all your stuff, you'd be wise to require a password and choose one of these options.

   Now you'll have to supply the user account password to wake up your computer after the length of time you selected.

The General System Preferences Pane

Computers don't care about appearances, but if you want your Mac to look a bit more festive (or, for that matter, businesslike), you have options in the General pane (see Figure 6-3) at your disposal. To open this pane, choose System Preferences, and then click the General icon.

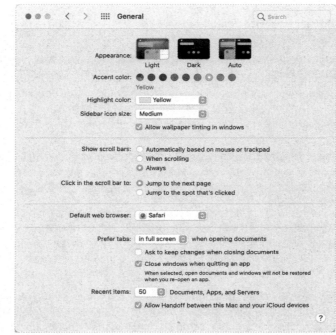

FIGURE 6-3:
The General
pane.

First up are the general appearance options:

TIP

>> **Appearance:** This option governs the appearance of buttons and other interface elements, including the menu bar and the three gumdrops (Close, Minimize, and Zoom) in the top-left corner of most windows.

Apple, however, in its infinite wisdom, provides only three choices: Light, Dark, or Auto.

>> **Accent Color buttons:** Change the color of buttons and other interface elements to one of eight choices.

To preview an accent color, click it. The check boxes, drop-down menus, and radio buttons in the General System Preferences pane instantly change to that accent color. Sweet!

>> **Highlight Color pop-up menu:** From here, you can choose the color that text is surrounded by when you choose it in a document or select an icon. This time, Apple isn't so restrictive: You have eight highlight colors you can choose, plus Other, which brings up a color picker from which you can choose almost any color.

I'm partial to yellow, which makes selections look like they've been run over by a yellow highlighter.

» **Sidebar Icon Size pop-up menu:** Choose Small, Medium, or Large for icons in your Finder sidebar.

NEW

» **Allow wallpaper tinting in windows check box:** This new option tints windows slightly. Enable and disable it to see its subtle effect on the System Preferences window (and any other open windows on your screen).

The next area in the General pane enables you to set the behavior of scroll bars:

» **Show Scroll Bars radio buttons:** These buttons let you choose when you want to see scroll bars on windows. Your choices are Automatically Based on Mouse or Trackpad, When Scrolling, or Always. I prefer Always; your mileage may vary.

» **Click in the Scroll Bar To radio buttons:** These buttons give you the option of moving your view of a window up or down by a page (the default) or to the position in the document roughly proportionate to where you clicked in the scroll bar. I prefer jumping to the spot that's clicked.

TIP

An easy way to try these options is to open a Finder window and place it side by side with the General pane, reducing the size of the window if necessary to make scroll bars appear. Select an option in the General pane, observe the behavior of the scroll bars, and then select a different option and observe again.

TIP

The Jump to the Spot That's Clicked option is handy for navigating long documents. And don't forget — the Page Down key does the same thing as choosing the Jump to the Next Page choice, so you lose nothing by choosing Jump to the Spot That's Clicked.

It would be even nicer if all third-party apps supported this feature, but some — including Microsoft Office 2011 (but not Office 2016 and later, which finally behave properly with respect to your scroll bar setting) — don't behave properly no matter what you choose for this setting.

Use the Default Web Browser drop-down menu to choose (what else?) your default browser. Unless you've installed another web browser, such as Chrome or Firefox, Safari is the only option.

» **Prefer Tabs pop-up menu:** This option determines when to use tabbed windows; your choices are Never, In Full Screen, or Always. I like tabbed windows all the time, so my option is set to Always. Try all three and choose the one you like best.

>> **Ask to Keep Changes when Closing Documents check box:** Monterey can save versions of your documents automatically and without any action on your part. So when you quit an application or close a document, your changes can be saved automatically. If you want to be able to close documents without having to manually save your changes, enable this option.

>> **Close Windows when Quitting an Application check box:** Your Mac's default behavior is to reopen documents and windows that were open when you quit that app. When you launch the app again, all the windows and documents magically reappear right where you left them. So enable this option to have your apps open to a clean slate, without reopening documents or windows from the previous session.

These last two items may not work as expected with older third-party applications. As a rule, the longer it's been since a program's last update, the more likely it is that the app will ignore these two settings.

WARNING

>> **Recent Items pop-up menu:** Use this to specify how many recent items will be remembered and displayed in your Recent Items submenu. The default is 10, but I like having access to more than 10 applications and documents in my Recent Items submenu, so I set mine to 50.

>> **Allow Handoff between This Mac and Your iCloud Devices check box:** When enabled, you can start working on a document, an email, or a message on any Apple device and pick up where you left off on another device, as described in Chapter 23.

Adjusting the Keyboard, Mouse, Trackpad, and Other Hardware

No two Mac users use the keyboard, mouse, or trackpad in the same way. Some folks don't use a mouse at all. (You might not even use the keyboard if you use voice-recognition software or other devices, as I explain in Chapter 23.) If you're using macOS on a notebook, you have a *trackpad*, that little surface where you move your finger around to control the cursor. Or perhaps you have a Bluetooth-enabled keyboard and mouse so you can hook them up wirelessly. Regardless of what you have, you should give some thought to customizing the way they work so it feels just right for you.

The Keyboard, Mouse, and Trackpad System Preferences panes offer several tabs that enable you to modify the behavior of your keyboard, mouse, and trackpad so it feels just right for you. The first thing to do is open the Keyboard System Preferences pane by choosing System Preferences and clicking the Keyboard icon.

The Keyboard System Preferences pane

The Keyboard System Preferences pane has five tabs: Keyboard, Text, Shortcuts, Input Sources, and Dictation.

Keyboard tab

On the Keyboard tab, you can adjust your settings in the following ways:

» Drag the Key Repeat slider to set how fast a key repeats when you hold it down. This feature comes into play when (for example) you hold down the hyphen (–) key to make a line or the asterisk (*) key to make a divider.

» Drag the Delay Until Repeat slider to set how long you have to hold down a key before it starts repeating.

If you have a notebook Mac (such as a MacBook, MacBook Pro, or MacBook Air), you also see one or more of these additional features:

» **Adjust Keyboard Brightness in Low Light:** This check box turns your laptop's ambient keyboard lighting on and off.

» **Turn Keyboard Backlight Off After (Choose 5, 10, or 30 seconds, or 1 or 5 minutes from the drop-down menu):** This option lets you determine how long the keyboard backlighting remains on when your computer isn't in use.

Of course, if your MacBook doesn't *have* ambient keyboard lighting, you don't see the last two items.

REMEMBER

Ambient keyboard lighting is a cool feature, but it reduces battery life. My recommendation is to use it only when you really need it.

» **Press the globe key To:** The options in this pop-up menu are Show Emoji & Symbols, Change Input Source, Start Dictation (Press Globe key twice), and Do Nothing.

» **Use F1, F2, etc. Keys as Standard Function Keys:** If this check box is selected, the F keys at the top of your keyboard control the active software application.

To use the special hardware features printed on each F key (display brightness, screen mirroring, sound volume, mute, and so on), you have to press the Fn (Function) key before pressing the F key. If the check box is left deselected, you have to press the Fn key if you want to use the F keys with a software application. Got it? Good.

Finally, these keys may not work if you use a third-party keyboard (one not manufactured by Apple).

>> **Set Up Bluetooth Keyboard button:** This button launches the Bluetooth assistant and walks you through pairing and setup as described in Chapter 23.

>> **Modifier Keys button:** With this button, you can change the action performed by the Caps Lock, Control, Option, and Command keys. This option is particularly useful if you use a non-Apple keyboard, although it works just fine on Apple keyboards, too.

TIP

I'm always engaging the Caps Lock key accidentally with my overactive left pinky, and I rarely engage it on purpose. So, I set *my* Caps Lock key to perform No Action. Now I never type half a sentence in ALL CAPS BECAUSE I ACCIDENTALLY PRESSED THE CAPS LOCK KEY.

Text tab

The Text tab is one of my favorite features in all of Macdom because it saves me countless keystrokes every day. Not because it's the tab with the Correct Spelling Automatically check box. Enable it (if it's not already enabled) and be done. Spelling correction is good, but the reason I love the Text tab so much is because it lets me create shortcuts to replace short phrases with longer ones.

When I type . . .	My Mac replaces it with . . .
wtf	what the heck
vty	Very truly yours,
	Bob "Dr. Mac" LeVitus
	Writer, Raconteur, and Troublemaker
blc	boblevitus@boblevitus.com

It's a handy trick, indeed. Plus, a preview pops up just below your typing so you can accept the replacement by pressing the spacebar or reject it by clicking the little X or pressing Esc.

To create your own shortcuts, click the little plus sign near the bottom-left corner of the window. Type the short phrase in the Replace field, click in the With field or press Tab, and then type the replacement phrase. You can see what happens when I type **wtf** in the TextEdit window in the foreground of Figure 6-4.

TIP

Although it's not obvious, you can create multiline substitutions. Just hold down Option and press Return to start a new line of text. Or paste multiline text from another application into the With field. You won't see the lines above (or below) the line you're typing, but with a bit of trial and error you can get it to work, as I did with my *vty* shortcut.

FIGURE 6-4:
The Text tab of the Keyboard System Preferences pane (left), and what I see when I type **wtf** in a TextEdit document (right).

Shortcuts tab

If you really hate to use your mouse or if your mouse is broken, keyboard shortcuts can be handy. I tend to use them more on my laptop because I really don't like using the built-in-touch-mouse thing (technically, it's a *trackpad*, and I talk more about it in the next section).

I introduce some commonly used keyboard shortcuts in Chapter 2. You probably don't want to mess with those, but you can assign other commands you use often to just about any key combination you like. By creating your own keyboard shortcuts, you can have whatever commands you need literally at your fingertips.

Not only can you add, delete, or change keyboard shortcuts for many operating system functions (such as taking a picture of the screen or using the keyboard to choose menu and dock items), but you can also add, delete, and change keyboard shortcuts for your applications.

To begin, choose the Shortcuts tab in the Keyboard System Preferences pane. Now you can do any or all of the following:

>> **To change a shortcut:** First, click the appropriate application, preference, or feature in the left column. Next, double-click the shortcut you want to change on the right side of the right column (for example, F3 or ⌘+G). The old shortcut becomes highlighted; when it does, press the new shortcut keys you want to use.

>> **To add a new shortcut:** Click App Shortcuts on the left and then click the + icon. Choose the appropriate application from the Application pop-up menu, type the exact name of the menu command you want to add in the Menu Title field, and then type the shortcut you want to assign to that command in the Keyboard Shortcut field. If the shortcut you press is in use by another application or preference, a yellow triangular caution symbol appears next to it. It really is that simple.

>> **To delete a shortcut you created:** Choose it and then click the – icon.

The Shortcuts tab also offers options for what happens when you press the Tab key in a window or dialog:

>> If you deselect (no check mark) the Use Keyboard Navigation to Move Focus Between Controls check box, the Tab key moves the cursor from one text box to the next or from one list item to the next item (usually alphabetically). This action is the default.

>> If you select the Use Keyboard Navigation to Move Focus Between Controls check box, you can avoid using the mouse for the most part, if that's your preference.

When the check box is selected, the Tab key moves the focus from one item to the next in a window or dialog. So (for example) every time you press the Tab key in an Open File dialog or sheet, the focus moves — say, from the sidebar to the file list to the Cancel button to the Icon view icon. Each item is highlighted to show it's selected, and you can activate the highlighted item from the keyboard by pressing the spacebar.

To move the focus backward (that is, to the previously selected item), press Shift+Tab.

You can toggle this setting by pressing Control+F7. And if you don't care for Control+F7 as its shortcut, you can change it by clicking Keyboard in the left column, double-clicking the Change the Way Tab Moves Focus item in the right column, and then pressing the new shortcut.

TIP

Input Sources tab

The Input Sources tab is where you can choose to display one or more foreign language keyboards in the Input menu (shown in the margin).

When you specify a foreign keyboard in this tab, the input menu icon in your menu bar changes from the rather tame default icon to the flag of the selected keyboard.

Last but not least, the Dictation tab is covered in Chapter 23; if you want to dictate to your Mac, you might want to read that section sooner rather than later.

The Mouse System Preferences pane

 The Mouse System Preferences pane is where you set your mouse tracking speed, scrolling speed, and double-click delays.

If you use a notebook or an Apple Magic Trackpad, you'll use the System Preferences pane named Trackpad instead. I tell you more about it in the upcoming section, "The Trackpad System Preferences pane."

The first item in this pane is a check box titled Scroll Direction: Natural. If scrolling or navigating in windows feels backward to you, try deselecting this box.

Moving right along, here are the features you'll find in the Mouse System Preferences pane (if you have a mouse connected):

>> Move the Tracking Speed slider to change the relationship between hand movement of the mouse and cursor movement onscreen. This slider works just like the slider for trackpads, as I explain in the upcoming section on trackpads.

>> The Double-Click Speed setting determines how close together two clicks must be for the Mac to interpret them as a double-click and not as two separate clicks. Move the slider arrow to the leftmost setting, Very Slow, for the slowest. The rightmost position, Fast, is the fastest setting. I prefer the setting one tick shy of Fast.

>> If your mouse has a scroll ball or scroll wheel, you also see a Scrolling Speed slider, which lets you adjust how fast the contents of a window scroll when you use the scroll wheel or ball.

>> If your mouse has more than one button, you see a pair of Primary Mouse Button radio buttons. These let you choose which button — left or right — you use to make your primary (regular) click. Conversely, the other mouse button (the one you didn't choose) becomes your secondary (Control or right) click.

Many lefties like to change this setting. Set the primary button as the right button, and you can click with the index finger of your left hand.

Being right-handed, I've chosen the defaults in Figure 6-5, so the left button is the primary click and the right button is the secondary (right or Control) click.

TIP

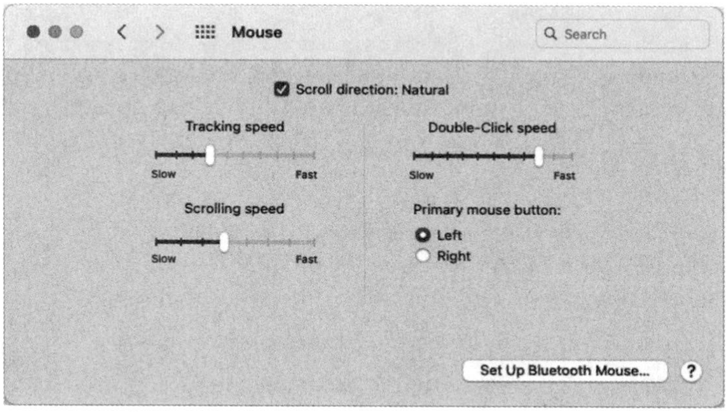

FIGURE 6-5:
The Mouse
System
Preferences pane
set up for a
right-hander.

One last thing: Changes in the Mouse System Preferences pane take effect immediately, so you should definitely play around with various speed settings to determine what works best for you.

The Bluetooth System Preferences pane

Bluetooth is a technology that lets you make wireless connections between your Mac and devices such as Bluetooth mice and phones. Most Macs manufactured in the past decade have Bluetooth built in; some older models don't.

TIP

You configure Bluetooth devices you want to use with your Mac elsewhere in the Bluetooth System Preferences pane (as I describe in Chapters 18 and 23).

If your Mac has Bluetooth built in, the Bluetooth tab shows you the battery level of your Bluetooth mouse or keyboard. It also offers a check box to add a Bluetooth status menu to your menu bar and a check box to let Bluetooth devices wake your computer from sleep.

The Trackpad System Preferences pane

If you use a notebook Mac — a MacBook, MacBook Air, or MacBook Pro — or a desktop Mac with a Magic Trackpad (version 1 or 2), you'll have an additional System Preferences pane called Trackpad. This pane lets you configure tracking and clicking speed as well as the gesturing behavior of your Mac's built-in trackpad.

TIP

If you're looking for a replacement for your mouse, consider Apple's $129 Magic Trackpad 2. This nifty wireless device can be used with any Mac or PC that has Bluetooth. It's also the biggest glass Multi-Touch trackpad yet. Yes, you can use the Magic Trackpad 2 with your MacBook Pro, and yes, that does mean you'll have dual trackpads.

I am trying to become more of a trackpad believer and make better use of the iPhone-like gestures available on my Mac. I have both a Magic Trackpad and a mouse on my desk and grab whichever is appropriate at the moment.

The Trackpad System Preferences pane has three tabs — Point & Click, Scroll & Zoom, and More Gestures — as shown in Figure 6-6.

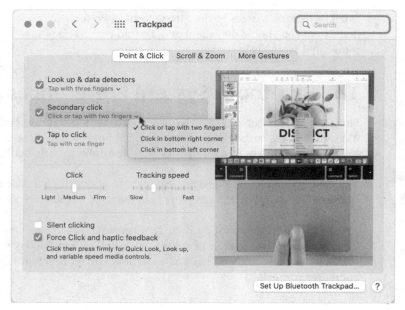

FIGURE 6-6:
The Trackpad System Preferences pane offers controls for one-finger and multi-finger gestures.

WARNING

If you have an older notebook with the older-style trackpad, you may not see all the controls in Figure 6-6. (For what it's worth, a Magic Trackpad 2 would cure it.)

All three tabs work the same way as the Point & Click tab shown in Figure 6-6. To enable or disable a feature, select its check box. To see how a feature works, just move your cursor over it (you don't even have to click), and a movie demonstrates that gesture on the right side of the window. In Figure 6-6, I'm pointing to the Secondary Click feature on the left; how it works is demonstrated in the movie playing on the right. Pretty cool, don't you think?

You need to know a couple of other things about the Trackpad System Preferences pane before you move on:

>> If you see a little v to the right of a feature's description (Click or Tap with Two Fingers in Figure 6-6), a drop-down menu is available; click near the v to display the options for that feature.

>> The Tracking Speed slider lets you change the relationship between finger movement on the trackpad and cursor movement onscreen. A faster tracking-speed setting (moving the slider to the right) sends your cursor flying across the screen with a mere flick of the finger; slower tracking-speed settings (moving the slider to the left) make the cursor crawl across in seemingly slow motion, even when your finger is flying. Set this setting as fast as you can stand it — I like the fastest speed. Try it: You might like it.

The Sound System Preferences Pane

Out of the box, macOS Monterey comes with a preset collection of beeps and controls. From the Sound System Preferences pane, however, you can change the way your Mac plays and records sound by changing settings on each of its three tabs: Sound Effects, Output, and Input.

Three items appear at the bottom of the Sound Effects tab, no matter which of the three tabs is active:

>> To make your Mac's volume louder or softer, use the Output Volume slider. You can also change or mute the volume with the designated volume and mute keys found on most Apple keyboards.

>> Select the Mute check box to turn off all sound.

>> Select the Show Sound in Menu Bar check box to add a volume control menu to your menu bar, and then choose when to add it — When Active or Always — from the pop-up menu.

Changing sound effects

On the Sound Effects tab, choose an alert (beep) sound by clicking its name; set its volume by using the Alert Volume slider control.

If your Mac can play a start-up sound, you can enable or disable that sound with the Play Sound on Startup check box.

You can also specify the output device through which sound effects play (if you have more than one device) by choosing it from the Play Sound Effects Through pop-up menu.

The Play User Interface Sound Effects check box turns on sound effects for actions, such as dragging a file to the Trash. The Play Feedback when Volume Is Changed check box tells your Mac to beep once for each key press when you increase or decrease volume.

Choosing output and input options

If you have more than one sound-output device (in addition to the built-in speakers), you can choose it on the Output tab. The Balance slider makes one stereo speaker — left or right — louder than the other.

If you have more than one sound-input device (in addition to the built-in microphone on many Macs), you can choose it on the Input tab. The Input Volume slider controls the Input Level (how loud input from that device will be), which is displayed as a row of blue dots. If the dots light up all the way to the right side, your input volume is too loud. Ideally, no more than three-fourths of the little dots on the Input Level meter should be lit when you're talking.

TECHNICAL STUFF

Some input sources (microphones) don't let you adjust their level in the Sound System Preferences pane.

Finally, you can choose to have Monterey flash the screen when an alert sound occurs, or have stereo recordings play back in mono, or both by enabling these options in the Audio tab of the Accessibility System Preferences pane.

» Checking out the macOS folder structure

» Saving your document before it's too late

» Opening icons

Chapter **7**

Opening and Saving Files

This might be the most important chapter in this book. If you don't understand how to open and save files by using the Open dialog and Save sheets or how to use the file and folder system, you'll have a heck of a time finding, opening, or saving files.

TECHNICAL STUFF

A *sheet* is nothing more than a dialog that is attached to a document window's title bar and can't be moved independently from the window itself. Some apps use sheets, which only prevent you from using the active window when they appear; other apps use modal dialogs that prevent you from using any open window. Either way you'll see the same options.

This chapter is a tonic for finding the file or folder you want. Knowing where your files are is something every Mac user should *grok* (fully understand). Hang with me and pay attention; everything will soon become crystal clear.

Later in the chapter, I look at using Open dialogs and Save sheets within applications to find files and folders. You see them only *after* you launch a program and use that program's File menu to open or save a file. (For more on launching applications, read the parts of Chapter 4 about icons; for more on creating and opening documents, see the documentation or Help file for the program you're using.)

A Quick Primer on Finding Files

Before we even look at organizing your files, let's look at the problem organizing files and folders can solve. Ask any longtime Mac user; the old lament is common: "Well, I saved the file, but I don't know where I saved it." It happens all the time with new users (and occasionally with longtime users like my wife).

If they don't master these essential techniques, they often become confused about where files are located on their hard drives. Sure, the sidebar has an item called Recents that displays all files you've used recently, and you can use Spotlight to find almost any file in milliseconds. But if you have tens of thousands of files, it's often faster to know precisely where to find the file you desire.

Recents (in the sidebar of Finder windows) is a fast and easy way to find a file or folder (although the sheer number of files it displays may overwhelm you, no matter how you sort or arrange them).

TIP

Recents is especially handy when you know you either created or worked on the file recently. Just use List view sorted or grouped by Date Last Opened, and the most recently used files will be at or near the top of the Recents list.

Chapter 10 is chock-full of tools and tips for finding files and folders when you misplace them. Furthermore, although you can often find files or folders by using Spotlight, you have to remember enough details about the file or its contents for Spotlight to find it.

At the end of the day, all the aforementioned techniques are useful and good to know, but I'll say it again: It's often faster and easier if you know exactly where a file or folder is than to hunt for it.

Understanding the macOS Folder Structure

Start by looking at the folder structure of a typical macOS installation. Open a Finder window and click the icon for your hard drive (typically called Macintosh HD; mine's been renamed Monterey SSD) in the sidebar.

TIP

If you don't see your startup disk in the sidebar, choose Finder ⇨ Preferences, click the Sidebar icon at the top of the window, and then enable the check box for hard disks.

You should now see a window with the contents of your startup disk: the Applications, Library, System, and Users folders (as shown in Figure 7-1).

FIGURE 7-1:
A bird's-eye view
of key folders on
your Mac.

In the Users folder, each user with an account on this Mac (see Chapter 18 for the skinny on users and accounts) have their own set of folders containing documents, preferences, and other information that belongs to that user and account.

TECHNICAL STUFF

If you're the sole person who accesses your Mac, you probably have only one user. Regardless, the folder structure that macOS uses is the same whether you have one user or dozens.

In the Users folder, you find your personal Home folder (which bears your account name), along with a Shared folder, where you can put files you want to share with other users. All these files are stored in a nested folder structure that's a bit tricky to understand at first. This structure makes more sense after you spend a little time with it and figure out some basic concepts.

TIP

The structure will start to make sense much sooner if you display the path bar at the bottom of the window, as shown in Figure 7-1. (Choose View ➪ Show Path Bar if yours isn't displayed.)

Examine Figure 7-1 to see how these four main folders are related to one another. In the sections that follow, you look at each of these folders in more depth and find out more about what's nested inside each one.

Understanding nested folders

Folders within other folders are often called *nested folders.* To get a feel for the way nested folders work in macOS, check out the example of nested folders on my desktop in Figure 7-2.

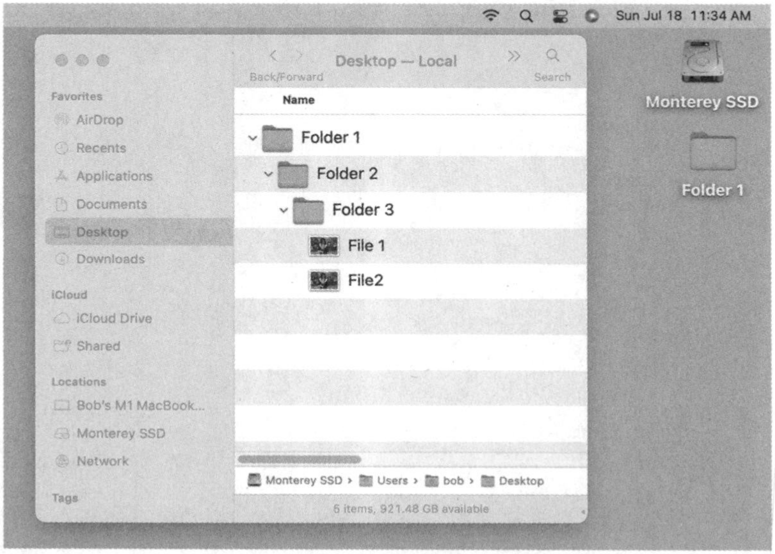

FIGURE 7-2: Nested folders, going four levels deep.

You can see the following in Figure 7-2:

» The Desktop is the top-level folder in this example; all other folders and files you see reside in the Desktop folder.

» Folder 1 is inside the Desktop folder, which is one level deep.

» Folder 2 is inside Folder 1, which is one level deeper than Folder 1, or two levels deep.

» Folder 3 is inside Folder 2 and is three levels deep.

» The two files inside Folder 3 are four levels deep.

REMEMBER

If the preceding list makes sense to you, you're golden. What's important here is that you can visualize the path to Folder 3. That is, to get to files inside Folder 3, you open Folder 1 and then open Folder 2 to be able to open Folder 3. Understanding this concept is important to understanding the relationships between files and folders. Keep reviewing this section and looking at the status bar, and eventually everything will click. You'll slap yourself in the head and say, "Now I get it!"

From the top: The Computer folder

I start with the Computer folder, which is the top level of the folder hierarchy. The Computer folder shows all the storage devices (hard drives, CD- or DVD-ROM, USB flash drive, and so forth) connected to your Mac. The following steps show how you can start at the Computer folder and drill down through the folder structure:

1. Choose Go ⇨ Computer; press Shift+⌘+C; or click your computer's name in the sidebar's Locations section.

Now you're at the Computer folder. In Figure 7-1, the Computer folder is called Bob's M1 MacBook Air (look in the title bar), and it contains a solid-state Drive icon (Monterey SSD) and a Network icon, from which you can access servers or other computers on your local network.

If that seems mysterious, read Chapter 18 for the scoop on sharing files (and more) with other users.

You might have more or fewer icons in your Computer folder than you see in Figure 7-1, depending on how many disks you have mounted.

You might also find an icon for your Mac in your sidebar (mine's called Bob's M1 MacBook Air). If you don't have your Mac in the sidebar but would like to, choose Finder ⇨ Preferences, click the Sidebar tab at the top, and then select the check box for your computer.

TIP

You can change a Mac's name (Bob's M1 MacBook Air in Figure 7-1) by opening the Sharing System Preferences pane (see Chapter 18) and changing the computer's name in the Computer Name field.

2. Double-click the icon for the drive that holds your macOS stuff.

Technically, this drive is called your boot drive. In Figure 7-1, that drive is called Monterey SSD. I have no idea what yours is called, of course, but if you haven't changed it, it's probably called Macintosh HD.

3. Check out the folders you find there.

You should see at least four folders on your boot drive. In the next few sections, I walk you through what you can find in each one.

Peeking into the Applications folder

You can access the Applications folder, located at the root level of your boot drive (the one with macOS installed on it), by clicking the Applications icon in the sidebar, by choosing it in the Go menu, or by pressing Shift+⌘+A. In this folder, you find applications and utilities that Apple includes with macOS as well as most (if not all) third-party apps and utilities you've installed.

Most users of a Mac have access to all the items in the Applications folder, with the exception of managed accounts or accounts with Parental Controls, as discussed in Chapter 18.

Visiting the Library folders

The Library folder, at the root level of your macOS hard drive, is like a public library; it stores items available to everyone who logs into any account on this Mac.

There are actually three (or more) Library folders on your hard drive:

>> At the root level of your macOS disk

>> In the root-level System folder

>> One in each user's Home folder

TECHNICAL STUFF

In Monterey, your Home/Library folder is hidden from view to protect you from yourself. Never fear: You'll discover the secret to making it visible if you need it in the "Your personal library card" section later in this chapter.

Now, here's the scoop on your various Library folders:

>> **/Library:** You find a bunch of folders inside the Library folder at the root level (the public Library folder). Most of them contain files that you never need to open, move, or delete.

By and large, the public Library subfolder that gets the most use is the Fonts folder, which houses many of the fonts installed on the Mac.

>> **/System/Library:** This is the nerve center of your Mac. In other words, you should never have to touch this particular Library folder.

WARNING

Leave the /System/Library folder alone. Don't move, remove, or rename it, or do anything within it.

>> **/Users/Username/Library (in each user's Home folder):** This is where macOS stores configuration and preferences files for each user account.

The location of each of these libraries is illustrated in Figure 7-3.

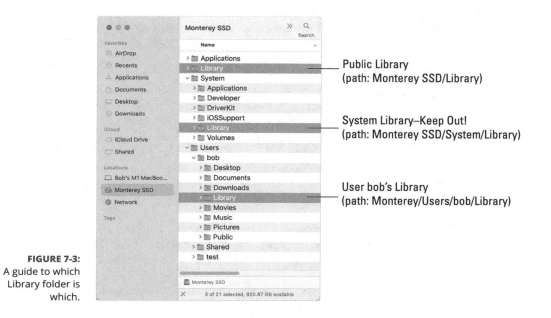

Public Library
(path: Monterey SSD/Library)

System Library—Keep Out!
(path: Monterey SSD/System/Library)

User bob's Library
(path: Monterey/Users/bob/Library)

FIGURE 7-3:
A guide to which
Library folder is
which.

If your Mac is set up for multiple users, only users with administrator (admin) privileges can put stuff in the public (root-level) Library folder. (For more information on admin privileges, check out Chapter 18.)

Let it be: The System folder

The System folder contains the files that macOS needs to start up and keep working.

WARNING

Leave the System folder alone. Don't move, remove, or rename it or anything within it. It's part of the nerve center of your Mac.

So now you can forget everything outside your Home folder because with few exceptions, that's where all *your* stuff will reside.

There's no place like Home

Your Home folder is inside the Users folder. When the user logs on to this Mac, the contents of their Home folder appear whenever they chooses Go⇨ Home, or uses the keyboard shortcut Shift+⌘+H.

REMEMBER

Your Home folder is the most important folder for you as a user — or at least the one where you stash most of your files. I strongly recommend that you always save files to a folder or subfolder within your Home folder — preferably, in sub-folders in your Home/Documents folder. The advantage of doing so is that your Home/Documents folder is easy to find, and many programs use it as the default folder for opening or saving a file.

When you open your Home folder, you see a Finder window with a little house icon and your short username in the title bar. Seeing your short username in the title bar tells you that you're in *your* Home folder. Every user has a Home folder named after their short username (as specified in the Users & Groups System Preferences pane). If you refer to Figure 7-1, you'll see that my Home folder contains seven subfolders — Desktop, Documents, Downloads, Movies, Music, Pictures, and Public — and that my Home folder is named *bob* — the short name I used when I first set up my Mac.

If your Mac has more than one user, you can see their Home folders in the Users folder (for example, *TheWoz* and *test* in Figure 7-1), but macOS prevents you from opening files from or saving files to other users' Home folders.

By default, your Home folder has several folders inside it created by macOS. The following four are the most important:

>> **Desktop:** If you put items (files, folders, applications, or aliases) on the desktop, they're actually stored in the Desktop folder.

>> **Documents:** This is the place to put all the documents (letters, spreadsheets, recipes, and novels) that you create.

>> **Library:** As I mention earlier in this chapter, this Library folder is invisible in macOS Monterey; I show you how to deal with that shortly. Rest assured that even though it's hidden, it's still one of the most important folders in your Home folder, containing Preferences (files containing the settings you create in System Preferences and individual applications' preferences), fonts available only to you (as described earlier in this chapter), and other stuff that you — and only you — expect to use.

>> **Public:** If others on your local area network (LAN) use file sharing to connect with your Mac, they can't see or use the files or folders in your Home folder (unless you explicitly share them), but they can share files you store in your Home folder's Public folder. (Read more about file sharing and Public folders in Chapter 18.)

You can create more folders, if you like. In fact, every folder that you *ever* create (at least every one you create on this particular hard drive or volume) *should* be within your Home folder. I explain more about creating folders and subfolders and organizing your stuff inside them later in this chapter.

The following are a couple more tidbits to keep in mind as you dig around your Home folder:

>> If you decide that you don't want an item on the desktop anymore, delete it by dragging its icon from the Desktop folder to the Trash or by dragging its icon from the desktop itself to the Trash. Both techniques yield the same effect: The file is in the Trash, where it remains until you empty the Trash. Or if you don't want it on the desktop anymore but don't want to get rid of it either, you can drag it from the desktop into any other folder you like.

>> The other four folders that you should see in your Home folder are Downloads, Movies, Music, and Pictures. All these folders are empty until you (or programs such as Music, GarageBand, Photos, or iMovie, which create files inside these folders automatically the first time you launch them) put something in them.

Your personal library card

The invisible Library subfolder of your Home folder is the repository of everything that macOS needs to customize *your* Mac to *your* tastes. If you want to add something to a Library folder, it's usually best to add it to your Home/Library folder. You won't spend much time (if any) adding things to the Library folder or moving them around within it, and that's probably why it's now hidden from sight. Still, I think it's a good idea for you to know what's in your Home/Library.

Earlier in this chapter I mention the root-level (which I call *public*) Library folder (refer to Figure 7-3), which is used to specify preferences for all users on this Mac. *This* Library folder, however, is all about you and your stuff.

Be cautious with all Library folders. macOS is persnickety about how the folders and files within it are organized. As I discuss earlier in the chapter, you can safely add items to and remove items from most public or Home/Library folders, but *leave the folders themselves alone.* If you remove or rename the wrong folder, you could render macOS inoperable. It's like the old joke about the guy who said to the doctor, "It hurts when I do that," and the doctor replies, "Then don't do that."

To find your hidden Home/Library folder, do this:

1. **Hold down the Option key on your keyboard and click the Go menu.**

The (formerly) invisible Library folder appears in the Go menu as long as the Option key is pressed.

2. **Select Library and release the mouse button.**

You should see several folders in the Home/Library folder; the exact number depends on the software that you install on your Mac. You probably have folders called Mail, Safari, Logs, and Preferences, for example.

TIP

If you don't want to do this dance every time you open your Home/Library folder, open your Home folder in Finder and choose View➪Show View Options (or press ⌘+J). Enable the Show Library Folder check box near the bottom of the View Options window and your Home Library will be visible evermore (or until you deselect the check box).

Some of the most important standard folders in the Library folder include the following:

>> **Application Support:** Some applications store their support files here; others store theirs in the main (root-level) public Library folder.

>> **Fonts:** This folder is empty until you install your own fonts here. The easiest way to install a font is to double-click its icon and let the Font Book utility handle it for you, as described in Chapter 21.

TIP

It might not be a great idea to add too many fonts because the Fonts menu will become long and unwieldy. Plus, too many fonts may cause degraded performance on older Macs.

>> **Preferences:** The files here hold the information about whichever things you customize in macOS or in the applications you run. Whenever you change a system or application preference, that info is saved to a file in the Preferences folder.

WARNING

Don't mess with the Preferences folder! You should never need to open or use this folder unless something bad happens — say, you suspect that a particular preferences file has become *corrupted* (that is, damaged). My advice is to just forget that you know about this folder and let it do its job. If you don't know why you're doing something to a folder (other than the Fonts folder) in your Home/Library, *don't do it.* There must be some good reasons why Apple decided to hide the Home/Library folder in macOS Monterey, and I'm sure that one of them is to keep you (or me) from accidentally screwing something up.

Saving Your Document Before It's Too Late

Now that you have a feel for the macOS folder structure, it's time to get down to the important stuff — namely, how to save documents and where to save them. You can create as many documents as you want, using one program or dozens of 'em, but all could be lost if you don't save the files (or versions of the files) to a storage device such as your startup drive, external hard drive, solid-state drive (SSD), or USB thumb drive (a.k.a. USB flash drive).

Another option is to save documents in iCloud, so they're available on all your Apple devices all the time without syncing or doing much of anything beyond saving the file.

When you *save* a file, you're committing a copy to a drive, whether it's a drive connected directly to your Mac, one available over a local area network, a removable disc such as a USB thumb drive or external hard or solid-state drive, or even a drive on a cloud-based server somewhere else, such as iCloud.

Speaking of iCloud, you'll be hearing a lot more about it — and especially the iCloud Drive feature — in Chapter 8 (once you get the hang of saving and opening files from drives or discs).

macOS's Resume feature automatically reopens all windows that were onscreen when you quit the app. So, when you launch the app again, all the windows are reopened in the same position onscreen as when you quit. Best of all, Resume seems to work with *most* (but not all) third-party apps.

Individual programs have offered Auto Save before, but it's been baked into macOS for years. Auto Save automatically saves *versions* (which you learn more about shortly) of your work as you work, when you pause, and every 5 minutes, whether you need it or not.

Versions are awesome. Every time you Save or Auto Save, a new version of the document is created. For as long as we've had Macs, we've saved unique versions of our files, creating and managing them with the Save As command or by duplicating and renaming them in Finder. Now macOS takes over version control for you by automatically saving versions, as described in the preceding paragraph.

The big advantage is that rather than ending up with a separate file on your hard drive each time you Save As or duplicate and rename a file, Versions saves them all in the same document icon. To access a previous version, select Choose File⇨Revert To⇨Browse All Versions or choose Enter Time Machine from the Time Machine icon on the menu bar while the document is active onscreen. (See Chapter 24 for more on Time Machine.)

That's the good news, but there's also bad news. Although Auto Save and Versions are built right into macOS, not all third-party apps choose to take advantage of these features. So please don't get too comfortable with Auto Save and Versions until you're sure that your applications offer them. Even a decade after the debut of these features in macOS, many third-party apps continue to rely on the old-school Save and Save As commands for versioning. Furthermore, if these features aren't in a third-party app by now (I'm looking at you, Adobe — even Microsoft has Versions now, though they work only if the file is stored on your Microsoft OneDrive), I wouldn't hold my breath waiting for their appearance.

The bottom line is that if the app you're using doesn't have Auto Save and Versions, macOS takes no responsibility for saving files and saving versions of files; it's all up to you. Apple apps that save files — Pages, Keynote, Numbers, and Logic Pro, to name a few — use Auto Save and Versions. I prefer to use apps that support Auto Save and Versions whenever possible.

In the following sections, I show you how to save your masterpieces. Prevent unnecessary pain in your life by developing good saving habits. I recommend that you save your work (or save a version in apps that support versions)

>> Every few minutes

>> Before you switch to another program

>> Before you print a document

>> Before you stand up

The keyboard shortcut for Save in almost every Mac program is ⌘+S, and it works with Auto Save and Versions as well as with Save and Save As. Memorize it. See it in your dreams. Train your finger muscles to do it unconsciously. Use it (the keyboard shortcut) or lose it (your unsaved work).

If you don't heed this advice — and then the program you're using crashes while switching programs, printing, or sitting idle (the three likeliest times for a crash) — you may lose everything you did since your last save or saved version. The fact that a program crash doesn't bring down the entire system or force a restart is small consolation when you've lost everything you've typed, drawn, copied, pasted, or whatever since the last time you saved.

Stepping through a basic save

This section walks you through the steps you use the first time you save a document. The process is the same whether your app supports Auto Save and Versions or not. It's only after the initial save that Auto Save and Versions come into play.

DOES IT HAVE AUTO SAVE AND VERSIONS OR NOT?

It can be hard to discern at a glance whether an app uses the Auto Save and Versions features.

The first way to discern if an app supports Auto Save and Versions is whether the app has a Save As or Duplicate command in its File menu. Programs with a Save As command are old-school and don't support the modern Auto Save and Versions features. Programs with a Duplicate command have usually been updated with support for Auto Save and Versions. (Interestingly, the shortcut for Duplicate and Save As is almost always the same: ⌘+Shift+S.)

The next way is to discern whether the app has Rename and Move To commands in its File menu. If it doesn't, it's old-school; if it does, it's Auto Save- and Versions-savvy.

The easiest way to tell, however, is to look at the title bar of a document. If it displays a little v to the right of the document's name when you hover your cursor over it (as shown on top of the figure here) and a pop-up window appears if you click the triangle, the app supports Auto Save and Versions. (You read more about the options in the pop-up window later in this chapter.)

Click the little v

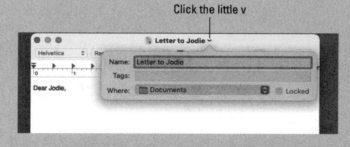

Everything I've said so far in this chapter applies to every app that saves files, with or without Auto Save and Versions. But I'd be remiss if I didn't reiterate that saving a file with Auto Save and Versions has one additional effect: It creates a new version of the file that you can access with Time Machine. To obtain that kind of functionality in apps without Auto Save and Versions, you'll need to use Save As to create a new version of the file periodically if you want to be able to roll back to an earlier version.

One last thing: Using Save As to create new versions uses more disk space (possibly much more) than using Auto Save and Versions and adds files on your drive — one file for each Save As versus one file for unlimited Versions. For example, after using Save As 11 times, you'll end up with 12 files on your drive; with Auto Save and Versions you'd still have 11 versions, but they're all contained in a single file.

In a few sections of this book, I ask you not only to read the instructions while sitting in front of your Mac but also to perform each step of the instructions as described. This section is one of them. If you read it and follow along, I can pretty much guarantee that it'll make sense. If you read it somewhere other than at your Mac, it could be a mite confusing.

Saving a file works pretty much the same way in any application you use to create documents. For this example, I use the macOS word-processing application, TextEdit, but the process will be similar in Microsoft Word, Adobe Photoshop, Apple Keynote, or any other application.

If you're going to follow along as I recommend, please launch the TextEdit program now (it's in your Applications folder), click the New Document button or choose File⇨New, and type a few words on the Untitled page that appears after you launch it.

Now that we're both on the same page (literally and figuratively), here's how saving a file works. When you choose to save a file for the first time (choose File⇨Save or press ⌘+S), a Save sheet appears in front of the document that you're saving, as shown in Figure 7-4. I call this a *basic* Save sheet (as opposed to an *expanded* Save sheet, which I get to in a moment):

1. **In the Save As field, type a name for your file.**

When a Save sheet appears for the first time, the Save As field is active and displays the name of the document. The document name (usually Untitled) is selected; when you begin typing, the name disappears and is replaced by the name you type.

2. **If the Where pop-up menu lists the location where you want to save your file, choose that location and proceed to Step 5. If not, click the disclosure button (labeled in Figure 7-4).**

You can choose from a short list of folders and volumes listed in the basic Save sheet's Where pop-up menu (which are the same devices and favorites you see in the sidebar of Finder windows). Or, if you click the disclosure button on the right of the Save As field, the sheet expands so that you can navigate folders just as you do in Finder: by opening them to see their contents.

If you click the Save button in Figure 7-4, your file will be saved to iCloud Drive, Apple's free online storage service (see Chapter 8). Or you can choose another location from the Where menu before you click Save, and save the file elsewhere.

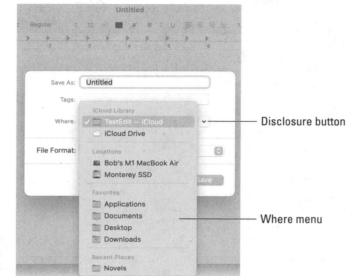

Disclosure button

FIGURE 7-4:
A basic Save
sheet looks a lot
like this.

Where menu

If you switch to expanded view (shown in Figure 7-5) by clicking the disclosure button, a standard Save sheet appears so you can save your file in any folder you like.

Note that the Where menu in the expanded Save sheet in Figure 7-5 doesn't have a Favorites section, but instead displays the path to the folder in which the file will be saved (Documents). I think that the Where menu should be the same in both basic and expanded Save sheets, as it was before macOS 10.5 Leopard. It seems more confusing to have the contents of this menu change based on whether the Save sheet is expanded or not. I've called it to your attention so it won't confuse you.

For what it's worth, Favorites are still available in an expanded Save sheet, but instead of being in the Where menu, they're in the sidebar.

TIP

Switch between the basic and expanded Save sheets a few times by clicking the disclosure button. Make sure that you see and understand the difference between what you see in the Where menu in a basic Save sheet and what you see in the Where menu in an expanded Save sheet. All the steps that follow assume you're using the expanded Save sheet.

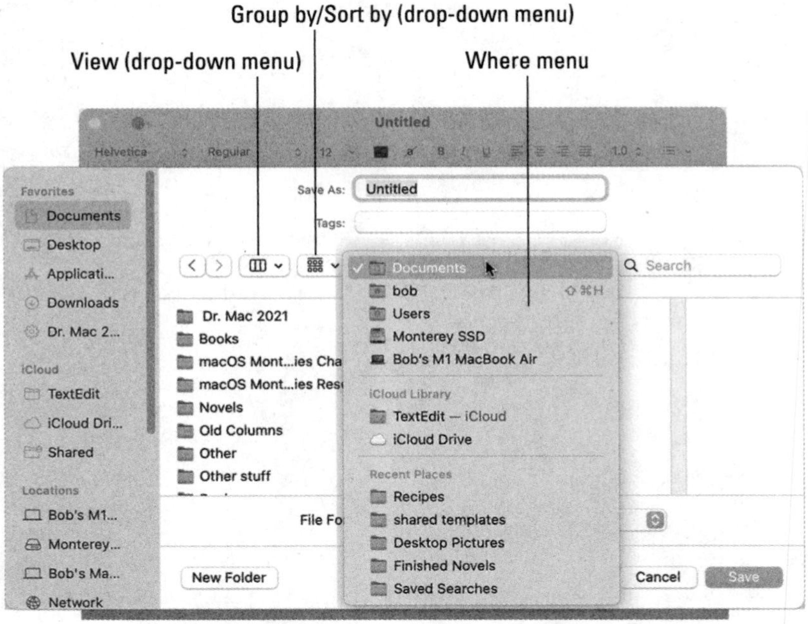

Group by/Sort by (drop-down menu)

View (drop-down menu)   Where menu

FIGURE 7-5:
An expanded
Save sheet looks
similar to this one
(shown in List
view).

3. **To make it easier to find the folder you want to save your file into, choose among views by clicking the View icon and making your choices from its drop-down menu.**

The View icon's drop-down menu, shown in Figure 7-5, allows you to choose the view that works best for you.

In Icons view, you double-click a folder to open it. List view offers disclosure triangles for folders and drives, so single-click the disclosure triangles of folders to see their contents. In Columns view, you click an item on the left to see its contents on the right, just as you do in a column-view Finder window.

You can also use the Forward and Back icons or the sidebar, both available only in an expanded Save dialog, to conveniently navigate your drive. Many of these navigation aids work just like the ones in Finder; see Chapter 4 for more details. You can enlarge the Save sheet to see more the same way you enlarge a Finder window: Drag an edge or corner of the sheet.

TIP

If you can't find the folder in which you want to save your document, type the folder name in the Search box. It works just like the Search box in a Finder window, as described in Chapters 4 and 8. You don't even have to press Return; the Save sheet updates itself to show you only items that match the characters as you typed them.

4. **Select the folder where you want to save your file in the Where pop-up menu or the sidebar.**

5. **If you want to create a new subfolder of the selected folder to save your file in, click the New Folder button (labeled in Figure 7-6), give the new folder a name, and then save your file in it.**

    In Figure 7-6, I selected an existing folder named Finished Novels. You can tell that it's selected because its name is displayed in the Where menu and highlighted below that in the first column.

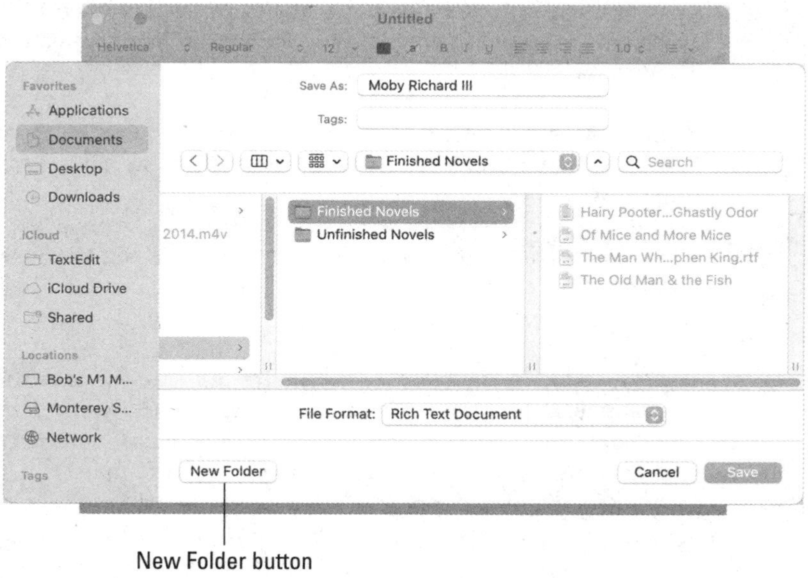

FIGURE 7-6:
Saving a file in the
Finished Novels
folder (which is in
the Documents
folder).

New Folder button

REMEMBER

The selected folder is where your file will be saved.

The keyboard shortcut for New Folder is Shift+⌘+N, regardless of whether you're in a Save sheet or Finder. If I want to create a folder inside the Finished Novels folder in Figure 7-6, I could click the New Folder button or press the shortcut.

6. **In the File Format pop-up menu (which says Rich Text Document in Figure 7-6), make sure the format selected is the one you want.**

    Double-check the Where pop-up menu one last time to make sure that the correct folder is selected.

7. **Click the Save button to save the file to the active folder.**

If you click Save, the file appears in the folder you selected. If you change your mind about saving this file, clicking Cancel dismisses the Save sheet without saving anything anywhere. In other words, the Cancel button returns things to the way they were before you displayed the Save sheet.

TIP

After you save a file for the first time, choosing File ⇨ Save or pressing ⌘+S won't bring up a Save sheet. Instead, what happens next depends on whether the app supports macOS's Auto Save and Versions. If the app *doesn't* support Auto Save and Versions, Save and its shortcut (⌘+S) merely resave your document in the same location and with the same name. If you want to save a unique version with a different name, you have to choose the Save As command and save the file under a new name.

If the app *does* support Auto Save and Versions, however, the upcoming section, "Save As versus Duplicate: Different names for the same result," explains how things work.

WARNING

When you use apps that don't support Auto Save and Versions, I beg you to get into the habit of pressing ⌘+S often. It can't hurt — and just might save your bacon someday.

One last thing: In Figures 7-4, 7-5, and 7-6, I used the Save sheet for TextEdit as an example. In programs other than TextEdit, the Save sheet might contain additional options, fewer options, or different options, and therefore might look slightly different. The File Format menu, for example, is a feature specific to TextEdit; it might not appear in other applications' Save sheets. Don't worry. The Save sheet always *works* the same way, no matter what options it offers.

Save As versus Duplicate: Different names for the same result

The two commands File ⇨ Duplicate and File ⇨ Save As serve the same purpose and achieve the same result. The difference is that you'll find File ⇨ Duplicate in apps that support Versions and Auto Save, and File ⇨ Save As in apps that don't. They're different names for achieving the same result: saving a file that's already been saved with a different name.

Before I get into the details, you may be wondering *why* you would want to save an existing file with a different name. So here's a good (albeit kind of rude) example: Suppose that you have two cousins, Kate and Nancy. You write Kate a long, chatty letter and save this document with the name Letter to Kate. Later, you decide that you want to send almost the same letter to Nancy, but you want to change a few things. So you change the part about your date last night and replace all references to Kate's husband, Kevin, with references to Nancy's husband, Norman. (Aren't computers grand?)

So you make all these changes in Letter to Kate, but you haven't resaved this document yet — and although the document on your screen is actually a letter to Nancy, its filename is still Letter to Kate. Think of what would happen if you were to save it now without using the Save As feature: Letter to Kate reflects the changes that you just made. (The stuff in the letter meant for Kate is blown away, replaced by the stuff that you just wrote to Nancy.) Thus the filename Letter to Kate is inaccurate. Even worse, you no longer have a copy of the original letter you sent to Kate! The solution? Just use Save As or Duplicate to rename this file Letter to Nancy by choosing File ⇨ Save As or File ⇨ Duplicate.

If you opt for Save As: A Save sheet appears, in which you can type a different filename in the Save As field. You can also navigate to another folder, if you like, and save the newly named version of the file there. Now you have two distinct files: Letter to Kate and Letter to Nancy. Both contain the stuff they should, but both started life from the same file.

If you choose Duplicate: The title bar of the document becomes editable so you can change its name without even seeing a Save sheet. (Refer to the figure in the earlier sidebar, "Does it have Auto Save and Versions or not?") By default it has the same name as the original with the word *copy* appended. Change its name or don't, and then press Return, and the duplicated file will be saved in the same folder as the original. Or, if you want to save the newly renamed file in a different location, choose File ⇨ Move To or click the little v to the right of the document's name, and select a different location in the Where menu.

Now that you understand what Save As or Duplicate are all about, here's an easier way to get the same result: Before you start, duplicate the document in Finder (choose File ⇨ Duplicate or press ⌘+D). Rename the copy and open it. This way, when you have finished making changes, you don't have to remember to choose Save As; you can just perform your habitual Save. This approach also protects you from accidentally saving part of the letter to Nancy without changing the file's name first (which you're likely to do if you're following my advice about saving often). So when you decide that you're going to reuse a document, choose Save As (or duplicate and rename the file) *before* you begin working on it, just to be safe.

TIP

For those who, like yours truly, prefer to use Save As, just press the Option key before you click the File menu and Duplicate magically transmogrifies into Save As. Sweet!

Versions gives you the benefits of Save As without any action on your part, but many programs still lack support for Auto Save and Versions nearly a decade after their introduction. And, in fact, some Apple apps, as well as most third-party apps, still use the Save As technique, and I expect that to be the status quo for quite some time. But because most of Apple's offerings (TextEdit, Pages, Numbers, Keynote, and more) use Auto Save and Versions, I'd be remiss if I glossed over Apple's current way of doing things.

REMEMBER

One last thing: If the app you're using supports Versions, it creates a snapshot called a *version* automatically as you work, when you pause, every 5 minutes, and every time you choose File ➪ Save (⌘+S). Choose File ➪ Revert To ➪ Browse All Versions or click the Time Machine icon in the dock while the document is active onscreen. (See Chapter 24 for more on Time Machine.) Either way, Time Machine displays versions of the document side-by-side, as shown in Figure 7-7.

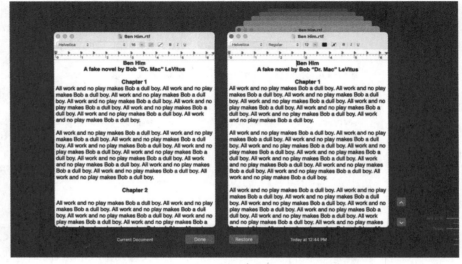

FIGURE 7-7:
Browse All Versions lets you compare all versions and revert to an earlier version.

Open, Sez Me

You can open any icon in Finder — whether it's a file or a folder — in at least six ways. (Okay, there are at least *seven* ways, but one of them belongs to aliases, which I discuss in great detail back in Chapter 4.) Anyway, here are the ways:

>> Click the icon once to select it and choose File ➪ Open.

>> Double-click the icon.

If the icon doesn't open, you double-clicked too slowly. You can test (and adjust) your mouse's sensitivity to double-click speed in the Mouse (or Trackpad) System Preferences pane, which you can access by launching the System Preferences application (from the Applications folder, the dock, or the menu) and then clicking the Mouse (or Trackpad) icon.

>> Select the icon and then press either ⌘+O or ⌘+↓.

>> Right-click or Control-click it and then choose Open from the contextual menu.

>> If the icon is a document, drag it onto the application icon (or the dock icon of an application) that can open that type of document.

>> If the icon is a document, right-click or Control-click it and choose an application from the Open With submenu of the contextual menu.

You can also open any document icon from within an application, of course. Here's how that works:

>> **Just launch your favorite program, and choose File ➪ Open (or press the shortcut ⌘+O, which works in most Mac programs).**

An Open dialog appears, like the one shown in Figure 7-8.

When you use a program's Open dialog, only files that the program knows how to open appear enabled (in black rather than light gray) in the file list. In effect, the program filters out the files it can't open, so you barely see them in the Open dialog. This method of selectively displaying certain items in Open dialogs is a feature of most applications. Therefore, when you're using TextEdit, its Open dialog dims all files it can't open, like the iBooks Author application in the Documents folder (first column) in Figure 7-8. Pretty neat, eh?

For what it's worth, TextEdit can open text, Rich Text Format, Microsoft Word, Microsoft Excel, and some picture files.

>> **In the dialog, simply navigate to the file you want to open (using the same techniques you use in a Save sheet).**

Click a favorite folder in the sidebar or use Spotlight (see Chapter 10) if you can't remember where the file resides.

>> **Select your file and click the Open button.**

For what it's worth, some applications allow you to select multiple files in their Open dialogs by holding down either Shift (for contiguous selections) or ⌘ (for noncontiguous selections). If you need to open several files, it's worth a try; the worst thing that could happen is that it won't work and you'll have to open the items one at a time.

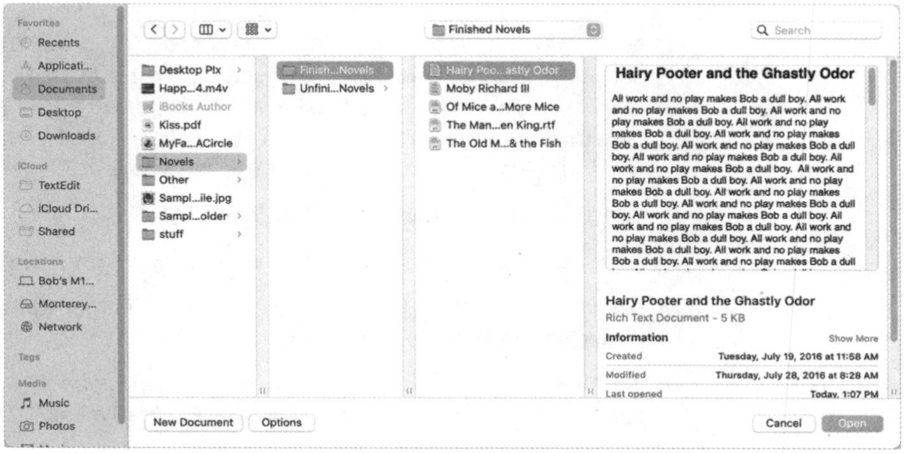

Figure showing the Open dialog using Column view, displaying a macOS file browser window with a sidebar (Favorites: Recents, Applicati..., Documents, Desktop, Downloads; iCloud: TextEdit, iCloud Dri..., Shared; Locations: Bob's M1..., Monterey..., Network; Tags; Media: Music, Photos) and multiple columns. A document "Hairy Pooter and the Ghastly Odor" is previewed with repeated text "All work and no play makes Bob a dull boy." Information panel shows Created Tuesday, July 19, 2016 at 11:58 AM, Modified Thursday, July 28, 2016 at 8:28 AM, Last opened Today, 1:07 PM. Buttons: New Document, Options, Cancel, Open.

FIGURE 7-8:
The Open dialog using Column view.

TIP

Some programs, including Microsoft Word and Adobe Photoshop, have a Show menu or a Format menu in their Open dialogs. This menu lets you specify the type(s) of files you want to see as available in the Open dialog. You can often open a file that appears dimmed by choosing All Documents from the Show or Format menu (in those applications with Open dialogs that offer such a menu).

With drag-and-drop

Mac drag-and-drop is usually all about dragging text and graphics from one place to another. But there's another angle to drag-and-drop — one that has to do with files and icons.

You can open a document by dragging its icon onto the icon of the proper application. You can open a document created with Microsoft Word, for example, by dragging the document icon onto the Microsoft Word application icon in the Applications folder, an alias of the Word icon, or Word's dock icon. The Word icon highlights, and the document launches. Usually, of course, it's easier to double-click a document's icon to open it; the proper application opens automatically when you do — or at least, it does most of the time. Which reminds me . . . .

With a Quick Look

The Quick Look window, shown in Figure 7-9, can display the contents of many types of files.

To use the Quick Look command to peek at the contents of most files in Open dialogs, right-click or Control-click the file and choose Quick Look, or use its easy-to-remember shortcut: Press the spacebar or ⌘+Y. Whichever way, you'll soon see the contents of that file in a floating window without launching another application.

Chapter 10 contains more information about Quick Look.

TIP

When your Mac can't open a file

If you try to open a file, but macOS can't find a program to open that file, macOS prompts you with an alert window. I tried to open a very old (1993) file created on a long-defunct Psion Series 3 handheld PDA (a file so old that most of you have probably never seen the .wrd file extension), shown in Figure 7-10.

FIGURE 7-10:
Oops! macOS
helps you find the
correct
application.

Click Cancel to abort the attempt to open the file, or click the Choose Application or Search App Store button to select another application to open this file.

If you click the Choose Application button, a dialog appears (conveniently opened to your Applications folder). Applications that macOS doesn't think can be used to open the file are dimmed. For a wider choice of applications, choose All Applications (instead of Recommended Applications) from the Enable pop-up menu.

REMEMBER

You can't open every file with every program. If you try to open an MP3 (audio) file with Microsoft Excel (a spreadsheet), for example, it just won't work; you get an error message or a screen full of gibberish. Sometimes, you just have to keep trying until you find the right program; at other times, you don't have a program that can open the file.

TIP

When in doubt, use a search engine to read about the file extension. You'll usually find out more than you need to know about what application(s) create files with that extension.

With the application of your choice

I don't know about you, but people send me files all the time that were created by applications I don't use . . . or at least that I don't use for that document type. macOS lets you specify the application in which you want to open a document in the future when you double-click it. More than that, you can specify that you want all documents of that type to open with the specified application. "Where is this magic bullet hidden?" you ask. Right there in the file's Info window.

Assigning a file type to an application

Suppose that you want all .jpg files that usually open in Preview to open instead in Affinity Photo, a more capable third-party image-editing program. Here's what to do:

1. **Click one of the files in Finder.**

2. **Choose File ⇨ Get Info (⌘ +I).**

    Or right-click, Control-click, or tap with two fingers on the file and then select Get Info from the contextual shortcut menu.

3. **In the Info window, click the gray triangle to disclose the Open With pane.**

4. **From the pop-up menu, choose an application that macOS believes will open this document type.**

    In Figure 7-11, I'm choosing Affinity Photo. Now Affinity Photo opens when I open this file (instead of the default application, Preview).

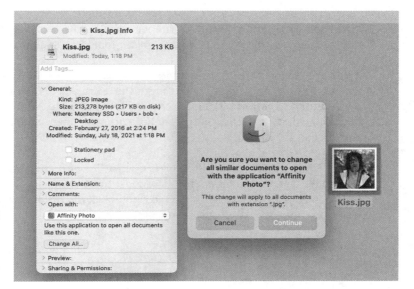

FIGURE 7-11:
Changing
the application
that opens this
document and all
others like it (that
is, .jpg files).

5. **(Optional) If you click the Change All button at the bottom of the Open With pane, as shown in Figure 7-11, you make Affinity Photo the new default application for all .jpg files that would otherwise be opened in Preview.**

Notice the handy alert that appears when you click the Change All button and how nicely it explains what will happen if you click Continue.

Opening a file with an application other than the default

TIP

Here's one more technique that works great when you want to open a document with a program other than its default. Just drag the file onto the application's icon or alias icon or dock icon, and presto — the file opens in the application.

If I were to double-click an MP3 file, for example, the file usually would open in Music (and, by default, would be copied into my Music library). But I frequently want to audition (listen to) MP3 files with QuickTime Player, so they're not automatically added to my Music library. Dragging the MP3 file onto QuickTime Player's icon in the Applications folder or its dock icon (if it's on the dock) solves this conundrum quickly and easily.

WARNING

If the icon doesn't highlight and you release the mouse button anyway, the file ends up in the same folder as the application with the icon that didn't highlight. If that happens, just choose Edit ➪ Undo (or press ⌘+Z), and the mislaid file magically returns to where it was before you dropped it. Just remember — don't do anything else after you drop the file, or Undo might not work. If Undo doesn't work, you must move the file back to its original location manually.

TIP

Only applications that *might* be able to open the file should highlight when you drag the file on them. That doesn't mean the document will be usable — just that the application can *open* it. Suffice it to say that macOS is usually smart enough to figure out which applications on your hard drive can open what documents — and to offer you a choice.

One last thing: If all you want to do is open a file with an application other than its default (and not change anything for the future), the techniques I just described work fine, but an even easier way is to right-click the file and choose another app from the contextual menu, as shown in Figure 7-12.

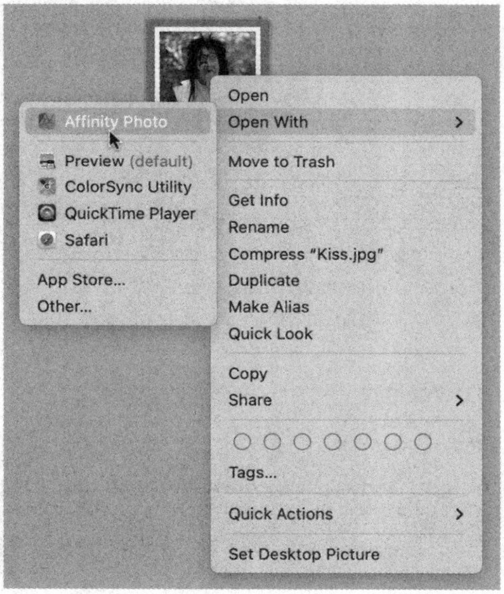

FIGURE 7-12:
To open a file with an app other than its default, right-click and choose the app you desire.

TIP

You can also change the default application to open *this* file by pressing Option after you right-click the file, which causes the Open With command to magically transform into Always Open With. Alas, you can't change the default application for *all* files of this type (.jpg in Figures 7-11 and 7-12); for that, you'll have to visit the Info window.

» Getting organized with folders

» **Moving around files and folders**

» **Introducing the incredible iCloud Drive**

Chapter **8**

File and Folder Management Made Easy

Y ou'll eventually accumulate a lot of files on your disk(s): tens, hundreds, thousands, even millions of files.

In Chapter 7, you can read about Finder and opening and saving files. In this chapter, it's time to take a look at how to organize all those files so you can find them when you need them.

Organizing Your Stuff in Folders

I won't pretend to be able to organize your Mac for you. Organizing your files is as personal as your taste in music; you develop your own style with the Mac. But after you know how to open and save documents when you're using applications, these sections provide food for thought — some ideas about how I organize things — and some suggestions that can make organization easier for you, regardless of how you choose to do it.

The upcoming sections look at the difference between a file and a folder; show you how to set up nested folders; and cover how some special folder features work. After you have a good handle on these things, you'll almost certainly be a savvier — and better organized — macOS user.

Files versus folders

When I speak of a *file*, I'm talking about what's connected to any icon except a folder or disk icon. A file can be a document, an application, an alias of a file or an application, a dictionary, a font, or any other icon that *isn't* a folder or disk. The main distinction is that you can't put something *in* most file icons.

TECHNICAL STUFF

The exceptions are icons that represent macOS packages. A *package* is an icon that acts like a file but isn't. Examples of icons that are really packages include many software installers and applications, as well as documents saved by some programs (such as Keynote, GarageBand, Pages, or TextEdit files saved in its .rtfd format). When you open an icon that represents a package in the usual way (double-click, choose File⇨Open, press ⌘+O, and so on), the program or document opens. If you want to see the contents of an icon that represents a package, right-click or Control-click the icon and choose Show Package Contents from the contextual menu. If you see an item by that name, you know that the icon is a package; if you don't see Show Package Contents on the contextual menu, the icon represents a file, not a package.

When I talk about *folders*, I'm talking about things that work like manila folders in the real world. Their icons look like folders, like the one in the margin to the left; they can contain files or other folders, called *subfolders*. You can put any icon — any file or folder — inside a folder.

WARNING

Here's an exception: If you try to put a disk icon in a folder, all you get is an alias to the disk — *unless* you hold down the Option key. Remember that you can't put a disk icon in a folder that exists on the disk itself. In other words, you can copy a disk icon only to a *different disk;* you can never copy a disk icon to a folder that resides on that disk. For more about aliases, flip to Chapter 4.

TIP

File icons can look like practically anything. If the icon doesn't look like a folder, package, or one of the numerous disk icons, you can be pretty sure that it's a file.

Organizing your stuff with subfolders

As I mention earlier in this chapter, you can put folders inside other folders to organize your icons. A folder nested inside another folder is a *subfolder*.

You can create subfolders according to whatever system makes sense to you — but why reinvent the wheel? Here are some organizational topic ideas and naming examples for subfolders:

>> **By type of document:** Word-Processing Documents, Spreadsheet Documents, Graphics Documents

>> **By date:** Documents May–June, Documents Spring 2017

>> **By content:** Memos, Outgoing Letters, Expense Reports

>> **By project:** Project X, Project Y, Project Z

When you notice your folders swelling and starting to get messy (that is, filling with tons of files), subdivide them again by using a combination of these methods that makes sense to you. Suppose that you start by subdividing your Documents folder into multiple subfolders. Later, when those folders begin to get full, you can subdivide them even further, as shown in Figure 8-1.

FIGURE 8-1:
Before (left) and after (right) organizing the Books and Novels folders with subfolders, shown closed (center) and open (right).

My point (yes, I do have one!): Allow your folder structure to be organic, growing as you need it to grow. Let it happen. Don't let any single folder get so full that it's a hassle to deal with. Create new subfolders when things start to get crowded. (I explain how to create folders in the next section.)

TIP

If you want to monkey around with some subfolders, a good place to start is the Documents folder, which is inside your Home folder (that is, the Documents folder is a *subfolder* of your Home folder).

If you use a particular folder a great deal, drag it to the right side of your dock, or make an alias of it and move the alias from the Documents folder to your Home folder or to your desktop (for more info on aliases, see Chapter 4) to make the folder easier to access. Or drag the folder (or its alias) to the sidebar, so it's always available, including in Open dialogs and Save sheets.

If you write a lot of letters, keep an alias to your Correspondence folder in your Home folder, on the dock, on your desktop, or in the sidebar for quick access. (By the way, there's no reason why you can't have a folder appear in all four places, if you like. That's what aliases are for, right?)

TIP

If you create your own subfolders in the Documents folder, you can click that folder on the dock to reveal them, as shown in Figure 8-2. I show you how to customize the dock in Chapter 3.

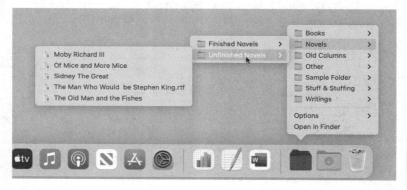

FIGURE 8-2:
It's super-convenient to have your Documents folder on the dock.

TIP

It's even more convenient if you choose to view the Documents folder as a list, as described in Chapter 3 and shown in Figure 8-2.

Creating new folders

So, you think that Apple has already given you enough folders? Can't imagine why you'd need more? Think of creating new folders the same way you'd think of labeling a manila file folder for a specific project. New folders help you keep your files organized, enabling you to reorganize them just the way you want. Creating folders is quite simple.

To create a new folder, just follow these steps:

1. **Decide which window you want the new folder to appear in — and then make sure that window is active.**

If you want to create a new folder right on the desktop, make sure that *no* window is active or that you're working in your Home/Desktop folder window. You can make a window active by clicking it, and you can make the desktop active if you have windows onscreen by clicking the desktop itself.

2. **Choose File ⇨ New Folder (or press Shift+⌘+N).**

A new, untitled folder appears in the active window with its name box already highlighted, ready for you to type a new name for it.

3. **Type a name for your folder.**

If you accidentally click anywhere before you type a name for the folder, the name box is no longer highlighted. To highlight it again, select the icon (single-click it) and press Return once. Now you can type its new name.

TIP

Give your folders relevant names. Folders with nebulous titles like Stuff, Untitled, or sfdghb will make it that much harder to find a file or folder six months from now.

REMEMBER

For folders and files that you might share with users of non-Mac computers, here's the rule for maximum compatibility: Use no punctuation and no Option-key characters in the folder name. Periods, slashes, backslashes, and colons in particular can be reserved for use by other operating systems. When I say Option-key characters, I'm talking about special-purpose ones, such as ™ (Option+2), ® (Option+R), ¢ (Option+4), and even © (Option+G).

Navigating with spring-loaded folders

A *spring-loaded folder* pops open when you drag something onto it without releasing the mouse button. Spring-loaded folders work with all folder or disk icons in all views and in the sidebar. Because you just got the short course on folders, subfolders, and various ways to organize your stuff, you're ready for your introduction to one of my favorite ways to get around my disks, folders, and subfolders.

Here's how spring-loaded folders work:

1. **Select any icon except a disk icon.**

The icon highlights to indicate that it's selected.

2. **Drag the now-selected icon onto any folder or disk icon — but don't release the mouse button.**

I call this *hovering* because you're doing just that: *hovering* the cursor *over* a folder or disk icon without releasing the button.

In a second or two, the highlighted folder or disk flashes twice and then springs open, right under the cursor.

Press the spacebar to open the folder instantly.

3. **After the folder springs open, perform any of these handy operations:**

- Continue to traverse your folder structure this way. Subfolders continue to pop open until you release the mouse button.

- If you release the mouse button, the icon you've been dragging is dropped into the active folder at the time and that window remains open.

- If you want to cancel a spring-loaded folder, drag the cursor away from the folder icon or outside the boundaries of the sprung window. The folder pops shut.

After you get used to spring-loaded folders, you'll wonder how you ever got along without them. They work in all four views, and they work with icons in the sidebar or dock. Give 'em a try, and you'll be hooked. And don't forget to slap the spacebar to spring folders open instantly.

Smart folders

As the late Steve Jobs was fond of saying near the end of his keynotes, "There is one more thing," and when it comes to folders, that one last thing is the smart folder.

A *smart folder* lets you save search criteria and have them work in the background to display the results in real time. In other words, a smart folder is updated continuously, so it displays all the files on your computer that match the search criteria at the moment.

So, for example, I created a smart folder that gathers all files with Dr. Mac in their name that were created after 1/1/2021, as shown in Figure 8-3. Or you can create a smart folder that displays graphics files, but only the ones bigger (or smaller) than a specified file size. Then all those files appear in one convenient smart folder.

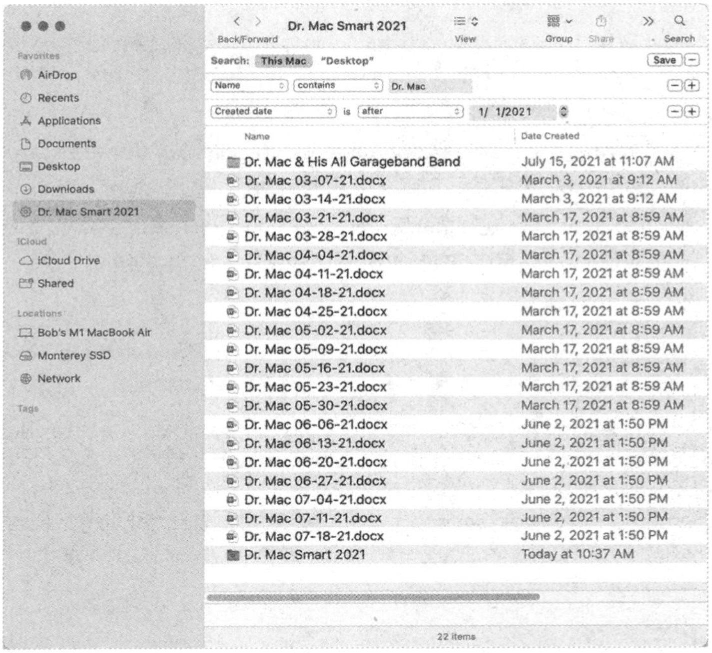

FIGURE 8-3:
A smart folder
that displays files
created after
1/1/2021 with
names that
contain the
phrase *Dr. Mac.*

The possibilities are endless. Because smart folders use alias-like technology to display items, the actual files reside in only one location: the folder where you originally put them. True to their name, smart folders don't gather the files themselves in a separate place; rather, they gather search results, leaving the originals right where you stashed them. Neat!

Also, because Spotlight (discussed in Chapter 10) is built deep into the bowels of the macOS file system and kernel, smart folders are updated in real time and so are always current, even after you add or delete files on your hard drive since creating the smart folder.

Smart folders are so useful that Apple provides four ways to create one. The following steps show you how:

1. **Start your smart folder by using any of the following methods:**

   - Choose File ⇨ New Smart Folder.
   - Choose File ⇨ Find.
   - Press ⌘+F.
   - Type at least one character in the Search box of a Finder window.

If you have Recents selected in the sidebar, you can't use the last method, because Recents is a smart folder itself — one with a weird icon, but a smart folder nonetheless.

2. **Refine the criteria for your search by clicking the + button to add a criterion or the – button to delete one.**

3. **When you're satisfied and ready to gather your criteria into a smart folder, click the Save button below the Search box.**

A sheet drops down.

4. **Type a name for your smart folder in the Save As field, choose where you want to save it, and then click the Save button.**

Select the Add to Sidebar check box before clicking Save to add this smart folder to the sidebar of all Finder windows.

Smart Folders are saved in the Saved Searches folder in your Library folder by default, but you can choose to save them anywhere on any drive and use them like any other folder.

If you want to *change* the criteria for a smart folder you created, right-click or Control-click the smart folder in the sidebar and choose Show Search Criteria.

When you're finished changing the criteria, click the Save button to resave your folder. Don't worry — if you try to close a smart folder that you modify without saving your changes, macOS politely asks whether you want to save this smart folder and warns that if you don't save, the changes you made will be lost. You may be asked whether you want to replace the previous smart folder of the same name; usually, you do.

Smart folders (with the exception of the sidebar's Recents, which has its own weird little icon) display a little gear icon, making them easy to tell apart from regular folders, such as the Dr. Mac 2021 smart folder icon shown in the sidebar in Figure 8-3.

Smart folders can save you a lot of time and effort, so if you haven't played with them much (or at all) yet, be sure to give 'em a try.

Shuffling Files and Folders

Sometimes, keeping files and folders organized means moving them from one place to another. At other times, you want to copy them, rename them, or compress them to send to a friend. These sections explain all those things and more.

TIP

All the techniques that I discuss in the following sections work at least as well for windows that use List, Column, or Gallery view as they do for windows that use Icon view. I use Icon view in the figures in this section only because it's the best view for pictures to show you what's going on. For what it's worth, I find moving and copying files much easier in windows that use List or Column view.

Moving files and folders

You can move files and folders around within a window to your heart's content — *as long as that window is set to Icon view.* Just click and drag any icon to its new location in the window.

TIP

If the icons won't move, make sure View⇨Arrange By is set to None.

Some people spend hours arranging icons in a window until they're just so. But because using Icon view wastes so much screen space, I avoid using icons in a window.

TIP

You can't move icons around in a window that is displayed in List, Column, or Gallery view, which makes total sense when you think about it. (Well, you can move them to put them in a different folder in List, Column, or Gallery view, but that's not moving them around, really.) And you can't move icons around in a window under the spell of the Arrange By command.

As you probably expect from Apple by now, you have choices for how you move one file or folder into another folder. You can use these techniques to move any icon (folder, document, alias, or program icon) into folders or onto other disks:

REMEMBER

>> **Drag an icon onto a folder icon.** Drag the icon for one or more folders or files onto another folder (or disk) icon, and then release when the second folder or disk icon is highlighted. The files or folders will then be inside the second folder or disk. This technique works regardless of whether the second folder is open in a separate window or tab.

If you *don't* release when the second folder is highlighted, the second folder will spring open, allowing you to see its contents *before* committing to moving the icon or icons you're dragging into it by releasing the button.

>> **Drag an icon into an open folder's window.** Drag one or more folders or files into the open window of a second folder (or disk), and then release it when the second folder's window is highlighted.

If you want to *move* an item from one *disk* to another disk, you can't use the preceding tricks. Your item is copied, not moved. If you want to *move* a file or folder from one disk to another, you have to hold down the ⌘ key when you drag an icon from one disk to another. The little *Copying* Files window reflects that you're moving and not copying by transmogrifying into the *Moving* Files window. Nice touch, eh?

Selecting multiple icons

Sometimes you want to move or copy several items into a single folder. The process is pretty much the same as it is when you copy one file or folder: That is, you just drag the icons to where you want it and drop them there. But you need to select all the items you want before you can drag them en masse to their destination.

If you want to move all the files in a particular folder, simply choose Edit ⇨ Select All or press ⌘+A. This command selects all icons in the active window, regardless of whether you can see them onscreen. If no window is active, choosing Select All selects every icon on the desktop.

But what if you want to select only some of the files in the active window or on the desktop? Here's the most convenient method:

1. **To select more than one icon in a folder, do one of the following:**

   - Click once in the folder window (don't click any one icon), and drag the cursor while continuing to hold down the mouse (or trackpad) button. You see an outline of a box (a *selection rectangle*) around the icons while you drag, and all icons within or touching the box become highlighted (the five icons with their names highlighted in Figure 8-4).

   - *Click one icon and hold down the Shift key while you click others.* As long as you hold down the Shift key, each new icon that you click is added to the selection. To deselect an icon, click it a second time while still holding down the Shift key.

   - *Click one icon and hold down the ⌘ key while you click others.* The difference between using the Shift and ⌘ keys is that the ⌘ key doesn't select everything between it and the first item selected when your window is in List, Gallery, or Column view. In Icon view, it really doesn't make much difference.

   To deselect an icon, click it while still holding down the ⌘ key.

2. **After you select the icons, click one of them (clicking anywhere else deselects the icons) and drag them to the location where you want to move them (or Option-drag to copy them).**

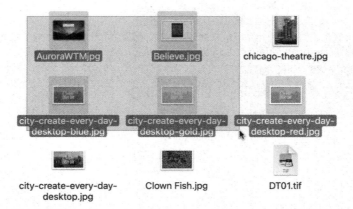

FIGURE 8-4:
The five icons
touched by the
selection
rectangle become
selected.

WARNING

Be careful with multiple selections, especially when you drag icons to the Trash. You can easily — and accidentally — select more than one icon, so watch out that you don't accidentally put the wrong icon in the Trash by not paying close attention. (I detail how the Trash icon works later in this chapter.)

Playing the icon name game: Renaming icons

Icon, icon, bo-bicon, banana-fanna fo-ficon. Betcha can change the name of any old icon! Well, that's not entirely true . . ..

TECHNICAL STUFF

If an icon is locked or busy (the application is currently open), or if you don't have the owner's permission to rename that icon (see Chapter 18 for details about permissions), you can't rename it. Similarly, you should never rename certain reserved icons (such as the Library, System, and Desktop folders).

To rename an icon, you can either click the icon's name directly (don't click the icon itself because that selects the icon) or click the icon and press Return once.

Either way, the icon's name is selected and surrounded with a box, and you can type a new name, as shown in Figure 8-5. In addition, the cursor changes from a pointer to a text-editing I-beam. An I-beam cursor is the Mac's way of telling you that you can type now. At this point, if you click the I-beam cursor anywhere in the name box, you can edit the icon's original name. If you don't click the I-beam cursor in the name box but just begin typing, the icon's original name is replaced by what you type.

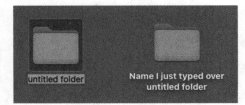

FIGURE 8-5:
Change an icon's
name by typing
over the old one.

If you've never changed an icon's name, give it a try. And don't forget: If you click the icon itself, the icon is selected, and you won't be able to change its name. If you do accidentally select the icon, just press Return once to edit the name of the icon.

WARNING

Don't change the name of a folder that contains open files because it might screw up the saving process and possibly cause data loss. So don't do that, okay?

Renaming multiple icons at once

To rename a group of files, first select them all, and then right-click anywhere in your selection and choose Rename from the pop-up menu. A sheet appears with options for adding or replacing text in the existing filename, or creating a custom format with indexes, counters, and dates before or after whatever new filename you choose.

Compressing files

TIP

If you're going to send files as an email enclosure, creating a compressed archive of the files first and sending the archive instead of the originals usually saves you time sending the files and saves the recipient time downloading them. To create this compressed archive, simply select the file(s) or folder(s) and then choose File⇨Compress. This creates a compressed .zip file out of your selection. The compressed file is smaller than the original — sometimes by quite a bit. Double-click a compressed (.zip) file to decompress it.

Getting rid of icons

To get rid of an icon — any icon — merely drag it onto the Trash icon in your dock.

REMEMBER

Trashing an alias gets rid of only the alias, not the parent file. But trashing a document, a folder, or an application icon puts it in the Trash, where it *will* be deleted permanently the next time you empty the Trash. The Finder menu offers a couple of commands that help you manage the Trash:

>> **Finder ⇨ Empty Trash:** This command deletes all items in the Trash from your hard drive, period.

I'll probably say this more than once: *Use this command with a modicum of caution.* After a file is dragged into the Trash and the Trash is emptied, the file is gone, gone, gone unless you have Time Machine or other backup. (Okay, maybe ProSoft Engineering's Data Rescue or some other third-party utility can bring it back, but I wouldn't bet the farm on it.)

If you put something in the Trash by accident, you can almost always return it from whence it came: Just click the Trash icon in the dock to open its window, right- or Control-click the icon you want to return, and choose Put Back in the shortcut menu.

You can also invoke the magical Undo command by choosing Edit ⇨ Undo or by pressing ⌘+Z. The accidentally trashed file returns to its original location. Usually. Unfortunately, Undo doesn't work every time — and it remembers only the very last action that you performed when it does work — so don't rely on it too much. (The right- or Control-click trick, however, works every time.)

One last thing: If you have two or more icons you want to move to a new folder, select the items and choose File ⇨ New Folder with Selection, press ⌘+Control+N, or right-click or Control-click one of the selected items and choose New Folder with Selection. All three techniques will create a new folder, move the selected icons into it, and select the name of the new folder (which will be New Folder with Items) so you can type its new name immediately.

The Incredible iCloud+ (and iCloud Drive)

iCloud has been around in various forms for years, but the service (known as iCloud+ in macOS Monterey) is Apple's remote storage service. iCloud Drive is a component of iCloud+ that lets you store files of any type in iCloud and access them from any device. It's built into Monterey and works like any other folder on your Mac. In other words, you can drag documents of any type into it, organize them with folders and tags (see Chapter 4) if you care to, and find them with Spotlight (see Chapter 10).

The best part is that the files are available not only on your Mac but also on your iPhone, iPad, or Windows PC as well. That's the good news. The bad news is that if you need more than the 5GB of free storage space, iCloud+ costs 99 cents per month for 50GB, $2.99 per month for 200GB, or $9.99 per month for 2TB.

Although iCloud Drive should be enabled by default, if yours isn't (you don't see it in the sidebar), launch System Preferences (⚫⇨System Preferences), click the Apple ID icon, and then enable the check box for iCloud Drive.

If you still don't see iCloud Drive in your sidebar, open Finder Preferences (Finder⇨Finder Preferences), click the sidebar icon, and then enable the check box to Show iCloud Drive in the sidebar.

One last thing: If your startup disk is getting close to full, you can choose to store the contents of your desktop and Documents folders on your iCloud Drive instead of your startup disk. The upside is that files in those folders are available to all your Macs and iDevices and via the iCloud website. The downside is that you may need to have internet access to access those files.

If storing your Desktop and Documents folders in the cloud appeals to you, choose ⚫⇨About This Mac, click the Storage tab at the top of the window, click the Manage button, click the Store in iCloud button, and (finally) enable the check box for Desktop & Documents Folders.

Monterey's Clipboard

» **Copying files and folders with the Clipboard**

» **Pasting files and folders with the Clipboard**

» **Introducing Monterey's Universal Clipboard**

Chapter 9

Comprehending the macOS Clipboard

B efore you start copying files, let me introduce you to the Clipboard. The *Clipboard* is a holding area for the last thing that you selected, and then cut or copied. That copied item can be text, a picture, a portion of a picture, an object in a drawing program, a column of numbers in a spreadsheet, any file or folder (except a drive), or just about anything else that can be selected.

Put another way, the Clipboard is your Mac's temporary storage area.

Introducing the Clipboard

Most of the time, the Clipboard works quietly in the background, but if you want to know what it currently contains, the Clipboard will reveal itself if you choose Edit ➪ Show Clipboard in Finder.

This command summons the Clipboard window, shown in Figure 9-1, which displays the type of item (such as text, an image, or sound) on the Clipboard, as well as either the item itself or a message letting you know that the item on the Clipboard can't be displayed.

FIGURE 9-1:
The Show
Clipboard
command
displays whatever
is on the
Clipboard if
it can.

As a storage area, the Clipboard's contents are temporary. *Very* temporary. When you cut or copy an item, that item remains on the Clipboard only until you cut or copy something else, logout, restart, or crash. When you cut or copy something else, the new item replaces the Clipboard's contents, and the newcomer remains on the Clipboard until you cut or copy something else (or log out, restart, or crash). And so it goes.

WARNING

Whatever is on the Clipboard heads straight for oblivion if you crash, lose power, log out, or shut down your Mac, so don't count on it too heavily or for too long.

If you want to preserve something on the Clipboard after you cut or copy something else, crash, lose power, log out, or shut down, paste it into a note in your Notes app (or into any other document, as long as that document is saved somewhere).

TIP

Myriad third-party clipboard enhancers remember the last 100 things (or more) that you copy or cut to the Clipboard. These utilities also preserve their contents if you crash, lose power, log out, or shut down. My favorites are CopyClip from FIPLAB (free) and its more powerful successor, CopyClip 2 ($7.99), both available from the Mac App Store (see Chapter 23).

TECHNICAL
STUFF

The Clipboard commands on the Edit menu are enabled only when they can be used. If the selected item can be cut or copied, the Cut and Copy commands in the Edit menu are enabled (black). If the selected item can't be cut or copied, the commands are unavailable and are dimmed (gray). If the Clipboard is empty or the current document can't accept what's on the Clipboard, the Paste command is dimmed. And when nothing is selected, the Cut, Copy, and Paste commands are dimmed (as in Figure 9-1).

One more thing: Files and folders can't be cut; they can only be copied (and pasted). So when a file or folder is selected, the Cut command is always gray.

Last but not least, if you don't see the Show Clipboard command in the Edit menu, chances are, an application other than Finder is active. Just activate Finder first and you'll see the Show Clipboard command in its Edit menu.

Copying Files and Folders

One way to copy files and folders from one place to another is to use the Clipboard. When a file or folder icon is selected, choose Edit ⇨ Copy (or use its shortcut, ⌘+C) to copy the selected item(s) to the Clipboard. To paste the copied item(s) in another location, navigate to that other location and then choose Edit ⇨ Paste (or use its shortcut, ⌘+V). The result is that you now have two copies of the files or folders in two places.

Other methods of copying icons from one place to another include these:

WARNING

>> **Drag the icon from one folder onto the icon of another folder while holding down the Option key.** Release the mouse button and Option key when the second folder is highlighted. This technique works regardless of whether the second folder's window is open.

If you don't hold down the Option key, you *move* the icon to a new location rather than *copy* it, as I explain a little later in this section.

When you copy something by dragging and dropping it with the Option key held down, the cursor changes to include a little plus sign (+) next to the arrow, as shown in the margin. Neat!

Note that when you drag an icon to a different disk, it is copied (rather than moved) with or without the Option key. But you can move an icon from one disk to another by pressing ⌘ when you drag.

Note that when you drag an icon to a different disk, it is copied (rather than moved) with or without the Option key. But you can move an icon from one disk to another by pressing ⌘ when you drag.

>> **Drag an icon into the open window for another folder while holding down the Option key.** Drag the icon for the file or folder that you want to copy into the open window for a second folder (or other hard drive or removable media, such as a USB flash drive).

>> **Choose File ⇨ Duplicate (⌘ +D) or right-click or Control-click the item you want to duplicate; then choose Duplicate from the contextual menu that appears.** This makes a copy of the selected icon, adds the word *copy* to its name, and then places the copy in the same window as the original icon. You can use the Duplicate command on any icon except a disk icon.

You can't duplicate an entire disk onto itself. But you can copy an entire disk (call it Disk 1) to any other actual, physical, separate disk (call it Disk 2) as long as Disk 2 has enough space available. Just hold down Option and drag Disk 1 onto Disk 2's icon. The contents of Disk 1 are copied to Disk 2 and appear on Disk 2 in a folder named Disk 1.

WARNING

If Disk 1 is a *startup disk* (macOS has been installed on the disk and it can start your Mac), Disk 2 will contain the same files but will not be a bootable startup disk (that is, it can't start a Mac). Also, some files may not be copied properly due to macOS permissions issues (see Chapter 18 for the story on permissions).

You can cut an icon's name, but you can't cut the icon itself; you may only copy an icon.

There are two ways to achieve the same effect as cutting an icon:

>> Select the icon, copy it to the Clipboard, paste it in its new location, and then move the original icon to the Trash.

>> Use the secret shortcut to move the icon via Copy and Paste. The secret is that you press the Option key before clicking the Edit menu. When you do, the Paste command transmogrifies into Move Item Here, providing the functional equivalent of cutting and pasting the icon. You can even use a keyboard shortcut — ⌘+Option+V — to move items from one location to another. Cool, eh?

If you're wondering why anyone would ever want to copy a file, trust me: Someday, you will. Suppose that you have a file called *Long Letter to Mom* in a folder called Old Correspondence. You figure that Mom has forgotten that letter by now, and you want to send it again. But before you do, you want to change the date and delete the reference to Clarence, her pit bull, who is no longer with us. So now you need to put a copy of *Long Letter to Mom* in your Current Correspondence folder. This technique yields the same result as making a copy of a file by using Save As, which I describe in Chapter 7.

WARNING

When you copy a file, it's wise to change the name of the copied file after you paste it. See, having more than one file on your hard drive with the same name isn't such a good idea, even if the files are in different folders. Trust me — having 12 files all named *Expense Report* or 15 files named *Consulting Invoice* is confusing no matter how well organized your folder structure is.

TIP

Add distinguishing words or dates to the names of files and folders you copy, such as *Expense Report Q3 2021* or *Dr. Mac Consulting Invoice 4-14-2021*.

You can have lots of files with the same name *on the same disk* (although, as I mention earlier, it's probably not a good idea). But your Mac won't let you have more than one file with the same name and extension (.txt, .jpg, .doc) *in the same folder.*

Pasting from the Clipboard

As I mention earlier in this chapter, to place the icon that's on the Clipboard someplace new, click where you want the item to go, and choose Edit➪ Paste or use the keyboard shortcut ⌘+V to paste what you've copied or cut.

REMEMBER

Pasting doesn't purge the contents of the Clipboard. In fact, an item stays on the Clipboard until you cut or copy another item, restart, shut down, log out, or crash. This means that you can paste the same item over and over and over again, which can come in handy at times.

And don't forget that most programs have Edit menus and use the Macintosh Clipboard, which means you can usually cut or copy something from a document in one program and paste it into a document in another program.

Usually.

Monterey's Universal Clipboard

The Universal Clipboard lets you copy or cut an item on one device (say, your Mac), and then paste it on another device (say, your iPhone or iPad). Because it performs this magic using iCloud, the requirements are as follows:

- » You must have an internet connection (wired or wireless).
- » Bluetooth must be enabled.

>> Both devices must have Handoff enabled. (It's in System Preferences ⇨ General on your Mac and Settings ⇨ General ⇨ AirPlay & Handoff on your iOS device.)

>> Both devices must be logged into the same iCloud account.

>> The devices must be within a few feet of each other.

When these conditions are met, Universal Clipboard just works. If you cut or copy something on one device, you can paste it on another device for approximately 2 minutes after you cut or copy it; after a couple of minutes, however, all bets are off.

If Universal Clipboard doesn't work for you, check the Apple website (www. apple.com/macos/continuity) to make sure both devices meet the system requirements. If both are supported and you still can't make Universal Clipboard work, try turning off Handoff on both devices, wait a minute or two, and then turn it back on. You might also try logging out of iCloud on both devices, restarting them, and then logging back into iCloud on both. Finally, some older Macs have issues with Continuity features such as Handoff and Universal Clipboard even though they meet the specifications.

One more thing before we move on: Monterey lets you use your iPhone or iPad camera (or camera roll) to add photos to documents on your Mac and to scan documents to your Mac. Look for the Insert from iPhone or iPad command on the File menu (or the shortcut menu, by right- or Control-clicking) of many apps. You discover more about this awesome Monterey feature in Chapter 23.

3
Getting Things Done

IN THIS PART . . .

Be more productive with Monterey's suite of time- and effort-saving tools.

Keep your life organized with Calendar, Reminders, and Notes (now with Quick Notes).

Master Siri — Siri-ously.

Go places with Maps.

Meet the many iOS apps that are now Mac apps, too!

» **Finding your files and folders, fast**

» **Taking charge with Mission Control**

» **Taking control with Control Center**

» **Learning to love the Monterey Launchpad**

Chapter **10**

Five Terrific Time-Saving Tools

In this chapter, I show you the ins and outs of five terrific time-saving tools: Quick Look, Spotlight, Mission Control, Control Center, and Launchpad. Each is designed to let you use your Mac better, faster, and more elegantly. Yes, you can use your mouse and click your way to any file or folder on any drive, but these features are built into Monterey for your convenience.

At the risk of repeating myself, Apple frequently provides more than one way to accomplish a task in macOS, so there's duplication and overlap among and between the tools in this chapter and tools I discuss elsewhere in this book. Don't worry. Take what you need, and leave the rest. Most users love Quick Look, but some never use it. Some people love Spotlight; others rarely invoke it. Mission Control is amazingly helpful, especially on laptops with small screens, but quite a few users find it inconsistent and confusing and don't care for it at all.

My advice: Try all the tools and techniques in this chapter at least a few times before you decide whether you want or need them. The good news is that unlike many Mac users, you will at least know what these five useful tools are about and how to use them if you choose to.

With a Quick Look

The Quick Look command displays the contents of the selected file in a floating window. The key point is that it's built into Monterey, so you can see what's in a file without double-clicking (to open) it and without launching an application.

This feature is handy when you want to peek at the contents of a file without having to open it.

To take a Quick Look yourself, select an icon and do any of the following:

>> Choose File ⇨ Quick Look.

>> Right-click or Control-click the file's icon and choose Quick Look from its contextual menu.

>> Choose Quick Look from the Action icon/menu on the toolbar.

>> Use one of its two keyboard shortcuts: ⌘+Y or the easiest shortcut ever, just press the spacebar while an icon is selected.

One of my favorite ways to use Quick Look is with a folder full of images, such as the one shown in Figure 10-1.

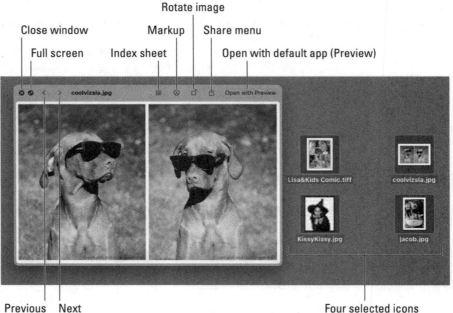

FIGURE 10-1:
The Quick Look window (right) displaying an image from one of the four selected icons in a folder full of pictures (left).

TIP

While the Quick Look window is open you can select different icons in the Finder window — use the arrow keys to select the next or previous icon — and see their contents in the Quick Look window!

The bad news is that although Quick Look works with many types of files — Microsoft Office, Apple iWork, plain-text, PDF, TIFF, GIF, JPEG, PNG, and most types of audio and video files — it doesn't work with *all* files. You'll know it doesn't work if Quick Look shows you a big document, folder, or application icon instead of the contents of that file.

If you select multiple items before you invoke Quick Look, as I did before snapping Figure 10-1, three icons appear at the top of the Quick Look window near the left side: Previous, Next, and Index Sheet. With these controls, you can view all selected items at the same time as an *index sheet* or view them one at a time by clicking the Next or Previous icons.

The outline around the jacob.jpg image indicates that the pointer is hovering over the image; if I were to click, that image would fill the window, and the icons shown at the top of the Quick Look window in Figure 10-1 would reappear.

REMEMBER

You can invoke Markup from the Quick Look window. Just click the Markup icon and the Markup tools appear. (Markup is described in loving detail in Chapter 5.)

Share and share alike with the Share menu

If you use an Apple iDevice, you're surely familiar with the rectangular icon with an arrow escaping from it, as shown in the margin and in the toolbar in Figure 10-1. That's the Share menu, with seven or more options (depending on the type of file you selected):

>> **Mail:** Launches the Mail app and attaches the selected file to a blank message, ready for you to address and send.

>> **Messages:** Launches the Messages app and puts the selected file in an outgoing message, ready for you to address and send. You become well acquainted with the Messages app in Chapter 17.

>> **AirDrop:** Sends the selected file to other Mac users or iDevice users. As long as you're on the same Wi-Fi network, your file transfer takes but a single click (or a single tap on iDevices).

>> **Notes:** Sends the selected file to the Notes app, where you can add it to an existing note or create a note for it. (You discover the Notes app in Chapter 11.)

>> **Reminders:** Creates a new reminder in the Reminders app. (To discover more on the Reminders app, see Chapter 11.)

>> **Add to Photos:** Adds the selected item to the All Photos album in the Photos app.

>> **More:** Monterey's extensible architecture lets you add other services (such as Vimeo or LinkedIn) and apps (such as Photos or Aperture) to your Share menu. To manage these extensions, choose More from the Share menu. Alternatively, you can launch the System Preferences application, click the Extensions icon, and then click the Share Menu item on the left side of the window.

If the file or folder you select is on your iCloud Drive, you'll see an additional option that lets you share the file or folder with others. You specify who can see it, who can modify it, and who can share it with others before sending them an invitation via Mail, Messages, Link, or AirDrop.

Slide into Slideshow (full-screen) mode

Quick Look really shines in its Slideshow (full-screen) mode, which you can start with any of these techniques:

>> Hold down Option and choose File ⇨ Slideshow.

>> Press ⌘+Option+Y.

>> If your file is already open in the Quick Look window, click the full-screen icon, as labeled in Figure 10-1 and shown here in the margin.

When you're in Slideshow mode, a completely different set of controls appears onscreen automatically, as shown in Figure 10-2.

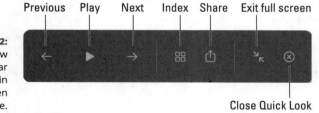

FIGURE 10-2:
The Slideshow controls appear automatically in full-screen Slideshow mode.

TIP

The Slideshow controls disappear after a few seconds of inactivity; if you don't see them when you need them, just wiggle the pointer anywhere onscreen, and they'll magically reappear.

To exit Slideshow (full-screen) mode, press Esc or click the Exit Full Screen icon to return to the Quick Look window or the Close Quick Look icon to both exit Slideshow mode and quit Quick Look.

When you're finished with the Quick Look window, click the X icon in the top-left corner (refer to Figure 10-1). If you're in full-screen mode, click the X icon in the control bar, as shown in Figure 10-2, or press ⌘+Y, which works in either mode.

Spotlight on Finding Files and Folders Faster

Even if you follow every single bit of advice provided in this chapter, a time will come when you won't be able to find a file or folder even though you know for certain that it's somewhere on your hard drive. Fortunately, Monterey includes a fabulous search technology called Spotlight, which can help you find almost anything on any mounted disk in seconds. Spotlight can search for

» Files

» Folders

» Text inside documents

» Files and folders by their metadata (creation date, modification date, kind, size, and so on)

Spotlight finds what you're looking for and then organizes its results logically, all in the blink of an eye (on most Macs).

Spotlight is both a technology and a feature. The technology is pervasive throughout Monterey, and is the underlying power behind the Search boxes in many Apple applications and utilities such as Mail, Contacts, System Preferences, and Finder. You can also use it by clicking the Spotlight menu — the little magnifying glass in your menu bar. Finally, you can reuse Spotlight searches in the future by turning them into smart folders (which I explain in Chapter 8).

Finding files and folders has never been faster or easier than it is in Monterey. So in the following sections, I look at the two separate but related ways that Spotlight helps you find files, folders, and even text inside document files and on the web: the Search box in the toolbar of Finder windows and the main Spotlight menu.

Using the Find command

With its power provided by Spotlight, this isn't your father's old search.

The following steps walk you through all the features:

1. **Choose File ⇨ Find or press ⌘+F to begin a new search or click in the Search box of any open window.**

   If you want to conduct a search limited to a specific folder (and its subfolders), open that folder first, and then click its Search box or press ⌘+F.

   You can then search for files by clicking This Mac (all files) or the active window's name, if there is one. If no windows are open, This Mac (all files) is used by default, as shown in Figure 10-3.

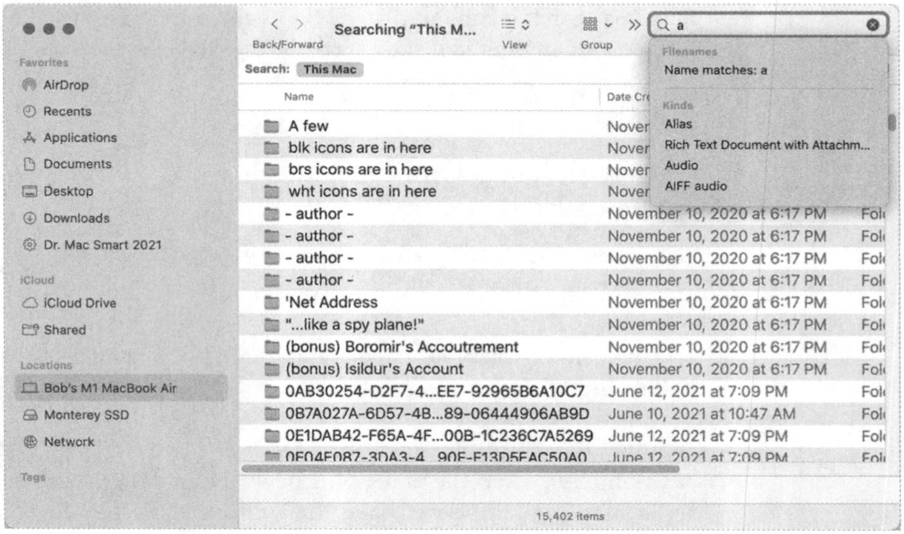

FIGURE 10-3: Type one character in the Search box, and the magic begins.

2. **In the Search box, type a single character.**

I typed the letter *a,* and the window starts displaying the results, as shown in Figure 10-3.

At the same time, a menu drops down below your pointer to offer search suggestions, in categories such as Filenames and Kinds, as shown in Figure 10-3.

Select an item from the menu to narrow the scope of your search. Or type additional characters: The more you type, the fewer matches and suggestions you'll see.

Spotlight's default behavior is to search files' contents if it can (and it can search the text inside files created by many popular applications).

TIP

Third-party Spotlight plug-ins are available that let you search the contents of file types not supported by Monterey, including old WordPerfect and QuarkXPress files and many others. Search the internet for *Spotlight plug-ins,* and you'll find plug-ins for dozens of popular apps.

If you know all or part of the file's name, you can limit your search to filenames (that is, exclude text in files and search only for files by name). Just choose Name Matches: (it's *a* in Figure 10-3) from the drop-down menu.

3. **When you find the file or folder, you can open any item in the window by double-clicking it.**

Keep these points in mind when you perform a search:

>> You have a choice of where to search. This Mac is selected in Figures 10-3 and 10-4.

>> You can choose additional search criteria — such as the kind (Folder in Figure 10-4) and the date the file or folder was created (Within Last 120 Days in the figure) — as well as other attributes, including Modification Date, Creation Date, Keywords, Label, File Contents, and File Size.

>> To add another criterion, simply click the + button on the right side of the window.

>> To save a search for reuse in the future, click the Save button on the upper-right side of the window.

TIP

Try choosing different options from the window's Group menu — Name, Kind, Date Last Opened, and so on — to see the search results presented in different ways.

FIGURE 10-4:
Search your
entire Mac or a
specific
folder (and its
subfolders) and
then narrow your
search using one
or more criteria.

![Screenshot of a Finder window searching "This M..." with search criteria: Kind is Folder, Created date is within last 120 days, showing three folder results for macOS Monterey For Dummies.]

So there you have it — fast searches made easy in Finder. But you can access the power of Spotlight in many ways, and the Search box in the toolbar of Finder windows is merely one of them.

Using the Spotlight menu and its keyboard shortcut

Another way to search for files and folders is to use the Spotlight menu itself — the magnifying-glass icon at the far-right end of your menu bar. Click the icon or use the keyboard shortcut ⌘+spacebar to open the Spotlight Search box. Now type a character, word, or series of words in the Search box begins your search.

Spotlight floats elegantly in the middle of your screen, as shown in Figure 10-5.

Check out the previews (*Monterey, California* in Figure 10-5), which is a nice touch. Also note that results may be culled from external sources, including Wikipedia and other websites, the iTunes Store, and Maps (in addition to results from files your hard drive).

TIP

Memorize and use the super-convenient and easy-to-remember keyboard shortcut for opening the Spotlight Search box, which is ⌘+spacebar by default. If you don't find ⌘+spacebar appealing as a shortcut, you can change it to whatever you like in the Spotlight System Preferences pane.

Spotlight is more than just a menu and a Search box; it also uses a technology that's pervasive throughout macOS and apps, including (but certainly not limited to) Mail and Contacts. The reason why it's so spectacularly speedy is that it indexes your files when your Mac is idle. The upshot is that Spotlight knows file locations and contents soon after a file is created or modified.

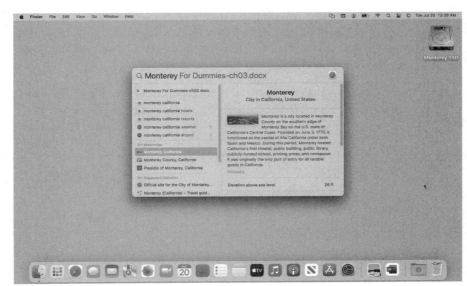

FIGURE 10-5:
This is Spotlight
in Monterey
searching for
Monterey.

REMEMBER

One last thing: The Search field in Finder windows finds items only on your hard drive. To include results from the internet, you have to use the Spotlight floating window via its menu icon or keyboard shortcut.

The bottom line is that regardless of which method you choose to invoke it — the Search box in a Finder window or the new floating Spotlight window — using Spotlight saves you time and effort.

Blast Off with Mission Control

Mission Control shows you big icons representing all open applications including full-screen apps, or all open document windows for the active application, presenting them in an organized and unified view. But before you start using Mission Control, you might want to configure it in the Mission Control System Preferences pane.

The Mission Control pane: It's painless

The top part of the pane contains four check boxes: Automatically Rearrange Spaces Based on Most Recent Use; When Switching to an Application, Switch to a Space with Open Windows for the Application; Group Windows by Application; and Displays Have Separate Spaces. These long-winded check boxes will all start to make sense shortly; for now, just know that they do what their lengthy names imply. You should experiment with the settings, turning them on and off, to see which way you prefer them.

Moving right along, the bottom part of the pane has three pairs of pop-up menus that govern keyboard and mouse shortcuts for Mission Control. Use them to specify the trigger for each of the three Mission Control features as a keystroke or mouse button. The default keyboard shortcuts appear in upcoming text, but yours may differ; to change them, click the appropriate pop-up menu and make a new selection.

TIP

Hold down the ⌘, Option, Control, or Shift key (or any combination thereof) when you choose an item from any of the shortcut menus to add modifier keys to the shortcuts you create. So, for example, if you were to hold down ⌘+Shift when you select F11 from a pop-up menu, the keyboard shortcut for that feature would be ⌘+Shift+F11.

Finally, most Apple keyboards made since April 2007 also include a dedicated Mission Control shortcut key (on the F3 or F4 key). If you see a tiny picture that looks like the Mission Control icon (shown in the margin) on your F3 or F4 key, you can use them in addition to the other shortcuts discussed in this section.

A picture is worth a thousand words, so check out Figure 10-6 as you read about each feature.

>> To see all open windows that aren't minimized or hidden in all open applications (as shown in Figure 10-6), press Control+↑ (up arrow).

>> To see all open windows belonging to the active application in a similar display, press Control+↓ (down arrow).

TIP

>> If you hover your cursor over a window on a Mission Control screen, a blue border appears around the item you're hovering over.

If you press the spacebar while a mini-window is highlighted, you'll see an overlay with a larger preview of the window's contents, which is especially helpful when a window is partially obscured by another window.

>> To hide all open windows so you can see icons on the desktop, press F11 or Fn+F11.

Note that when you're using Mission Control, windows appear as reduced-size thumbnails. Identifying information — either the program or window name — appears when you hover the pointer over a thumbnail (Mission Control) or below it (Application Windows), making it easier to discern what each item contains. When you click any of these small windows, Mission Control deactivates, and the window you clicked becomes the active window.

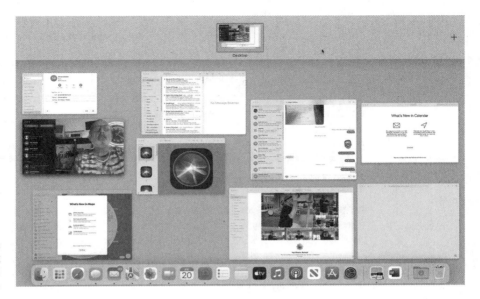

One last thing: If you use a trackpad, check out the More Gestures tab in the Trackpad System Preferences pane, where you can enable gestures to invoke Mission Control, App Exposé, Launchpad, and Show Desktop.

Hot corners are hot stuff!

In the bottom-left corner of the Mission Control System Preferences pane is a Hot Corners button, which lets you designate any or all of the corners of your screen as hot spots to trigger Mission Control, Launchpad, Screen Saver, Display Sleep, or Lock Screen. Click the menu for a corner, and select the feature you want associated with that corner. Then, whenever you move your pointer onto that corner and leave it there for a second or two, the feature executes.

TIP

Hot corners have been part of Mac OS since time immemorial and are still as useful as ever. For example, I like to set the top-right corner to start my screen saver and the bottom-right corner to disable it.

Mission Control is enabled by default, but you can disable any or all of its features by turning off its trigger: Just choose the minus sign from a pop-up menu instead of a keyboard shortcut.

TIP

Hold down the ⌘, Option, Control, or Shift key (or any combination thereof) when you choose an item from any of the Active Screen Corner menus to add modifier keys to the hot corners you create. So, for example, if you were to hold down ⌘+Shift when you select Mission Control as the shortcut assigned to the top-left corner, you'd have to press ⌘ and Shift and move the pointer to the top-left corner to trigger it. Or if you were to hold down Shift when you select Application Windows from the pop-up menu, you'd have to hold down Shift when you move the pointer to the top-left corner to invoke the command. If you don't press a modifier key when you select an item from a hot corner menu, merely moving the pointer to that corner will invoke the command.

Mission Control's Spaces from 30,000 feet (an overview)

If Mission Control lets you manage your windows in real time, its spaces let you manage windows by organizing them in groups called *desktops,* and switch from desktop to desktop with a keystroke or trackpad gesture.

In earlier versions of macOS, what are now called desktops were called *spaces.* Mission Control, improbably, uses the words *spaces* and *desktops* more or less interchangeably, so as you see in Figure 10-7, three spaces have been named Desktop 1, Desktop 2, and Desktop 3 for me. I think it's dumb, and I'm going to continue to call a space a space regardless of what Mission Control labels them (because calling them desktops would be even more confusing).

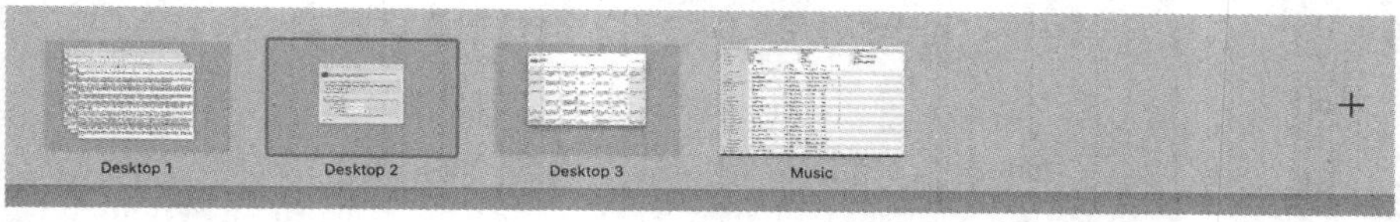

FIGURE 10-7: Mission Control showing off my four spaces (named Desktop 1, 2, 3, and Music).

By the way, apps running in full-screen mode are automatically considered a space of their own, which bears the name of the app (Music in Figure 10-7) instead of being named Desktop *x* by Monterey.

Think of a space as being a single screen, set up just the way you like it, with its windows arranged just the way you like them. When you use spaces, only two kinds of windows are shown in the space you're using: windows from applications associated with the active space and windows from applications launched while that space is active.

If you find yourself spending too much time moving and resizing windows onscreen, consider setting up spaces for specific tasks. You might have one space dedicated to a specific project, another for web surfing, and a third for email, each with all its windows arranged just the way you like them.

Take, for example, the four spaces shown in Figure 10-7. I have one for writing (Desktop 1), one for System Preferences (Desktop 2), one for my calendar (Desktop 3), and one for music, each with its windows arranged exactly as I like 'em (which is "big enough to read easily").

Moving right along, you manage your spaces with Mission Control, which provides an overview of what's running on your Mac, including all your spaces and all open windows. In a nutshell, this dynamic duo makes it easier than ever to manage and maintain the mélange of Finder and application windows that conspire to clutter and eventually consume your screen.

To see spaces in action, press the Mission Control key (Control+↑ by default). If you have a trackpad, you can also swipe upward using three fingers to see Mission Control, which will look something like Figure 10-7 based on the four spaces just described.

TIP

Try this: To see a thumbnail above a desktop's name, hover your cursor over the name. Its thumbnails (and thumbnails of all your Mission Control desktops) magically appear, as shown in Figure 10-7.

To add a new space, first enter Mission Control; then move the pointer to the top-right corner of the screen and click the Add (+) button. Note that if you have your dock on the right side of the screen, you have to move your pointer to the top-left corner for the + to appear.

You can use this technique to add as many spaces as you like. When you're finished using Mission Control, you can

>> Click a space at the top of the screen to switch to it.

or

>> Press the Mission Control key, press the Esc key, or swipe downward with three or four fingers to return to the space you were using when you entered Mission Control.

REMEMBER

The three-finger gesture requires a Magic Mouse, Magic Trackpad, or laptop with a buttonless trackpad.

TIP

If you're using a notebook Mac, I implore you to learn to use gestures with Mission Control. Visit the Trackpad System Preferences pane's More Gestures tab and make sure you've enabled three- or four-finger swipes. I love swiping between Mission Control spaces on my laptop. Swipe, and I've got my writing setup; swipe again, and I've got System Preferences; swipe again, and I have Calendar; and finally, one more swipe to see the Music app. Try it — I think you'll like swiping to switch spaces (desktops) as much as I do.

One last thing: macOS Monterey takes full advantage of multiple displays no matter how many displays are connected to your Mac. So, for example, you can work in Finder's desktop on one display and use a full-screen app on another. And finally, each display has its own exclusive set of Mission Control spaces associated with it.

TIP

If you use multiple monitors (like I do), you can drag and drop a space (desktop) from one display to another. Try it — it's way cool!

Getting around in space(s)

The preceding section shows you one way to move from one space to another — enter Mission Control, and click the space you want to use. You can also navigate spaces in the following ways:

>> Press the Control key and ← (left-arrow key) or → (right-arrow key) to move to the previous or next space.

>> Swipe left or right with three fingers to move to the next or previous space.

TIP

You can enable or disable these keyboard shortcuts in the Shortcuts tab of the Keyboard System Preferences pane.

There will be times when you want to move a window from one space to another. Do one of the following:

>> Drag a window to the top of the screen; when Mission Control appears, drag it onto a different space (desktop).

>> Press and hold down the mouse button on the window you want to move while pressing the Control key and the left-arrow key (←) to move the window to the space on the left of the current space or the right-arrow key (→) to move the window to the space on the right of the current space.

>> Start in the space that has the window you want to move. Enter Mission Control, press Control, and drag the window to the thumbnail of the appropriate space at the top of the screen. When you release the mouse button, the window will move to that space.

Finally, should you want to delete one or more spaces, simply enter Mission Control, and move the pointer over the space. A Delete icon — an X that should look familiar if you use the an iPhone, iPad, or iPod touch — appears in its top-left corner. Click it to delete that space.

Deleting a space doesn't delete or quit any applications or close any documents. Applications and windows in a deleted space move to the first desktop.

The bottom line is that spaces can be particularly useful for those with a smaller display. And it can be even more useful for users with more than one display.

REMEMBER

Using Mission Control can be an acquired taste, so even if you have a small screen or multiple screens, you may not care for it at first. My advice: Try it for a while, and if you decide that you hate it, turn its triggers off (by selecting the minus sign) and be done with it.

Taking Control of Essential Settings

Control Center lets you quickly manage Wi-Fi, Bluetooth, AirDrop, and other settings quickly, easily, and without launching System Preferences.

To access Control Center, click its icon in the menu bar, as shown on the left in Figure 10-8 (and in the margin). To see the options for each control, click the control or, for Display and Sound, click the little icon to the right of the slider. The options for Wi-Fi are shown in Figure 10-8, right.

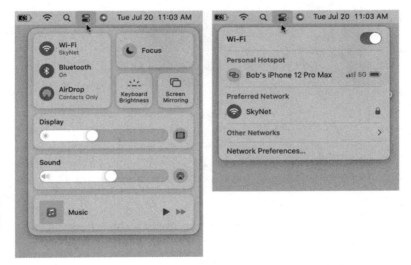

FIGURE 10-8:
The default
Control Center
(left), and its Wi-Fi
controls (right).

To add additional controls to Control Center or your menu bar, open System Preferences and click the Dock & Menu Bar icon. Here you can add Accessibility Shortcuts, Battery, and Fast User Switching to Control Center as well as manage other menu bar icons.

Launchpad: The Place for Applications

Launchpad presents all the applications in your Applications folder in a view that looks like the home screen of any iOS device (that is, iPhone, iPad, or iPod touch). In fact, if you use one of these devices, I suspect that you could skip everything that follows about Launchpad, because it works almost exactly like the home screen on an iPhone or other iDevice.

 Click the Launchpad dock icon (shown in the margin). It fills your screen with big, beautiful application icons, as shown in Figure 10-9.

FIGURE 10-9:
Launchpad, in all
its glory.

If your Launchpad has more than one page of apps, you'll see dots (two in Figure 10-9) near the bottom of the screen. To switch pages, click a gray dot; press ⌘ + right arrow (→) or ⌘+left-arrow (←) to move to the next or previous page, respectively; or click anywhere (except on an icon) and flick left or right. Trackpad users can also use a three-finger swipe left or right to move from page to page.

To launch an app, single-click its icon. In a heartbeat, Launchpad disappears, and the app replaces it on your screen.

Launchpad is configurable, just like home screens on iDevices. As you're about to see, you can rearrange app icons on a page, move them from one page to another, organize them in folders, and delete them. Say it all together now: "Just like on iDevices."

For those who are unfamiliar with iOS or devices that run it, here's how these things work on your Mac:

>> **To find an app:** Type the first few characters of its name in the Search box at the top of the screen.

>> **To rearrange app icons:** Click and drag the app to its new location.

>> **To move apps to the next or previous page:** Click and drag the app to the left or right edge of the screen. When the next page of apps appears, drag the app to its new location on that page.

>> **To add an app to your dock:** Click and drag the app onto the left side of the dock.

>> **To create a folder for apps:** Drag one app's icon on top of another app's icon to create a folder (such as Other in Figure 10-9).

>> **To add an app to a folder:** Drag the app onto that folder to add it.

>> **To move an app out of a folder:** Click the folder to open it and drag the app out of the folder to a new location.

>> **To change a folder's name:** Click to open the folder, click the current name, and then type a new name.

>> **To uninstall apps:** Click an app's icon, but don't release the mouse button until all the icons begin to wiggle. Apps that can be uninstalled display a Delete icon (X); click to uninstall the app.

>> **To stop the wiggling:** Press Esc or click the background.

TIP

Many Apple apps don't have a Delete icon because they're integral pieces of macOS Monterey and can't be removed.

Finally, you may notice that some items from the Applications and Utilities folders on your startup disk are in a folder named Other in Launchpad. Why? Which apps and for what reason? Nobody knows. It's been like that for as long as I can remember, but the logic behind it remains a mystery.

» **Creating and using Calendar calendars**

» **Creating and organizing Calendar events**

» **Remembering events with Reminders and Notification Center**

» **Taking notes with Notes**

» **Tracking productivity with Screen Time**

Chapter **11**

Organizing Your Life

When you install macOS Monterey, the folks at Apple generously include applications that can help simplify and organize your everyday affairs — Calendar, Reminders, and Notes (to name three you discover in this chapter).

In fact, macOS Monterey comes with a folder full of applications — software you can use to do everything from surfing the internet to capturing an image of your Mac's screen to playing QuickTime movies to performing numeric calculations.

Technically, most of these applications aren't even part of macOS. Rather, the vast majority of them are what are known as *bundled* apps — programs that come with the operating system but are unrelated to its function. Readers (bless them) tend to complain when I skip bundled applications, so I mention almost all of them in this book.

But in this chapter, you get a look at only the applications that help you organize your everyday life — appointments, to-do items, and notes — and how to keep them in sync with your other Macs and iDevices.

The applications discussed in this chapter are stored in (where else?) the Applications folder, which you can get to in four ways:

>> Click the Applications folder in the sidebar of any Finder window.

>> Choose Go ➪ Applications from Finder.

>> Press ⌘+Shift+A in Finder.

>> Click the Launchpad icon on the dock to see all the applications installed on this Mac (refer to Chapter 10).

TIP

Other bundled apps you might be especially interested in include Safari (Chapter 15), Contacts (Chapter 16), Mail (Chapter 17), Music (Chapter 19), a whole handful of multimedia applications that enable you to play video and more on your Mac, including Preview, which lets you view and annotate PDF and other image files (Chapter 20), and TextEdit (Chapter 21).

Keeping Track with Calendar

Calendar is a wonderful program that provides one or more appointment calendars with alerts. More precisely, you can have multiple color-coded calendars; several types of visual, audible, and emailed alerts; repeating events; and more. You can publish your calendar(s) on the web for others to view (which requires an iCloud account or other WebDAV server), and you can subscribe to calendars published by other Calendar users.

In the sections that follow, I share some of the features I think you'll find most useful.

Navigating Calendar views

Calendar lets you display the main Calendar window just the way you like it. You can find the following useful items (most of which have shortcuts) in the View menu, which provides nearly total control over what you see and how you navigate.

>> **To move back or forward:** Click the arrow buttons on either side of the Today button (upper right) or use the keyboard shortcuts ⌘+left arrow and ⌘+right arrow, respectively. You then see the previous or next week in Week view, yesterday or tomorrow in day view, and so on.

>> **To go to today's date:** Click the Today button or use its keyboard shortcut, ⌘+T.

>> **To add a new calendar:** Choose File ➪ New Calendar or use its keyboard shortcut, ⌘+Option+N.

>> **To view your calendar by day, week, month, or year:** Click the Day, Week, Month, or Year buttons at the top of the calendar. Figure 11-1 shows the Week view (keyboard shortcut: ⌘+2). Other views in the eponymous menu include By Day, By Month, and By Year, or use their keyboard shortcuts ⌘+1, ⌘+3, or ⌘+4, respectively.

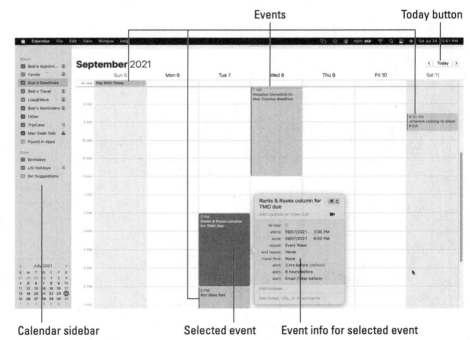

Events   Today button

FIGURE 11-1: The Calendar main window displaying the view I use most: Week view.

Calendar sidebar   Selected event   Event info for selected event

TIP

If you want to master Calendar, it would behoove you to spend some time experimenting with these views and with their navigation commands and options.

Creating calendars

If you refer to Figure 11-1, you see a list of my calendars in the top-left corner: Bob's Appointments, Family, Bob's Deadlines, Bob's Travel, Lisa@Work, and so on. The check boxes turn the visibility of a calendar on (selected) and off (deselected).

To create a calendar in Calendar, follow these steps:

1. Choose File ⇨ New Calendar.

If you have more than one account enabled (in Calendar ⇨ Preferences ⇨ Accounts or the Internet Accounts System Preferences pane), choose File ⇨ New Calendar ⇨ iCloud (or whichever account you want to use for this calendar).

A new calendar named Untitled is created and added to the appropriate account in the sidebar.

2. The default calendar name (Untitled) is selected after you create the calendar, so type a more descriptive name.

3. (Optional) To color-code the entries for this calendar, right-click or Control-click it in the sidebar to select a color from its shortcut menu.

In my humble opinion, Custom Color is the coolest choice because it lets you select from thousands of colors — including the lovely dusky rose hue I use for my Bob's Appointments and Bob's Reminders calendars.

If you have an iCloud account (or access to another WebDAV server), you can publish your calendars and invite others to subscribe to them by right- or Control-clicking the iCloud calendar in the list and choosing Share Calendar. Type their email address in the Share With field, and then click Done. Each invitee receives an email asking that person to join your calendar. This is what my wife and I do. Each of us maintains and publishes our own calendar and joins the other's. That way, we can see at a glance who's doing what and when they're doing it. This is by far the slickest solution we've found.

Deleting a calendar

To delete a calendar, select it in the list and press ⌘+Delete. An alert will appear to ask if you're sure.

This alert has a useful button, Merge, which provides an opportunity to merge the calendar with another rather than just blowing it (and all the events it contains) away.

Click Merge to select another calendar to merge this one with, click Delete to delete it, or click Cancel to do neither. Note that you can't merge calendars you subscribe to such as Found in Apps, Birthdays, US Holidays, and others — you can only turn them off.

When you delete a calendar, all the events and reminder items in that calendar are also deleted. Although you *can* undo a deleted calendar (choose Edit ➪ Undo or press ⌘+Z), you must do so before you quit Calendar. If you quit Calendar without undoing a calendar deletion, everything on that calendar (or calendars) will be gone forever (unless, of course, you have Time Machine or another backup, as I explain in Chapter 24).

If you sync your calendars with iCloud or another cloud-based service, deleting the calendar will delete it from all your devices.

Creating and managing events

The heart of Calendar is the event. To create a new one, follow these steps:

1. **Choose File ➪ New Event, press ⌘+N, double-click a date or time on the calendar in any view, or drag up or down anywhere on a date in Week or Day view.**

If you double-click or click and drag on the day of the event, you can skip Step 2, and you don't need to specify the date in Step 3.

2. **If the event doesn't appear in the proper place, just click it and drag it wherever you like.**

3. **To edit an event, select it and choose Edit ➪ Edit Event, press ⌘+E, or double-click it to open its event info window.**

All the items can be edited. For example, click the date or time to change it. The other items — Repeat, Travel Time, and Alerts — are pop-up menus. The colored square in the upper-right corner of the event info window is a pop-up menu that lets you assign this event to a different calendar.

The Travel Time item lets you add travel time to and from an event (and blocks out that time on your calendar) while preserving the event's start and end times.

4. **When you're satisfied with all of the event's items, press Return or click anywhere outside the event bubble.**

If you prefer working with event information in a context-sensitive window, choose Edit ➪ Show Inspector (⌘+Option+I). It looks the same as an event bubble with one difference: If you click a different event, that event's info instantly fills the Inspector window. Try it; you might like it.

TECHNICAL STUFF

What's the difference between the Event Info and Event Inspector? The Inspector window changes contextually and displays information about the currently selected event. Get Info windows, on the other hand, display info for a specific event. Put another way, a Get Info window displays the info for a specific event, and you can have as many Get Info windows on the screen as you like. There's only one Inspector window, though, and it displays info for whichever event is currently selected.

Inviting others to attend an event

To invite other people to your event, open the Contacts app or the Calendar Address panel (Window ⇨ Contacts) and drag the contacts onto the event in Calendar. Alternatively, you can type the first few letters of the name in the Invitees field for an event, and names that match magically appear. In Figure 11-2, I typed the letters *stan L*, and Calendar offered me a choice of my two contacts with names that start with *stan L* — Stan LeVitus and Stan Lee. Sweet! (If you're unfamiliar with Contacts, flip to Chapter 17 for details.)

FIGURE 11-2:
Invite people to your event.

After you add one or more invitees, click the Send button to invite them to the event. If the invitees have a compatible calendar application (Calendar, its predecessor iCal, Microsoft Outlook, and most calendar programs on most platforms), they can open the enclosure (included with your invitation email), which adds the event to Calendar with Accept, Decline, and Maybe buttons. All they have to do is click the appropriate button, and you receive an email informing you of their decision along with an enclosure that adds their response to the event in Calendar. Nice, eh?

It doesn't always work with some third-party mail programs, but the majority of people use either Apple Mail, Google Calendar, or Microsoft Outlook, which do the right thing with Calendar invitations.

If the invitee doesn't have a compatible calendar app (or doesn't open the enclosure that was included with the email invitation), the person has to respond the old-fashioned way: by replying to your email, texting, or calling you on the telephone.

Setting an alert

What's the point of putting an event on your calendar if you forget it? If you set an alert, Calendar won't let you forget. To set an alert, click None (just to the right of the word *alert)* in the Event Info window or Inspector. Now choose a time for the alert from the menu or choose Custom for more options. I find the custom Email alerts so useful that I use at least one for almost every event I create.

You can have as many alerts as you like for each event. When you add the first alert to an event, a +-in-a-circle will appear to its right when you hover the cursor over the alert pop-up menu; click the + to create a second (or third or fifteenth) alert.

To remove an alert, click the pop-up menu to the right of the word *alert* and choose None from the pop-up menu.

TIP

You can choose separate default alerts for Events, All Day Events, and Birthdays in Calendar Preferences. Choose Calendar ⇨ Preferences or press ⌘+, (type the comma), and then click the Alerts tab at the top of the window.

All the features mentioned so far are wonderful, but my favorite Calendar feature is the alert. I rarely miss an important event anymore; Calendar reminds me of them with time to spare. Better still, I sync events and alerts among my Mac, iPhone, iPad, and Apple Watch. So, when I create an event or alert on any device, within a few minutes — through the magic of iCloud — it appears on the other devices.

Reminders: Protection Against Forgetting

Reminders help you stay organized. Unlike an event, a reminder item isn't necessarily associated with a particular day or time (although it can be). Furthermore, reminders can be associated with a location, which is handier on an iDevice than on a Mac, but a great feature if you have such a device. Finally, reminders can have a priority level of low, medium, high, or none.

If you have an iDevice and sync with iCloud, Microsoft Exchange, or Office 365, your reminders will appear simultaneously on all your Apple devices — other Macs, iPhones, iPads, and iPod touches — which means you should never miss a reminder. Just set a reminder on your Mac or any iDevice, and you'll never forget anything.

Getting started with Reminders

Before you create or manage your own reminders, you should know a couple of things, starting with the concept of lists. Reminders includes a list called Reminders by default. You can delete or rename it if you like, and you can create additional lists if you care to by choosing File ➪ New List, pressing ⌘+Shift + N, or clicking the Add List icon (+) at the bottom of the window.

I like to have a bunch of lists with names such as Sooner, Later, and Out and About. And Reminders creates a separate section for completed items after you click the circle before a reminder's name to indicate a task is done, like *A completed reminder* in Figure 11-3.

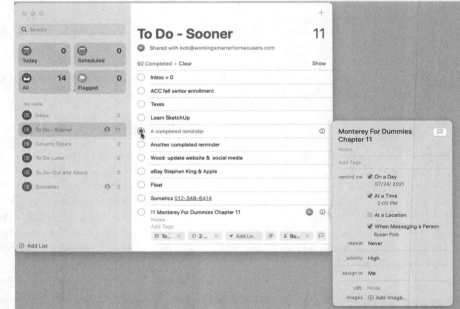

FIGURE 11-3:
When a list
(To Do – Sooner)
is selected in the
sidebar, its
reminders are
displayed on
the right.

After you select the circle for an item, the item is moved to the completed list. To see completed items, click Show near the upper-right corner of the window, choose View ➪ Show Completed, or press ⌘+Shift+H. When shown, completed items appear at the end of the list below uncompleted items.

The aforementioned Show commands change to Hide when completed items are showing; click Hide, choose View ➪ Hide Completed, or press ⌘+Shift+H again.

Here are more helpful techniques for working with lists:

>> **To rename a list:** Right- or Control-click the list, choose Rename from the contextual menu, type the new name, and press Return when you're done. Or select the list, press Return, type the new name, and then press Return again when you're done.

>> **To display a list in a separate window:** Double-click the list name; right- or Control-click the list, and choose Open List in New Window from the contextual menu; choose Window ⇨ Open in New Window; or press ⌘+Return.

>> **To show or hide the sidebar:** Choose View ⇨ Show/Hide Sidebar or press ⌘+Option+S.

TIP

You don't have to have more than one list. You don't even have to change the default list name (Reminders). That being said, I like having Reminders organized into separate To-Do lists. The point is that you can make a bunch of lists or dump everything into a single list; just use lists to organize your reminders so they make sense to you.

Finally, the boxes near the top of the sidebar — Today, Scheduled, All, Flagged, and Assigned (which appears only if one or more tasks is assigned) — are preconfigured smart lists. To hide a smart list, choose View ⇨ Show Smart List ⇨ and then select the smart list to remove its check mark and hide it. Or right- or Control-click the smart list and choose Hide.

To do or not to do: Setting reminders

The preceding sections tell you pretty much everything about reminders except how to create one, so it's time to find out how to create a reminder. It couldn't be easier: If you have more than one Reminders list, select the one that you want to contain the new reminder and then choose File ⇨ New Reminder; press ⌘+N; click the + at the top-right corner of the Reminders window; or click the first blank line in a list and begin typing.

Ah, but there's much more to a reminder, including:

>> Reminding you at a specific time on a specific date (refer to Figure 11-3)

>> Repeatedly reminding you at a specified interval

>> Reminding you at a specific location (as shown in Figure 11-4)

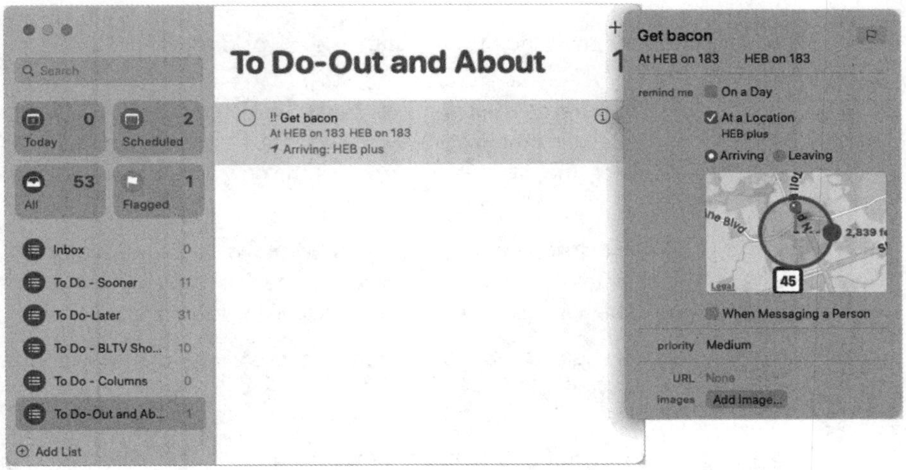

FIGURE 11-4: Location-based reminders are super handy.

If you have an iPhone, location-based reminders are the best. Give them a try, and I'm sure you'll be as hooked as I am. As you can see in Figure 11-4, the next time I am near HEB (our local grocery store), I'll receive an alert notification from Reminders that says *Get bacon.* That's sweet!

Reminders can also have a priority, a URL, and notes. To access these features, you need to Show Info for the reminder by choosing View ⇨ Show Info; pressing ⌘+I; clicking the little *i* that appears on the right side of the reminder (hover your cursor over the reminder if you don't see it); or double-click a blank spot on the reminder.

To change the order of reminders in a list, choose View ⇨ Sort By and then choose Due Date, Priority, Creation Date, or Title. Or choose Manual and control the item order yourself by clicking a blank spot on any reminder and then dragging it to its new position.

Also, reminders can have subtasks, which you create by choosing Edit ⇨ Indent Reminder or press ⌘ +]; to promote a subtask, choose Edit ⇨ Outdent Reminder or press ⌘ + [. If the subtask is below the wrong reminder, click a blank spot on the subtask and drag it where you want it. You can show or hide all subtasks by choosing View ⇨ Show/Hide All Subtasks or by pressing ⌘+E (show) or ⌘+Shift+E (hide).

Sharing lists and assigning reminders

Because you can assign a reminder only to someone you've shared a list with, let's look at sharing lists first.

To share a list, right- or Control-click the list and choose Share List, or click the list to select it and then choose File ⇨ Share List. A sheet appears with options for Mail, Messages, AirDrop, and Copy Link. Enable the Anyone Can Add More People check box if you want invitees to be able to share this list with others. Click Share and the recipient(s) get a link that adds the list to their reminders, synchronizing changes in (almost) real time.

I share a shopping list called Groceries with my wife. That way, either of us can pull out our iPhone and see what's on the Groceries list in Reminders. We mark items we buy as Completed, which is also synced in near-real-time. It's convenient, handy, and easy to set up.

After you've shared a list, you can assign its reminders to anyone with whom you've shared the list. To assign a reminder, right- or Control-click the reminder and then choose Assign ⇨ *person's name,* or click the reminder to select it and then choose Edit ⇨ Assign ⇨ *person's name.*

One more thing: You can view your Reminders in any web browser on any device by logging into www.icloud.com and clicking Reminders. You'll see the same lists and reminders that you see on your Macs and iDevices. You can't share lists or assign reminders (at this time), but you can manage existing reminders or create ones at icloud.com, which can be handy when you're stuck somewhere without your Apple devices.

Everything You Need to Know about Notification Center

The item in Figure 11-5 should look familiar to those of you who use an iPhone, iPad, or iPod touch — it's Monterey's rendition of Notification Center.

Notification Center manages and displays alerts from any app that supports Apple's notifications protocol. You can show or hide Notification Center by either clicking the clock icon in your menu bar or by swiping from the right edge of your trackpad to the left with two fingers.

Tweaking Notification settings

You manage which apps display notifications in the Notifications tab of the Notifications System Preferences pane. Choose ⇨ System Preferences or click the System Preferences icon in the dock, click the Notifications icon, and then click the Notifications tab at the top.

FIGURE 11-5:
Calendar and
Reminders alert
banners (top),
Calendar's Up
Next widget
(middle), with a
Reminders widget
(lower left), and
Weather widget
(lower right).

On the left side of the Notification tab, you'll find a list of all installed apps that
support notifications. To specify the settings for an app, click it once in the list to
select it. The selected app offers some or all of the following options:

>> **Turn off notifications for the app:** Deselect the Allow Notifications on/off
switch near the top of the window.

>> **Specify the alert style for the app:** Click the Alert Style you prefer: None,
Banners, or Alerts. Alerts remain onscreen until you dismiss them; banners
appear in the upper-right corner for a few seconds before fading away.

TIP

To make a banner reappear after it fades away, just click the clock in your
menu bar or use the two-fingered trackpad swipe as just described.

>> **Allow time-sensitive alerts:** Enable the Allow Time Sensitive Alerts check
box. (See the "Getting focused" section)

>> **See notifications for this app on the Lock Screen:** Enable the Show
Notifications on Lock Screen check box.

>> **See notifications for this app in Notification Center:** Enable the Show in
Notification Center check box.

>> **See the number of new notifications for the app on its dock icon:** Select the Badge App Icon check box.

>> **Hear a sound when receiving notifications:** Select the Play Sound for Notifications check box.

>> **Display a preview for this app's notifications:** Choose Always, When Unlocked (the default), or Never in the Show Previews pop-up menu.

>> **Change how apps are grouped in Notification Center:** Click the Notification Grouping pop-up menu and choose Off, By App, or Automatic (which groups them by time with the most recent notifications first).

Widget management 101

To manage the Widgets displayed in Notification Center, click the clock to display Notification Center, and then click the Edit Widgets button at its bottom.

A list of widgets available in Notification Center appears on the left side of the screen, with details displayed in the middle. Note that most widgets offer three sizes — Small, Medium, and Large, which you select by clicking the three little buttons (S, M, L) below the Up Next calendar widget. Small widgets display less information than Medium widgets; Medium widgets display less info than Large widgets; and not all widgets come in all sizes. I suggest trying all sizes of widgets you prefer to determine which size works best given your work style and screen size.

To add a widget to Notification Center, start by clicking a size button (if available), and then double-clicking the widget.

To move a widget to a different spot, click and drag it (on the right side of the screen) to its new location.

Finally, many widgets offer additional options, such as the Reminder list or Calendar. To access such options, click the widget on the right side of the screen. If options are available, the widget will spin around to display them on its backside. When you've finished working with a widget's options, click Done.

Finally, to rearrange widgets, click a widget on the right side of the Edit Widgets screen and drag it to its new location.

When you're happy with your widget lineup and arrangement, click the Done button.

Using Notification Center

Now, here's a quick rundown of ways you can use Notification Center:

TIP

>> **To respond to a notification:** Click the banner or alert before it disappears. Or open Notification Center, and then click the notification to launch its app.

If you hover the pointer over banners, you may see additional options such as the ability to reply to an email or message without launching Mail or Messages. Give it a try!

>> **To repeat a notification in nine minutes:** Click its Snooze button.

>> **To close all notifications for an app:** Hover the pointer over a notification. If the app has more than one notification, the little X in its upper-left corner (which would close only this notification) transmogrifies into Clear All. Click Clear All to close all notifications from that app.

Getting focused

NEW

Previous versions of macOS offered Do Not Disturb, which silenced all alerts and notifications. But it was on or off, period. Monterey replaces it with Focus, which does everything DND used to do but also enables you to customize who and what is allowed to notify you and when.

You can have one or more focuses, which you manage in the Notifications System Preferences pane's new Focus tab. In the Focus tab, you'll find one focus named Do Not Disturb, which works like Do Not Disturb worked prior to Monterey — it's on or off, with no exceptions. What's new is that you can specify which apps and people are allowed to notify you when Do Not Disturb is enabled. Also new is the capability to create more than one focus, with different settings for each.

TIP

The following instructions apply to the Do Not Disturb focus, but while you can customize its settings, I recommend that you create at least one custom focus. That way, you can use the Do Not Disturb focus when you want to shut off all notifications from all apps and people, and use your custom focus to allow interruptions from important people or apps.

To create a focus, click the + button at the bottom of the list on the left. Give the focus a name, select its color and icon, and click Add.

To customize a focus (including the default Do Not Disturb), select the focus in the list on the left. Use the Allowed Notifications From section to specify which people and apps (if any) can notify you while the focus is enabled.

To add a person or group, click the People button at the top of the Allowed Notifications From section and then click the + button at the bottom. Select a contact, contacts, or group and then click the Add button.

To add an app, click the Apps button at the top of the Allowed Notifications From section and then click the + button at the bottom. Select an app or apps and then click the Add button.

Now click the Options button at the top of the Allowed Notifications From to

>> **Allow time-sensitive notifications:** Enable this check box to allow people and apps to notify you immediately even with this focus enabled.

>> **Allow calls from:** Enable this check box to choose a group (or all contacts) to allow their phone or FaceTime calls when this focus is enabled.

>> **Allow repeated calls:** Enable this check box if you want don't want to silence a second call from the same person within three minutes.

Click the + button at the bottom of the Turn On Automatically section to add a time-based automation, a location-based automation, or an app-based automation.

Finally, enable the Turn On iCloud Syncing check box to share your focus settings with your other Apple devices. And enable Share Focus Status to tell apps you have notifications silenced and allow people to notify you anyway if something is important.

 To enable or disable a focus, click the focus icon on the menu bar (and shown in the margin) or click Do Not Disturb in Control Center.

Use Notes for Making Notes

Notes is an electronic notepad for your Mac. A note is a convenient place to jot quick notes, recipes, phone numbers, or whatever. Some notes are shown in Figure 11-6.

To create a new note, choose File ⇨ New Note; press ⌘+N; or click the button with the little square and pencil in the toolbar.

Notes is supremely flexible; here are just a few things you can do:

>> **Double-click a note to open it in its own window** so you can drag it around onscreen by its title bar.

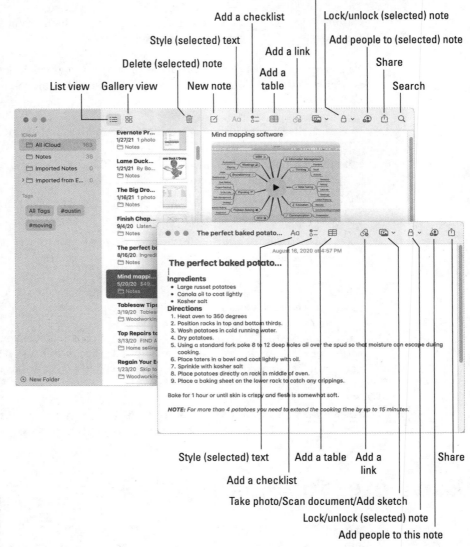

Take photo/Scan document/Add sketch

Add a checklist

Lock/unlock (selected) note

Style (selected) text

Add people to (selected) note

Add a link

Share

Delete (selected) note

Add a table

List view   Gallery view   New note   Search

Style (selected) text   Add a table   Add a
link   Share

Add a checklist

Take photo/Scan document/Add sketch

Lock/unlock (selected) note

Add people to this note

FIGURE 11-6:
Notes is for
making notes on
your Mac.

TIP

After opening a note in its own window, if you want the note to float in front
of other windows so it's always visible, choose Window ➪ Float on Top.

» **Change text** to any font, color, size, and style by selecting it and using the
myriad of tools in the Format menu and Style icon (Aa).

» **Search for a word or phrase** in any note by typing your query in the
Search box.

>> **Create bulleted, numbered, or dashed lists** by selecting the text and choosing Format ⇨ Bulleted List (cmd+Shift+7), Format ⇨ Dashed List (cmd+Shift+8), or Format ⇨ Numbered List (cmd+Shift+9).

In Figure 11-6, Ingredients is a bulleted list, and Directions is a numbered list.

>> **Create folders** (Notes and Imported Notes in Figure 11-6) to organize your notes by choosing File ⇨ New Folder, pressing ⌘+Shift+N, or clicking the New Folder button at the bottom of the Folder list.

REMEMBER

Folders in the Notes application are exclusive to Notes. In other words, the folders described in the following bullets aren't folders in Finder. You won't find them on your hard drive; they live only in the Notes app (and iCloud or other internet accounts if you've enabled them). And also remember that folders are optional. If you don't have a ton of notes, keeping them all in a single folder and using the Search box to filter them may work for you.

>> **Show or hide the Folders list** by choosing View ⇨ Show/Hide Folders or pressing ⌘+Option+S.

>> **Show only notes in a folder** by clicking the folder name in the Folders list, or click All iCloud to see all your notes.

>> **Automatically sync notes with your iDevice by using iCloud or other internet Accounts** by choosing Notes ⇨ Accounts, which will open the Internet Accounts System Preferences pane; then click the appropriate internet account — such as Office 365 or Gmail — and enable its check box to sync Notes.

>> **Send the contents of a note via the Mail or Messages app** by choosing File ⇨ Share or clicking the Share icon.

>> **Print a note** by choosing File ⇨ Print or pressing ⌘+P.

TIP

Whatever you type in a note is saved automatically as you type it, so Notes has no Save, Save As, or Duplicate commands.

Moving right along, here are more useful features in Notes:

>> You can drag and drop photos, PDFs, videos, and other files into any note.

>> The Attachments browser displays every external file you've dragged into every note in a single place, making it easier to find things. Choose View ⇨ Show/Hide Attachments Browser or use its keyboard shortcut ⌘+3 to see the Attachments Browser in action.

>> Use the Share menu in apps such as Safari and Maps to add content to Notes.

>> You can add checklists (in addition to bulleted, numbered, and dashed lists) by clicking the Checklist icon in the toolbar, by choosing Format ⇨ Checklist, or by using the shortcut ⌘+Shift+L.

And here are three more features you may find useful when creating notes:

>> You can add a table to any note by choosing Format ⇨ Table, by using its keyboard shortcut, ⌘+Option+T, or by clicking the Table icon in the toolbar.

>> You can format text as a title, heading, or body by choosing Format ⇨ Title, Heading, or Body or using their keyboard shortcuts ⌘+Shift+T, ⌘+Shift+H, or ⌘+Shift+B, respectively.

NEW

Choose Notes ⇨ Preferences to specify which format new notes start with.

>> Notes appear in the list in chronological order with the most recently created note on top. You can pin a note to the top of the list, where it remains until you unpin it. To pin or unpin a note, click it once to select it and then choose File ⇨ Pin Note (or Unpin Note). Or right- or Control-click the note in the list and choose Pin Note (or Unpin Note).

You can also share your notes with others and allow them to edit them. Here's how it works: Click the Add People icon in the toolbar and choose how you'd like to send your invitation: Mail, Messages, Link, or AirDrop.

If the people you invite are also running Monterey (or Big Sur, Catalina, or Mojave), they'll see the note in their copy of Notes; if they're running any other operating system, the note will open in the iCloud website for editing. When they're done, you'll see their edits in Notes on your Mac (and other devices) within a few minutes.

Other Notes goodies include a spell checker, spoken notes, text substitutions (such as smart quotes and smart dashes), and transformations (such as Make Upper or Lowercase). You can find all these options on the Edit menu.

NEW

macOS Monterey has two more new features in Notes: Activity view and Tag Browser. Activity view (View ⇨ Show/Hide Note Activity) provides information on who created, edited, or shared this note, and when they did it. Tags, which you can add to any note by preceding the note's name with #, (for example, *#Monterey* or *#Clients)*, are another way of organizing and filtering your notes. After you create a tag, it appears in the sidebar's Tag Browser as a button (All Tags, #austin, and #moving in Figure 11-6). When you click a button, notes with that tag are displayed. Or click All Tags to see notes that have any tag.

If you've created one or more tags but don't see buttons in your sidebar, hover your cursor over the word Tags and click the > that appears to its right.

One more thing: Don't forget that you can use your iDevice as a camera or scanner by using Continuity Camera. (Chapter 23 has the details.)

Take a Quick Note with Quick Note

I saved the best for last: Quick Note, a new and welcome feature that lets you jot a note instantly. To do so, drag the cursor to the lower-right corner of your screen and click the blank note that appears. The Notes app launches (if it's not already open) and a new note appears in the middle of the screen.

If you tap the link icon, you can add an app link to the note. Then, because Notes knows which website you're on, what story you're reading in the News app, who you're communicating with in the Messages app, and much more, the next time you visit that website or store or correspond with a person, Notes will automatically display that Quick Note in the lower-right corner.

The links are contextual, so the Quick Note will appear when Notes thinks you need it. There's also a smart list in the Notes app with all Quick Notes you've created.

You now know everything you need to know to use and enjoy Monterey's Notes app!

Tracking Productivity with Screen Time

We can all use a break from our digital devices, and Apple's solution is Screen Time. Although Screen Time includes the parental controls that used to appear in the Parental Controls System Preferences pane, this new feature is about policing your own behavior as well as the behavior of others in your family (if you so desire).

If you have an iDevice, you're probably familiar with Screen Time, which provides insight into how you spend your time on your iPhone or other iDevices, including which apps you used and websites you visited and for how long you. On the Mac, Screen Time is a System Preferences pane (choose ⇨ System Preferences or click the System Preferences Dock icon).

Today's date appears at the top of the pane by default. Use the arrows on either side of the Today button near the upper-right corner to view days before or after the day being displayed, or click the Today button to return to your stats for today.

If you have other devices using Screen Time, you'll see a pop-up menu at the bottom of the pane, allowing you to display Screen Time information for all devices combined or for a particular device. And if you're using Family Sharing, click your name below your picture to set Screen Time options for other family members.

All action takes place in the eight tabs in the sidebar on the left, namely:

>> **App Usage:** Displays details about the apps you used and how long you used them.

>> **Notifications:** Displays the number of notifications you received on this day and the time you received them.

>> **Pickups:** Shows you how many times you picked up your devices.

>> **Downtime:** Sets a schedule for times when only apps you have specifically allowed during downtime are available. A reminder appears 5 minutes before downtime starts.

>> **App Limits:** Sets time limits for apps and app categories such as Social, Games, and Productivity & Finance.

>> **Communication:** Set a limit on who is allowed to contact you via phone, FaceTime, or iMessage during screen time and downtime.

>> **Always Allowed:** Limit contacts and apps available during downtime.

>> **Content & Privacy:** Replaces the Parental Controls options in earlier versions of macOS. Enable or disable content by type, Apple online store, or specific app, as well as allow or disallow passcode changes, account changes, and other options for which you may want to restrict changes.

Finally, the Options button at the bottom of the sidebar offers two choices. Share Across Devices enables reporting for this Mac to be shared with your other devices. Screen Time Passcode lets you secure your Screen Time settings with a passcode and allow more time when limits expire.

Chapter **12**

Are You Siri-ous?

If you aren't familiar with Siri, Apple's intelligent digital assistant, you will be after reading this chapter.

Siri is designed to help you get things done using your voice, including capabilities designed specifically for your Mac, which means you can search for information, find files, send messages, and much, much more using only your voice.

Finally, Siri is optimized to work well with your Mac's built-in microphone, so you don't have to buy or connect a mic. That said, I think Siri (along with Dictation and Voice Control) works even better with a wired or wireless headset, as I explain in Chapter 23.

If you haven't tried Siri, you should. And if you're already a Siri fan, the latest rendition works just as you would expect.

What Siri Can Do for You

Before we get to the "how," let's look at what, exactly, Siri can do for you. Here's a short list of some cool things you can ask Siri to do:

» **"Open the Microsoft Word document I worked on yesterday."**

» **"Remind me to take the pizza out of the oven in 14 minutes."**

>> **"Add a meeting to my calendar at 11 a.m. tomorrow with Dr. Spock."**

>> **"Call Jacob LeVitus with FaceTime."**

>> **"Play songs by The Beatles."** This one works only if you have songs by The Beatles in your iTunes Library or subscribe to Apple Music, of course.

>> **"Call me 'Your Highness.'"** Replace "Your Highness" with, "Sir," "Madam," or anything else you like; Siri will refer to you by that name forevermore.

>> **"Who am I?"** If you forget who you are, Siri will remind you.

>> **"Call my wife on her cellphone."**

>> **"What song is this?"** If you've ever used Shazam to identify songs, Siri uses its technology. So, like the Shazam app, it can identify millions of songs after a brief listen.

>> **"Send a message to Lisa to reschedule dinner tomorrow."**

>> **"Find an ATM near here."**

>> **"Send an email to Jack Black that says, 'You rock.'"**

>> **"Show me pictures I took in Florence Italy"** or **"Show me all the pictures I took on Thanksgiving."**

>> **"What is the Dow at?"**

>> **"Send a tweet: 'Going on vacation. Smiley-face.'"** Siri will replace "Smiley-face" with a smiley-face emoji in the tweet.

>> **"I need directions to House of Blues."**

>> **"Who was the 19th president of the United States?"**

>> **"How many calories are in a blueberry muffin?"**

>> **"Wake me up at 8:30 in the morning."**

>> **"Who is pitching for the Yankees tonight?"**

>> **"Who won the Academy Award for Best Actor in 2003?"**

>> **"What is trending on Twitter?"**

Siri is relatively intelligent and understands many things in context. So, for example, if you ask, "Will I need an umbrella this weekend?" Siri will grok that you're looking for a weather forecast. Siri is also smart about using your personal information, so you can say, "Remind me to call Mom at 8 p.m." When the time comes, Siri will offer a list of your mom's phone numbers. And if Siri can't determine who "Mom" is, it will ask you — and then, in the future, Siri will remember your mother.

You can also ask things such as, "What's the traffic like around here?" or "Where can I get cheap gas around here?" Siri knows where, precisely, "here" is based on your Mac's current location.

Now that you've had a glimpse of the kinds of things Siri will do for you, let's dive in and take a look at how to actually *use* Siri.

Working with Siri

You can summon Siri in five easy ways. The first four ways are to click its menu bar icon or its icon in the Launchpad (shown in the margin), double-click its icon in the Applications folder; or use its keyboard shortcut (⌘+spacebar by default or whatever you selected in the Siri System Preferences pane).

TIP

If you pressed and held down ⌘+spacebar and Spotlight appeared instead of Siri, you didn't press and hold down long enough. Keep both keys pressed for two or three seconds and Siri will be at your beck and call. Pressing and releasing them any faster summons Spotlight, not Siri.

NEW

The fifth way is new — say "Hey Siri." Alas, this way is disabled by default. If you want to summon Siri by saying "Hey Siri," enable the "Listen for 'Hey Siri'" check box in the Siri System Preferences pane.

Moving right along, when you've summoned Siri, a bubble will appear near the top-right corner of your screen, and Siri asks its favorite question: "What can I help you with?" as shown in Figure 12-1.

FIGURE 12-1:
Speak now or Siri
will bug you . . . .

That's really all there is to it. Just remember two things: how to invoke Siri, and how to ask it a question or give it a command. That's all. Well, that's all except for one last thing: how to customize Siri to your liking.

Making Siri Your Own

Using Siri couldn't be easier: You summon it, ask or tell it to do something, and then wait for that something to be done. But you can invoke several tweaks that can help make Siri sound and behave the way you prefer.

You manage Siri in its System Preferences pane (➪ System Preferences ➪ Siri).

You can't change much, but here's what you can customize and how to do it:

>> **Enable Ask Siri check box:** Select the box to enable Siri (if it's not enabled already).

>> **Keyboard Shortcut menu:** If you don't care for the default ⌘+spacebar keyboard shortcut, this menu lets you change it to anything you like.

>> **Language menu:** Use this menu to select the language Siri will speak and understand from a long list — including nine varieties of English; four varieties each of Chinese, French, and Spanish; and dozens of others.

TIP

Siri is known to have difficulty understanding people with distinct accents. If it has trouble understanding you, look in the Languages menu for a different version of the language. It couldn't hurt, and it might just help.

>> **Voice Variety menu:** Select an American, an Australian, a British, an Irish, a South African, or an Indian accent. Note that this menu won't appear for other languages such as German.

>> **Siri Voice menu:** Choose one of the voices offered — the number of voices you see here depends on which language and voice variety you choose.

>> **Voice Feedback radio buttons:** These buttons allow you to enable or disable voice feedback. Do you want to hear Siri's dulcet tones? Click the On button. Do you prefer that Siri keep its mouth shut and just type its replies? If so, click the Off button.

>> **Delete Siri & Dictation History button:** If you say something you shouldn't have said and want to eradicate any record of it, click this button.

>> **Show Siri in Menu Bar check box:** This option does what you'd expect — it allows you to disable Siri's menu bar icon, which is enabled by default when you enable Siri.

And that's pretty much all you need to know to use and customize Siri in Monterey.

TIP

I'd like to mention two more things before we move on:

>> Siri requires an active internet connection. If you aren't connected to the internet, you can't use Siri.

>> Although I mentioned that Siri isn't great with heavily accented voices, I forgot to tell you that it's just as bad at recognizing your words when your environment is noisy. If Siri misunderstands you frequently and changing languages didn't help, try moving your face closer to your Mac and speaking in the direction of its microphone. Or try using a headset or other higher-quality microphone; most third-party headsets and microphones work better with Siri than the built-in mic on your Mac.

IN THIS CHAPTER

» **Finding yourself**

» **Zooming, panning, and viewing in Maps**

» **Finding addresses and other places of interest**

» **Getting from here to there**

Chapter **13**

Maps Are Where It's At

 f you know how to use the Maps app on your iPhone, iPad, or iPod touch, you already know most of what you need to know to use Maps on your Mac.

As for the rest of you — the ones without iOS devices — I'll have you up to speed RealSoonNow™.

Finding Your Current Location with Maps

I'll start with something supremely simple yet extremely useful: determining your current location. At the risk of sounding like a self-help guru, here's how to find yourself. Launch the Maps application from the dock, Launchpad, or Applications folder, and then click the Current Location icon, which is a little arrowhead (shown in the margin) and found on the toolbar at the top of the window.

Your location is indicated by a blue dot. I clicked the arrowhead in the toolbar, and the blue dot displayed my location, as shown in Figure 13-1.

REMEMBER

If you click or drag the map, your Mac continues to update your location but won't re-center the blue marker — meaning that the blue dot can scroll (or zoom) off the screen. If that happens, click the Current Location icon again to center the map on your current location again.

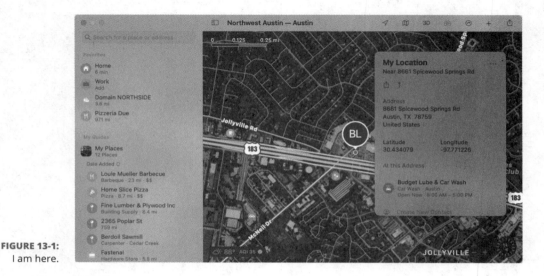

FIGURE 13-1:
I am here.

Of course, this and many other Maps features rely on an active internet connection and having Location Services enabled (System Preferences ⇨ Security & Privacy ⇨ Privacy tab).

TIP

Use the – and + icons in the lower-right corner (or the scroll control on your mouse or trackpad) to zoom in and out on the map.

Finding a Person, Place, or Thing

To find a person, place, or thing with Maps, choose Edit ⇨ Find, press ⌘+F, or click in the Search field in the sidebar (where it says Search Maps), and then type what you're looking for. You can search for addresses, zip codes, intersections, towns, landmarks, and businesses by category and by name, or combinations, such as *New York, NY 10022, pizza 60645,* or *Texas State Capitol.*

TIP

If the letters you type match names stored in your Mac (or iDevice) Contacts app (see Chapter 16), the matching contacts appear in a list below the Search field. Click a name to see a map of that contact's location. The Maps app is smart about it, too, displaying only the names of contacts that have a street address.

If you don't find a match in the list, press Return, and with any luck, a map will appear within a few seconds. If you search for a single location, it's marked with a single bubble. If you search for a category (*BBQ Lockhart TX,* for example), you may see multiple bubbles, one for each matching location (4 BBQ joints in Lockhart, TX), as shown in Figure 13-2.

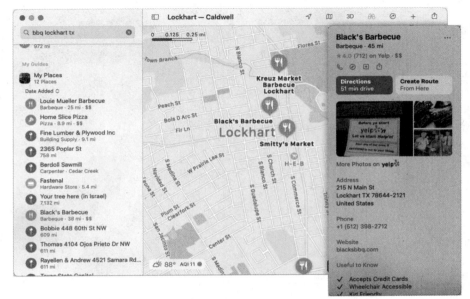

FIGURE 13-2:
Bubbles indicate matching locations; click a bubble to see its details.

TIP

You can search for all sorts of things, including intersections, neighborhoods, landmarks, restaurants, and businesses. Furthermore, you can combine several items, such as pizza and a zip code. The Maps app is adept at interpreting search terms and finding the right place. After you use the app a few times, you'll be as addicted as I am.

To find out more, click a name in the list below the Search field or click a pin. An overlay with details appears (refer to Figure 13-2).

This handy little info window sometimes contains reviews, photos, or both (only photos are visible in Figure 13-2), so scroll down through the overlay to read reviews or view pictures.

Views, Zooms, and Pans

The preceding section talks about how to find just about anything with Maps, and the following section shows ways to use what you find. But before doing that, I want to take a little detour and explore how you can work with Maps.

Click the View icon on the toolbar to choose Default, Transit, or Satellite view (see Figure 13-3), all of which can be viewed also in 3D. Just FYI, Figure 13-1 shows Satellite view in 2D; Figure 13-2 shows Default view in 2D; Figure 13-3 shows Transit view in 2D; and Figure 13-4 shows Satellite view in 3D.

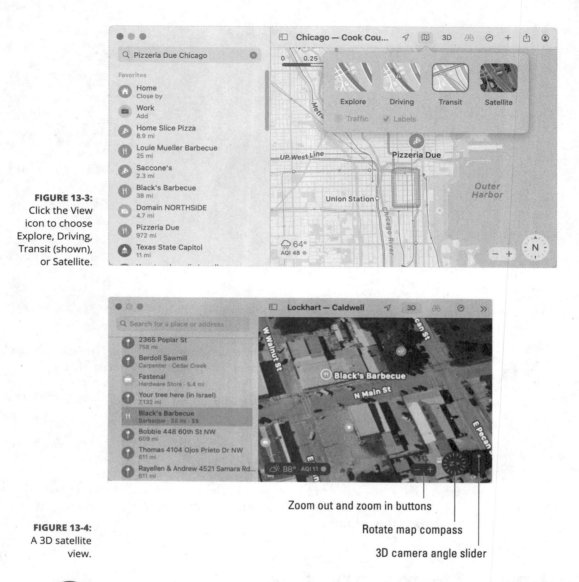

FIGURE 13-3:
Click the View
icon to choose
Explore, Driving,
Transit (shown),
or Satellite.

Zoom out and zoom in buttons

Rotate map compass

3D camera angle slider

FIGURE 13-4:
A 3D satellite
view.

3D maps aren't available in every area. It appears that the more populated the area, the more likely it is available in 3D.

WARNING

Speaking of which, to display a 3D map click the 3D icon in the toolbar (shown in the margin), choose View ➪ Show 3D Map, or press Shift+⌘+1. You may have to zoom in for the map to appear in 3D.

Moving right along, these tools are available in all views, in 2D or 3D:

>> **To zoom in:** Choose View ➪ Zoom In or press ⌘++ (plus sign). If you have a trackpad, you can also expand (spread two fingers) to zoom in (just like on an iPhone).

>> **To zoom out:** Choose View ➪ Zoom Out or press ⌘+− (minus sign). If you have a trackpad, you can also pinch to zoom out (just like on an iPhone).

TIP

If you have a scroll-wheel mouse, you can use the wheel to zoom in and out. You can also click the tiny + (zoom in) and − (zoom out) icons in the lower-right corner of the window.

TIP

If you click and then fling your mouse in any direction (or flick with two fingers on a trackpad), you'll "fly over" the ground below. It's usually not useful, but it's fun and looks cool.

NEW

Monterey has a new interactive globe view that you'll see if you zoom out as far as you can. Then you can manipulate the globe with your mouse or trackpad, and zoom in wherever you like to see additional details.

>> **To scroll:** Hold down the mouse or trackpad button and drag left, right, up, or down. If you have a trackpad, drag using two fingers.

>> **To rotate the map:** Click the compass in the lower-right corner and drag.

Finally, to adjust the camera angle in 3D views, press the Option key before you click and drag on the map (Option+drag with two fingers on a trackpad), or click and drag on the little slider in the lower-right corner (shown in Figure 13-4).

Maps and Contacts

Maps and Contacts (see Chapter 16) go together like peanut butter and jelly. For example, if you want to see a map of a contact's street address, type a few letters of the contact's name in the Search field and click the name in the list that automatically appears.

If you're in the Contacts app, it's even easier: Hover your pointer over a street address and click the little blue pin that appears to its right, as shown in Figure 13-5. Maps will then open with a pin at the address.

After you find a location by typing an address in Maps, you can add that location to your contacts.

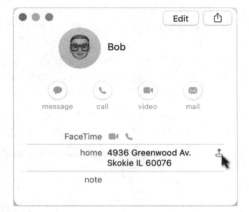

FIGURE 13-5:
Click the little
blue pin to see
this address
in Maps.

First, click the location's bubble on the map. Then, either click the ellipsis in the upper-right corner of the Info sheet and choose Create New Contact or scroll to the bottom of the Info sheet and click Create New Contact near the bottom of the sheet.

You can also get driving directions to and from most locations, including a contact's address, to most other locations, including another contact's address. You see how to do that in the "Smart Map Tricks" section, later in the chapter.

Time-saving Map Tools: Favorites, Guides, and Recents

The Maps app offers three tools in its sidebar that can save you from having to type the same locations over and over.

Favorites

Favorites in the Maps app, like favorites in Safari, lets you return to a location without typing a single character. To make a location a favorite, click its bubble on the map, and then either click the ellipsis in the upper-right corner of the Info sheet and choose Add to Favorites or scroll to the bottom of the Info sheet and click the Add to Favorites button.

You can also add a favorite by clicking the little + that appears to the right of Favorites in the sidebar when you hover over it. The little chevron that also appears when you hover your cursor over Favorites is a disclosure triangle. Click it and you'll see either all or none of your favorites.

After you add a favorite, you can recall it at any time.

TIP

The first items you should add as favorites are your home address and work address. You use these addresses all the time with Maps, so you might as well add them now to avoid typing them over and over.

Here's how to manage your favorites:

>> **To move a favorite up or down in the Favorites list:** Click and drag the favorite upward to move it higher in the list or downward to move it lower in the list.

>> **To delete a favorite from the Favorites list:** Right- or Control-click the favorite and choose Delete from the pop-up menu.

Guides

Guides are collections of places that you can create and share with others. A few big cities such as San Francisco, New York, London, and Los Angeles will have guides created by "brands you trust" (at least according to Apple). The cool thing about guides is that they update automatically, so if you share them with others, their guide will update when you add or delete locations.

To create a guide, hover your cursor over the words My Guides in the sidebar and then click the little + that appears to its right. A new guide named New Guide appears. Change its name to something meaningful and then right- or Control-click your new guide to do the following:

>> **Edit the guide.** Changes the name of this guide, add or change its photo, or delete it.

>> **Add a new place.** Opens an overlay where you can search for a place or choose one from your Recents list by clicking its + button.

>> **Duplicate the guide.** Creates a copy of this guide.

>> **Open the guide in a new tab or window.** Does what it says.

>> **Share.** A submenu that provides the standard share options — Mail, Messages, AirDrop, Notes, and Reminders.

>> **Send the guide to a device.** A submenu that lists all Apple devices nearby; select one to send this guide to it.

And there you have all you need to know to create and share Monterey's guides.

Recents

The Maps app automatically remembers every location you've searched for in its Recents list (unless you've cleared it, as described next). Click Recents to see your recent searches; click the item's name to see it on the map.

To clear the Recents list, scroll down if necessary until you see Clear Recents at the bottom of the list.

To clear a single location from your Recents list, right- or Control-click it and choose Delete.

Smart Map Tricks

The Maps app has more tricks up its sleeve. This section lists a few nifty features you may find useful.

Get route maps and driving directions

You can get route maps and driving directions to any location from any other location in a couple of ways:

>> **If a bubble is already on the screen:** Click it, and then click the Directions button on its Info sheet Click in the My Location field to choose where the directions begin.

>> **When you're looking at a map screen:** Click the Directions button on the toolbar (shown in the margin). The Directions overlay appears with Start and End fields at the top. When you click in either field, a drop-down list appears with your current location and a few recent locations. If you don't see what you need, type a few letters and choose the location in the list that appears. To swap the starting and ending locations, click the little swirly arrow to the right of the Start and End fields.

If you need to change the start or end location, click the little x-in-a-circle to the right of its name to erase it and try again.

When the start and end fields have been filled, press Tab or Return and step-by-step directions appear in an overlay, as shown in Figure 13-6.

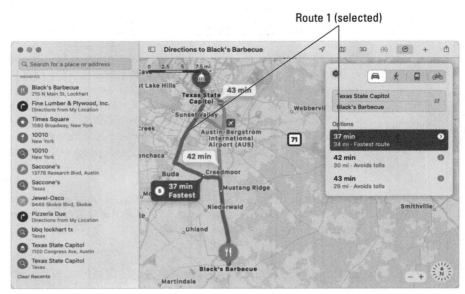

Route 1 (selected)

FIGURE 13-6:
Routes from the Texas State Capitol in Austin to Black's Barbecue in Lockhart, TX.

Maps will often suggest several routes. The suggestions appear on the map with the selected route in darker blue (the 37-minute route is selected in Figure 13-6). The alternate routes are shown on the map in lighter blue, and cartoon balloons that tell you how long it will take (42 or 43 minutes, respectively). Click a cartoon balloon or alternate route in the list to select it. The selected route always appears in dark blue; alternate routes always appear in a lighter shade of blue.

Click a blue line or cartoon balloon to select a route, as in Figure 13-6, where the first (and fastest) route is selected.

Click the chevron to the right of a route to see step-by-step directions for it.

After you've selected your route, you can print the directions (File ⇨ Print or ⌘+P), share them (File ⇨ Share), or send them to any nearby Apple device (File ⇨ Send to Device).

When you're finished with the step-by-step directions, click the Directions button to close the Directions overlay.

Get walking directions

For step-by-step directions for walking, click the Walk icon above the Start and End fields. Walking directions generally look a lot like driving directions except for your travel time.

Get directions for public transportation

Monterey's Maps app offers directions for using public transportation in more cities than ever. That's the good news. The bad news is that unless you live in a relatively large city, it may be a while (and possibly a long while, depending on the size of your city) before such directions are available for your hometown.

As far as I can tell, public transit directions work the same as driving directions; specify your start and end points and Maps suggests several routes via public transit.

TIP

If you zoom in far enough you can see the entrances to transportation facilities such as train stations. Also, to see the effect of leaving at a time other than right now, click the Plan tab and specify a departure or an arrival time.

Get traffic info in real time

You can find out the traffic conditions for whatever map you're viewing by choosing View ⇨ Show Traffic or clicking the Show drop-down menu lower-left on the map and choosing Show Traffic. When you do this, major roadways are color-coded to inform you of the current traffic speed.

TIP

Reverse this process to hide traffic.

Here's the key to those colors: Orange means 25 to 50 miles per hour; red means under 25; and no color means no data is available at this time.

WARNING

Traffic info isn't available in every location, but the only way to find out is to give it a try. If color codes don't appear, assume that traffic information doesn't work for that particular location.

Flyovers and look arounds

Certain cities and landmarks include cool additional features such as 3D flyover tours and *look around,* which you can use to explore select cities in an interactive 3D experience, panning 360° and moving smoothly through streets.

Flyovers

To try a flyover, first search for a city or landmark by name and select it; if a 3D flyover tour is available for it, you'll see the Flyover Tour button on its Info sheet, as shown in Figure 13-7. Click the button to watch the flyover tour; click the little x-in-a-circle at the bottom of the window to end the tour.

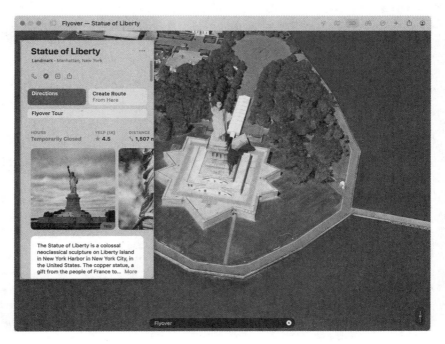

Look arounds

Look arounds are rare but interesting when you find them. You can start a look around by clicking the Look Around icon in the toolbar. The map screen changes to look around view, where you can click to move (or look) in any direction, as shown in Figure 13-8. If the Look Around icon is light gray and nothing happens when you click it, a look around doesn't exist for that location.

Do more on the Info sheet

As I explain earlier in this chapter, after clicking a location's bubble you can get directions to or from that location, add the location to your favorites or contacts, or create a new contact from it. But you can do three more things with a location from its Info sheet:

>> Click the phone number to call it.

>> Click the email address to launch the Mail app and send an email to it.

>> Click the URL to launch Safari and view its website.

And that, my friends, should be all you need to know to get you anywhere you want to go with Maps.

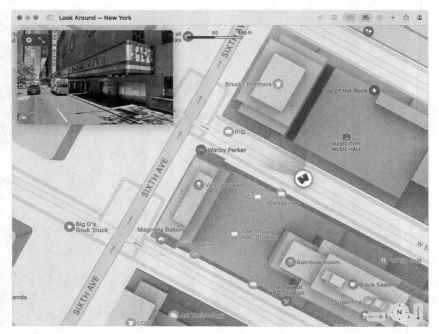

FIGURE 13-8:
A look around view near Rockefeller Center in Manhattan.

» **Staying current with News**

» **Making voice memos with Voice Memos**

» **Automate repetitive tasks with the Shortcuts app**

» **Smartening your home with the Home app**

Chapter **14**

Apps Born in iOS

This chapter covers five apps that have been around on the iPhone and iPad for many years, but only made their debut on the Mac recently. They should be familiar to anyone who uses an iOS device:

» Stocks lets you monitor information about specific stocks and the market in general.

» News gathers stories from myriad publications in one convenient place.

» Voice Memos lets you record (what else?) memos with your voice.

» Shortcuts lets you automate repetitive tasks.

» Home lets you control your HomeKit-enabled smart devices such as lights, thermostats, and locks.

None of the five is earthshattering as a Mac app, but all can be useful if you need what they provide. More Mac apps that started out as iOS apps are coming up in Chapters 19 and 20. For now, just dive right in with Stocks.

Taking Stock of the Market with Stocks

If you're familiar with the Stocks app from your iDevices, you're in for a treat because the Monterey Stocks app features an all-new design that makes it easy to view stock quotes, interactive charts, and top business news (from Apple News, which is covered in the next section).

When you launch Stocks for the first time, it's populated with a default set of quotes and indexes that Apple thinks you might appreciate, as shown in Figure 14-1. Note that if you have an Apple ID and have selected securities in the Stocks app prior to Monterey, your selections will appear instead.

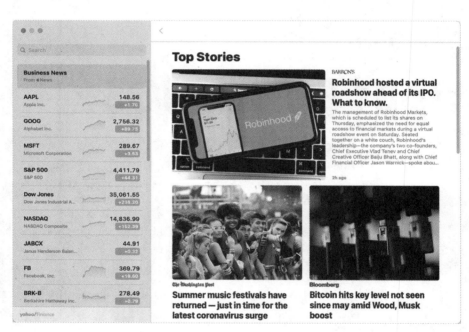

FIGURE 14-1:
The Stocks app comes stocked with a handful of securities and indexes chosen by Apple.

The default stocks, funds, and indexes are listed in the sidebar on the left; news items appear in the pane on the right. Figure 14-1 shows only a handful of stocks and news items; scroll down either pane to see more.

When you open the Stocks app, it displays the latest price for the listed stocks, with two provisos:

>> The quotes are provided in near-real time.

>> The quotes are updated only if your Mac can connect to the internet.

Your stocks also appear by default in Notification Center. If you don't see stocks in yours, click the Edit Widgets button at the bottom of Notification Center to add the Stocks app. (Flip back to Chapter 11 if you don't remember how to add widgets.)

Adding and deleting stocks, funds, and indexes

Your chance of owning the exact group of stocks, funds, and indexes displayed by default is slim, so this section shows you how to add your own stocks, funds, or indexes and delete any or all default ones.

Here's how to add a stock, a fund, or an index:

1. **In the Search field in the top-left corner of the Stocks window, type the name of a stock, fund, or index you want to add.**

   As you type, the list updates with companies, indexes, and funds that match what you've typed so far, with items already in your watchlist appearing in a separate section.

2. **Do one of the following:**

   - *Right- or Control-click the stock, fund, or index you want to add and choose Add to Watchlist.*

   - *Click the stock, fund, or index and then click the Add to Watchlist button, near the top-right corner of the stocks window.*

3. **When you've finished adding stocks, funds, and indexes, click < (Back) above the Search field to return to your watchlist.**

To delete a stock, fund, or index, select it and then press Delete. Or right- or Control-Click the item and choose Remove from Watchlist.

That's all there is to adding and deleting stocks.

To change the order of the items on your watchlist, click and hold down on the item and drag it up or down to its new place in the list.

Details, details, details

To see the details for an item, click it; the right side of the window will offer additional information on the item. The interactive chart described in the next section appears at the top of the pane. Scroll down for additional news; click More Data from Yahoo! for even more additional news.

Charting a course

When you select a stock, fund, or index, you'll see a graph with the following numbers and letters above it: 1D, 1W, 1M, 3M, 6M, 1Y, 2Y, 5Y, 10Y, and ALL. They stand for 1 day, 1 week, 1 month, 3 months, 6 months, 1 year, and 2, 5, 10, and all recorded years, respectively. These numbers and letters are labels; click one and the chart is updated to reflect that period of time.

You can do two other very cool things with charts:

>> Hover your cursor over the chart to see the value for that day.

>> Click and drag to see the difference in values between two days.

By default, the Stocks app displays the change in a stock's price in dollars. You can instead see the change expressed as a percentage or as the stock's market capitalization. Just choose Price Change, Percentage Change, or Market Cap from the View menu.

While the View menu is open, check out its other Stocks-related commands:

>> Refresh (⌘+R)

>> Hide Sidebar (⌘+Control+S)

>> Back (⌘+[)

>> Next Story

>> Previous Story

>> Actual Size (⌘+Shift+0)

>> Zoom In (⌘+plus sign)

>> Zoom Out (⌘+minus sign)

>> Enter Full Screen (⌘+Control+F)

Finally, Stocks lets you open multiple windows or tabs to keep more information available on the screen.

And that's about all you need to know to enjoy and be educated by Monterey's Stocks app.

Read All about It in News

The Apple News app gathers articles, images, and videos you might be interested in and displays them in a visually appealing fashion. Participating publishers include ESPN, *The New York Times,* Hearst (publisher of the newspaper I write for, the *Houston Chronicle*), Time, Inc., CNN, Condé Nast, Bloomberg, and many more.

What are your interests?

You can customize what appears in your News app by choosing File ⇨ Discover Channels, as shown in Figure 14-2.

FIGURE 14-2:
The Follow Your Favorites screen with NPR and the *New Yorker* selected to follow.

When the Follow Your Favorites screen appears, click the little red plus sign for each source you want to follow in the News app. When you click, a red check mark in a circle appears to indicate that you're following this source (such as NPR and the *New Yorker* in Figure 14-2).

Click the item again and the check mark turns back into a small red plus (like all items but NPR and the *New Yorker* in Figure 14-2) to indicate that you're not following this source.

When you've clicked all the sources you want to follow, click Done and they'll appear in the Following section of your sidebar.

To remove an item from the sidebar's Following section, either:

» Select the item and choose File ⇨ Unfollow Channel.

» Select the item and press ⌘+Shift+L.

» Right- or Control-click the item and choose Unfollow Channel.

How News works

News creates a customized real-time newsfeed based on the sources you're following, highlighting stories it expects you to be interested in. The more you read, the better its suggestions become, or at least that's what Apple says.

Click a story to read it; click < (Back) at the top of the pane to return to the main News screen. Or use the handy commands and shortcuts in the View menu, including the following:

» Check for New Stories (⌘ + R)

» Next Story

» Previous Story

» Actual Size (⌘ + 0)

» Zoom In (⌘ + plus sign)

» Zoom Out (⌘ + minus sign)

Managing your news

In addition to the useful commands in the View menu, the News app's File menu also offers myriad commands that help you manage your news.

For example, to help News find stories you'll enjoy, choose File ⇨ Suggest More Stories Like This (⌘ + L) if you love the story you're reading, choose File ⇨ Suggest Fewer Stories Like This (⌘ + D) if you don't love it.

REMEMBER

The more you use these two commands, the more insightful News will be when suggesting stories of interest.

Choose File ⇨ Save Story (⌘ + S) to save the story for future reading (in the Saved Stories section near the bottom of the sidebar).

The History section in the sidebar can help you find that story you read the other day and now want to share.

Finally, check out the other commands in the File menu, which can help fine-tune what you see in News, including the following:

>> Follow Channel (⌘ + Shift + L)

>> Block Channel (⌘ + Shift + D)

>> Manage Notifications & Email

>> Manage Blocked Channels and Topics

>> Manage Subscriptions

In 2019, Apple began offering a subscription news service called News+, which offers access to hundreds of newspapers and magazines for $9.99 a month. Click News+ in the sidebar for more information or to begin a free one-month trial.

And that's about all you need to know to customize and enjoy news in the News app.

Recording Memos with Voice Memos

The third addition from iOS is called Voice Memos, a simple one-trick-pony of an app that lets you record, play back, and share short audio recordings.

Consider all the times you'd find it useful to have an audio recorder in your MacBook — perhaps when you're attending a lecture or interviewing an important source (a big deal for writers). Or maybe you just want to record a quick reminder ("Pick up milk after work"). Well, you're in luck. Monterey includes the same built-in digital voice recorder you know and love on your iPhone (and other iDevices).

Recording a voice memo

Launch Voice Memos and you'll see a simple window with a sidebar that sports your previous recordings (if you have them) and a big red button.

TIP

Recordings use your Mac's built-in microphone by default. If you prefer to use a different microphone, select it in the Sound System Preferences pane's Input tab before you begin recording.

To record a voice memo, click the big red button. To pause the recording, click the red Pause button, which becomes the Resume button, as shown lower left in Figure 14-3. Click Resume to continue recording, or click Done to finish and save the recording.

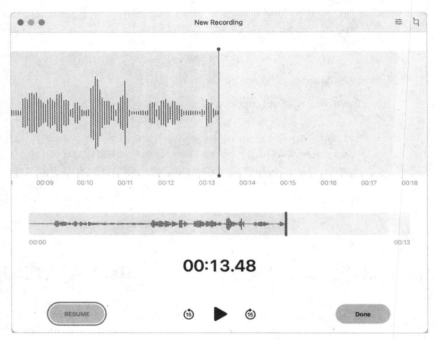

FIGURE 14-3:
You can pause at any time, then click Resume or Done.

Listening to a voice memo

After you capture your thoughts or musings, you'll probably want to play them back. To do so, just click the voice memo you want to hear, and then click the triangular Play icon to listen.

TIP

You can drag the playhead (the vertical blue line in the middle of the waveform) to move forward or back in the memo.

Naming a voice memo

When a memo is added to your list of recordings, it shows up with the date and length of the recording and the uninspiring title *New Recording.* You could have named it something else at that point, but if you didn't, you may have a tough time remembering which recording was made for which purpose. Fortunately, you can easily create a custom title after the fact:

1. **Click any Voice Memo in the sidebar.**

2. **Double-click the name Apple assigned (New Recording, New Recording 1, and so on).**

3. **Type your own name for the voice memo.**

    Professor Snookins on Biology, for example.

That's it. Your recording is duly identified.

Trimming a voice memo

Maybe the professor you were recording rambled on and on. Fortunately, it's easy to trim the audio. To do so, first click a recording and then choose Edit ⇨ Trim Recording.

Now, drag the start marker (<), end marker (>), or both to specify the portion of the audio you want to keep.

To conclude the process, click the Trim button — but before you do, I recommend that you preview your edit by clicking the Play icon. Then if you're happy, click the Trim button.

If you make a mistake, choose Edit ⇨ Undo immediately to restore the audio you trimmed.

You may want to share a Voice Memo with others. No problem. Just click a Voice Memo to select it, and then click the share icon (shown in the margin) in the toolbar. You then have the option to email the memo or send it in a message. Or you can share it instantly with Mac or iDevice users via AirDrop (covered in Chapter 4), or add it to the Notes or Reminders app.

When you have no further use for a recording, you can remove it from the Voice Memos app by selecting it and pressing Delete (or Backspace).

TIP

To see all your voice memos on all your Apple devices:

>> **On your Mac:** Open System Preferences, click Apple ID, click iCloud in the sidebar, click the iCloud Drive Options button, click the Documents tab, and enable Voice Memos in the list of apps.

>> **On your iOS or iPadOS device:** Tap Settings ➪ *your name here* ➪ iCloud, and then enable Voice Memos.

Automating Repetitive Tasks with Shortcuts

NEW

Making its Mac debut in Monterey is Shortcuts, which helps you automate repetitive tasks and trigger those automations from the menu bar, from Quick Actions, or with Siri. I could write an entire chapter (or book) about Shortcuts, and very well might someday. The best I can do in the limited space available is give you a glimpse into the things you can do with Shortcuts on your Mac.

Figure 14-4 is that glimpse — just a few of the premade shortcuts included with Shortcuts.

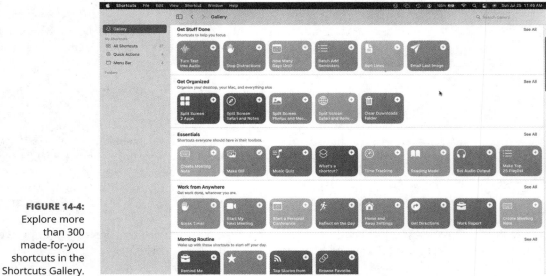

FIGURE 14-4:
Explore more than 300 made-for-you shortcuts in the Shortcuts Gallery.

In a nutshell, the Gallery displays ready-made shortcuts for you to use as-is or modify to your liking. Click any shortcut to see a description of what it does. If you like it, click the Add Shortcut button to open the Setup dialog and configure the shortcut for your Mac.

Once you've added a shortcut, drag it from your All Shortcuts folder to the Quick Actions or Menu Bar folder to trigger it from the right-click shortcut menu or from the menu bar, respectively, or ask Siri to perform the shortcut by name.

Controlling Lights, Locks, and More with Home

The Home app is all about using your Mac to remotely control smart *HomeKit* accessories, such as smart door locks, lightbulbs, thermostats, garage-door openers, and other devices.

Sadly, it's worthless on your Mac unless you've added smart HomeKit accessories to the Home app on an iDevice.

So, if you've used Home on an iDevice to add your smart devices, you already know how to use the Home app on your Mac since it works the same on both platforms (except that the Mac app can't add new smart devices).

4

Getting Along with Others

Get the internet working on your Mac (and find out what to do with it after that).

See how to surf the internet with Safari.

Explore video chatting with FaceTime and SharePlay.

Make imaginatively named apps such as Mail, Contacts, and Messages work for you.

Share files and more.

IN THIS CHAPTER

» **Getting an overview of the internet**

» **Pre-surfing with the Network System Preferences pane**

» **Surfing the web with Safari**

» **Searching the web**

» **Going face to face with FaceTime**

Chapter **15**

(Inter)Networking

These days, networking online is easier than finding a log to fall off: You simply use the internet to connect your Mac to a wealth of information residing on computers around the world. Luckily for you, macOS Monterey has the best and most comprehensive internet tools ever shipped with a Mac operating system.

macOS offers built-in internet connectivity right out of the box. macOS Monterey comes with the following:

» Apple's Safari web browser, which you use to navigate the web, download remote files, and more

» The FaceTime app for video chats with other Mac or iDevice users

» The Messages app, used for instant messaging (text), audio and video chatting, screen sharing, and file transfers

» The Mail application (for email)

In this chapter and the two that follow, I cover the top things most people use the internet for: surfing the web and video and audio chatting. You discover Safari in this chapter, Contacts and FaceTime in Chapter 16, and Mail and Messages in Chapter 17.

But before I can talk about any of those things, I first have to walk you through configuring your internet connection, given that none of these apps work well without it. The good news is that after you finish making the connection, you can play with your internet-enabled applications to your heart's content.

And here's more good news: If you're already able to surf the web, send and receive email, or send and receive text messages, you're connected and could skip many (if not most) of the steps in the "Getting Connected to the Internet" section. However, I suggest that you don't skip that section, even if your internet already works perfectly, because it offers a number of useful tips and techniques. (Do you know what Locations are? Or why you might want to use them?)

Onward!

Getting Connected to the Internet

Before you can use (or surf) the internet, you need to connect to the internet. If you're a typical home user, you need three things to surf the internet:

>> **A connection to the internet,** such as a cable modem, digital subscriber line (DSL) modem, fiber, or a satellite internet service (referred to generically as your *internet box*).

REMEMBER

If you use technology other than DSL, cable, fiber, or satellite to connect your computer to the internet, your network administrator (the person you run to at work when something goes wrong with your computer) or ISP (internet service provider) might have to help you set up your Mac because setting up those other configurations is (sigh) beyond the scope of this book.

>> **An account with an ISP,** such as AT&T or Comcast.

TIP

The technical reviewer for previous editions of this book reminded me that these days, that's not necessarily true. All you really need is free Wi-Fi, which is available almost everywhere — in stores, restaurants, parks, libraries, and other places — and a free email account from Apple's iCloud, Microsoft's Outlook.com, Google's Gmail, or Yahoo! Mail.

>> **A Mac,** preferably one running macOS 12 Monterey.

You might need to tweak a few settings, as I explain in the upcoming section "Plugging in your internet-connection settings."

After you set up each of these components, you can launch and use Safari, Mail, Messages, and any other internet applications.

Your internet service provider and you

You may have to select a company to provide you access to the internet: an ISP. The prices and services that ISPs offer vary, often from minute to minute. Keep the following in mind when choosing an ISP:

>> **If your connection comes from a cable or telephone company, your ISP is probably that company.** In effect, the choice of ISP is pretty much made for you when you decide on cable or DSL service.

>> **Broadband access to the internet starts at around $25 or $30 per month.** If your service provider asks for considerably more than that, find out why.

  If you think you're paying too much for internet service or you don't like your current provider, by all means do your homework and determine what other options are available in your neighborhood.

TIP

Because most Mac users like things to be easy, macOS includes a cool feature in its Setup Assistant to help you find and configure an account with an ISP. When you installed macOS Monterey (assuming that you did and that it didn't come preinstalled on your Mac), Setup Assistant may have asked you a bunch of questions about your internet connection and set up everything for you.

If you didn't have an internet connection (an ISP) at that time, you may need to configure the Network System Preferences pane yourself. Chances are you'll be good to go as soon as you connect the cable, but in the event it doesn't just work, these settings could be something you'll have to hash out with your ISP.

If you have questions or problems not answered by this book, your ISP should be able to assist you. And if your ISP can't help, it's probably time to try a different ISP (if you can).

Plugging in your internet-connection settings

If you didn't set up your internet connection when you installed macOS, you need to open System Preferences (from the Applications folder, the dock, Launchpad, or the menu) and click the Network button. The Network pane offers options for connecting your Mac to the internet or to a network. Setting up your internet connection in the Network System Preferences pane is beyond the purview of this book, so the easiest way to do it is to search for *network setup* in Mac Help (Help ⇨ Search).

WARNING

If you're part of a large office network, check with your system administrator before you change anything in this pane. If you ignore this advice, you run the risk of losing your network connection completely.

TIP

If your Mac asks you a question you can't answer during setup, ask your ISP (or search its online help if you can) or contact your network administrator for the answer. I can't possibly tell you how in this book because there are just too many possible configurations, and each depends on your particular ISP and service.

If you use your Mac in more than one place, you can set up a separate configuration for each location and choose it from the Location menu. A *location*, in this context, consists of all settings in all items in the Network System Preferences pane.

TIP

My technical editor for a previous edition reminded me that you probably don't need to create separate locations these days. My MacBook Pro just works. I may have to choose a Wi-Fi network and provide a password the first time I visit a hotel, cafe, or office; after that, my Mac remembers everything so the next time I'm at that hotel, cafe, or office, it just works.

After you have this entire pane configured the way that you like, follow these steps to create separate locations:

1. **Pull down the Location menu and choose Edit Locations.**

2. **Click + at the bottom of the Locations list.**

   A new, untitled Location appears in the list.

3. **Type a descriptive name for the new location, such as AirPort at Starbucks or Ethernet at Joe's Office.**

4. **Click Done, and then click Apply.**

   From now on, you can change all your network settings at the same time by choosing the appropriate location from the Location pop-up menu.

If, on the other hand, your Mac has a single network or internet connection (as most home users have), just leave the Location menu set to Automatic and be done with it.

REMEMBER

And while this may be beyond the purview of this book, I'd like to remind you to use only wireless networks that you know and trust, especially in public places such as hotels and airports, and consider using a virtual private network (VPN) when you're out and about as an alternative to free public Wi-Fi (which is often less secure than a VPN).

Finally, if you have any reservations about using public Wi-Fi, use your mobile phone's hotspot feature (if available — not all carriers and plans include it) instead of an unsecured public Wi-Fi network. Why? Because cellular networks encrypt all traffic, making them more secure than Wi-Fi networks.

Also look for *https* (not *http*) at the beginning of URLs to ensure your wireless connection to that website is encrypted (more secure).

Browsing the Web with Safari

With your internet connection set up, you're ready to browse the web. In the following sections, I concentrate on browsing the web with Safari because it's the web browser installed with macOS Monterey.

TIP

If you don't care for Safari, check out Firefox or Chrome, which are both free browsers and have features you won't find in Safari. It never hurts to have a spare in case Safari has issues with a particular website.

To begin, just open your web browser. No problem. As usual, there's more than one way. You can launch Safari by any of these methods:

>> Single-click the Safari icon on the dock or Launchpad (look for the big blue compass that looks like a stopwatch, as shown in the margin).

>> Double-click the Safari icon in your Applications folder.

>> Single-click a URL link in an email, an iMessage, or a document.

>> Double-click a URL link document (a .webloc file) in Finder.

The first time you launch Safari, you see a generic start page, as shown in Figure 15-1.

In the sections that follow, I show you the highlights of using Safari, starting at the top of its window.

Note that if you're upgrading from an earlier version of macOS, Safari will open to the same page it opened to before you upgraded.

You can customize your start page by clicking the little settings icon in the lower-right corner of the start page (shown in Figure 15-1 and in the margin). Enable or disable an item by selecting or clearing its check box, respectively.

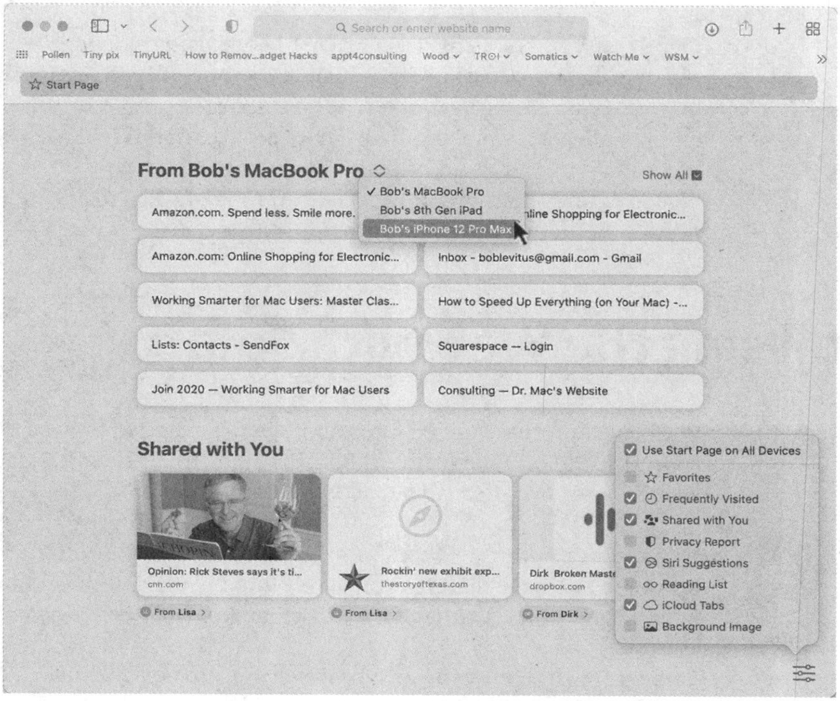

FIGURE 15-1:
Safari first
displays a generic
start page.

TIP If you have more than one Apple device near your Mac, hover the pointer over the current device's name (Bob's MacBook Pro in Figure 15-1), and then click the little up and down arrow icon that appears on its right to see the open Safari tabs from a different device (Bob's iPhone 12 Pro Max or 8th Gen iPad in Figure 15-1).

TIP You can choose what appears in new Safari windows and tabs by choosing Safari ⇨ Preferences and clicking the General tab at the top of the Preferences window.

Owning your toolbar

The Safari toolbar, at the top of every Safari window, consists of a narrow row of icons and the Search or Enter Website Name field. The icons do pretty much what their names imply. From left to right, they are

>> **Show/Hide Sidebar:** Click to see your favorites or Reading list in the sidebar; click it again to hide the sidebar.

>> **New Tab Group:** Click this icon (shown in the margin) to create a new empty tab group. And if you don't already know what a tab group is, you will shortly.

>> **Back/Forward:** When you open a page and move to a second page (or third or fourth), Back takes you to previously visited pages. Remember that you need to go back before the Forward icon will work.

>> **Privacy Report:** Click to see an overlay with a brief privacy report; click the little *i*-in-a-circle on the overlay to see a more comprehensive report.

>> **Search or Enter Website Name:** This field, to the right of the Show Sidebar button, is where you type web addresses, or URLs (Uniform Resource Locators) that you want to visit. Just type one, and press Return to surf to that site.

To the right of the Search or Enter Website Name field are three more icons. Keep reading.

>> **Share/More:** When you find a page of interest or a page you know you'll want to remember, click this icon (which is actually a drop-down menu) to tell Safari to remember it for you in Monterey's cool Reading list or as a bookmark — two topics I explore further a little later in this chapter. Or send a link to it via Mail or Messages, both covered in Chapter 17, or post it on Facebook or tweet it on Twitter.

>> **Create a New Tab (+):** Click to create a tab; press and hold down to see a drop-down menu of recently closed tabs.

>> **Show/Hide Tab Overview:** Click the Show/Hide Tab Overview icon to see previews of all your open tabs (which you learn about shortly) or all tabs in the selected tab group. If you have other Macs or iDevices, you'll also see the open tabs in Safari on other devices that have Safari enabled in iCloud. This feature is so handy you can also find it in the View menu, where you'll also spy its handy keyboard shortcut, ⌘+Shift+\.

TIP

You can add other useful icons to your toolbar by choosing View⇨ Customize Toolbar and then dragging icons such as Home Page, History, Bookmarks, Auto-Fill, and Print from the Customize Toolbar dialog to the toolbar.

Using the Safari sidebar

Click the Sidebar icon on the toolbar, choose View⇨ Show Sidebar, or press ⌘+Shift+L to display the sidebar, where you'll find links to your start page, tab groups, received links, and collected links (where you'll find Bookmarks and Reading List).

Click the first sidebar item, Start Page, to see your Start Page (as discussed previously).

Tab groups are the new pinned tabs

NEW

Earlier releases of macOS offered pinned tabs that persisted until you unpinned them. In Monterey, they've been replaced by tab groups, a more flexible approach for managing multiple tabs.

Here's how to set up and use tab groups:

To create a new tab group, click the New Tab Group icon on the right above the sidebar (shown in the margin) and choose New Empty Tab Group. Or, if you currently have more than one tab open, choose New Tab Group with *x* Tabs (where *x* is the number of open tabs).

Another way to create a new empty tab group is by choosing File ⇨ New Empty Tab Group or pressing ⌘+Control+N.

To add a web page to a tab group, drag it from the tab bar (or URL field) onto the group in the sidebar. If the sidebar isn't visible, choose View ⇨ Show Sidebar or press ⌘+Shift+L.

To see the Tab Overview page for a tab group with thumbnails of all the pages it contains (as shown in Figure 15-2), click the Show/Hide Tab Overview icon next to its name in the sidebar (visible for Mac Stuff in Figure 15-2 and shown in the margin).

To preview an inactive tab, hover the pointer over that tab until a small preview appears (as shown for the Is Apple Silicon Ready? tab in Figure 15-2).

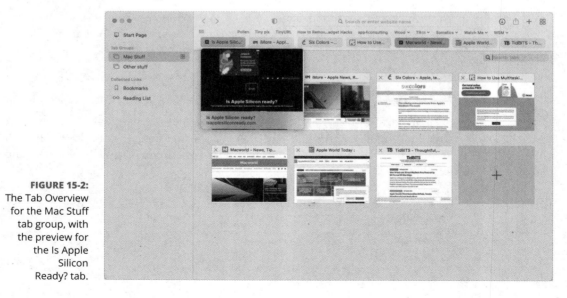

FIGURE 15-2:
The Tab Overview for the Mac Stuff tab group, with the preview for the Is Apple Silicon Ready? tab.

Now that you know how to create and manage tabs and tab groups, it couldn't be easier to use them. To activate a tab group, click its name in the sidebar. The tab group's tabs replace your current tabs.

Note that if you open a new tab with a tab group active (selected in the sidebar), the new tab becomes part of the active group. Conversely, if you close a tab with a tab group selected in the sidebar, the tab is removed from the group.

Shared with You: links from others

NEW

The next entry in the sidebar is new in Monterey: Shared with You automatically gathers content that's been shared with you. Click Shared with You and an overview page appears with thumbnails of all the photos, videos, articles, and more that have been shared with you by friends and family in the Messages app.

Bookmarking your favorite pages

When you find a web page you want to remember and return to, you *bookmark* it. Here's how it works:

1. **Choose Bookmarks ⇨ Add Bookmark, press ⌘ + D, or click the Share icon and choose Add Bookmark.**

2. **Choose where to store the bookmark from the pop-up menu.**

   By default, Safari puts new bookmarks in the Favorites folder.

3. **Rename the bookmark or use the name provided by Safari.**

4. **(Optional) Add a brief description in the Description field if you care to.**

5. **Click the Add button to save the bookmark.**

Finding your bookmarks in the sidebar

To return to a bookmarked page, click it in the Favorites bar, choose Bookmarks ⇨ Show Bookmarks, press ⌘+Option+B, or click the Show Sidebar icon to see all your bookmarks.

If you add a bookmark to the Favorites folder, it automatically appears in the Favorites bar. If you add the bookmark outside the Favorites folder in the sidebar, it will not appear in the Favorites bar but will be available at the bottom of the Bookmarks menu and in the Bookmarks sidebar.

Open bookmarked pages in the sidebar by clicking them once. View the contents of a folder by single-clicking the folder name in the list.

To delete a bookmark, right- or Control+click it and choose Delete.

⌘+click a folder in the Bookmarks window or Favorites bar to simultaneously open all the bookmarks it contains.

Managing your favorites and the Favorites bar

Below the Search or Enter Website Name field is the Favorites bar, which is populated by default with icons for web pages that Apple thinks you might enjoy, including Apple, Yahoo!, Google Maps, YouTube, and Wikipedia.

If you don't see your Favorites bar, choose View ➪ Show Favorites Bar or press ⌘+Shift+B.

I've replaced all those default icons on my Safari Favorites bar with folders that are drop-down menus, as denoted by the little chevron after each name, as shown in Figure 15-3.

FIGURE 15-3:
All the icons in my Favorites bar are actually drop-down menus.

One last thing: Favorites and bookmarks are not exactly the same in Monterey. Favorites is a folder of bookmarks that appear in the Favorites bar and Favorites page. Not all bookmarks are favorites, but all favorites are bookmarks. Which makes total sense when you think about it.

What's on your Reading list?

The last item in the Safari sidebar is your Reading list, which serves as a repository for pages or links you want to read but don't want to read right now. It's a lot like a bookmark but easier to create on the fly, which makes the Reading list perfect for sites or links you don't need to keep forever (that's what bookmarks are for).

To add the page you're viewing to your Reading list, hover your cursor over the left side of the Search or Enter Website Name field and then click the +-in-a-circle. (You can also use the keyboard shortcut ⌘+Shift+D or click the Share icon and choose Add to Reading List from its menu.)

To add a link to your Reading list without visiting the page, just press the Shift key before you click that link. It's fast and easy, and it works even if the sidebar is closed. Or you can right- or Control-click the link and choose Add Link to Reading List from the contextual menu.

Right-click any item in your Reading list for additional options.

To delete an item from the Reading list, right- or Control-click the item and then choose Remove Item. To remove all items from the Reading list, right- or Control-click any item and then choose Clear All Items.

TIP

If you have other Macs or iDevices, you can sync your Reading list among your devices by enabling Safari in the iCloud System Preferences pane.

Website-specific settings

To specify settings for the active website, choose Safari ⇨ Settings for *website name*. The website-specific settings overlay appears with the following options:

>> Use Reader view when available.

>> Enable/disable content blockers.

>> Set page zoom.

>> Auto-Play: Allow All Auto-Play; Stop Media with Sound; or Never Auto-Play.

>> Pop-up Windows: Block and Notify; Block; or Allow.

>> Ask, Deny, or Allow use of the camera, microphone, screen sharing, and your location.

Reader view

Finally, Reader view reformats the page for easier reading while hiding ads, navigation, and other distractions. It's available for a page if the icon in the margin appears at the left edge of the Search or Enter Website Name field.

Click the icon to enter Reader view; click it again to exit Reader view.

Checking out Help Center

I could write an entire book about Safari, but one of the rules we *Dummies* authors must follow is that our books can't run 1,000 pages. So I'm going to give you the next best thing: Open Help Center (by choosing Help ➪ Safari Help). A special Safari Help window appears; you can search for any Safari-related topic or solution to any Safari-related problem right there.

TIP

As Steve Jobs used to say, there is one last thing: I'd like to share one of my favorite Safari features, namely, the little blue speaker icon, which appears on the right side of the Search or Enter Website Name field whenever audio is playing on a web page. Click that little speaker and Safari will go silent even if the audio is coming from an inactive tab or a hidden window.

Safari now blocks audio and video from playing automatically by default. If you want to enable it for all sites or specific sites, choose Safari ➪ Preferences, click the Websites tab, and then click Auto-Play in the sidebar on the left to allow or disallow sound globally or from individual sites.

Thanks, Apple; we needed that.

IN THIS CHAPTER

» **Collecting your contacts**

» **Managing your contacts**

» **Syncing your contacts with other devices**

» **Making audio and video calls with FaceTime**

Chapter **16**

Dealing with People

I n this chapter and the next, you discover a quartet of programs that work beautifully together and make managing your contacts, email, and messages (chats) a breeze. You're about to find out how these eponymous programs — Contacts and FaceTime in this chapter, and Mail and Messages in Chapter 17 — work, and how to use them individually and as a team.

REMEMBER

I cover a lot of material in not a lot of space in these two chapters, so if you want to find out something about Contacts, FaceTime, Mail, or Messages that I don't cover, remember the capable assistance you can find in Help ⇨ Contacts Help (or FaceTime Help, Mail Help, or Messages Help).

Collecting Your Contacts

Contacts stores and manages information about your family, friends, companies, and any other entity you want to keep in touch with. It works seamlessly with the Mail, Messages, and Maps applications, enabling you to quickly look up phone numbers or email addresses when you're ready to communicate with someone.

In fact, Contacts works with several applications, both on and beyond your Mac, including the following:

» Use it with FaceTime (covered later in this chapter) to video chat with friends and family.

>> Use it with Calendar (covered in Chapter 11) to display your contacts by choosing Window ⇨ Contacts. You can then drag any person in your contacts from the Address Panel to any date and time on the calendar, and a special meeting event is created automatically by Calendar. The event even has a Send Invitation button; if you click it, it launches Mail and sends the person an invitation to this meeting. Very cool stuff.

>> The Contacts application can also work with any other application whose programmers choose to make the connection or with any device that's compatible with Contacts.

>> Contacts is available also in most programs that have a Share icon or menu so you can share with your contacts via whichever method is appropriate, usually their phone number, email, or iCloud.com or Mac.com address (for an iMessage).

>> If you use iCloud, you can choose to sync contacts with devices that include (but are not limited to) other Macs, iPhones, iPads, and iPod touches. And you can also sync contacts via Google, Microsoft Exchange, Microsoft Office 365, or any combination.

In the following sections, you find out the best ways to fill Contacts with your own contacts and how to keep those contacts organized.

Adding contacts

Follow these steps to create an entry in Contacts:

1. **Launch the Contacts application by double-clicking its icon in the Applications folder, clicking its dock icon, or clicking its Launchpad icon.**

    The Contacts window appears. The first time you open Contacts, you see two cards: Apple Computer and the one with whatever personal identification information you supplied when you created your account.

2. **To create an entry, click the + button at the bottom left of any Contact card and choose New Contact from the drop-down menu.**

    An untitled address card appears. The First name text field is initially selected.

3. **In the First text field, type the person's first name.**

    Here, I typed *Bob "Dr. Mac."*

4. **Press Tab.**

    Your cursor should now be in the Last text field.

You can always move from one field to the next by pressing Tab. In fact, this shortcut works in almost all Mac programs with fields. (Move to the previous field by pressing Shift+Tab.)

5. **Type the last name for the person you're adding to your Contacts.**

Here, I typed *LeVitus*. Continue this process, filling in the rest of the fields shown in Figure 16-1.

If you don't see the field you need, click the + icon at the bottom of the card and choose More Fields to add a field.

The contact I created with this step appears in Figure 16-1.

6. **When you've finished entering information, click the Done button to exit editing mode.**

The little triangles (actually up and down arrows) between the labels and their content fields in Figure 16-1 are pop-up menus that offer alternative labels for the field. For example, if you were to click the arrows next to Mobile, you would be able to choose iPhone, Apple Watch, Home, Work, and so on, to replace the Mobile label.

To add more info about any Contacts entry, click the name in the list on the left (Bob "Dr. Mac" LeVitus in Figure 16-1). Click the Edit button at the bottom of the Contacts window (where the Done button appears in Figure 16-1), make your changes, and click Done.

Repeat these steps for everyone you want to keep in touch with.

Importing contacts from other programs

If your contacts are on another Mac or an iDevice, or stored by Google or Microsoft, you won't need to import your contacts. Just enable the appropriate account in the Internet Accounts System Preferences pane, and enable syncing for contacts.

Those who have contacts in another program (such as FileMaker Pro or ACT) might be able to import them into Contacts, which can import contacts in vCard, LDIF, or text file format.

The first thing is to export the data from the other program in one of these formats.

I always export the file to the desktop, so that the file is easy to find in the next step.

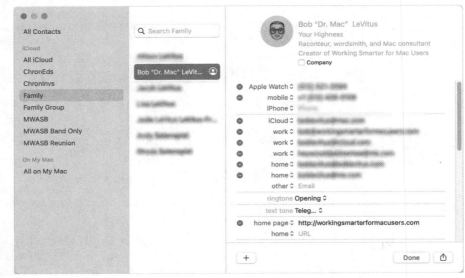

FIGURE 16-1:
My address card
displayed in the
Contacts window.

Then, back in the Contacts app, choose File ⇨ Import, select the exported data file in the Open File dialog, and then click the Open button.

Creating a basic group

Now let me explain how to organize your contacts into groups. Why would you want to organize your contacts into groups? The main reason, at least for me, is practical: I can send email with a single click to everyone in a group that I've defined. For example, when it's time to send out a press release, I can simply send it to my Press/PR group, shooting the email off to all 68 people I have in that group. And when I want to send an email to all the parents of kids on my son's indoor football team, I merely address it to my Flag Football Parents group, and all 12 families in that group receive it.

Here's how to create a group and add contacts to it:

1. **Launch the Contacts application by double-clicking its icon in the Applications folder or clicking its dock icon.**

2. **Create the new group by choosing File ⇨ New Group, pressing ⌘+Shift+N, or clicking the + icon at the bottom of the window and choosing New Group.**

   An untitled Group appears in the Group column with Untitled Group highlighted.

3. **Type a descriptive name for this group and then press Return.**

   I named mine Family.

4. **Click All Contacts on the left side of the window to show all your contacts on the right side.**

5. **Click the contacts you want in the group from the contacts list.**

   To select more than one contact, hold down the ⌘ key when clicking the contacts.

TIP

You can use the Search field at the top of the window to find a contact or contacts, and then drag them onto the group to add them, as shown in Figure 16-2.

...to here   Drag from here...

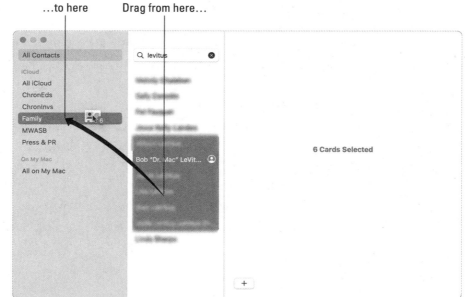

FIGURE 16-2:
Adding six
contacts to the
Family group.

6. **Drag the selected contact names onto the group, as shown in Figure 16-2.**

   Contacts displays the number of contacts you're dragging, which happens to be six in this instance.

TIP

Another way to create a group is to select contacts by clicking, ⌘-clicking, or Shift-clicking contacts and then choosing File ➪ New Group from Selection.

Setting up a smart group (based on contact criteria)

A second type of group — a smart group — might be even more useful to you because it gathers contacts in your Contacts based on criteria you specify. For example, say I create a group that automatically selects Apple staff members who have email addresses that end in @apple.com.

REMEMBER

The big advantage of using a smart group instead of a regular group is that when I add, say, a new Apple contact, that contact automatically becomes a member of the Apple smart group with no further action on my part. And if you delete a card or modify it so the contact no longer matches the smart group criteria, the contact is removed from the group automatically.

To create a smart group, follow these steps:

1. Choose File ➪ New Smart Group or press ⌘+Option+N.

   A Smart Group sheet appears in front of the Contacts window, as shown in Figure 16-3.

2. Give the smart group a name.

   I named mine @Apple.

3. Select the appropriate items from the menus: Company, Contains, Email, and so on.

   In Figure 16-3, I created a smart group that includes any contact that contains *Apple* in the company field or *@apple.com* in any email field.

4. When you're happy with the criteria specified, click OK.

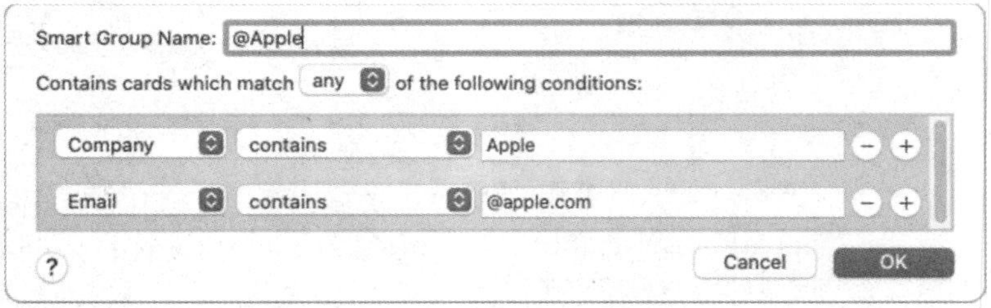

Smart Group Name:	@Apple	

Contains cards which match any ⬦ of the following conditions:

| Company ⬦ | contains ⬦ | Apple | — + |
| Email ⬦ | contains ⬦ | @apple.com | — + |

?   Cancel   OK

FIGURE 16-3:
Creating a smart group.

Deleting a group or smart group

To delete a group or a smart group from your Contacts, click to select it, and then press Delete or choose Edit ➪ Delete Group.

Sync + Contacts = your contacts everywhere

If you're not syncing contacts with iCloud, Google, or Microsoft Exchange/Office 365 (I discuss syncing calendars and reminders with iCloud in Chapter 11; you're on your own with Google or Microsoft), your contacts will be stored locally on your hard drive. iCloud, Google, and Microsoft users, on the other hand, can choose to store their contacts locally or in iCloud, Google's cloud, or Microsoft's cloud. The difference is if you store your contacts in the cloud, you can sync all your devices so they all display the same information. In other words, if you add a contact to your iPhone, you'll see it on your Mac in the Contacts app within a few minutes. Conversely, if you add a contact on your Mac, within a few minutes, it magically appears in the Contacts app on your iDevice.

Here is how to enable cloud syncing for Contacts:

1. **Choose System Preferences from the menu (or click its dock icon or double-click its icon in the Applications folder).**

   The System Preferences window appears.

2. **Click the Internet Accounts icon.**

   The Internet Accounts pane appears.

3. **In the list on the left, if you see the account you want to use for syncing contacts, click it and skip to Step 5.**

4. **At the bottom of the window, click the + icon, and then on the right side of the window click the name of the provider you want to sync with (iCloud, Exchange, Google, and so on).**

   Provide your user name and password and follow the prompts to add the account.

5. **In the list on the left, click iCloud (or Exchange or Google or other).**

6. **In the list on the right, select the check box for Contacts.**

   If you previously enabled contact syncing with a service provider, reenabling it is even easier: Click its name in the list on the left, and then select the check box for Contacts in the list on the right.

Now you'll see the same contacts on all your devices. More precisely, you'll see them on devices that are signed in to the same Apple ID as your Mac and have iCloud Contacts syncing enabled.

Audio and Video Calls with FaceTime

FaceTime works beautifully for Mac-to-Mac audio or video calls and has several exciting and useful new features in Monterey.

By the way, at this time there's no Windows version of FaceTime, so you'll have to use a third-party solution such as Skype or Zoom for cross-platform video chats with your less fortunate PC-using brethren (or sisteren).

TIP

A feature known as Wi-Fi Calling lets you use your Mac to make and receive voice calls with the FaceTime app on your Mac by routing them through your iPhone. When enabled, you can make or receive phone calls by using your Mac's microphone and speakers (as long as your iPhone is nearby). It's easy and trouble-free if your wireless carrier supports it; find the details at `https://support.apple.com/en-us/HT203032`.

But FaceTime can do much more than be an ersatz telephone. And with new features like improved noise reduction, portrait mode (on M1-powered Macs), and SharePlay introduced in Monterey, it's never been more useful or fun.

If you want to follow along at home, launch FaceTime from the Applications folder, Launchpad, or the dock. The main (only) FaceTime window appears.

To make a FaceTime call, click the New FaceTime button. The FaceTime overlay appears with a field for typing a contact's name above a few suggestions, as shown in Figure 16-4.

FIGURE 16-4:
The FaceTime window, ready to make a call to my wife.

If your contact appears in the list of recent calls in the sidebar, you can click the camera icon to initiate a video call that the recipient can answer on an iPad, an iPhone, or a Mac.

As it happened, when I called my wife to capture Figure 16-5, she wasn't there. Fortunately, her iPad was, so I answered my own FaceTime call on her iPad. What each of us saw is shown in Figure 16-5.

FIGURE 16-5:
A FaceTime call: What I saw on my Mac screen (left) and what Lisa saw on her iPad screen (right).

TIP

FaceTime uses Contacts, so if you have friends or family members who have an iPhone 4 or later, iPad 2 or later, iPad mini, iPod touch (fourth-generation or later), or a Mac, type the contact name in the field, select them in the resulting list, and click the FaceTime button to begin your video chat.

If you're running Mojave V10.14.3 or later (which includes Monterey), you can also host Group FaceTime chats. I've never been able to get it to work reliably, but feel free to give it a try. In theory, you start a video chat with someone, and then click the little video camera icon next to another contact's name in the sidebar. You should be able to add up to 31 other people, but I've never been able to get it to work with more than one person at a time, so good luck.

About SharePlay

NEW

This space was reserved for a very cool new feature called SharePlay, which Apple describes as "a powerful set of system features that enables users to have shared experiences while on a FaceTime call. Users can share their favorite music, TV shows, movies, projects, and more with friends and family in real time — kicking off a shared listening party, watching movies and shows, collaborating in apps through screen sharing, and more."

You now know as much about SharePlay as I do. Just before this book went to press, Apple announced that SharePlay will not be available in the initial release of Monterey:

We're reaching out to let you know that SharePlay has been disabled for use in the developer beta 6 versions of iOS 15, iPadOS 15, and tvOS 15, and will be disabled in the upcoming beta 6 release of macOS Monterey. SharePlay will also be disabled for use in their initial releases this fall. SharePlay will be enabled for use again in future developer beta releases and will launch to the public in software updates later this fall.

So visit www.dummies.com and type **macOS Monterey For Dummies Cheat Sheet** in the Search box. The cheat sheet will (soon) include an article titled "How to use SharePlay in Monterey."

Chapter **17**

Communicating with Mail and Messages

You can see how to use Contacts and Maps to find people and places in Chapters 16 and 13, respectively. In this chapter, I take a look at two more terrific programs — Mail and Messages — that work with Contacts to make managing your email and messages (chats) a breeze.

Sending and Receiving Email with Mail

I cover a lot of material in not a lot of space in this chapter, so if there's something you want to find out about Mail or Messages that I don't cover, don't forget about Help ⇨ Mail Help or Help ⇨ Messages Help.

TIP

Mail is a program for sending, receiving, and organizing your email. Mail is fast and easy to use, too. Click the Mail icon on the dock or Launchpad or double-click the Mail icon in the Applications folder to launch Mail. The Mail icon looks like an envelope, as shown in the margin.

You can use other applications to read email. The App Store has dozens of other mail readers, and most versions of Microsoft Office include the Outlook application, which handles email and more. And most email services, including Google's Gmail and Apple's iCloud (to name a couple), offer a web-based interface you can use from a web browser in a pinch. You can continue to use any or all of these options for your email if you like, but when you're using your Mac, the easiest and best mail reader around (meaning the best one on your hard drive by default) is almost certainly Mail. And of course, you can't beat the price; it's free!

Setting Up Mail

If this is your first time launching Mail, you need to set up your email account(s) before you can proceed. A set of Choose a Mail Account Provider screens appears automatically. Just follow the instructions on each screen, fill in the fields as requested, and keep clicking the Continue button until you're finished.

If you've signed into your iCloud account on this Mac, your iCloud email should be set up already. If it's not, choose Mail ➪ Accounts and enable it.

If this is the first time you've enabled iCloud mail on this Mac, you'll also see a Mail Privacy Protection dialog the next time you launch Mail. Click a button — Protect or Don't Protect Mail Activity — and then click Continue. (To change this setting at any time, choose Mail ➪ Preferences ➪ Privacy and enable or disable the Hide IP Address and Block All Remote Content check boxes.)

TIP

If you don't know what to type in one or more of these fields, contact your ISP (internet service provider) or mail provider for assistance.

After you set up one or more email accounts, you see a Welcome message asking whether you'd like to see what's new in Mail. If you click Yes, Help Viewer launches and shows you the What's New in Mail page; the Mail main window, which looks like Figure 17-1, appears in the background. Or if you click No, the Mail main window appears immediately.

TECHNICAL STUFF

The Mail main window is called a *viewer window* or *message viewer window*. You can have more than one of them on your screen, if you like; just choose File ➪ New Viewer Window or press ⌘+Option+N.

A quick overview of the toolbar

Before you go any further, look at Figure 17-1, which shows the 12 handy icons and a Search field on the viewer window's toolbar by default:

>> **Filter:** Click to enable or disable filtering for this mailbox; press and hold down to change filtering criteria.

>> **Get Mail:** Checks for new email.

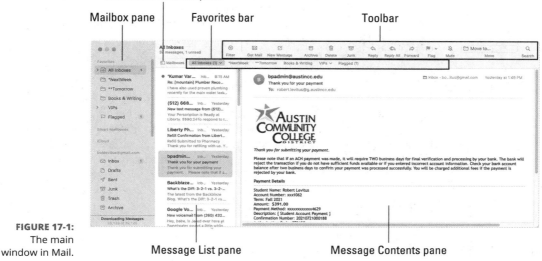

FIGURE 17-1:
The main
window in Mail.

Message List pane   Message Contents pane

>> **New Message:** Creates a new, blank email message.

>> **Archive:** Archives selected message or messages.

>> **Delete:** Deletes selected message or messages.

TIP

To select more than one message in the list, hold down the ⌘ key when you click the second and subsequent messages.

>> **Junk:** Marks the selected message or messages as junk mail.

Mail has built-in junk-mail filtering that can be enabled or disabled in Mail Preferences. (Choose Mail ➪ Preferences and click the Junk Mail icon on the toolbar.) If you receive a piece of *spam* (junk mail), select it and click the Junk icon to help train the Mail junk-mail filter. If a selected message has been marked as junk mail, the icon changes to read Not Junk.

TIP

For more info on junk-mail filtering, click the question mark icon in the Junk Mail pane of the Mail Preferences window.

>> **Reply:** Creates a reply to the sender only.

>> **Reply All:** Creates a reply to the sender and everyone who was sent the original message.

>> **Forward:** Creates a copy of this message you can send to someone other than the sender or other recipients.

>> **Flag/Unflag:** From this drop-down menu, you can mark or unmark one or more messages with any of seven colored flags, which you can specify in searches and smart mailboxes (as you discover shortly).

>> **Mute:** Clicking this icon (or choosing Message ⇨ Mute, or using the keyboard shortcut Control+Shift+M) turns off notifications for new messages in the selected message thread.

>> **Move:** This drop-down menu moves the selected messages to the folder of your choice.

Finally, the Search field on the toolbar finds a word or phrase in any item stored in Mail. When you begin typing, a drop-down menu appears so you can narrow the search to people or subjects matching your search phrase. Note that you can click the buttons on your Favorites bar to limit the search to a specific mailbox.

TIP

If you don't see your Favorites bar, choose View ⇨ Show Favorites Bar or press ⌘+Option+Shift+H.

TIP

If you see little numbers next to the mailbox buttons on the Favorites bar or Mailbox pane, they indicate the number of unread messages in that mailbox. A message is considered read after you click it.

Searching in Mail should be familiar because it works the same way as searching in Finder. So, for example, if you want to save a search as a smart mailbox (Mail's version of a smart folder in Finder), click the + icon below the search field to add criteria.

Mail populates the Favorites bar with mailboxes it expects you to use often, namely Inbox, VIPs, Sent, and Flagged. In Figure 17-1, I've added three of my mailboxes — *Next Week, **Tomorrow, and Books & Writing — by dragging them from the Mailbox pane onto the Favorites bar (or into the Favorites section of the sidebar).

Composing a new message

Here's how to create an email message:

1. **Choose File ⇨ New Message, click the New Message icon on the toolbar, or press ⌘+N.**

   A new window appears. This is where you compose your email message, as shown in Figure 17-2.

   Don't be concerned if your new message doesn't have a pop-up Signature menu like the one in Figure 17-2. That menu is displayed only after you've created at least one signature, as described later in this chapter.

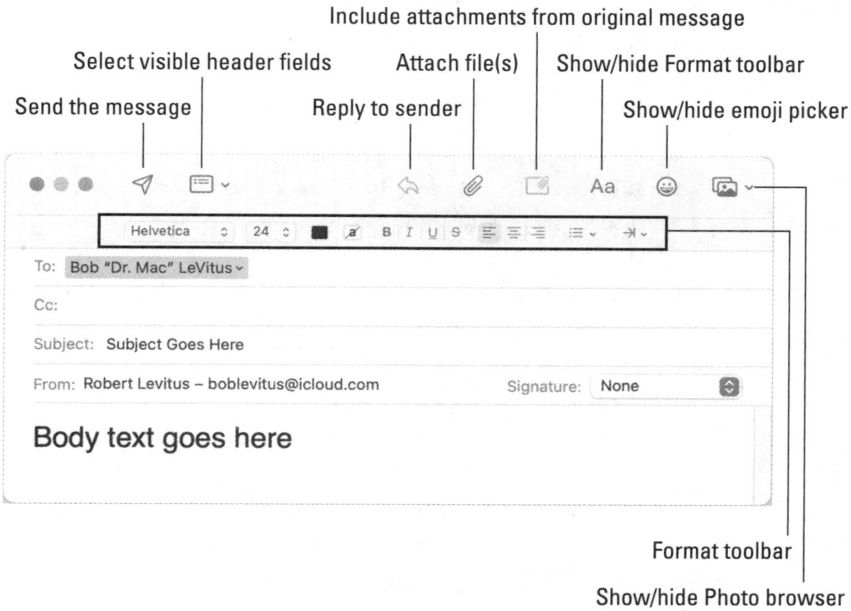

Include attachments from original message

Select visible header fields   Attach file(s)   Show/hide Format toolbar

Send the message   Reply to sender   Show/hide emoji picker

To: Bob "Dr. Mac" LeVitus ⌄

Cc:

Subject: Subject Goes Here

From: Robert Levitus – boblevitus@icloud.com   Signature: None

Body text goes here

Format toolbar

Show/hide Photo browser

FIGURE 17-2:
Composing an
email message.

2. **Click in the To field, and type someone's email address.**

   Use my address (MontereyForDummies@boblevitus.com) if you don't know anyone else to send mail to.

TIP

   If the recipient is in your Contacts, just type a few letters, and Mail's intelligent autocomplete function matches it up with names in your Contacts database. When the list appears, you can choose an item by either clicking it or using the arrow keys to select it and then pressing Return.

3. **Press the Tab key twice and type a subject for this message in the Subject text field.**

   I typed *Subject Goes Here* in Figure 17-2.

4. **Click in the main message portion of the window, and type your message there.**

   I typed *Body Text goes here* in Figure 17-2.

5. **When you're finished writing your message, click the Send button to send the email immediately, or close it to save it in the Drafts mailbox so you can work on it later.**

TIP

   If you save your message to the Drafts mailbox (perhaps so you can write more later on), you can send it when you're ready by opening the Drafts mailbox, double-clicking the message, and then clicking the Send button.

Just for the record, here's what the icons on the toolbar in Figure 17-2 are all about:

>> **Send:** Duh. Sends the message.

>> **Select visible header fields:** This drop-down menu lets you select which header fields — CC, BCC, Reply-To, and Priority — you want to see when you create new messages.

>> **Reply to sender:** Lets you reply to the sender directly from the message window. It's inactive in Figure 17-2 because this is a brand new message, so there is no sender to reply to.

>> **Attach:** Opens a standard Open File sheet so you can choose a file or files to enclose with this message. To enclose multiple files, hold down the ⌘ key while you click each file you want to enclose.

If the recipients of this message use Windows, you probably want to click the Options button and select the Send Windows-Friendly Attachments check box, which appears at the bottom of the Open File sheet (if it's not already selected).

TIP

I recommend that you select it even if you don't think you have Windows-using recipients because there's no downside for Mac or iOS users.

>> **Include attachments from original message:** This icon includes any files that were attached to the message you're replying to or forwarding. It's inactive in Figure 17-2 because this is a new message, not a reply.

>> **Format toolbar:** Shows or hides the Format toolbar, which is displayed (between the toolbar and the To field) in Figure 17-2.

>> **Show/hide emoji and symbol picker:** Opens the emoji picker; double-click an emoji to add it to your message at the insertion point.

>> **Photo Browser:** Opens the Photo Browser panel, which displays the images in your photo library and lets you drag and drop them into a mail message.

Sending email from the Contacts app

TIP

You don't even have to open the Contacts app to send an email to a contact or group contained in your Contacts. In the preceding section, you see how Mail finds contacts (or groups) for you without launching Contacts. But if you already have Contacts open, the following technique for sending email to a contact or group is probably most convenient.

To create a blank email message to a contact, click and hold down on the field label next to the desired email address, and choose Send Email from the pop-up menu that appears, as shown for the iCloud label in Figure 17-3. Or move the pointer over an email address and then click the tiny envelope icon that appears to the right of its name, as shown for my iCloud email address in Figure 17-3.

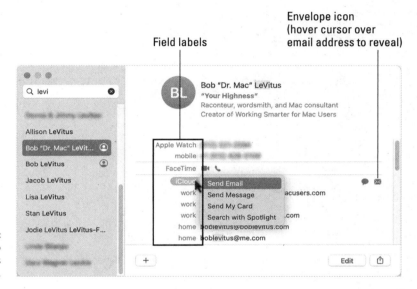

FIGURE 17-3: Sending email to a contact is as easy as clicking.

The Mail program becomes active, and a blank email message addressed to the selected contact appears on your screen. Just type your email as you normally would.

As you can see in Figure 17-3, the pop-up menu next to email addresses lets you do the following:

>> Send an email.

>> Send a message (see the "Communicating with Messages" section, later in this chapter).

>> Send your vCard (see the following Tip) to this email address.

>> Search for this email address in documents on your Mac using Spotlight (see Chapter 10).

TIP

The information for each contact can be sent to others in an industry-standard file format known as a *vCard* (virtual business card). Choosing Send My Card works the same as Send Email, but instead of starting with a totally blank email message, the message starts with your vCard enclosed. When the recipient opens the vCard file, all your contact information will be added to their Contacts (or other contact manager in Windows).

Checking your mail

How do you check and open your mail? Easy. Just click the Get Mail icon at the top of the main Mail window (refer to Figure 17-1) or press ⌘+Shift+N.

>> **To read a new message,** select it. Its contents appear in the Message Content pane.

>> **To delete a selected message,** click the Delete icon on the toolbar or press Delete (or Backspace) on your keyboard.

You can delete a message in one other way if you have a trackpad. Swipe with two fingers from right to left a little bit and the Trash icon appears. Now you can click the Trash icon or continue your swipe to the left a bit farther. Either way, the message will disappear into Mail's Trash folder.

>> **To retrieve a message you accidentally deleted,** click Trash on the left and drag the message to the Inbox or another mailbox.

TIP

>> **To configure Mail to send and check for your mail every *x* minutes,** choose Mail ➪ Preferences and click the General icon at the top of the window. Click the Check for New Mail pop-up menu and make a selection — Automatically; every 1, 5, 15, 30, or 60 minutes; or Manually. The default is to check for new mail automatically, which means every few minutes. If you don't want Mail to do that, choose Manually.

>> **To add a sender to Contacts:** When someone who isn't already in your Contacts sends you an email message, simply choose Message ➪ Add Sender to Contacts.

Adding a sender to your Contacts has an additional benefit: It guards future messages from that person against being mistaken for junk mail. If a sender appears in your Contacts, their messages will never be mistakenly marked as junk mail. In other words, your Contacts is a white list for the spam filter. See the next section in this chapter for how to deal with spam.

TIP

When you receive an email containing details for an event, such as a flight or a dinner reservation, or even an invitation that says something like, *Let's have a beer at 6,* a smart suggestion appears between the message's header and body, so you can add the event to Calendar with just a click if you so desire.

Dealing with spam

Speaking of junk mail . . .. Although email is a wonderful thing, some people out there try to spoil it. They are *spammers,* and they're lowlifes who share their lists among themselves — and before you know it, your email inbox is flooded with get-rich-quick schemes, advertisements for pornographic websites and chat rooms, pills and powders that claim to perform miracles, and plenty of the more traditional buy-this-now junk mail.

Fortunately, Mail comes with a pretty darn good junk mail filter that analyzes incoming message subjects, senders, and contents to determine which ones are likely to contain bulk or junk mail.

Start by choosing Mail ⇨ Preferences and clicking the Junk Mail tab. If Junk Mail Filtering is not enabled, enable it and then click the Mark as Junk Mail, But Leave It in My Inbox radio button.

The rest of the check boxes let you specify which types of messages are exempted from junk mail filtering; enable or disable them to suit your needs and then close the Preferences window.

Now Mail is running in what I call training mode, which is how Mail learns to differentiate between what it considers junk mail and what you consider junk mail; all it needs is your input. Mail identifies messages it thinks are junk, but if you disagree with its decisions, here's what you do:

>> Click the Not Junk icon on the toolbar for any message that *isn't* junk mail.

>> Conversely, if a piece of junk mail slips past Mail's filters and ends up in the Inbox, select the message and click the Junk icon on the toolbar.

After a few days (or weeks, depending on your mail volume), Mail should be getting it right almost all the time. When you reach that point, choose Move It to the Junk Mailbox on the Junk Mail tab of Mail's Preferences dialog. Now Mail starts moving junk mail automatically out of your Inbox and into a Junk mailbox, where you can scan the items quickly and trash them when you're ready.

If you prefer to use your email provider or third-party spam filters, you can turn off junk mail processing in Mail by disabling it on the Junk Mail tab of Mail's Preferences dialog. Or use both.

Mailboxes smart and plain

After reading mail, you can either delete it or file it in a mailbox. The following sections take a closer look at the two types of mailboxes you have at your disposal — plain and smart.

Plain old mailboxes

Plain mailboxes are just like folders in Finder; you create them and name them, and they're empty until you put something in them. They even look like folders in the Mailboxes sidebar in Mail. You use mailboxes to organize any messages you want to save.

Here are three ways to create a plain mailbox:

>> Choose Mailbox ⇨ New Mailbox.

>> Click the + that appears to the right of each top-level Mailbox in the mailbox pane. If you don't see the +, it will magically appear if you hover your cursor over mailbox name (such as iCloud or Gmail).

>> Right-click or Control-click in the Mailboxes sidebar and choose New Mailbox from the shortcut menu.

Whichever way you choose, the next thing that happens is that a sheet drops down with a Location pop-up menu and a field for you to type the name you want to give this mailbox. Choose On My Mac from the Location menu to store your filed messages locally, on your hard drive; or choose iCloud or another email provider to store filed messages remotely, on the mail server.

TIP

Choosing iCloud or your email provider means messages you move to that mailbox will be stored remotely. If you access your email from more than one device, I recommend you create all your mailboxes on the email server so they'll be available to you no matter where you are or what device you're using to check your mail.

Finally, name the mailbox anything you like and click OK, and the mailbox is created in the Mailboxes sidebar.

If you right- or Control-click a mailbox and choose New Mailbox, the Location menu in the sheet will show the name of the mailbox you clicked. So, if you were to click OK now, the new mailbox would be a sub-mailbox of the mailbox you clicked. *Sub-mailboxes* — mailboxes inside other mailboxes — are a useful feature if you care to further subdivide your message storage system.

You can also drag and drop a mailbox or mailboxes from the top level of the list into another mailbox to make *them* sub-mailboxes. If you drag a mailbox into a sub-mailbox, it becomes a sub-sub-mailbox.

To delete a mailbox (and its sub-mailboxes if it has any), do one of the following:

>> Click it to select it and then choose Mailbox ⇨ Delete Mailbox.

>> Right-click or Control-click the mailbox, and choose Delete Mailbox.

Intelligent smart mailboxes

A smart mailbox is Mail's version of Finder's smart folder. In a nutshell, *smart mailboxes* are mailboxes that display the results of a search. The messages you see in a smart mailbox are *virtual;* they aren't really in the smart mailbox itself. Instead, the smart mailbox displays a list of messages stored in other mailboxes that match whatever criteria you defined for that smart mailbox. Like smart folders in Finder, smart mailboxes are updated automatically when new messages that meet the criteria are received.

To create a smart mailbox:

>> Choose Mailbox ⇨ New Smart Mailbox.

>> Click the +-in-a-circle on the right side of the Smart Mailboxes header in the Mailboxes pane.

Whichever method you choose, a sheet drops down with a field for the smart mailbox's name, plus some pop-up menus, buttons, and check boxes, as shown in Figure 17-4. This smart mailbox gathers messages with the words *Monterey* in either the body or subject.

Name your smart mailbox, determine its criteria (by using the pop-up menus, plus and minus buttons, and check boxes), and then click OK. The smart mailbox then appears in the Mailboxes pane with a little gear icon to denote that it's smart.

I use a smart mailbox I call *Family* that gathers every mail message to or from my wife and children. And I use another to see all my Dummies email in a single place. Since smart mailboxes don't use up any additional disk space, they're a great way to organize mail, automatically making it easier to find a message with no effort on your part (after you set them up).

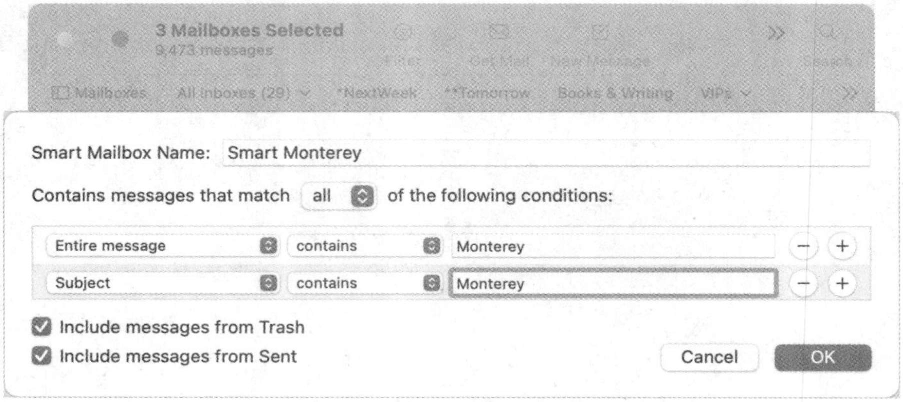

3 Mailboxes Selected
9,473 messages

Filter   Get Mail   New Message   Search

Mailboxes   All Inboxes (29) ∨   *NextWeek   **Tomorrow   Books & Writing   VIPs ∨

Smart Mailbox Name: Smart Monterey

Contains messages that match [all ⬍] of the following conditions:

| Entire message ⬍ | contains ⬍ | Monterey | − + |
| Subject ⬍ | contains ⬍ | Monterey | − + |

☑ Include messages from Trash

☑ Include messages from Sent   Cancel   OK

FIGURE 17-4:
Set criteria for a
smart mailbox.

TIP

When you select a mailbox or multiple mailboxes (plain, smart, or both) in the mailbox pane, you'll see how many mailboxes are currently selected along with how many messages they contain in the toolbar above the message list (in Figure 17-4 that's 3 mailboxes and 9,473 messages).

Changing your preferences

Mail's preferences (Mail ➪ Preferences or ⌘+,) are more than you might expect from the name. The Mail Preferences window is the control center for Mail, where you can do the following:

» **Create and delete email accounts.**

» **Determine which fonts and colors are used for your messages.**

» **Decide whether to download and save attachments (such as pictures).**

» **Decide whether to send formatted mail or plain text.**

» **Decide whether to turn on the spell checker.** The default is to check spelling as you type, which many people (myself included) find annoying.

» **Decide whether to have an automatic signature appended to your messages.**

» **Establish rules to process mail that you receive.**

The first five items are up to you to decide. The last two are the most important features of the Preferences window — namely, automatically adding your signature(s) to outgoing messages and inbound-mail processing rules.

Sign here, please

If you're like me, you'd rather not type your entire signature every time you send an email message, and you don't have to with Mail. If you create canned signatures, you can use them in outgoing messages without typing a single character.

Here's how it works:

1. **Choose Mail ⇨ Preferences or press ⌘+, (comma).**

2. **On the Preferences dialog's toolbar, click the Signatures icon.**

3. **In the left column, click the name of the mail account for which you want to create this signature.**

   I clicked iCloud.

4. **To create a new, blank signature, click the little + sign at the bottom of the middle column.**

5. **Type a descriptive name for this signature to replace the default name Signature #1.**

   My new name is *BL Long*.

6. **In the right column, type the signature exactly as you want it to appear in outgoing messages.**

   I typed *All the best, Bob "Dr. Mac" LeVitus – Technology Columnist* and so on in Figure 17-5.

7. **(Optional) Drag a scanned image of your signature to the appropriate place in your document.**

   I dragged it between *All the best* and *Bob "Dr. Mac" LeVitus*.

8. **Drag the name you assigned this signature to the mail account you're using it with.**

   I dragged BL Long to iCloud.

If you have more than one signature, you can select the one you want to use as the default: Choose the account in the column on the left, and then choose the signature from the Choose Signature pop-up menu at the bottom.

TIP

As soon as you add your first signature, another cool thing happens. The Signature pop-up menu appears in new messages and replies, so you can choose a different signature (or no signature) without opening the Signatures System Preferences pane.

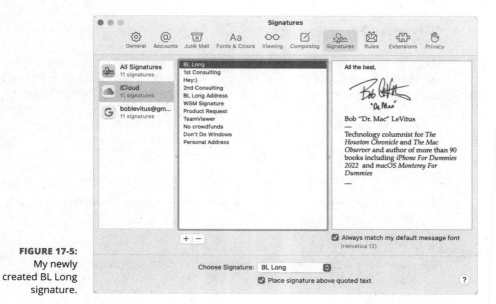

FIGURE 17-5:
My newly
created BL Long
signature.

Mail rules rule

If you really want to tap the power of Mail, you need to set *rules*. With some cool rules, you can automatically tag messages with a color; file them in a specific mailbox; reply to, forward, or redirect the messages automatically (handy when you're going to be away for a while); automatically reply to messages; and *kill-file* messages (just delete them without even bothering to look at them — what better fate for mail from people you hate?).

There's no way I can do rules justice in a page or so, but here's a quick look at how to create one. In broad terms, you create a condition and then an action. In this example, I create a filter named Message From LeVitus, with the action to sound a funky alert, as shown in Figure 17-6.

Here are the steps:

1. **Choose Mail ⇨ Preferences.**

2. **Click the Rules icon on the toolbar of the Preferences dialog.**

3. **Click the Add Rule button.**

4. **In the Description field, type a description.**

   I typed *Message From LeVitus*.

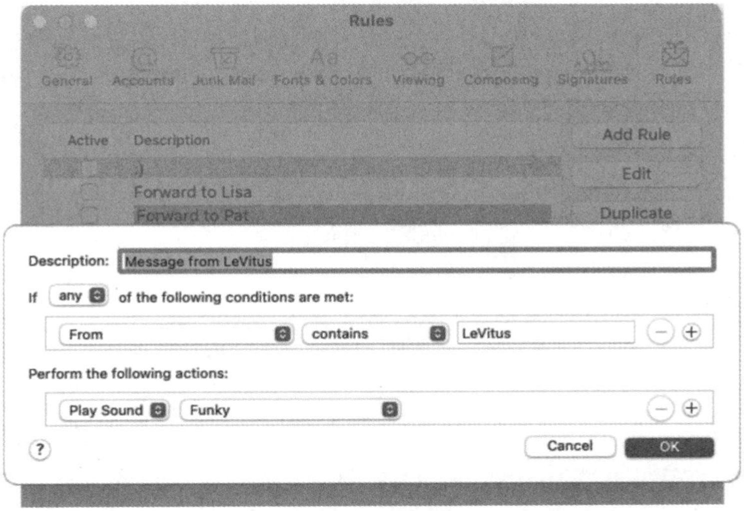

FIGURE 17-6:
Setting a rule.

5. **Click the first pop-up menu (which says Any in Figure 17-6) to determine when to apply this rule.**

The options are Any or All. I chose Any, which is the default. Note that my choice in this menu doesn't matter for this rule, which only has one condition.

6. **Click the first pop-up menu in the Conditions section to define the condition.**

I chose From in Figure 17-6, but there are myriad other options: Date Sent, Date Received, Sender Is or Isn't in My Contacts, and dozens more, which I implore you to explore at your leisure.

7. **Click the second pop-up menu in the Conditions section (Contains in Figure 17-6) and make a selection.**

Your choices are Contains, Does Not Contain, Begins With, Ends With, or Is Equal To.

8. **In the field on the right side of the Conditions section, type a word or phrase.**

I typed *LeVitus,* so my condition reads: From Contains LeVitus.

9. **Click the first pop-up menu in the Perform the Following Actions section (Play Sound in Figure 17-6).**

Look at your options in this pop-up menu (too numerous to mention) and choose one.

10. **Click the second pop-up menu in the Perform the Following Actions section (Funky in Figure 17-6) to specify the sound you'll hear when this action is triggered.**

11. **Click OK.**

    Mail asks whether you want to apply your rule(s) to the selected mailboxes.

12. **Choose Apply if you want Mail to run this rule on the selected mailboxes, or choose Don't Apply if you don't.**

    And that's how you build a rule. From this point forward, every time you get a message from someone named LeVitus, you hear the Funky sound.

TIP

Note the little − (minus) and + (plus) buttons to the right of the conditions and actions. Use + to add more conditions or actions and − to delete a condition or action. If you have multiple conditions, you can choose Any or All from the pop-up menu above them, which executes this rule when either any condition is met or all conditions are met. All the actions you create are always executed when this rule is triggered.

Take a (Quick) look and (Slide) show me some photos

One last cool feature, and you're finished with Mail. That cool feature is Quick Look, which includes a slick Slideshow option. If you press and hold down on the paper clip icon in a message you've received and then choose Quick Look from the resulting drop-down menu, a new window appears showing one of the enclosed pictures.

If you don't see a paperclip, hover your cursor over the line between the message header and the message body and the paper clip will magically appear. Or click any image in the message body to highlight it, and then press the spacebar to take a Quick Look.

To close the Quick Look window, click the little X in its top-left corner or press the spacebar.

Markup and Mail Drop

Last but not by any means least, two more excellent Mail features: Markup and Mail Drop.

Markup

Markup lets you annotate images or PDF documents. When you're composing a message that has an image or a PDF you've attached or dragged in, hover the pointer over the picture and a little chevron *(v)* appears in its upper-right corner. Click it to use the Markup tools on this image.

Details on using Markup appear in Chapter 5.

Mail Drop

Mail Drop, on the other hand, is an elegant solution for large email attachments. If you enclose files or a folder full of files in a message and Mail thinks the enclosure(s) might be too big to send via email, an alert appears when you try to send the message. A picture is worth a thousand words, so check out my alert in Figure 17-7.

If I opt for Try Sending in Email, Mail will go ahead and try to send my message even though the file is 88.4MB. Chances are pretty good, though, that the mail server I send the message through will bounce it back to me for being too large. But if I choose Use Mail Drop, which uses iCloud, the enclosure's size can be huge and the message still won't bounce. If I go this route, the recipient will receive a link to download the files from iCloud, as shown on the bottom in Figure 17-7.

Mail Drop should be enabled by default. If it's not, choose Mail ⇨ Preferences and click the Accounts icon at the top of the window. Then click the account you want to use it with, click the Account Information tab, and select its Send Large Attachments with Mail Drop check box.

Another feature I'm fond of is the Unsubscribe button. When you receive an email from a mailing list, just click the Unsubscribe button (between the header and the body of the message) and you're done (at least you're done if the list honors unsubscribe requests, which some apparently do not).

You'll also find a toolbar icon (a bell with a slash) to mute the selected conversation. Clicking this icon (or choosing Message ⇨ Mute, or using the keyboard shortcut Control+Shift+M) will turn off notifications for new messages in this thread.

Finally, you can block a sender by right- or Control-clicking a sender's name and choosing Block Sender from the pop-up menu. You'll then see This Message Is from a Blocked Sender, along with a Preferences button. Click the button to specify how you want your blocked mail handled: marked as blocked but left in your inbox or moved directly to the Trash.

Finally, to unblock a sender you've blocked, choose File ⇨ System Preferences, click Junk Mail, and then click the Blocked tab.

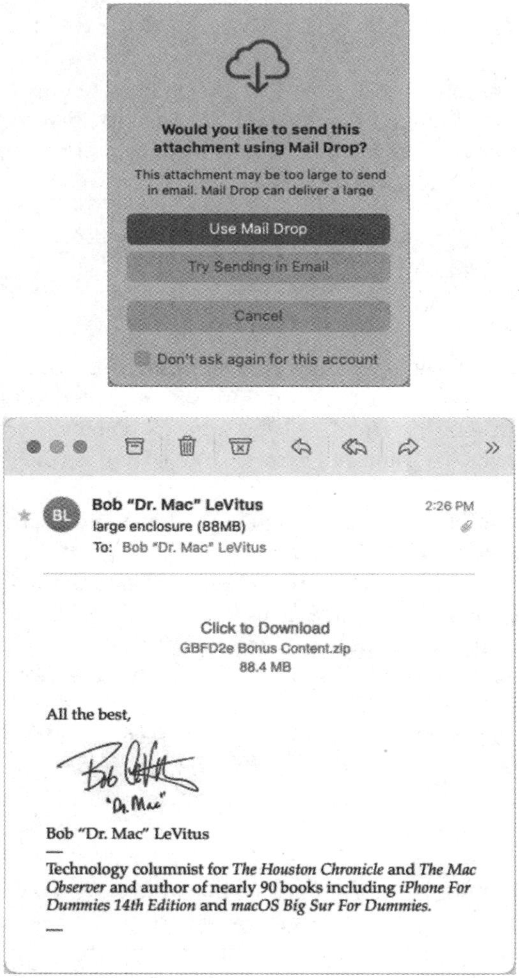

FIGURE 17-7:
Choose Use Mail
Drop in the alert
box (top), and
your recipient
sees this message
(bottom).

Communicating with Messages

Instant messaging (IM) enables interactive communication among users all over the world. Messages gives you immediate access to all the other users of AIM, Google Talk, and iCloud. All you need are their screen names, and you're set to go.

To get started, launch Messages from your Applications folder, Launchpad, or the dock.

What the heck is an iMessage?

iMessage is Apple's inter-device messaging protocol. That means you can send unlimited iMessages to anyone with an iPhone, iPad, or iPod touch running iOS 5 (or later) or a Mac running Mountain Lion (OS X 10.8) or later.

Think of it as MMS messaging, similar to what you find on smartphones, but you can send and receive messages from your Mac. Better still, an iMessage can include photos, audio recordings, videos, locations, and contacts in addition, of course, to text. And if you have more than one iOS device or Mac, iMessage keeps all your conversations going across all of them. You can also get delivery receipts letting you know your messages went through. You'll know it's been read, too, if your friend has enabled read receipts.

If you have an iPhone 4 or newer, the Continuity feature allows all SMS and MMS text messages you send and receive on your iPhone via your wireless carrier's messaging system to appear also in the Messages app on your Mac, iPad, and iPod touch almost simultaneously — even if the person you're messaging doesn't have an iPhone. Better yet, you can reply from whichever device is closest to you, regardless of what kind of cellphone the person has.

For this to happen, all devices need to be using the same Apple ID for Messages on all devices, and Enable Messages in iCloud must be enabled (Messages ➪ Preferences ➪ iMessage tab).

TIP

You can start a new iMessage also by clicking a phone number in Safari, Contacts, or Calendar.

Chit-chatting with Messages

Your chats can be one to one, or they can be group bull sessions. Messages is integrated with Contacts, so you don't have to enter your buddies' information twice.

Here's all the essential info you need to get started:

>> **To start a text chat,** open Messages, click the New Message icon above the Search field (shown in the margin) and then either begin typing a contact's name in the To field or click the little plus-in-a-circle to see a list of contacts with its own search field.

If you've already shared a message with someone, click their name in the list on the left to send a new message or use the Search field to find your chat with that person.

After you've chosen a recipient, type your text in the iMessage field at the bottom of the window and press Return or Enter to send it.

In Figure 17-8, I clicked my wife's name in the list on the left and saw a message that she left home without her driver's license. I asked if that was going to be a problem. She replied "No" and asked me if it was on the table, to which I replied "Yes."

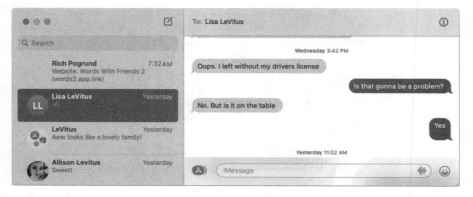

FIGURE 17-8:
A chat between
my wife and me.

In a chat, each participant's text appears in a different color and orientation; my words are in blue bubbles with white text on the right; her words are in gray bubbles with black text on the left.

>> **To start a group text chat,** click the New Message icon, and add each person you want to include as described above.

When you finish adding names to the To field, type and send your message as just described and everyone in the To field will receive it. From then on, everyone will see every message from every participant.

TIP

Click the little *i*-in-a-circle at the top right to open the Info window for this conversation. Now you can use your iPhone (if it's nearby) to call someone by clicking the phone icon next to their name. Or choose Hide Alerts to mute notifications for this conversation only, which is great if one or more participants is a serial texter. Other options in the Info window such as sharing your location, sending an email, starting a FaceTime video call, and hiding alerts for this conversation. Finally, click Leave This Conversation (near the bottom of the Info window) when you want to, well, leave this conversation permanently.

>> **To attach a picture to a person in your Contacts:** Copy a picture of the person to the Clipboard in your favorite graphics application (Preview, for example). Now open Contacts, and display the card for the person you want to add a picture to. Click the empty picture box at the top of the card, and paste the picture from the Clipboard. You should now see that picture on the Contacts card and also when you chat in Messages with the person. Neat!

TIP

If you already attached a picture to a contact in Contacts, that picture will appear automatically when you chat.

>> **To transfer a file or files,** just drag the icon(s) to the iMessage field (where you type your messages), and then press Return. The file zips across the ether. This is a convenient way to share photos or documents without resorting to file sharing or email.

When you drag an image file onto the Messages window's message box, you see an oversize semitransparent preview, letting you know you're sure you're sending the right image and not something totally embarrassing. Way to go, Monterey.

You could also choose Conversations ⇨ Send File or press ⌘+Option+F and then select the file(s) from a standard Open File sheet, but the drag-and-drop method is faster and easier.

>> **To send a voice message,** click the sound wave to the right of the iMessage field and begin talking. When you're finished, click the red Record icon and then click Cancel or Send.

>> **To start a FaceTime video or audio call,** select the person you want to call in the list on the left, and then choose Conversations ⇨ FaceTime Video or Conversations ⇨ FaceTime Audio.

>> **To share your Mac screen with a contact** (or ask a contact to share their Mac screen with you), choose Conversations ⇨ Invite to Share My Screen or Conversations ⇨ Ask to Share Screen.

TIP

This semi-hidden feature is awesome for providing technical support to other Mac users. I use it all the time to help my family with their Mac issues. Solving a Mac problem is much easier when I can see the person's Mac screen and control it remotely.

>> **To search for a person, a word, a phrase, or an image,** begin typing in the Search field or press ⌘+F.

» **To pin a conversation to the top of the list,** right- or Control-click the conversation and choose Pin. To unpin a pinned conversation, right- or Control-click and choose Unpin.

» **To add message effects (balloons, confetti, lasers, fireworks, and more), create a memoji, use memoji stickers, or search for images on the internet,** click the Applications icon (A) on the left side of the iMessage field.

» **To send an email from Messages,** just select a conversation in the list and choose Conversations ⇨ Send Email (or press ⌘+Option+E). Mail launches (if it's not already open) and addresses a new message to the selected buddy, ready for you to begin typing.

IN THIS CHAPTER

» **Comprehending networks and file sharing**

» **Setting up file sharing**

» **Finding out about users**

» **Understanding access and permissions**

» **Sharing files, folders, and disks with other users**

» **Sharing remotely**

» **Changing your password**

Chapter **18**

Sharing Your Mac and Liking It

Have you ever wanted to grab a file from your Mac while you were halfway around the world, around the corner, or in the next room? If so, I have good news for you: It's not difficult with macOS (believe it or not) even though computer networking in general has a well-deserved reputation for being complicated and nerve-wracking. The truth is that you won't encounter anything scary or complicated about sharing files, folders, and disks (and printers, for that matter) among computers as long as the computers are Macs. And even if some of the computers are running Windows, Monterey even makes that (almost) painless.

Your Macintosh includes everything that you need to share files and printers, except the printers and the cables (and maybe a router). So here's the deal: You supply the hardware, and this chapter supplies the rest.

The first sections of this chapter provide an overview and tell you everything you need to know to set up new user accounts and share files successfully. I don't show you how to actually share a file, folder, or disk until the "Connecting to a Shared Disk or Folder on a Remote Mac" section, later in this chapter. Trust me, there's a method to my madness. If you try to share files without doing all the required prep work, the whole mess becomes confusing and complicated pretty fast — kind of like networking PCs.

One last thing: If you're the only one who uses your Mac, you don't intend to share it or its files with anyone else, and you never intend to access your Mac from another computer in a different location, you can safely skip this chapter.

Introducing Networks and File Sharing

Monterey's file sharing enables you to use files, folders, and disks from other Macs on a network — including the internet — as easily as though they were on your own local hard drive. If you have more than one computer, file sharing is a blessing.

Before diving in and sharing, allow me to introduce a few necessary terms:

>> **Network:** For the purposes of this chapter, a *network* is two or more Macs connected by Ethernet cables, wireless networking (Apple refers to this as AirPort or Wi-Fi), or FireWire cables (rarely seen anymore).

>> **Ethernet:** This network protocol and cabling scheme lets you connect two or more computers so they can share files, disks, printers, or whatever.

>> **Ethernet port:** This is where you plug an Ethernet cable into your Mac (as long as your Mac has one — not all Macs do).

Be careful to match the cable to its specific jack. On your Mac and printer, the Ethernet ports look a lot like a phone jack, and the connectors on each end of an Ethernet cable look a lot like phone cable connectors — but they aren't the same. Ethernet cables are typically thicker, and the connectors (RJ-45 connectors) are a bit larger than the RJ-11 connectors that you use with old-fashioned telephones. (See examples of both types of ports in the margin.) Standard phone cables fit (very loosely) into Ethernet ports, but you shouldn't try that, either; they'll probably fall out with the slightest vibration. It's unlikely that such a mistake will cause damage, but it won't work and will be frustrating.

If your Mac didn't include an Ethernet port but you'd like one, you can find Thunderbolt and USB adapters that will let you have your cake (and an Ethernet port) and eat it too (plug an Ethernet cable into a Thunderbolt or USB port).

>> **Local devices:** Such devices are connected directly to your computers, such as hard or optical drives. Your internal SSD or hard drive, for example, are local devices.

>> **Remote devices:** You access (share) these devices over the network. The hard drive of a computer in the next room, for example, is a remote device.

>> **Protocols:** These are the languages that networks speak. When you read or hear about networks, you're likely to hear the words *Bonjour, Ethernet, SMB,* and *TCP/IP* bandied about with great regularity. These are all *protocols*. Macs can speak several different protocols, but every device (Mac or printer) on a network needs to speak the same protocol at the same time to communicate.

REMEMBER

Support for the TCP/IP protocol is built into every Mac, and macOS Monterey includes all the software you need to set up a TCP/IP network. The hardware you provide consists of Ethernet cables and a hub (if you have more than two computers) or Wi-Fi provided by a wireless router. Here, I'm using the term *hub* generically for hubs and their more powerful cousins, switches and routers, any of which may be used to connect devices to each other on a network.

Portrait of home office networking

A typical Mac home office network consists of two Macintoshes, a wireless Wi-Fi router (or other type of Ethernet hub, switch, or router), and a network printer. Check out Figure 18-1 to see the configuration of a simple network. In the figure, the black lines between the devices are Ethernet cables; the rectangular device with those cables going into it is an Ethernet hub, switch, or router. (I tell you more about cables and such devices in the section "Three ways to build a network," later in this chapter.) You need enough Ethernet cable to run among all your devices.

TIP

With the setup shown in Figure 18-1, either Mac can use the other Mac's files, and both Macs can print to the same printer. If you have a broadband internet connection, you can also connect the cable or DSL modem to the hub or switch or router so all Mac users on the network can share the internet connection.

TECHNICAL STUFF

A network can — and often does — have dozens or hundreds of users. Whether your network has two nodes (machines) or two thousand, the principles and techniques in this chapter apply.

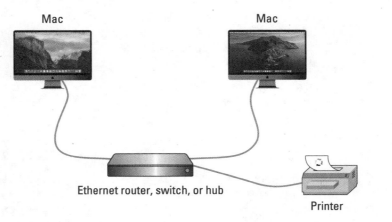

Mac   Mac

FIGURE 18-1:
Two Macs and a printer make up a simple Mac network.

Ethernet router, switch, or hub

Printer

FILE SHARING MADE EASY WITH AIRDROP

Perhaps all you want to do is share an occasional file (not necessarily a printer or a home internet connection or a folder of music files or pictures). In that case, check out AirDrop (available on all Macs built in the past few years), which uses Bonjour, Apple's proprietary zero-configuration network protocol. It's a big part of the secret sauce in macOS that makes Mac networking so simple.

Here's how it works: If two devices speak Bonjour, you don't have to do any configuration other than possibly turning on the sharing capability (and holding them near each other), as I explain in "Setting Up File Sharing," later in this chapter. Bonjour queries the other available networked devices to see what services they support and then configures the connections for you automatically. Sweet!

It gets even better if you're using macOS 10.7 Lion or later (which I suspect most of you are), because you can use the nifty sharing feature called AirDrop. It appears in your Finder window sidebar and locates all other AirDrop-capable Macs on your local wireless network.

And it's better still if you're using macOS 10.10 Yosemite or later, because in these versions, AirDrop can also locate and share files with AirDrop-capable iPhones, iPads, and iPod touches. Sweeter!

The only caveats are that AirDrop uses both Bluetooth and Wi-Fi, and users must enable AirDrop from Control Center on iDevices or by selecting it in the sidebar on a Mac's Finder window. On a Mac, you see AirDrop in the Finder window, as shown in the figure here.

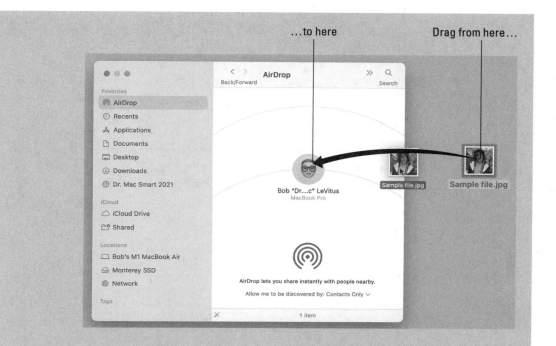

...to here

Drag from here...

To send a file (or multiple files and/or folders) to the other Mac or iDevice, just drag it (or them) onto the other Mac's or iDevice's icon as shown. AirDrop displays a dialog on the other Mac asking whether the user wants to accept delivery; if so, the items are transferred immediately to the Downloads folder on the Mac. If you're sending to an iDevice, its user gets an alert asking whether to accept the file, and then is asked what app to open it in using a familiar Share sheet-like interface.

When you close the AirDrop window, you're no longer visible to other AirDrop users.

Three ways to build a network

In this chapter, I assume you're working on a small network, the kind typically found in a home or small business. If you're part of a megamonstrous corporate network, and you have questions about your particular network, talk to the PIC (*person in charge,* also known as your *network administrator*). In other words, if you're trying to build a meganetwork, you're going to need a book a lot thicker and harder to understand than this one.

The following list gives you three common ways to build a modern small home or office network:

- » **Wi-Fi:** All Macs come equipped with Wi-Fi; if you have an AirPort, AirPort Extreme, Time Capsule, or any other Wi-Fi router, you don't need cables at all.

  For what it's worth, you can use most third-party Wi-Fi routers, which is a good thing since Apple stopped producing AirPort products, including Time Capsule, early in 2018. You can still find them and they still work, but I advise against buying one now because they are no longer in production and may or may not work with future versions of macOS.

  For the sake of convenience, from here on I'm going to refer to wireless routers — including the discontinued Apple products — generically as Wi-Fi routers.

  Just plug in a Wi-Fi router, and Macs can communicate with one another. If you use an Ethernet printer (connected to your Mac by Ethernet cable), you have to connect it to the Wi-Fi router before you can print from your wireless Macs. Both the Wi-Fi router and printer have Ethernet ports, so you can use an Ethernet cable (more about that in a minute) to make the connection.

  Although this setup is more expensive than connecting everything with Ethernet cables and a cheap hub or router, it's also more flexible because you can move your devices anywhere. (Well, almost anywhere; you're limited to a maximum of 150 to 200 feet from each Wi-Fi router, and that's assuming that nothing is in the way to block your signal. Your mileage may vary.) That said, Ethernet is usually significantly faster than Wi-Fi.

TIP

  I've been using wireless printers for years. If you have a Wi-Fi network available, many inexpensive printers (and expensive ones, too) now offer wireless printing, which means you can stash your printer in a closet or another room if you care to.

- » **Traditional Ethernet:** Most desktop Macs still have an Ethernet port, while most laptops don't. If you need an Ethernet port for a Mac that doesn't have one, you can buy an inexpensive Ethernet-to-USB dongle (adapter).

  To connect Ethernet-equipped Macs to a wired network, you need Ethernet cables for each Mac and a little device called a *switch* or *router,* which acts as the center of a wheel; the cables to computers and printers are the spokes.

  A typical Ethernet switch or router includes two to eight Ethernet ports. You plug the device into an electrical outlet and then connect Ethernet cables from each of your Macs and printers (from their Ethernet ports) to the router or switch. *Voilà* — instant network. These gadgets are pretty cheap, starting at around $30; cables start at a few bucks, increasing in price with the length and quality.

>> **Small Ethernet:** If you have only two devices to network (two Macs, or a Mac and an Ethernet printer, in most cases), you can use an Ethernet cable to connect them directly to each other via the Ethernet ports. You can purchase an Ethernet cable at your local electronics store. Plug one end of the Ethernet cable into one device and the other end into the other device.

If you use a Wi-Fi router, you may not need an Ethernet router or switch because most Wi-Fi routers incorporate small switches, often with several Ethernet ports. If you have more Ethernet devices than your Wi-Fi router offers, you'll need a switch with additional Ethernet ports to accommodate them all.

TIP

If you have a cable modem, digital subscriber line (DSL), or fiber as your internet connection, you might need a router or switch if you need to connect more Ethernet devices to the network than the equipment provided by your ISP offers. Your ISP can tell you whether you need one and what they recommend.

Last, but not least, if your Mac doesn't have an Ethernet port built-in but you wish it did, pick up an inexpensive Ethernet-to-USB adapter for less than $20 at Amazon.com or your favorite tech store.

Setting Up File Sharing

Before you get into the nitty-gritty of sharing files, you must complete a few housekeeping tasks, such as enabling the appropriate type of file sharing. Follow these steps to do so:

1. **Choose ⇨ System Preferences and then click the Sharing icon.**

   The Sharing System Preferences pane appears. The first word of the long username of the first admin account created on this computer appears in the Computer Name field by default, followed by the type of Mac (for example, Bob's MacBook Air).

2. **If you want to change the name of your computer from whatever Monterey decided to call it to something more personal, do that now in the Computer Name text field at the top of the Sharing pane.**

   I renamed mine *Bob's M1 MacBook Air*. You can name yours anything you like.

3. **Enable the check box for File Sharing on the left side of the pane.**

   Now other users on your network can access files and folders on your computer, as you see later in this chapter.

By default, only one folder in your Home folder is shared, and that folder is your Public folder. If you want to access files or folders on this computer while you're using another computer on the network, you can so long as you first provide your username and password. Everyone else on the network can see only your Public folder.

WARNING

These are the safest settings. Unless you have good reason to tinker with them, you should probably not change anything here. That said, if you feel you must change these settings, you find out how to do so in the next section of this chapter.

4. **(Optional) If you want remote users to upload and download files to and from this computer, make sure that File Sharing is selected in the sidebar. Then click the Options button, and select the Share Files and Folders Using SMB check box.**

   Doing so gives users on the internet but not on your local area network (LAN) an alternative to file sharing by allowing any client program that uses Server Message Block (Samba, or SMB) protocol.

   If you want to enable Windows or Linux users — or users of other operating systems — to share files with you, the SMB check box must be selected.

   Select the On check box (in the leftmost column) for each account you want to enable to use these protocols to access your Mac, providing the password when prompted.

5. **Click the Done button when you're done, and then proceed to the following section to continue setting up your network.**

Access and Permissions: Who Can Do What

After you set up file sharing (as I explain in the preceding section), your next step on the path to sharing files on a network is telling your Mac who is allowed to see and access specific folders. Fortunately, this happens to be what I cover in the following sections.

Users and groups and guests

Mac file sharing (and indeed, macOS as well) is based on the concept of users. You can share items — such as drives or folders — with no users, one user, or many users, depending on your needs.

Before you can understand how file sharing works, you need to grok the terminology. So here are brief descriptions of users, administrators, groups, and guests:

>> **Users:** People who share folders and drives (or your Mac) are *users.* A user's access to items on your local hard drive is entirely at your discretion. You can configure your Mac so only you can access its folders and drives, or so only one other person or group — or everyone — can share its folders and drives.

When you first set up your Mac, you created your first user. This user automatically has administrative powers, such as adding more users, changing preferences, and having the clearance to see all folders on the hard drive.

REMEMBER

For the purposes of this book, I assume that some users for whom you create identities will be not folks who sit at your Mac but those who connect to it only from remote locations when they need to give or get files. But you could allow such a user to use the same name and password to log in while sitting at your desk.

TECHNICAL STUFF

For most intents and purposes, a remote user and a local user are the same. Here's why: After you create an account for a user, that user can log in to your Mac while sitting in your chair in your office, from anywhere on your local area network via Ethernet or Wi-Fi, or from anywhere in the world via the internet — as long as that person has an Administrator, Standard, or Sharing account on your Mac.

>> **Administrative users:** Although a complete discussion of the special permissions that a user with administrator permissions has on a Mac running macOS is far beyond the scope of this book, note two important things:

- The first user created (usually when you install macOS for the first time) is automatically granted administrator (admin) powers.

- Only an administrator account can create users, delete some (but not all) files from folders that aren't in the administrator's Home folder, lock and unlock System Preferences panes, and do a bunch of other stuff. If you try something and it doesn't work, make sure you're logged in as an administrator or can provide an administrator username and password when prompted.

TIP

You can give any user administrator permissions by selecting that user's account in the Users & Groups System Preferences pane and selecting the Allow User to Administer This Computer check box. You can select this check box when you're creating the user account or anytime thereafter.

>> **Groups:** As you may recall, macOS is based on the Unix operating system and *Groups* are the Unix-level designations for privilege consolidation. For example, there are groups named Staff and Everyone (as well as a bunch of

others). A user can be a member of multiple groups. For example, your main account is in the Staff, Admin, and Everyone groups (and others, too). Don't worry — you find out more about groups shortly.

>> **Guests:** Two kinds of guests exist. The first kind lets your friends log into your Mac while sitting at your desk without user accounts or passwords. But they have no access to your data. When they log out, all information and files in the guest user account's Home folder are deleted automatically.

TIP

If you want this kind of guest user account, you need to enable the account in the Users & Groups System Preferences pane. To do so, click Guest User account in the list of accounts on the left and select the Allow Guests to Log In to This Computer check box.

The second kind of guest is people who access Public folders on your Mac via file sharing over your LAN or the internet. They don't need usernames or passwords. If they're on your LAN, they can see and use your Public folder(s), unless you or the Public folder's owner has altered the permissions. If they're on the internet and know your IP address, they can see and use your Public folder(s) if you don't have a firewall blocking such access. Public folders are all that guests can access, luckily. You don't have to do anything to enable this type of guest user account.

Creating users

Before users can share folders and drives they must have an account on your Mac. You can create two different kinds of accounts for them — a user account or a sharing only account.

>> **When you create a user account** for a person (I call that person and account *User 1*), the account has its own Home folder (called — what else? — User 1), which is filled with User 1's files. Nobody but User 1 can access files in this Home folder unless, of course, User 1 has provided someone the account name and password.

>> **When you create a sharing only account** for a person (I call that person and account *Sharing 1*), the person using that account doesn't have a Home folder and can't access other users' Home folders. Sharing 1 can access only the Public folders inside all the Home folders on that Mac.

You can create a new *user* account only in the Users & Groups System Preferences pane. You can create a new *sharing only* account in either the Users & Groups or Sharing System Preferences panes.

REMEMBER

Anyone can remotely access files or folders in your Public folder(s) over a LAN or the internet. But if you want them to be able to access folders or files other than those in the Public folder(s) on your Mac, they need either a user account or a sharing only account.

When you add (create) a user, you need to tell your Mac who this person is. This is also the time to set passwords and administrative powers for this new user. Here's the drill:

1. **Choose ⇨ System Preferences (or click the System Preferences icon on the dock), click the Users & Groups icon, and then make sure that the Password tab is selected.**

The Users & Groups System Preferences pane appears. In this pane you can see the name of the first user (Bob LeVitus) and the administrative control that this user is allowed (Admin).

REMEMBER

The first user created (usually at the same time you installed macOS or turned on a brand-new Mac) always has administrator permissions. This is why the Allow User to Administer This Computer check box is selected but dimmed for the first user created, who is *always* an admin.

2. **Click the + button below the list of users.**

A sheet appears in which you enter the new user's information.

REMEMBER

If the + button is dimmed, here's how you get it functioning: Click the lock (at bottom left), supply an administrator name and password in the resulting dialog, and then click OK.

3. **Choose Standard from the New Account menu.**

4. **In the Full Name text box, type the full name of a user you want to add.**

In the Account Name text box, your Mac inserts a suggested account name (formerly known as the *short name*). Check out Figure 18-2 to see both.

In Figure 18-2, I added Steve Wozniak as a user, typing his full name in the Full Name field. You don't really need to type the user's full name, but I do so in this example to show you the difference between a full name and an account name.

5. **Press the Tab key to move to the next field.**

macOS suggests an abbreviated version of the name in the Account Name field.

Because he's not the only Steve who matters around here, I changed the account name suggested by macOS (stevewozniak) to TheWoz, which is shorter. (In other words, I typed TheWoz in the Account Name field, replacing the suggested stevewozniak.) The name of each user's folder (in the Users folder) is taken from the account name that you enter when you create a user.

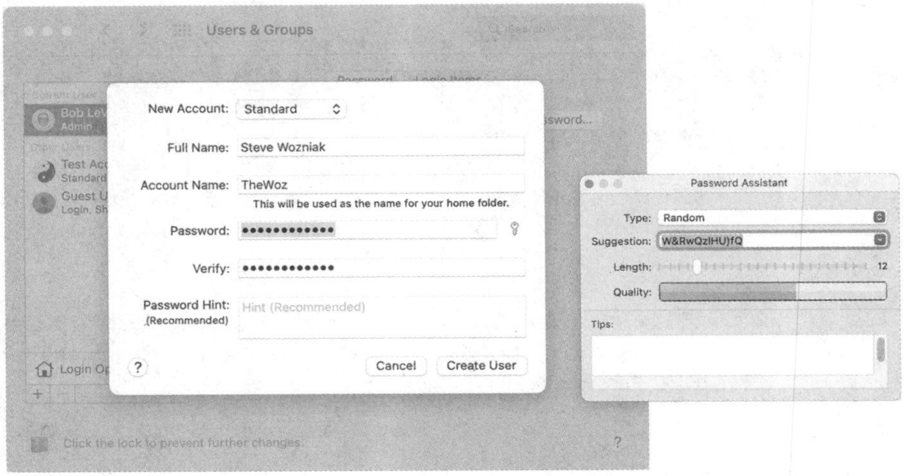

FIGURE 18-2:
Name the new user, and your Mac suggests a shortened name and password.

Users can connect to your Mac (or log in from their own Macs, for that matter) by using the account name, rather than having to type their full names. The account name is also used in environments in which usernames can't have spaces and are limited to eight or fewer characters. Although macOS Monterey allows longer usernames (but no spaces), you might be better off keeping your account name shorter than eight characters, just in case.

6. **Tab to the Password field and enter an initial password for this user.**

The small, square icon with the key to the right of the Password field, when clicked, displays the Password Assistant. You can use the Password Assistant, as seen to the right of the New Account sheet in Figure 18-2, to help you generate a password that will be hard for a cracking program to guess.

To make your password even harder to guess or crack, choose Random or FIPS-181–compliant from the Password Assistant's Type pop-up menu. It will also make it harder for you to remember, so make sure you either memorize it or store it in a safe place.

7. **Press the Tab key to move your pointer to the Verify text field.**

8. **In the Verify text box, type the password again to verify it.**

9. **(Optional) To help remember a password, type something in the Password Hint text box to jog the user's memory.**

If a user forgets the password and asks for a hint, the text that you type in the Password Hint field pops up, ideally causing the user to exclaim, "Oh, yeah . . . *now* I remember!" A password hint should be something simple enough to jog the user's memory but not so simple that an unauthorized person can guess. Perhaps something like "Your first teddy bear's name backward" would be a good hint. And, of course, you should never include the password in the hint.

10. **Click the Create User button to create the account.**

The sheet disappears, and the new user now appears in the Users & Groups System Preferences pane's Users list.

11. **(Optional) Click the account picture and choose a different one.**

TIP

macOS suggests a picture from its default collection for each account, but you can select a different one from the sheet that appears when you click the account picture. Or choose Camera in the sheet and take a photo with an attached or built-in camera.

Changing a user

If circumstances dictate a change to a user's picture or administrator privileges, do the following:

>> **Change a user's picture:** Click the user you want to modify, click the user's picture, and select a replacement. Click Done when you're done.

>> **Grant a user administrator privileges:** Click the user you want to modify and then click the Allow User to Administer This Computer check box.

Removing a user

To delete a user — in effect, to deny that user access to your Mac — select the user you want to delete in the list of accounts and click the – (minus) button. A sheet appears, offering three choices:

>> **Save the Home Folder in a Disk Image** saves a disk image of the user's Home folder in a folder named Deleted Users (which it creates inside the Users folder).

>> **Don't Change the Home Folder** removes the user from the Users & Groups System Preferences pane and login screen but leaves that user's Home folder in the Users folder. *(Deleted)* is appended to the folder's name, so if I had selected this option in the previous example, Steve Wozniak's Home folder would be renamed *TheWoz (Deleted)*.

>> **Delete the Home Folder** does what it says. You have the option of a secure erase (the contents get overwritten multiple times) if you select this option.

WARNING

Be certain you really want to kiss that Home folder goodbye, because after you delete it there's no way to get it back.

REMEMBER

To remove a user from your Mac, you must be logged in using an account that has administrator permissions. And you can't remove the first user ever created on this Mac.

macOS knows best: Folders shared by default

When you add users in the Users & Groups System Preferences pane as I describe earlier, macOS automatically does two things behind the scenes to facilitate file sharing: It creates a set of folders, and it makes some of them available for sharing.

Each time you add a standard, administrator, or sharing-only user, macOS creates a Home folder hierarchy for that user on the Mac. The user can create more folders (if necessary) and also add, remove, or move anything inside these folders. Even if you create a user account solely to allow the person to exchange files with you, your Mac automatically creates a Home folder for that user. Unless you, as the owner of your Mac, give permission, the user can't see inside or use folders outside the Home folder (which has the user's name), with only four exceptions: the Shared folder in the Users folder, the top level of other user account folders; the Public folders in every user's folder; and the Shared folder within the Users folder. A description of the latter follows:

>> **Public:** A Public folder is located inside each user's Home folder. That folder is set up to be accessible (shared) by any user who can log in to this Mac. Furthermore, any user can log in (as a guest) and copy things out of this folder as long as they know your Mac's IP address, even if they don't have an account on this Mac at all. Files put into the Public folder can be opened or copied freely.

WARNING

It's not hard for someone to obtain your IP address. For example, when you visit most web pages, your IP address is saved to that site's log file. So be careful what you put in your Public folder. Protecting your data is also a fine reason to employ a firewall. Monterey has an excellent software implementation available via the Firewall tab in Security & Privacy System Preferences, and most routers include a hardware firewall.

Inside each user's Public folder is a Drop Box folder. As the name implies, this folder is where others can drop a file or folder for you. Only the owner can open the Drop Box to see what's inside — or to move or copy the files that are in it. Imagine a street-corner mailbox: After you drop your letter in, it's gone, and you can't get it back out.

A popular cloud-based storage service is called Dropbox. The Drop Box folder in your Public folder has nothing to do with that Dropbox service beyond having a similar name.

>> **Shared:** In addition to a Public folder for each user, macOS creates one Shared folder on every Mac for all users of this Mac. The Shared folder *isn't* available to guests, but it is available to all users who have an account on this Mac. You find the Shared folder within the Users folder (the same folder where you find folders for each user). The Shared folder is the right place to put stuff that everyone with an account on this Mac might want to use. (Check out my introduction to the Mac OS Monterey folder structure in Chapter 8.)

Sharing a folder or disk by setting permissions

As you might expect, permissions control who can use a given folder or any disk (or partition) other than the startup disk.

TECHNICAL STUFF

Why can't you share the startup disk? Because macOS won't let you. Why not? Because the startup disk contains the operating system and other stuff that nobody else should have access to.

REMEMBER

Throughout the rest of this chapter, whenever I talk about *sharing a folder,* I also mean *sharing disks and disk partitions other than your startup disk* (which, when you think of it, are nothing more than big folders anyway). Why am I telling you this? Because it's awkward to keep typing *a folder or any disk (or partition) other than your startup disk.* So anything that I say about sharing a folder also applies to sharing any disk (or partition) other than your startup disk. Got it?

You can set permissions for

>> The folder's owner

>> A subset of all the people who have accounts on the Mac (a group)

>> People who have the Mac's address, whether they have an account or not (guests)

To help you get a better handle on these relationships, a closer look at permissions, owners, and groups is coming right up.

Contemplating permissions

When you consider who can use which folders, three distinct kinds of users exist on the network. I describe each of them in this section. Then, in the "Useful settings for permissions" section, later in this chapter, I show you how to share folders with each type of user. Here's a quick introduction to the different user types:

» **Owner:** The *owner* of a folder or disk can change the permissions to that folder or disk at any time. The name you enter when you log in to your Mac — or the name of your Home folder — is the default owner of Shared folders and drives on that machine. Ownership can be given away (more on that in the "Useful settings for permissions" section, later in this chapter). Even if you own the Mac, you can't change permissions for a folder on it that belongs to another user (unless you get Unix-y and do so as root). The owner must be logged in to change permissions on his folders.

macOS is the owner of many folders outside the Users folder. If macOS owns it, you can see that "system" is its owner if you select the folder and choose File ➪ Get Info (or press ⌘+I).

Folders that aren't in the User directories generally belong to system; it's almost always a bad idea to change the permissions on any folder owned by system.

WARNING

If you *must* change permissions on a file or folder, select its icon and choose File ➪ Get Info (⌘+I) and then change the settings in the Sharing & Permissions section at the bottom of the resulting Get Info window. I urge you not to change permission settings if you're not absolutely sure of what you're doing and why. And by all means think twice before deciding to apply changes to all the items in a folder or disk; change permissions on the contents of the wrong folder and you could end up with a mess.

» **Group:** In Unix systems, all users belong to one or more *groups.* The group that includes everyone who has an account with administrator permissions on your Mac is called Admin. Everyone in the Admin group has access to Shared and Public folders over the network, as well as to any folder that the Admin group has been granted access to by the folder's owner.

For the purpose of assigning permissions, you can create your own groups the same way you create a user account: Open the Users & Groups System Preferences pane, click the little plus sign, choose Group from the New Account pop-up menu, type the name of the group, and then click the Create Group button.

The group appears in the list of users on the left, and eligible accounts appear with check boxes on the right, as shown in Figure 18-3.

FIGURE 18-3:
This group, The
Outsiders,
contains the Mac
the Knife and
Miss Kitty
accounts.

>> **Everyone:** This category is an easy way to set permissions for everyone with an account on your Mac at the same time. Unlike the Admin group, which includes only users with administrative permissions, this one includes, well, everyone (everyone with an account on this Mac, that is).

If you want people without an account on this Mac to have access to a file or folder, that file or folder needs to go in your Public folder, where the people you want to see it can log in as guests.

REMEMBER

Sharing a folder

Suppose you have a folder you want to share, but it has slightly different rules than those set up for the Public folder, for the Drop Box folder in the Public folder, or for your personal folders. These rules are *permissions*, and they tell you how much access someone has to your stuff.

Actually, the rules governing Shared and Public folders are permissions, too, but they're set up for you when macOS is installed.

TIP

I suggest that you share only those folders located in your Home folder (or a folder within it). Because of the way Unix works, the Unix permissions of the enclosing folder can prevent access to a folder for which you *do* have permissions. Trust me, if you share only the folders in your Home folder, you'll never go wrong. If you don't take this advice, you could wind up having folders that other users can't access, even though you gave them the appropriate permissions.

By the way, you can set permissions for folders in your Public folder (like the Drop Box folder) that are different from those for the rest of the parent folder.

REMEMBER

I said this before, but it bears repeating: Whenever I talk about *sharing a folder,* I also mean sharing disks — and disk partitions other than your startup disk (which you just can't share, period). So don't forget that anything I say about sharing a folder also applies to sharing any disk (or partition) other than your startup disk. Although you can't explicitly share your startup disk, anyone with administrator access can mount it for sharing from across the network (or internet).

To share a folder with another user, follow these steps:

1. Choose ⇨ **System Preferences (or click the System Preferences icon on the dock).**

The System Preferences window appears.

2. **In the System Preferences window, click the Sharing icon.**

The Sharing System Preferences pane appears.

3. **Click File Sharing in the list of services on the left.**

The lists of Shared folders and their users appear on the right, as shown in Figure 18-4.

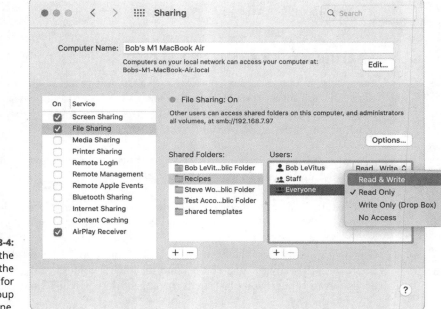

FIGURE 18-4:
Changing the privileges of the Recipes folder for the group Everyone.

4. **Click the + (plus) button under the Shared Folders list or drag the folder from Finder onto the Shared Folders list to add the folder you want to share (Recipes in Figure 18-4).**

   If you select the Shared Folder check box in a folder's Get Info window, that folder already appears in the list of Shared Folders, so you won't have to bother with Step 4.

WARNING

   Alas, although selecting the Shared Folder check box in a folder's Get Info window causes it to appear in the Sharing System Preferences pane's Shared Folders list, you still have to complete the steps that follow to assign that folder's users and privileges.

5. **Click the + (plus) button under the Users column to add a user or group if the user or group you want isn't already showing in the Users column.**

6. **Click the double-headed arrow to the right of a user or group name and change its privileges.**

   I'm changing the permission for Everyone from Read Only to Read & Write (refer to Figure 18-4). You can choose among three types of access (in addition to no access) for each user or group, as shown in Table 18-1. If you're the folder's owner (or have administrator access), you can click the padlock icon and change the owner or group or both for the file or folder.

TABLE 18-1   ## Privileges

Permission	What It Allows
Read and write	A user with read and write access can see, add, delete, move, and edit files just as though they were stored on the user's own computer.
Read only	A read only user can see and copy files that are stored in a Shared folder but can't add new files, or delete, move, or edit existing ones.
Write only (Drop Box)	Users can add files to this folder but can't see what's in it. The user must have read access to the folder containing a write only folder.
No access	With no permissions, a user can neither see nor use your Shared folders or drives.

Useful settings for permissions

The following sections show you some of the most common ways that you can combine permissions for a folder. You'll probably find one option that fits the way you work and the people you want to share with.

REMEMBER

Owner permissions — Bob (single silhouette) in the example in Figure 18-5 — must be at least as expansive as Group permissions (double silhouette; Staff in the figure), and Group permissions must be at least as expansive as Everyone's permissions (triple silhouette; Everyone in the figure). So to set the Everyone privilege to read and write, the Group and Owner privileges must also be set to read and write.

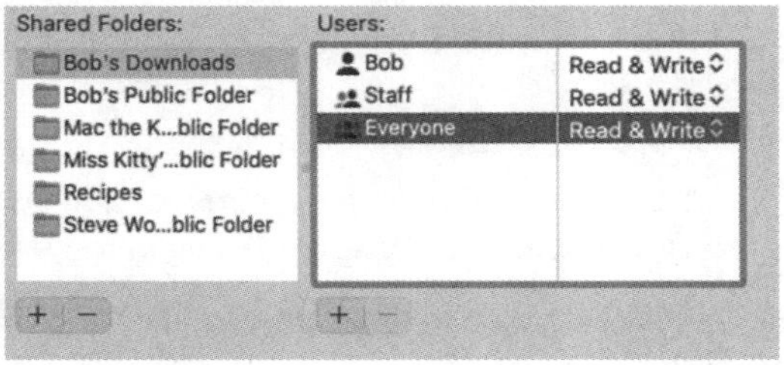

FIGURE 18-5:
Allow everyone access, if you want.

In the following examples, I show how to set permissions in the Sharing System Preferences pane. Another way to set permissions is by selecting an icon in Finder and choosing File ⇨ Get Info (⌘+I) and then changing the settings in the Sharing & Permissions section at the bottom of the resulting Get Info window. The two methods are pretty much interchangeable, so you can use whichever is more convenient:

TIP

>> **Allow everyone access:** In Figure 18-5, I configure settings that allow everyone on a network to access the Bob's Downloads folder. Everyone can open, read, and change the contents of this Shared folder. Do this by choosing Read & Write for Others from the pop-up menu to the right of the user's name in the Sharing System Preferences pane or the folder's Get Info window.

>> **Allow nobody but yourself access:** The settings shown in Figure 18-6 reflect appropriate settings that allow owner-only access to the Bob's Downloads folder. No one but me can see or use the contents of this folder. Members of the Staff group can drop files and folders into this folder (see the later bullet "Allow others to deposit files and folders without giving them access: A drop box"). Use the pop-up menus to choose Write Only (Drop Box) as the Staff privilege and No Access as the Everyone privilege.

>> **Allow all administrative users of this Mac access:** Check out Figure 18-7 to see settings that allow the group Staff (in addition to the owner, Bob) access to see, use, or change the contents of the Bob's Downloads folder. Use the pop-up menu to choose Read & Write for the Staff privilege.

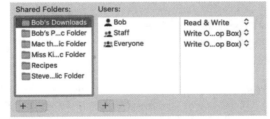

FIGURE 18-6:
Allow access for
no one but the
folder's owner.

FIGURE 18-7:
Allow access for
the Staff group
and the folder's
owner.

>> **Allow others to deposit files and folders without giving them access: A drop box:** The settings in Figure 18-8 enable people to drop their own files or folders in the Bob's Downloads folder without being able to see or use the contents of the Shared folder. After a file or folder is deposited in a drop folder, the dropper can't retrieve it because the person doesn't have permission to see the items in the drop folder.

FIGURE 18-8:
Everyone can
drop files and
folders into this
folder.

>> **Read-only bulletin boards:** If you want everyone to be able to open and read the files and folders in this Shared folder — but not to modify them — choose Read Only from the pop-up menus for Group and Others. If you do this, however, only the owner can make changes to files in this folder.

>> **One more privilege:** The Apply to Enclosed Items icon (click the gear at the bottom of the Sharing and Permissions section of a Get Info window in Finder) does exactly what its name implies. This feature (which is available only in Get Info windows and doesn't appear in the Sharing System Preferences pane) is a fast way to assign the same permissions to many subfolders at the same time. After you set permissions for the enclosing folder the way you like them, click this icon to give these same permissions to all folders inside it.

Be careful — there is no Undo for this action.

WARNING

What is true of Get Info windows is also true of their Inspector window variant. Show Inspector replaces Get Info on the File menu when the Option key is pressed (also Option+⌘+I).

Unsharing a folder

To unshare a folder that you own, change the permissions for every user and group to No Access. When you do, nobody but you has access to that folder. If you're not sure how to do this, see the "Sharing a folder" and "Useful settings for permissions" sections, earlier in this chapter.

Connecting to a Shared Disk or Folder on a Remote Mac

After you set up sharing and assign permissions, you can access folders remotely from another computer. (Just make sure first that you have the correct administrative permissions to it.)

TIP

File sharing must be activated on the Mac where the shared files/folders reside; it doesn't have to be activated on the Mac that's accessing the files/folders. When file sharing is turned off, you can still use that Mac to access a remote Shared folder on another machine as long as its owner has granted you enough permissions and has enabled file sharing. If file sharing is turned off on your Mac, others won't be able to access your folders, even if you've assigned permissions to them previously.

TIP

If you're going to share files, and you leave your Mac on and unattended for a long time, logging out before you leave it is a very good idea. This prevents anyone who just walks up to your Mac from seeing your files, email, applications, or anything else that's yours — unless you've given that person a user account that has permissions for your files. If you don't want to log out, at least consider requiring that your password be entered when waking from sleep or dismissing the screen saver (General tab of Security & Privacy System Preferences).

Move along now and see how to access your Home folder from a remote Mac — a supercool feature that's bound to get more popular as the internet continues to mature.

REMEMBER

The following steps assume that you have an account on the remote Mac, which means you have your own Home folder on that Mac.

To connect to a Shared folder on a Mac other than the one you're currently on, follow these steps:

1. **Make sure that you're already set up as a user on the computer that you want to log in to (LisaMBP in Figure 18-9).**

   If you need to know how to create a new user, see the "Creating users" section, earlier in the chapter.

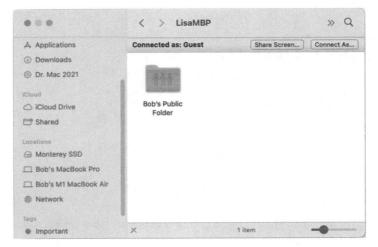

FIGURE 18-9:
I am connected to LisaMBP as a guest.

2. **On the computer that you're logging in from (my MacBook Air in this example), click Network in the sidebar's Locations section.**

   If you don't see anything below the Locations header, click the Locations header to expand its contents.

   All available shared servers appear. (Three are visible in the sidebar in Figure 18-9 — Monterey SSD, Bob's MacBook Pro, and Bob's M1 MacBook Air.)

3. **If the computer you want doesn't appear in the Locations section, click Network (also in the Locations section), and then double-click the icon of the remote Mac that you want to access.**

So, in Figure 18-9 I clicked Network in the sidebar, double-clicked LisaMBP in the main pane, and am connected to the remote Mac (LisaMBP) as a guest, as shown in Figure 18-9.

4. **Click the Connect As button.**

The Connect dialog appears. The name of the person logged in and using this Mac automatically appears in the Name field (my account name, bob, in Figure 18-10).

If that's not your username on the Mac you're trying to access, type the username in the Name field.

TIP

If you select the Remember This Password in My Keychain check box in the Connect dialog, macOS remembers your password for you the next time you connect to this server. Sweet!

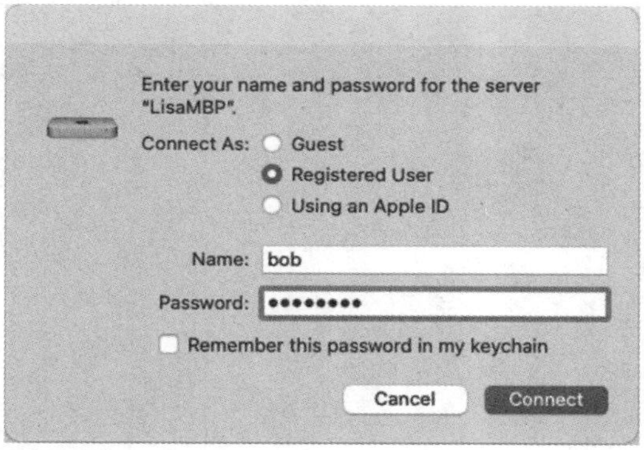

FIGURE 18-10:
The Connect
dialog needs my
password.

> Enter your name and password for the server
> "LisaMBP".
>
> Connect As: ○ Guest
> ● Registered User
> ○ Using an Apple ID
>
> Name: bob
> Password: ••••••••
> ☐ Remember this password in my keychain
>
> Cancel   Connect

5. **Select the Guest radio button if you don't have an account on the remote computer and then click Connect; if you're logging in as a user, skip to Step 6.**

Pressing ⌘+G is the same as selecting the Guest radio button, and pressing ⌘ + R is the same as selecting the Registered User radio button.

6. **Type your password and click the Connect button.**

After you connect as a registered user, you see your Home folder (bob in Figure 18-11) and everyone else's Public folders.

File sharing must be active on LisaMBP (the Mac I'm accessing remotely in the example). If file sharing weren't active on LisaMBP, its name wouldn't appear in the Locations section of the sidebar, and I wouldn't be able to connect to it. But file sharing doesn't have to be active on the computer *you're* using (my MacBook Pro in this example) to give you access to the remote computer and make this trick work.

When you access your Home folder on a remote Mac, as I did in this example, you see an icon with the short name of your Home folder on that Mac (bob in Figure 18-12) on the desktop of the Mac you're using (unless you've deselected Connected Servers in Finder's General Preferences pane, under Show These Items on the Desktop).

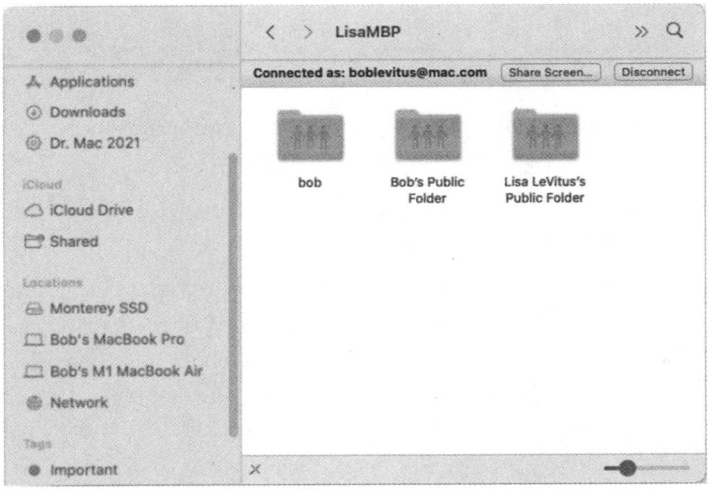

LisaMBP

Connected as: boblevitus@mac.com   Share Screen...   Disconnect

bob   Bob's Public Folder   Lisa LeVitus's Public Folder

Applications
Downloads
Dr. Mac 2021

iCloud
iCloud Drive
Shared

Locations
Monterey SSD
Bob's MacBook Pro
Bob's M1 MacBook Air
Network

Tags
Important

FIGURE 18-11:
Connecting to LisaMBP as Bob LeVitus (bob).

7. **When you finish using the remote Mac, disconnect by using one of these methods:**

- Drag the shared-volume icon (bob in Figure 18-12) to the Eject icon on the dock.

- Right-click or Control-click the shared volume icon and choose Eject from the contextual menu that appears.

- Select the shared volume icon and choose File ⇨ Eject.

- Select the shared volume icon and press ⌘ + E.

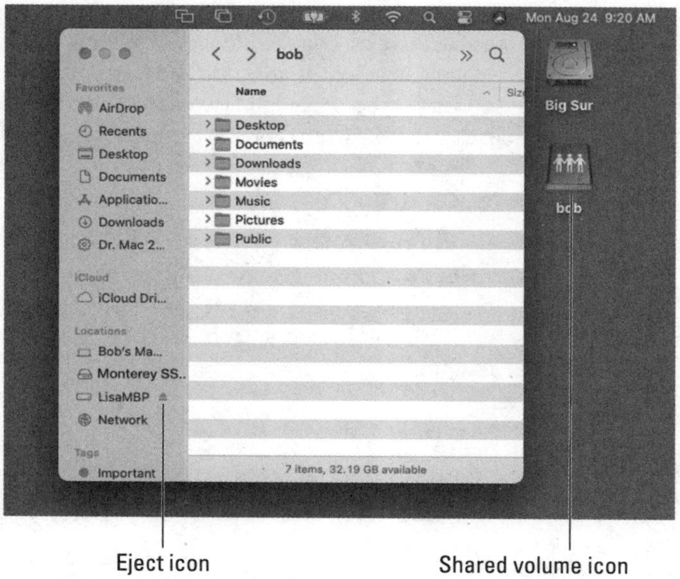

FIGURE 18-12:
Accessing my
Home folder on
LisaMBP
remotely.

Eject icon   Shared volume icon

- In a Finder window sidebar, click the little Eject symbol to the right of the remote computer's name (LisaMBP in Figure 18-12).

  When a disk or volume is selected (highlighted), the Trash icon turns into a little arrow, which represents eject. Nice touch, eh?

TIP

- If you've finished working for the day, and you don't leave your Mac on 24/7 (as most folks do), choose ➪ Shut Down or Log Out. Shutting down or logging out automatically disconnects you from shared disks or folders. (Shut Down also turns off your Mac.)

Changing Your Password

You can change your password at any time. Changing your password is a good idea if you're concerned about security — for example, if there's a chance your password has been discovered by someone else.

You can change the password for your account on your own Mac, you can change the password you use to connect to your account on a remote Mac, and you can change another account's password. I show you how to do all this (and more) in the following sections.

Changing your account password on your Mac

To change the password on your own Mac, just follow these steps:

1. **Choose ⇨ System Preferences, or double-click its icon in your Applications folder and click the Users & Groups icon.**

The Users & Groups System Preferences pane appears.

2. **In the list on the left, select your account.**

Your account information appears in the area on the right.

3. **Click the Change Password button.**

A sheet drops down.

4. **In the Old Password field, type your current password.**

This demonstrates that you are who you're supposed to be, not someone who just walked up to your unattended Mac.

5. **In the New Password field, type your new password.**

6. **In the Verify field, retype your new password.**

7. **(Optional but recommended) In the Password Hint field, type a hint.**

8. **Click the Change Password button.**

Assuming that you entered your old password correctly, the sheet disappears.

9. **Close the System Preferences window.**

Changing the password of any account but your own on your Mac

To change a password for a different account on your Mac, just follow these steps:

1. **Choose ⇨ System Preferences or double-click its icon in your Applications folder and click the Users & Groups icon.**

The Users & Groups System Preferences pane appears.

You may have to click the lock (at bottom left), supply an administrator name and password in the resulting dialog, and then click OK before you can proceed.

2. **In the list on the left, select the account for which you want to change the password.**

   The account information appears in the area on the right.

3. **Click the Reset Password button.**

   A sheet drops down.

4. **In the New Password field, type the new password.**

5. **In the Verify field, retype the new password.**

6. **(Optional but recommended) In the Password Hint field, type a hint.**

   It's a terrible idea to type the password here.

7. **Click the Reset Password button.**

8. **Close the System Preferences window.**

More Types of Sharing

Several more types of sharing exist, and I'd like to at least mention a few in passing. All are found in (where else?) the Sharing System Preferences pane, which you can find by launching the System Preferences application (from the Applications folder, ⌘ menu, or dock) and clicking the Sharing icon.

Sharing a screen

Here's the sharing that I consider the coolest. Screen Sharing lets you control another Mac on your network from your Mac. In essence, you see the other Mac's screen on *your* Mac — and control it using *your* mouse and keyboard.

To set up Screen Sharing on the Mac you want to control remotely, follow these steps:

1. **Open the Sharing System Preferences pane by launching the System Preferences application (from the Applications folder, the ⌘ menu, Launchpad, or the dock) and clicking the Sharing icon.**

2. **In the list of services on the left, select the check box for Screen Sharing.**

3. **Select either the All Users or Only These Users radio button.**

4. **If you opt for Only These Users, click the + (plus sign) button and add the user or users you want to allow to control this Mac remotely.**

   Note that the Administrators group is included by default.

To take control of your Mac from another Mac, follow these steps:

1. **If the Locations section of the sidebar isn't displayed, expand it by clicking the Locations header in the sidebar.**

    All available servers appear. If you don't see the server you desire in the list, click Network in the Locations section and look there.

2. **Click the name of the remote Mac you want to control.**

3. **Click the Share Screen button.**

    Depending on whether you selected the All Users or Only These Users radio button, you may have to enter your name and password, and then click the Connect button.

    A window with the name of the remote Mac in its title bar appears. In it, you see the screen of the Mac you're looking to control remotely.

4. **Go ahead and click something.**

    Pull down a menu or open a folder. Isn't that cool? You're controlling a Mac across the room or in another room with your mouse and keyboard!

When you're finished with your session, click the Disconnect button to end it.

Sharing the internet

If your Mac has an internet connection and another Mac nearby doesn't, you can enable Internet Sharing, and the other Mac can share your internet connection. The following steps show you how:

1. **Open the Sharing System Preferences pane by launching the System Preferences application (from the Applications folder, the menu, Launchpad, or the dock) and clicking the Sharing icon.**

2. **Choose the connection you want to share from the Share Your Connection From pop-up menu.**

    Your choices will be some or all of the following (depending on the ports and wireless protocols supported by your Mac): Wi-Fi, Bluetooth, Ethernet, and Thunderbolt.

3. **In the list of services on the left, select the Internet Sharing check box.**

4. **Select the check boxes next to connections other computers will use.**

    Again, your options will depend on the ports and protocols.

5. **(Optional) Click the Wi-Fi Options button to name, select a wireless channel for, enable encryption for, and/or set a password for your shared network.**

That's all there is to it.

And yet more ways to share

A few more cool ways to share your Mac follow:

>> **Printer (and Scanner) Sharing:** If you turn on Printer Sharing in the Sharing System Preferences pane, other people on your LAN can use any printer or scanner connected to your computer.

>> **Media Sharing:** Enable this option to allow devices on your network to browse and play downloaded music, movies, and TV shows from your Library.

>> **Bluetooth Sharing:** If you have a Bluetooth mobile phone or PDA and your Mac has Bluetooth, you can configure many of the default behaviors for transferring files to and from your Mac. A picture is worth a thousand words, so Figure 18-13 shows all the things Bluetooth Sharing lets you configure.

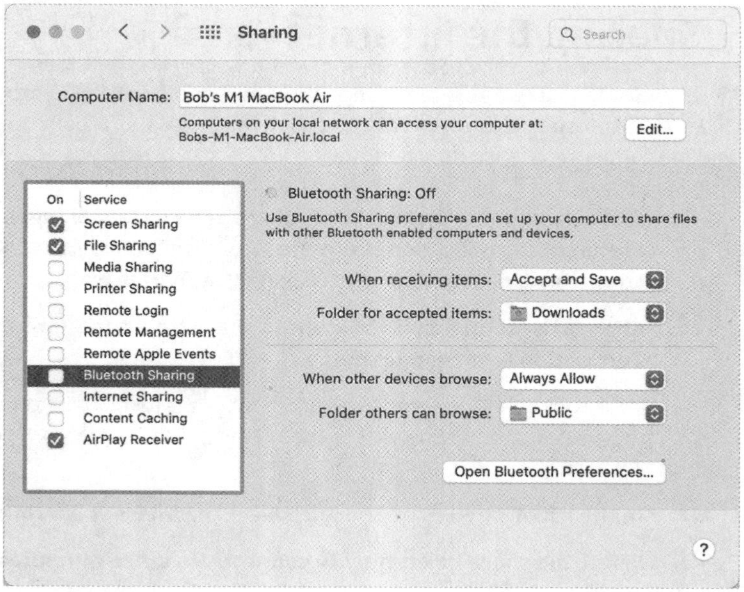

FIGURE 18-13:
Configure items for wireless Bluetooth file transfers between other devices — such as iPhones and iPads — and your Mac.

5

Getting Creative

Enjoy music on your Mac with Music.

Read any good Books lately?

Work with photos.

Import and export media.

Get enough information about fonts and typefaces to impress your friends and family.

Set up a printer without tearing out your hair.

Make sense of the myriad print options.

iTunes Match

» **Using Music (the app formerly known as iTunes)**

» **Working with media**

» **Playing with playlists**

Chapter **19**

The Musical Mac

A long time ago, before the iPod and the iTunes Store were even born, iTunes was a program that stored, managed, and played your MP3 music files. Over the ensuing years, it grew into a bloated monstrosity barely resembling the iTunes we old-timers knew and loved. It was so awful, in fact, that I wrote, produced, and released a song called "iTunes Must Die." (To snag a free copy, search for *iTunes Must Die free download* or go to `https://tinyurl.com/4jxnfdna`.)

Apple finally listened; iTunes died with the release of macOS Catalina and was replaced by three apps: Music, Podcasts, and TV. We look at Music in this chapter, and Podcasts and TV in the next.

Entire books have been dedicated to the app formerly known as iTunes. (I once wrote one called *The Little iTunes Book,* now out of print.) So, the best I can do in this chapter is show you a handful of things you really need to know.

Before you can look at Music, however, you need to know a few things about the Apple Music and iTunes Match subscription services because what you see in your Music app might be different if you subscribe to one or both.

Apple Music and iTunes Match Rock!

iTunes Match and Apple Music are a pair of subscription music services offered by Apple.

iTunes Match is the older of the two, designed to let you store all your music in iCloud so you can stream songs to any Mac, PC, or iDevice. iTunes Match performs its magic by first determining which songs in your iTunes library are already available in the iTunes iCloud library. Because Apple's vast iCloud repository contains tens of millions of songs, chances are that much of your music is already there. Then iTunes proceeds to upload a copy of every song it *can't* match (which is much faster than uploading your entire Music library). The result is that you can stream any song in your iTunes library on any of your Macs, PCs, or iDevices, regardless of whether the song file has been downloaded to the device. As a bonus, all the music iTunes matches plays back from iCloud at 256Kbps AAC DRM-free quality even if your original copy was lower quality. (You can even download higher-quality versions of those songs to replace your lower bit-rate copies if you want.)

Subscribers can store up to 100,000 songs in iCloud, and songs you purchased from the iTunes Store don't count. Only tracks or albums you specify are stored locally on your devices, saving tons of precious storage space.

At just $24.99 a year, iTunes Match is a bargain for those with extensive collections of music *not* purchased from Apple.

But Apple Music may be a better (albeit more expensive) option. For $9.99 a month (or $14.99 a month for you and up to five family members), an Apple Music subscription provides instant access to more than 75 million songs on all your devices. Whatever you want to hear is usually just a few clicks away.

Now, here's my favorite part: You can ask Siri to play whatever you want to hear on your Mac, as well as on your iPhone and other iDevices. Following are some of the phrases I like to use:

>> Play popular songs by The Beatles (or another artist).

>> Play "While My Guitar Gently Weeps" by The Beatles (or another song by a different artist).

>> Play *Greetings from Asbury Park, N. J.* by Bruce Springsteen (or another album by another artist).

>> Play some smooth jazz (or almost any other genre).

>> Play the number 1 song on April 1, 1955.

>> Play music you think I'll like.

If you find yourself with a song playing in your head (which some call an earworm), just ask Siri to play it, and in seconds the song will be playing in real life. Usually.

One more thing: When asking for an album or song, I've found that it helps if you also name the artist. So, rather than saying, "play Rubber Soul," try saying "play Rubber Soul by The Beatles."

WARNING

It would behoove you to make a complete backup of your Music library before enabling either iTunes Match or Apple Music, just in case. There were reports early in their existence that enabling one or both scrambled the data in some users' iTunes libraries.

Both subscription services require internet access (of course), but as long as you're connected you can have your entire Music library (iTunes Match) or access to a library of over 75 million songs (Apple Music) on your Mac, iPhone, or other device. You'll never have to worry about filling up your device's storage space with your music.

TIP

And here's a tip for subscribers to either service (one I learned the hard way): Before you travel on a plane or ship, remember to tap the iCloud download button (or right-click and choose Download from the shortcut menu) for all songs, albums, and playlists you want to listen to when internet access isn't available.

You're entirely welcome.

Introducing Music (the App Formerly Known as iTunes)

To open Music, click its icon on the dock or double-click its icon in the Applications folder. If this is your first time opening Music, click the Start Listening button. An ad for Apple Music (the subscription service, not the app) appears. Click Try It Free or Already a Subscriber, or press the Esc key to dismiss the ad.

The main Music window then appears, as shown in Figure 19-1. The important items are labeled, but I encourage you to click whatever you want on the screen — you won't break anything.

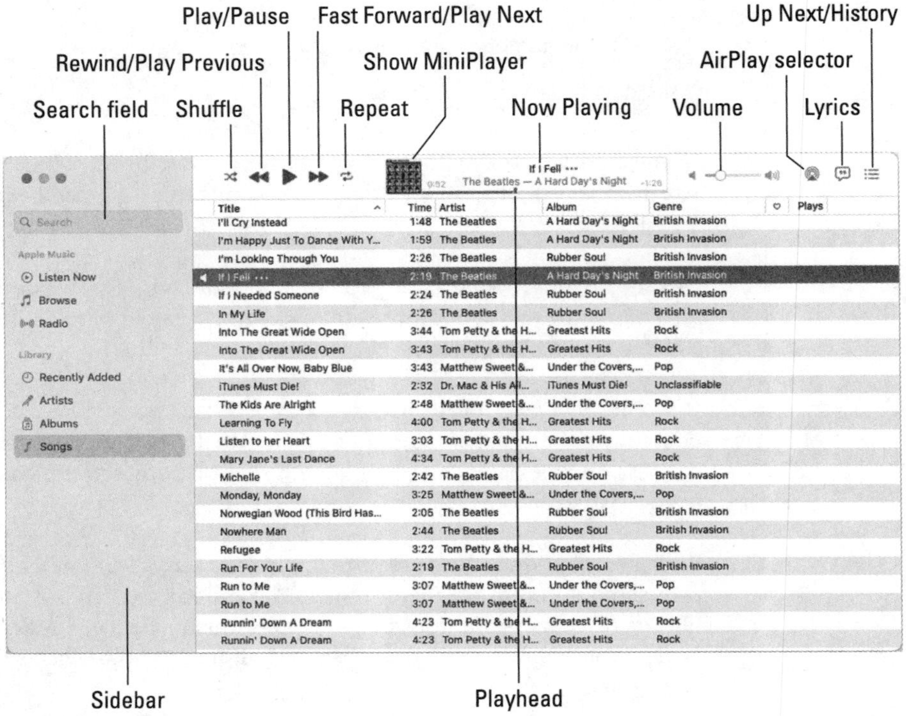
Play/Pause
Fast Forward/Play Next
Up Next/History
Rewind/Play Previous
Show MiniPlayer
AirPlay selector
Search field
Shuffle
Repeat
Now Playing
Volume
Lyrics
If I Fell •••
The Beatles — A Hard Day's Night
Search
Apple Music
Listen Now
Browse
Radio
Library
Recently Added
Artists
Albums
Songs
Title
Time
Artist
Album
Genre
Plays
I'll Cry Instead 1:48 The Beatles A Hard Day's Night British Invasion
I'm Happy Just To Dance With Y... 1:59 The Beatles A Hard Day's Night British Invasion
I'm Looking Through You 2:26 The Beatles Rubber Soul British Invasion
If I Fell ••• 2:19 The Beatles A Hard Day's Night British Invasion
If I Needed Someone 2:24 The Beatles Rubber Soul British Invasion
In My Life 2:26 The Beatles Rubber Soul British Invasion
Into The Great Wide Open 3:44 Tom Petty & the H... Greatest Hits Rock
Into The Great Wide Open 3:43 Tom Petty & the H... Greatest Hits Rock
It's All Over Now, Baby Blue 3:43 Matthew Sweet &... Under the Covers,... Pop
iTunes Must Die! 2:32 Dr. Mac & His A... iTunes Must Die! Unclassifiable
The Kids Are Alright 2:48 Matthew Sweet &... Under the Covers,... Pop
Learning To Fly 4:00 Tom Petty & the H... Greatest Hits Rock
Listen to her Heart 3:03 Tom Petty & the H... Greatest Hits Rock
Mary Jane's Last Dance 4:34 Tom Petty & the H... Greatest Hits Rock
Michelle 2:42 The Beatles Rubber Soul British Invasion
Monday, Monday 3:25 Matthew Sweet &... Under the Covers,... Pop
Norwegian Wood (This Bird Has... 2:05 The Beatles Rubber Soul British Invasion
Nowhere Man 2:44 The Beatles Rubber Soul British Invasion
Refugee 3:22 Tom Petty & the H... Greatest Hits Rock
Run For Your Life 2:19 The Beatles Rubber Soul British Invasion
Run to Me 3:07 Matthew Sweet &... Under the Covers,... Pop
Run to Me 3:07 Matthew Sweet &... Under the Covers,... Pop
Runnin' Down A Dream 4:23 Tom Petty & the H... Greatest Hits Rock
Runnin' Down A Dream 4:23 Tom Petty & the H... Greatest Hits Rock
Sidebar
Playhead

FIGURE 19-1: Dissecting the Music interface.

The Music app is pretty straightforward, so I'll just highlight a few of the more useful items in Figure 19-1 before we move on to actually doing stuff in the Music app.

In a nutshell, whatever you select in the sidebar on the left is displayed in the large pane on the right. In Figure 19-1, Songs is selected, so you see a list of songs on the right.

To play a song, double-click it, click it and then click the Play/Pause icon, or click it and choose Controls ⇨ Play.

💡 TIP

The spacebar is the shortcut for Play/Pause. It's way easier and more convenient than the options just listed.

After you've selected a song, you can use the Fast Forward/Play Next, Play/Pause, and Rewind/Play Previous controls to manage its playback.

I'd like you to take note of a few other interface items before we move on to doing stuff in Music:

» You can use the more manageable MiniPlayer (on the left in Figure 19-2) by clicking the MiniPlayer icon (labeled in Figure 19-1), choosing Window ⇨ MiniPlayer, or pressing ⌘+Option+M.

The main window is hidden when you invoke the MiniPlayer and returns when you close MiniPlayer by clicking the x in its upper-left corner.

Finally, you can toggle between the main window and MiniPlayer by choosing Window ⇨ Switch To/From MiniPlayer or by using the shortcut ⌘+Shift+M.

Although MiniPlayer works in any category, it's most useful for listening to audio — music, podcasts, and audiobooks.

» Music offers a ten-band graphic equalizer that can make your music (or video) sound significantly better. Just choose Window ⇨ Equalizer or use the shortcut ⌘+Option+E to invoke it onscreen. You can see the equalizer on the right in Figure 19-2.

 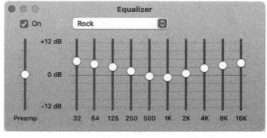

FIGURE 19-2:
The Music MiniPlayer window (left) and equalizer (right).

» Don't miss Music's Visualizer, which offers a groovy light show that dances in time to the music (see Figure 19-3). You turn it on by choosing Window ⇨ Visualizer or pressing ⌘+T. If you like the default Visualizer, also check out Classic Visualizer, which you'll find in the Visualizer Settings submenu.

When you get sick of Visualizer (as you surely will), just choose Window ⇨ Visualizer again or press ⌘+T again to make it disappear.

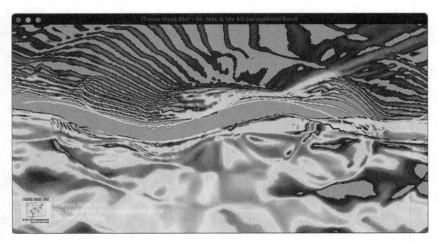

FIGURE 19-3:
The psychedelic light show that is Music Visualizer.

Working with Media

Music is, first and foremost, a music manager and player, so the next thing I examine is how to get your favorite media *into* Music.

Of course, you can acquire media a number of ways, depending on the type of media and where the files reside. For example, you can add song files that you download from websites or receive as enclosures in email messages. Or you can add songs by ripping audio CDs. You can buy music at the iTunes Store (and, to be fair, from many other online vendors, including www.amazon.com). You can listen to all sorts of music on the internet radio stations included with Music. Finally, Apple Music subscribers can listen to pretty much any song they can think of.

REMEMBER

To use the iTunes Store, internet radio, or Apple Music, you must be connected to the internet.

In the following sections, you discover the various ways to add music to your Music library, followed by a quick course in listening to Music internet radio stations.

Adding songs

You can add songs from pretty much any source, and how you add a song to Music depends on where that song comes from. Here are the most common ways people add songs:

>> **Add a song file (such as an MP3 or AAC file) from a disk drive.** Drag the document into the Music window, as shown in Figure 19-4, drag the song document (or documents or folders) onto the Music dock icon, or choose File ⇨ Import (⌘+O) and choose the file or folder in the Open File dialog.

...to here   Drag from here...

FIGURE 19-4:
Drag and drop songs to the Music content pane or library to add them to your Music library.

>> **Add songs from a store-bought or homemade audio CD.** Insert the CD, and Music will launch itself and offer a dialog asking whether you want to import the CD to your Music library. Click the Yes button, and the songs on that CD are added to your Music library. If you don't see a dialog when you insert an audio CD, you can import the songs on that CD by selecting the CD in the sidebar's Devices section and then clicking the Import CD button.

TIP

If your computer is connected to the internet, Music magically looks up the song title, artist name, album name, song length, and genre for every song on the CD. Note that this works only for store-bought CDs containing somewhat popular music; Music might not be able to find information about an obscure CD by an even more obscure band, even if the disc is store-bought. And in most cases it can't look up information for homemade (home-burned) audio CDs. Finally, it sometimes gets things wrong.

>> **Buy your songs from the iTunes Store.** Click the iTunes Store in the sidebar to visit the iTunes Store. If you don't see the iTunes Store in the sidebar, choose Music ⇨ Preferences, click the General tab, and select the Show iTunes Store check box (in the Show section).

From the home page, you can either click a link or type the song title, album title, artist name, keyword, or phrase in the Search field. Press Enter or Return to start the search. When you find an item that interests you, double-click any song to listen to a short preview (or the entire song if you're an Apple Music subscriber) or click the Buy Song or Buy Album button to purchase the song or album, as shown in Figure 19-5.

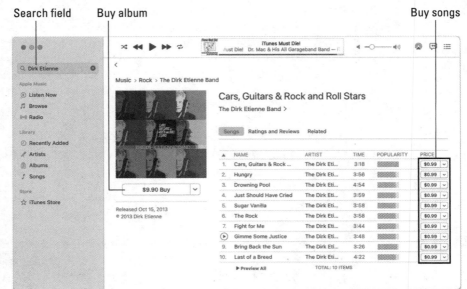

Search field   Buy album   Buy songs

FIGURE 19-5:
At the iTunes
Store, buying
music is as easy
as clicking the
Buy Song or Buy
Album button.

>> **Buy your songs from other online vendors.** Amazon (www.amazon.com) has a huge downloadable music store on the web. Its MP3 Downloads section has more than a million songs, with more added every day. The prices at Amazon are often lower than the prices for the same music at the iTunes Store. If you're concerned about audio quality, carefully read the details for each track or album and buy tracks that meet your criteria. For what it's worth, I prefer a bit rate of 160 or higher for both AAC audio files (Apple) and MP3 audio files (Amazon and most of the rest of the universe).

To make a purchase from the iTunes Store, you first have to create an Apple account, if you don't already have one. To do so, just choose Account ⇨ Sign In and then click the Create New Apple ID button in the Sign In dialog. After your account is established, future purchases require just one or two clicks.

Note that iTunes Store purchases made with this Apple account appear automatically on all other Apple devices signed into the same account.

Listening to Radio

Streaming audio is delivered over the internet in real time. Think of streaming audio as being just like radio but using the internet rather than the airwaves as its delivery medium.

To listen to Radio, select Radio in the sidebar. The first thing you see, at the top of the screen, are Apple's own live radio stations — Music 1, Music Hits, and Music Country. These stations are on the air worldwide 24 hours a day, 7 days a week offering world-class programming, interviews, and music. Scroll down to see more radio stations organized in categories such as Hosted by Artists, Discover New Shows, and Stations by Genre. To listen to a radio station, just click it.

Sadly, most radio stations are available to only Apple Music subscribers. So, rather than enjoying glorious music when you click them, you'll instead be treated to yet another Apple Music sales pitch. Sigh.

And that, friends, is pretty much all you need to know to use and enjoy radio stations in Music.

Moving right along, the more music you have in your Music library, the more you're going to love Filter Field and Column Browser.

Enabling and using the Filter Field

To enable Filter Field, choose View ⇨ Show Filter Field (or use its keyboard shortcut, ⌘+Option+F). To hide it, choose View ⇨ Hide Filter Field (or press ⌘+Option+F).

Type a word or phrase in Filter Field; all items that match that word or phrase appear below. You can type the name of a song, an album, an artist, a genre, or a composer, and the results will appear instantly as you type.

Enabling and using Column Browser

To enable Column Browser, choose View ⇨ Column Browser ⇨ Show Column Browser (or use its keyboard shortcut, ⌘+B). To hide it, choose View⇨Column Browser ⇨ Hide Column Browser (or press ⌘+B).

The Column Browser submenu allows you to choose which categories are displayed. Genres, artists, and albums are displayed by default. Disable or enable the Composers or Groupings columns by selecting them in the Column Browser submenu. A check mark next to a category means it's enabled.

When enabled, Column Browser appears above the main content area. Narrow your search by clicking one or more items in each column. So, for example, if you selected Rock in the first column (Genre by default), and selected The Beatles in the second column (Artist by default), you'd see every Beatles album in every genre in the third (Albums) column.

Column Browser is an easy, visual way to narrow your search. I leave it enabled at all times. Try it! I predict that the bigger your music library, the more you'll like using Column Browser.

All about Playlists

Playlists are a big deal in Music; they let you manage otherwise unmanageable amounts of media. Playlists let you create subsets of a large collection, such as the 23,000+ songs in my Music library, so it's easier to enjoy exactly the kind of music you want in Music or on your iDevices. Put another way, playlists are the high-tech equivalent of mixtapes.

You can create three types of playlists:

>> **Regular playlists,** which contain the songs (or videos, podcasts, or radio stations) that you specify by adding them to the playlist.

>> **Smart playlists,** which select songs from your library based on criteria you specify. Furthermore, you can set your smart playlists to update automatically when you add items to your library that meet the criteria.

>> **Genius playlists,** which use artificial intelligence to choose songs from your library that the Genius thinks will go great together (and often do).

TIP

If you're an Apple Music subscriber, you can use songs from your personal Music library, as well as the more than 75 million songs available to Apple Music subscribers in any type of playlist.

Creating a regular playlist

To create a regular playlist, follow these steps:

1. **Choose File ➪ New ➪ Playlist, or press ⌘+N.**

A new playlist named Playlist appears in the main pane.

2. **(Optional) The playlist's name, Playlist, is selected and ready to be edited, so you might want to rename it something meaningful by typing a new name for it.**

I typed *A Shiny New Playlist* in Figure 19-6.

TIP

If you decide not to name your playlist now, you can double-click it and type a new name anytime.

3. **(Optional) In the Add Description field, type a description of the playlist.**

4. **To add a song or songs to a playlist, click an item in your library and then drag the song or songs onto the playlist's name in the sidebar.**

   The playlist (A Shiny New Playlist in Figure 19-6) is highlighted, indicating that it's selected and the song or songs will be added to it when you release the mouse button.

   Note that adding a song to a playlist doesn't remove it from the library. And if you delete a song from a playlist, the song isn't deleted from your library. Furthermore, if you delete a playlist from the sidebar, the songs it contains aren't deleted from your library. In other words, think of songs in playlists as being aliases of songs in your library.

5. **To listen to the songs in a playlist, click it in the sidebar to select it, and then click Play to hear all the songs on the list or double-click a specific song to listen to it.**

...onto the playlist   Drag songs from your library...

FIGURE 19-6:
Adding songs to a playlist is as easy as dragging them onto the playlist.

If you don't want to drag songs to your playlist one by one, there's an easy way to do it in one fell swoop. First, ⌘-click all the songs you want to include in the playlist. Then choose File ➪ New ➪ Playlist from Selection or use the keyboard shortcut, ⌘+Shift+N.

You can also use the ⌘-click technique to select and then drag a batch of songs onto an existing playlist.

Finally, you can add any song to a new or existing playlist by right- or Control-clicking it and choosing Add to Playlist.

Working with smart playlists

To create a *smart playlist* that gathers its contents based on criteria you specify and updates itself automatically, follow these steps:

1. **Choose File ⇨ New Smart Playlist (⌘+Option+N).**

The Smart Playlist dialog appears, as shown in Figure 19-7.

2. **Use the pop-up menus to select the criteria — song or album name, genre, or other attributes — that will build your smart playlist.**

To add more criteria, click the + button(s) on the far right.

3. **Click OK when you're done.**

The playlist appears alongside your other playlists in the sidebar. You can tell it's a smart playlist by the gear on its icon. To modify the criteria of a smart playlist after it's been created, click Edit Rules (below the Smart Playlist's name and description) or right-click (or Control-click) the smart playlist in the sidebar and choose Edit Rules.

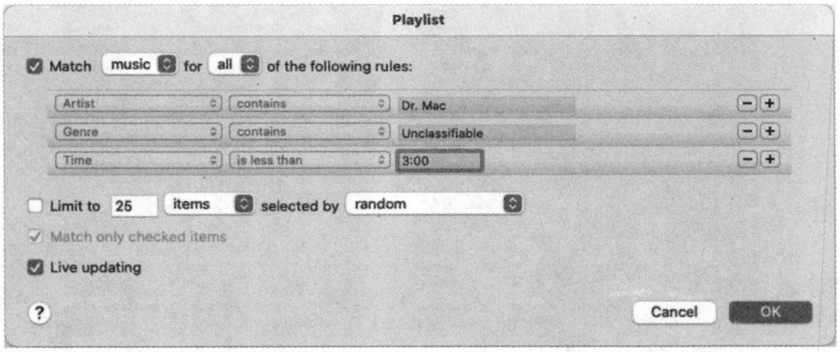

FIGURE 19-7:
Specify the criteria for your smart playlist.

Playlist

☑ Match [music ⬥] for [all ⬥] of the following rules:

(Artist ⬥)	(contains ⬥)	Dr. Mac	⊟ ⊞
(Genre ⬥)	(contains ⬥)	Unclassifiable	⊟ ⊞
(Time ⬥)	(is less than ⬥)	3:00	⊟ ⊞

☐ Limit to [25] [items ⬥] selected by [random ⬥]
☑ Match only checked items
☑ Live updating

(?) [Cancel] [OK]

TIP

Right- or Control-click any playlist to see additional options: Play, Shuffle, Play Next, Play Later, Love, Dislike, Open in New Window, Edit Rules (as mentioned), Burn Playlist to Disc, Copy to Play Order, Duplicate, and Delete.

I use smart playlists for many things. I have one that gathers Beatles songs and songs by individual Beatles; another for songs in my library that have never been played; another for Classical and Jazz (which I find soothing while working); and one that gathers all of Doctor Mac & His All GarageBand Band's greatest hits in one playlist.

Smart playlists are fabulous. Try 'em and I'm pretty sure you'll like 'em.

Working with the Genius playlist

Last but certainly not least, I'd like to draw your attention to one more playlist: Genius.

Who is Genius?

Genius is more of a *what* than an *is:* It's a Music feature that lets you find new music — in your Music library or the iTunes Store — related to a song of your choosing. Or, as Apple puts it: "Genius makes playlists and mixes from songs in your library that go great together. And the Genius selects music from the iTunes Store that you don't already have."

To use Genius, you must (for some unknown reason) have an iTunes Store account, even though the information Genius sends to Apple about your Music library is stored anonymously. No purchase is required, but I still think it's a dumb requirement. However, that's the way it works, so take it or leave it.

Assuming you take it, sign in to your iTunes Store account if you have one (or create one if you don't). After you agree to the Genius terms of service, Genius gathers info about your Music library, sends the info to Apple, and then (finally) delivers your results. When all of this is done, you can create Genius playlists and peruse Genius suggestions.

How does Genius work?

How? Glad you asked! Select at least one song (or a bunch of songs) in your library or a playlist and then choose File ➪ New ➪ Genius Playlist. After a bit of cogitation, Music presents you with a Genius playlist based on the song you clicked, as shown in Figure 19-8.

Or try a Genius shuffle, which is an instant Genius playlist without the playlist. Select a song and then choose Controls ➪ Genius Shuffle (or press Option+spacebar) and a selection of songs that go great together will play. To see the songs selected by Genius, just click the Up Next/History button in the toolbar (and shown in the margin).

By the way, if you're not a fan of Led Zeppelin and classic British rock, let me assure you that most of the songs in the Thank You Genius playlist in Figure 19-8 do, mostly, "go great together."

That said, the tech editor of some of the previous editions of this book, the late Dennis R. Cohen, said Genius was not so hot with classical music or comedy. And I've noticed that it works better with big names than lesser-known indie artists.

Even so, it's free. So if you don't have issues with all the legal mumbo jumbo, the iTunes Store account, or sending information about your Music library to Apple, give Genius a try.

Burning a playlist to CD

Another use for playlists is for burning audio CDs you can listen to on almost any audio CD player. The only trick is to make sure the total playing time of the songs in the playlist is less than the capacity of the blank CD you're using, which is usually 74 to 80 minutes. Don't forget to account for the gap between tracks, which is two seconds by default. When you have all the songs you want on your CD on the playlist, choose File ⇨ Burn Playlist to Disc. The Burn Settings dialog appears.

Note that although the default type of disc Music burns is an audio CD, it can also burn two other types — MP3 CDs or data CDs (and DVDs):

>> **MP3 CD** is a special format that can be played in many CD audio players and set-top DVD players. The cool thing about an MP3 CD is that rather than holding a mere 74 to 80 minutes of music, it can hold more than 100 songs! The uncool thing about MP3 CDs is that many older audio CD players won't play them.

>> **A data CD or DVD** is nothing more than a disc formatted to be read and mounted by any computer, Mac or Windows.

If you click the Burn button now, you'll get an audio CD. To burn an MP3 CD or Data CD or DVD, select the appropriate radio button in the Burn Settings dialog.

When you're satisfied, click the Burn button. In a few minutes, you'll have an audio CD that contains all the songs on the playlist — and plays the songs in the order in which they appeared on the playlist (unless, of course, you elected to burn a data CD or DVD).

To learn more about the Music app, I suggest exploring the excellent Music Help which you'll find in the Help menu along with other excellent Help resources, including a list of keyboard shortcuts!

TIP

One last thing: I'd be remiss not to mention that unlike iTunes, the Music app doesn't sync music with iDevices. These days (that is, in Monterey), you use Finder to sync your iPhones, iPads, and iPod touches.

» **Watching movies and TV shows with the TV app**

» **Reading books with Books**

» **Taking pictures and movies with Photo Booth**

» **Importing media — photos and videos — to your Mac with Image Capture**

Chapter **20**

The Multimedia Mac

edia content is more than just music (the topic of Chapter 19), and your Mac is ready, willing, and able to handle almost any type of media (with almost any type of content) you can throw at it. Which is why, in addition to the aforementioned Music app, macOS Monterey includes applications for viewing and working with media (such as DVD movie discs and QuickTime movie files) as well as graphics in a variety of file formats (including PDF, TIFF, and JPEG).

In this chapter, you look at some bundled applications you can use to work with such media — namely QuickTime Player, TV, Books, Podcasts, Photo Booth, and Preview — followed by a brief section about importing your own media (photos and videos) into your Mac and the Image Capture app.

Playing Movies and Music in QuickTime Player

QuickTime is Apple's technology for digital media creation, delivery, and playback. It's used in myriad ways by programs such as Apple's iMovie, by websites such as YouTube (www.youtube.com), and in training videos delivered on CD or DVD.

QuickTime Player is the macOS application that lets you view QuickTime movies as well as streaming audio and video, QuickTime VR (Virtual Reality), and listen to many types of audio files as well. The quickest way to launch it is by clicking its icon in Launchpad or double-clicking its icon in the Applications folder. This is the default application for most QuickTime movie document files.

TIP

I say most QuickTime movies because some will open QuickTime Player, and others will open the TV app or another video player. To change the app that opens for a particular movie, right- or Control-click its icon in Finder and choose the application you prefer from the Open With submenu. However, this action opens the file with that program only this one time. To make the change permanent, press Option, and the Open With command becomes the Always Open With command.

To play a QuickTime movie, merely double-click its icon, and QuickTime Player launches itself.

Using QuickTime Player couldn't be easier. All its important controls are available right in the player window, as shown in Figure 20-1.

FIGURE 20-1:
QuickTime Player
is simple to use.

TIP

The QuickTime Player's controls disappear when you're not using them (for obvious reasons). So, if you don't see the controls floating in front of your video, just hover the cursor over the QuickTime Player window and the controls will magically reappear.

Here are a few more QuickTime Player features you might find useful:

>> **The Movie Inspector window** (Window ⇨ Show/Hide Movie Inspector or ⌘+I) provides a lot of useful information about the current movie, such as its location on your hard drive and the file format, frames per second, file size, and duration.

>> **The Trim control** (Edit ⇨ Trim or ⌘+T) lets you delete frames from the beginning and end of a movie.

>> **The Share/More Menu** (click >> on the floating control window) lets you send your movies to others via the Mail, Messages, Notes, or Photos apps or via AirDrop, or upload them to YouTube.

See Chapter 23 for details about Monterey's cool AirPlay Mirroring option, which lets you mirror what's on your Mac screen and view it on an HDTV wirelessly. The only thing you need is a smart TV with AirPlay or an Apple TV connected to your HDTV.

Watching TV

The TV app took over video storage and discovery duties from iTunes in 2019 (in macOS Catalina)— and it was about time. Now your video content lives in one place; it's easy to find more to rent or buy; and it's simple to add your own videos, too.

The TV app's main window features five tabs: Watch Now, Apple TV+, Movies, TV Shows, and Library. All but Library suggest video content you can rent or buy from the iTunes Store.

Shopping for video is almost the same as shopping for music. Here are the steps:

1. **Select the appropriate tab.**

2. **Either click a link in the content pane or type in the Search field and press Return.**

   You can search for a movie title, a music video name, a TV show, an actor's or a director's name, or another keyword or phrase.

3. **When you find a video item that interests you, double-click it to see a preview or click the Buy button to purchase the episode or video.**

Speaking of movies, don't forget to check out the picture-in-picture option, which works with most video content in the TV app, as well as videos on many websites. Just look for the little picture-in-picture icon (shown in the margin) at the bottom of the video player and click it to make your video float above all other pictures, as shown in Figure 20-2.

TIP

If you don't see a picture-in-picture icon on a video player, try right- or Control-clicking the video. If it supports picture-in-picture, you'll see it in the pop-up menu.

FIGURE 20-2:
The picture-in-picture video (lower right) continues to play and remains in front of TextEdit (left) or Safari (center), even if I'm using them.

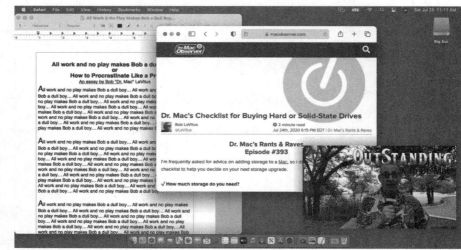

TIP

You can also add your own movies, TV shows, and home videos. To add a video file (such as MOV or MP4) from your hard drive, drag the file to the TV window or the TV dock icon, or choose File ➪ Import (⌘+O) and choose the file in the Open File dialog. In all cases, the file is added to your video library (click the Library tab to see it).

Using the Books App

Don't be surprised if you have to answer this question from an inquisitive child someday: "Is it true, Grandpa, that people once read books on paper?"

Books, the app formerly known as iBooks, is Apple's answer to Amazon's Kindle. It's a combination e-book reader and bookstore. You can view your purchases (and free downloads) on any Apple device.

 Don't get me wrong; I still love physical books as much as anyone and think they'll be around a lot longer than you or I. But I also recognize the real-world benefits that e-books have over paper ones.

Everything that follows will make more sense if you have at least one e-book in your library. So the first thing to do is stock your virtual library with an e-book from the app's built-in Book Store. Don't worry. This won't cost you a penny unless you want it to — the store is chock-full of free books!

So without further ado, here's how to acquire some e-books (and audiobooks).

Buying an e-book or audiobook

First things first. The Books app needs to be running, so launch it by one of these routes:

>> Double-click its icon in the Applications folder.

>> Single-click its icon in Launchpad.

If this is your first time launching Books, you may be asked to sign in with your Apple ID and password. Do so (or don't) and then click the Get Started button.

Now, click Book Store (or Audiobook Store) in the sidebar.

If you've purchased Books with iTunes in the past, they should appear automatically in your Books library.

TIP

You can look for books or audiobooks in many ways. After you select the Book Store tab, scroll down to see books organized into sections, which might include For You, Featured, Top Charts, New and Trending, More to Explore, and Bestsellers by Genre.

Of course, you can also search for a book or an author; just type a word or two in the Search field near the upper-left corner of the Books window and press Return.

When you see a book or ad that interests you, click it, and details will fill the screen, as shown in Figure 20-3.

Click the Buy button (which says $14.99 in Figure 20-3) to buy the book. Or for free books, click the Get button (not shown) to add the book to your library for free.

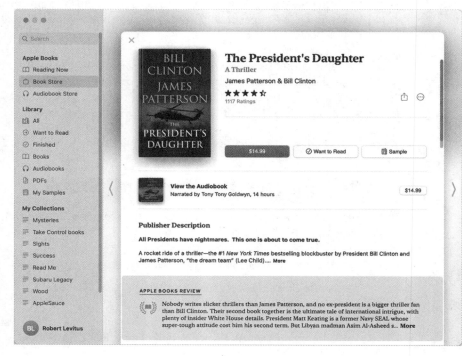

FIGURE 20-3:
Buy books from the Book Store and add them to your Books library.

TIP

Many books offer a free sample, or a chapter or chapters that you can download for free. Click the Sample button, and a sample will appear in your Books library within a few minutes.

One last thing: The big angle brackets to the left and right of the book description in Figure 20-3 are Previous and Next buttons. Click the one on the left to see the previous book in this section; click the one on the right to see the next book in this section.

When you finish shopping, click All in the sidebar's Library section to return to your Books library.

Shopping for e-books without Apple

Books can also handle books you acquire elsewhere, and it supports a technical standard called *ePub*, which is a format that offers hundreds of thousands of free and public domain books on the web. You can import such files into Books, so you don't ever have to shop (or only shop) in the Book Store. The only possible gotcha is that the ePub titles must be *DRM-free*, which means free of any digital rights restrictions.

You can find ePub titles at numerous cyberspace destinations:

>> **Baen:** www.baen.com

>> **Feedbooks:** www.feedbooks.com

>> **Google Play:** Not all the books here are free, and Google has a downloadable app. http://play.google.com/store/books.

>> **Project Gutenberg:** www.gutenberg.us

>> **Smashwords:** www.smashwords.com

To import an ePub title, download the file to your Mac, fire up Books, and then do one of the following:

>> Choose File ⇨ Add to Library (or use its shortcut, ⌘+Shift+O), select the ePub file in the Open sheet, and click Add.

>> Drag the ePub file from Finder onto your Books library.

Before I move on to reading Books, I feel obliged to mention that between the free books in the Book Store and ePub books available from the sites in the preceding list and elsewhere, tons of great books out there are free and tons more are good, pretty good, or okay (and free). The point is that you can read a lot without spending a dime.

WARNING

You can't add books made for the Amazon Kindle to Books, not even ones that are DRM-free. You have to download the free Kindle app from the Mac App Store if you want to read Kindle books.

TIP

You *can* add PDF files to Books; it works the same as adding an ePub title. After they're imported, they appear in the PDF section of your Books library.

Finally, for those who'd rather listen than read, you'll love that the Books app can read text aloud. To listen instead of reading, do the following:

1. **Click at the spot where you want to begin from or select the text you want to hear.**

2. **Choose Edit ⇨ Speech ⇨ Start Speaking.**

   In a few seconds, a robotic voice will begin reading.

3. **To stop, simply choose Edit ⇨ Speech ⇨ Stop Speaking.**

It may not be quite like having Mom or Dad read you to sleep, but it can be a potential godsend for people with impaired vision.

Finding and Listening to Podcasts with the Podcasts App

Podcasts are like radio or television shows, except when you subscribe to them, you can listen to or watch them (using the Podcasts app on your iPod, iPad, or iPhone) at any time you like. Thousands of podcasts are available and many (or most) are free.

 To find podcasts, launch the Podcasts app and follow these steps:

1. **Click Browse or Top Charts in the sidebar.**

2. **Click a link in the content pane on the right or type a keyword or phrase in the Search field at the top of the sidebar.**

3. **When you find a podcast that appeals to you, do one of the following:**

   - *Click the Follow button to receive all future episodes of that podcast automatically.*

   - *Click the Latest Episode button to listen to the latest episode immediately.*

   - *Click the down arrow button to download the current episode of that podcast.*

4. **Click the ellipsis (. . .) for additional options.**

Figure 20-4 shows all these things for the Mac Geek Gab audio podcast from *The Mac Observer*.

For more information on most podcasts, just click the ellipsis to the right of the +Follow button, as shown in Figure 20-4.

Play/pause latest episode   Follow this podcast

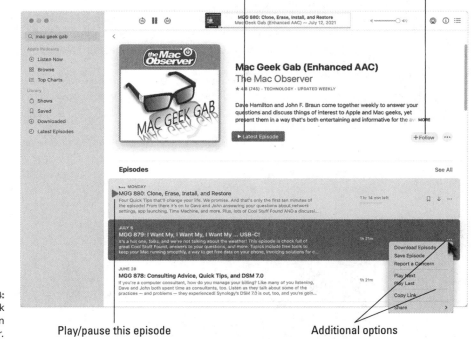

FIGURE 20-4:
The Mac Geek
Gab podcast from
The Mac Observer.

Play/pause this episode   Additional options

Following (formerly subscribing to) a podcast offers myriad options. You can configure how often the Podcasts app checks for new episodes (hourly, daily, weekly, or manually), what to do when new episodes become available (download the most recent one, download all episodes, or do nothing), and how many episodes to keep in your iTunes library (all, all unplayed, or a specific number between 2 and 10). To specify these settings, click a podcast you've followed in your library, click the ellipsis (. . .), and choose the appropriate option from the shortcut menu.

When you start listening to a followed podcast on your Mac in the Podcast app and switch to an iDevice, the podcast will pick up where it left off on your Mac. Or at least that's what's supposed to happen — and it usually does.

You're the Star with Photo Booth

The Photo Booth application provides all the fun of an old-time (or new-time) photo booth, like the ones you sometimes see in malls or stores. It lets you shoot one photo, shoot a burst of four photos in a row, or shoot a movie using your Mac's built-in camera. If yours is one of the rare Macs with no built-in camera (such as the Mac mini) or you own a USB webcam better than the built-in model, you'll be pleased to hear that most USB webcams work with Photo Booth right out of the box with no drivers or other software necessary. Just launch Photo Booth and look in the Camera menu, where all compatible cameras appear.

TIP

If you have only one camera available — mine is called FaceTime HD Camera (Built-In) — it's selected automatically, so you shouldn't have to even bother with the Camera menu.

Photo Booth couldn't be easier to use. Start by clicking one of the three icons in the lower-left corner of the Photo Booth window — Burst (of four photos), Single Photo (selected in Figure 20-5), or Movie — and then click the big, red camera button to take a picture, as shown in Figure 20-5.

FIGURE 20-5:
Photo Booth about to take a picture of yours truly.

Before you shoot, you may want to explore the five pages of special effects — Sepia Tone, Color Pencil, Pop Art, and dozens more — by clicking the Effects button (lower right) and then clicking the particular effect you want to try. If you like it, click the big, red camera button and shoot a picture, pictures, or video; if you don't, click the Effects button again and click another effect. Or if you prefer to shoot with no effects, click the Normal effect in the center of all the Effects pages.

TIP

Photo Booth includes a feature called Screen Flash, which uses your computer display as a camera flash by turning the screen all-white as it shoots the photo. If *your* screen isn't flashing when you shoot, look in the Camera menu and make sure that the Enable Screen Flash command has a check mark. Finally, Screen Flash is (understandably) disabled when you're shooting movies.

After you shoot, your pictures or movies drop into the tray at the bottom of the window (there's one photo in Figure 20-5). You can then select one or more photos in the tray and then do any of the following:

>> **Delete them** by pressing the Delete or Backspace key.

>> **Share them** by clicking the Share button, which replaces the Effects button when one or more photos are selected in the tray.

>> **Export them as JPEG files** by choosing File ➪ Export.

>> **Print them** by choosing File ➪ Print or pressing ⌘+P.

>> **Drag them from the tray** to the desktop, a folder, an email, or an iMessage, where they appear as JPEG files; or drag them onto an image editor icon such as Photos (on the dock or in the Applications folder). Note that they're not automatically saved in your Photos library or elsewhere, so if you don't drag them somewhere, they exist only in the tray of the Photo Booth app.

So that's the scoop on Photo Booth. It's fun and easy, and if you have a camera (as most of you do), you should definitely launch Photo Booth and give it a try.

TIP

If you have kids who are old enough to trust with a Mac, Photo Booth and its effects will entertain them for hours (or, more likely, for a few minutes).

Viewing and Converting Images and PDFs in Preview

You use Preview to open, view, and print PDFs as well as most graphics files (TIFF, JPEG, PICT, and so on). *PDF files* are formatted documents that can include text and images. User manuals, books, and the like are often distributed as PDF files. You can't edit the existing text in a PDF file with Preview, but you can leaf through its pages, annotate and mark it up, and print it. You can often select text and graphics in a PDF file, copy them to the Clipboard (⌘+C), and paste (⌘+V) them into documents in other applications. Preview is also the application that pops open when you click the Preview button in the Print dialog, as I describe in Chapter 22.

TIP

Actually, that's not entirely true. You can edit one certain type of PDF file: a form that has blank fields. Preview allows you to fill in the blanks and then resave the document. And although it's technically not editing, you can annotate a PDF document by using the Annotate tools on the toolbar, and add, delete, or reorder pages in the sidebar.

One of the most useful things Preview can do is change the file format of a graphic file. For example, say you're signing up for a website and want to add a picture to your profile. The website requires pictures in the JPEG file format, but the picture file on your hard drive that you'd like to use is in the TIFF file format. Preview can handle the conversion for you:

1. **Double-click the TIFF file to open it with Preview.**

   If another program (such as Adobe Photoshop) opens instead of Preview, drag the TIFF document onto the Preview icon or launch Preview and choose File ⇨ Open (⌘+O) to open the TIFF file.

2. **Choose File ⇨ Export.**

3. **Choose the appropriate file format — such as JPEG or PNG — from the Format pop-up menu.**

4. **(Optional) If you want to make sure you don't confuse your original image with the one in the new format, change the name of your file in the Export As field.**

5. **(Optional) Add a tag or tags if you like.**

6. **Click Save.**

Preview lets you convert any file it can open to any of the following file formats: HEIC, JPEG, JPEG-2000, OpenEXR, PDF, PNG, and TIFF. Or choose File ⇨ Export as PDF to export the current file as a PDF.

HEIC is Apple's High Efficiency Image format, which creates smaller files with a higher image quality than JPEG. The upside is smaller files; the downside is that not all apps that will open a JPEG file will open an HEIC file.

You'll probably never need to convert a file to most of these formats, but it's nice to know that you can if you need to.

TIP

Almost every macOS program with a Print command allows you to save your document as a PDF file. Just click and hold down on the PDF button (found in all Print dialogs) and choose Save as PDF. Then, should you ever need to convert that PDF file to a different file format, you can do so by using the preceding steps.

Chapter **21**

Words and Letters

As I discuss in previous chapters, your Mac is well equipped for creating and managing media — music, movies, and photos — but it is also ready to handle more common tasks, such as typing a letter or composing an essay. I think it's fair to say that the TextEdit application we're about to explore is all the word processor many users will ever need for casual everyday writing.

TIP

If you need more control over your pages than TextEdit provides, try Pages from Apple, a powerful word processor and page layout program. It comes preinstalled on some Macs, so you may already have it. If not, get it for free in the Mac App Store.

Furthermore, macOS comes with a wide variety of fonts (sometimes called *typefaces*) plus a handy little app called Font Book for managing those fonts. Fonts allow you to change how text looks on the screen and the printed page.

In this chapter, you look at the macOS text composition and text-editing program — TextEdit — and then explore fonts and how to manage them.

Processing Words with TextEdit

TextEdit is a word processor and text editor that you can use to write letters, compose notes, open Read Me files, and much more. It's not as sophisticated as Microsoft Word or Apple's Pages, but you can use it for many word-processing and text-editing tasks. It's been included with every Mac sold since time immemorial.

TextEdit is capable of performing a respectable amount of text formatting, and it can even check your spelling and read text to you in a natural-sounding (if somewhat creepy) voice.

TextEdit supports images, too. Just copy an image from another program and paste it into a TextEdit document. Or drag and drop an image into a TextEdit document from many applications or Finder.

TextEdit can even open Microsoft Word documents (.doc and .docx files), which is fabulous if you don't happen to have a copy of Microsoft Word on your hard drive. It can also open .rtf, .odt, .htm, .html, and .txt files, should you need to view a document saved in any of these popular file formats.

 Like most apps included with Monterey, you find TextEdit in the Applications folder at the root level on your hard drive.

The dock doesn't have TextEdit's icon preinstalled, but if you like TextEdit, use it regularly, or would just like to have it on your dock, do one of the following:

>> Drag its icon from the Applications folder to anyplace on the left side of the dock.

>> Launch it, and then right- or Control-click its dock icon and choose Options ➪ Keep in Dock.

Creating and composing a document

You'll get the most from the rest of this chapter if you have TextEdit open. So go to your Mac, if necessary, and launch TextEdit. Otherwise, you'll find it hard to follow (and remember) the information in this section.

When you launch TextEdit, an Open File dialog (see Chapter 7) appears. Click the New Document button in the lower-left corner, and an Untitled document appears. Let its default (and ambiguous) name — Untitled — be a message to you that before you begin working on this document, you should give it a name and save it to your hard drive or iCloud Drive. To do so now, choose File ➪ Save or press ⌘+S, replace Untitled with your title, and then click Save to save it. (If you're new to macOS Save sheets, flip to Chapter 7 for details.)

TextEdit uses macOS's modern version support and auto-save features, so your work is saved automatically on the fly. However, don't be lulled into a false sense of security; many third-party apps still don't support these features. (Chapter 7 has the lowdown on versions and saving.)

It's a good idea to choose File ➪ Save or use its shortcut, ⌘+S, every so often regardless of whether the app supports versions and auto-save. Better safe than sorry.

Now begin typing your text. When you type text in a word processor, here are three tips for processing words properly:

» **Press the Return key only when you want to start a new paragraph.** You don't need to press Return at the end of a line of text; the program automatically wraps your text to the next line, keeping things neat and tidy.

» **Type a single space after the punctuation mark at the end of a sentence, regardless of what your typing teacher told you.** Word processors and typewriters aren't the same. With a typewriter, you want two spaces at the end of a sentence; with a word processor, you don't. (Typewriters use *fixed-width* fonts; computers mostly use fonts with variable widths. If you put two spaces at the end of a sentence in a computer-generated document, the gap looks too wide.) Trust me on this one.

» **Limit most documents to a maximum of two different fonts.** macOS offers hundreds of fonts, but that doesn't mean you should use them all in one document.

Working with text

TextEdit operates on the "select, then operate" principle, as do most Mac programs, including Finder. Before you can affect (style, or format) text in your document — that is, change font face, style, size, margins, and so on — you need to select the text you want formatted.

You can use several methods to select text in a document:

» **Select a word.** Double-click the word.

» **Select a paragraph.** Triple-click a word in that paragraph.

>> **Select a chunk.** Click anywhere in the document, hold down the Shift key, and then click again somewhere else in the document. Everything between the two clicks will be selected.

>> **Extend the selection.** Click anywhere in the document, hold down the Shift key, and use the keyboard arrow keys to extend the selection. You can also click, hold down the mouse button, and drag to select text; release the mouse button when you've finished selecting.

>> **Select all text in the document.** Choose Edit ➪ Select All or use the shortcut ⌘ + A.

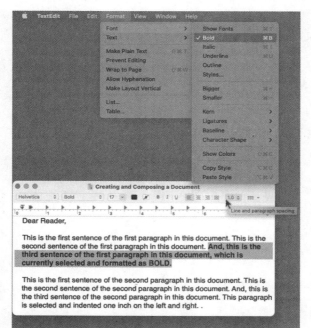

TIP Give all these methods of selecting text a try, decide which ones feel most comfortable, and then memorize them for future use.

TIP Rather than bore you with a rundown of what the icons on the TextEdit toolbar do, just hover the cursor over any item to display its tooltip, as I've done for the Line and Paragraph Spacing drop-down menu in Figure 21-1.

After your text is selected, you can format it. For example, you can use the Format menu's Font submenu to choose Bold, Italic, Outline, or Underline (among others), as shown in Figure 21-1. I opted for bold in Figure 21-1, and you can see in the figure how the selected sentence is now bold.

FIGURE 21-1:
Only the selected text is affected by these formatting commands.

Another way to apply the Bold style to the text in Figure 21-1 is by clicking the B (for Bold) icon on the toolbar. Note that the toolbar and ruler won't be visible if you're working on a plain text (.txt) document. So if you choose Format ➪ Make Plain Text (⌘+Shift+T) while working on any document, the toolbar and ruler disappear.

The same idea applies to tabs and margins. In Figure 21-2, I dragged the left and margin markers in one inch. Note that the selected text is now indented by one inch from the left margins.

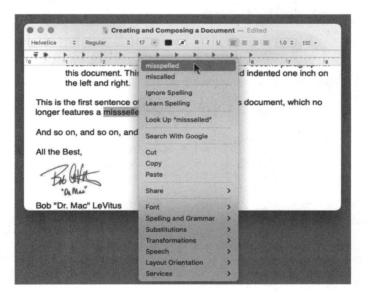

FIGURE 21-2:
The selected paragraph is now indented.

Select some text in your document, and try all the items in the Format menu's Font and Text submenus. As you see, you have a great deal of control over the way your words appear on the screen. And because TextEdit, like most Mac software, is WYSIWYG (What You See Is What You Get), when you print the document (by choosing File ➪ Print), the printed version should look exactly like the version you see on the screen. For help with printing, see Chapter 22.

The View menu is your friend. Choose View ➪ Actual Size or use its shortcut (⌘+0) to see your document just as it will print. Use the View menu's Zoom In and Zoom Out commands or their shortcuts — ⌘+Shift+. (period) and ⌘+Shift+, (comma) — to make everything appear larger or smaller.

Before you print your masterpiece, however, you may want to check your spelling and grammar — something that TextEdit makes extremely simple. Merely choose Edit ⇨ Spelling and Grammar ⇨ Check Document Now or press ⌘+; (semicolon). TextEdit highlights and underlines what it perceives to be mistakes in your document. Right-click (or Control-click) to bring up a menu with correction choices.

TIP

Don't put too much faith in the Monterey spelling and grammar checker. It's good, but it's not perfect and no substitute for a good proofreading.

Adding graphics to documents

Last but not least, you have a couple of ways to add pictures to a TextEdit document. The first works as follows:

1. Copy an image in another program — Preview, Safari, or whatever.

2. Put the pointer where you want the picture to appear in your TextEdit document.

3. Choose Edit ⇨ Paste.

The image magically appears on the page.

Or you can drag an image from Finder (or another application such as Safari or Mail) to a TextEdit document, as I did in Figure 21-3.

Drag an image from the desktop, a folder, or another app...

...onto the TextEdit document

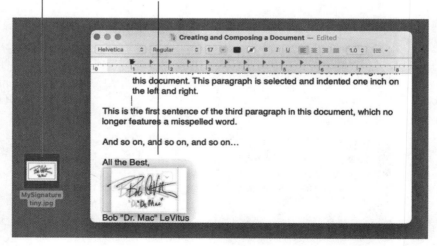

FIGURE 21-3:
Drag an image into a TextEdit document.

You may see an alert asking if you want to convert this document to RTFD format before you drop (or paste) the image. You do, because otherwise you can't add images to the document.

Note that you can't wrap text around images in TextEdit. So if you drag an image to the middle of a sentence by accident, you'll have text before and after the image but a huge gap on either side. To fix it, click and drag the image between paragraphs. (You may find it necessary to add an extra Return between paragraphs to get the image where you want it.)

TIP

Finally, to put special characters such as mathematical symbols, arrows, ornaments, stars, accented Latin characters, and emoji (such as smiley faces) in your TextEdit document, choose Edit ⇨ Emoji & Symbols (⌘+Control+spacebar). This opens the Character palette, from which you can choose characters. To insert a character, make sure your cursor is in the document where you want (the insertion point), and then double-click the character in the palette.

Font Mania

You can jazz up your documents — or make them a little more serious — with different fonts. To a computer user, *font* means *typeface* — what the text characters look like. Although professional typographers will scream at my generalization, I'll go with that definition for now.

Tens of thousands of different fonts are available for the Mac. You don't want to use the same font for both a garage-sale flyer and a résumé, right? Luckily for you, Monterey comes with hundreds of fonts. Some are pretty predictable, such as Times New Roman, but macOS gives you some artsy ones, too, such as Brush Script.

If you *really* get into fonts, you can buy single fonts and font collections anywhere you can buy software. Plenty of shareware and public domain fonts are also available from online services and user groups. Some people have thousands of fonts. Don't judge me.

To see how to manage third-party fonts you collect, check out the upcoming section, "Managing your fonts with Font Book."

Types of fonts

You can find many font formats with names such as OpenType, Mac TrueType, Windows TrueType, PostScript Type 1, bitmap, and dfont. No problem — macOS supports them all.

The only font format I know that macOS *doesn't* support is PostScript Type 3.

TECHNICAL STUFF

All you really need to know is that pretty much any font you buy or download will probably work with Monterey.

Managing your fonts with Font Book

Font Book lets you view your installed fonts, install new fonts, group your fonts into collections, and enable and disable installed fonts. As usual, you find the Font Book application in the Applications folder at the root level on your hard drive.

The easiest way to install a new font is to double-click it in Finder. Font Book opens and displays the font. Click the Install Font button to install the font.

Other ways you can install new fonts are to choose File ➪ Add Fonts or press ⌘+O. A standard Open dialog allows you to select a font or fonts to be installed.

Note that, by default, new fonts are installed in your Home folder's Fonts folder, which is inside your invisible Library folder (Users/Home/Library/Fonts). You can change the default installation location in Font Book's Preferences (Font Book ➪ Preferences or ⌘ +, [comma]).

TIP

To view a font or font family, click its name in the Font list. Click the disclosure triangle before the name of a font to see all the variants that are installed.

To change the size of the viewed font, click the triangle next to the font size (36, in Figure 21-4) in the top-right corner of the Font Book window and choose a new size from the drop-down list that appears, or type a different number where the number 36 appears in Figure 21-4, or move the size slider — the white dot with a blue line below it near the lower-right corner of the window — up or down.

To disable a font so it no longer appears on any applications' Font menus, choose Edit ➪ Disable or click the Disable icon (the check mark in a square on the toolbar).

To enable a previously disabled font, choose Edit ➪ Enable or click the Enable icon (same as the Disable icon).

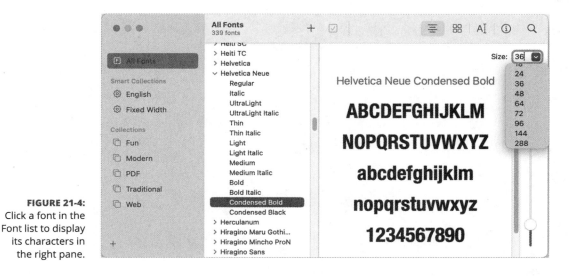

FIGURE 21-4:
Click a font in the
Font list to display
its characters in
the right pane.

If a font name is gray instead of black, that font is available but not yet downloaded to your Mac. To download and enable it, first select it and then choose Edit ⇨ Download or click the Enable icon.

Font Book looks out for your best interests; it won't allow you to disable or delete any fonts required by Monterey — including (but not limited to) Lucida Grande, Helvetica, and Helvetica Neue.

One last thing: Try to refrain from installing more fonts than you'll use. Having tons of installed fonts can slow down some apps and make the Font menu long and unmanageable. And the longer your Font menu gets, the longer it will take the menu to appear after you click it.

Bottom line: Install only the fonts you need — your Mac will thank you for it.

Chapter **22**

Publish or Perish: The Fail-Safe Guide to Printing

When you want to get what's on your screen onto paper, printing under Monterey should be as simple as pressing the keyboard shortcut ⌘+P and pressing Return. Happily, that's usually just how easy printing something is. Unfortunately, when it isn't just that easy, printing can turn into a nightmare. After you configure a printer and confirm that things work as expected, printing is generally a simple affair forevermore.

In this chapter, I scare away the bogeymen to help you avoid any printing night-mares. I walk you through the entire process as though you just unpacked a new printer and plugged it in.

Before Diving In . . .

Before I even start talking about hooking up printers, you need to know a few essential things. So here's a little list that tells you just what those things are:

REMEMBER

>> **Read the documentation that came with your printer.** Hundreds of different printer makes and models are available for the Mac, so if I contradict something in your printer manual, follow your manual's instructions first. If that effort doesn't work, try the techniques in this chapter.

>> **The Print and Page Setup sheets differ slightly (or even greatly) from program to program and from printer to printer.** Although the examples I show you in this chapter are representative of what you'll *probably* encounter, you might come across sheets that look a bit different. For example, the Print and Page Setup sheets for Microsoft Word include choices that I don't cover in this chapter (such as Even or Odd Pages Only, Print Hidden Text, and Print Selection Only). If you see commands in your Print or Page Setup sheet that I don't explain here, they're specific to that application; look in its documentation for an explanation. Similarly, many graphics-related apps — such as Adobe Illustrator and Photoshop — have added their own Print dialog, which appears before the Monterey print sheet with check boxes, radio buttons, and other controls, to the point where you might not even recognize them as Print dialogs.

TIP

>> **Don't forget about Help.** Of course, it's built into Monterey and just keeps getting better and better. Plus, many third-party programs support this excellent Apple technology, which can be the fastest way to figure out how to use a feature that has you stumped. So don't forget to check out the Help menu before you panic. (I cover the Help menu in Chapter 1.)

Ready: Connecting and Adding Your Printer

Before you can even think about printing something, you have to connect a printer to your Mac and inform your Mac (and Monterey) that the printer exists.

REMEMBER

If you have a printer and are able to print documents already, you can skip ahead to the "Set: Setting Up Your Document with Page Setup" section. The info between here and there pertains only to setting up a *new* printer for the first time.

Connecting your printer

Once again, I must remind you that you *could* connect your Mac to thousands of printer models, and each one is a little different from the next. In other words, if what you're about to read doesn't work with the printer you're trying to connect, RTFM (Read the Fine Manual). It should tell you how to load your ink or toner cartridges, and anything else you might need to know to set up your printer successfully.

That said, here are some very general steps to connect a printer to your Mac:

1. **Connect the printer to your Mac with the cable snugly attached to both your printer and Mac.**

   You may ignore this step if your printer supports wireless printing and you intend to print only wirelessly.

   For your printer to work, you have to somehow connect it to a data source. For what it's worth, connecting with a cable is more reliable than connecting wirelessly.

2. **Plug the printer's AC power cord into a power outlet.**

   Yup, I mean the regular kind of outlet in the wall; on a power strip; or, best of all, on a UPS (uninterruptible power supply). Some printers require you to plug one end of the AC power cord into the printer; others have the AC power cord attached permanently. The point is that your printer won't work if it's not connected to a power source.

   TIP

   If you decide to plug it into a UPS, make sure it's rated to provide more power than your printer consumes, because some laser printers use more power than a desktop computer.

3. **Turn on your printer.**

   Look in the manual if you can't find the power switch.

Setting up a printer for the first time

After you connect your computer and printer and provide a power source for your printer, you're ready to configure your Mac running Monterey. You have to do this configuration so that your Mac and your printer will be able to communicate.

REMEMBER

Many, if not all, of the steps involving the Printers & Scanners System Preferences pane require that your printer be turned on and warmed up (that is, already through its diagnostics and start-up cycle) beforehand. So before doing anything else, make sure your printer is turned on, warmed up, and connected to your Mac.

The first time you connect your printer, you may see an alert asking whether you want to download and install software for your printer.

You do, so click the Install button. At this point, you may see a License Agreement window. If so, click the Agree button to proceed. (You may click Disagree if you want, but that halts the installation process.)

TIP

If you connect a new printer and *don't* see an alert, don't worry; just follow the upcoming instructions.

After clicking the Install and Agree buttons, a Software Update window may appear and tell you it's finding software. If it does, just leave it alone; it disappears after a minute or two. Don't click the Stop button unless you want to abort the installation.

Here are the steps to set up a printer for the first time:

1. **Launch System Preferences, click the Printers & Scanners icon, and then click your printer's name in the Printers list on the left side of the window.**

REMEMBER

   You can open System Preferences from the menu, or launch it from the Applications folder, dock, or Launchpad.

   Monterey is a pretty smart cat; it should have already recognized your printer at this point. If so, your printer's name appears in the Printers list of the Printers & Scanners System Preferences pane, as shown on the left in Figure 22-1. The new printer I'm setting up in Figure 22-1 is an Epson ET-4750 Series.

   - *If your printer isn't in the list at this point:* Click the + button at the bottom of the Printers list, and then select it from the list in the Add Printer dialog that appears (the right image in Figure 22-1), and then click the Add button.

   - *If you still can't see your printer in the Add Printer dialog:* You need to install (or reinstall) its driver software manually, by downloading the latest driver software from your printer manufacturer's website. See the nearby sidebar "Go for a driver" for more on drivers.

REMEMBER

   You can't proceed until the Printers & Scanners System Preferences pane recognizes your printer. So download and install that driver if necessary and then proceed onward.

2. **In the Default Printer pop-up menu, choose the printer you want selected by default when you print documents (Last Printer Used is selected in Figure 22-1).**

3. **In the Default Paper Size menu, select the default paper size you want to use with this printer (usually US Letter, if you live in the United States).**

That's all there is to it. Close System Preferences, and you're ready to print your first document! Before you do, however, make sure you have the document set up to look just the way you want it to look printed. Read through "Set: Setting Up Your Document with Page Setup" later in this chapter for more info.

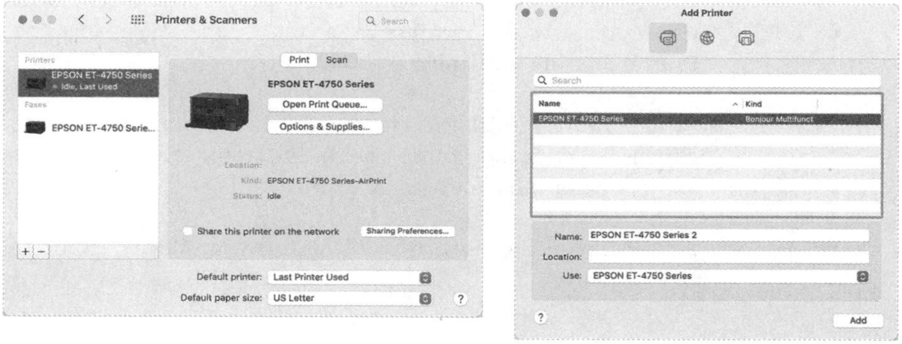

FIGURE 22-1:
The only printer that Monterey recognizes here — Epson ET-4750 Series — is displayed on the left side of the System Preferences window.

GO FOR A DRIVER

Apple includes a library of printer drivers with Monterey, which covers many popular printer brands and models. These drivers are installed by default. Monterey also checks to see whether a newer driver is available — for every driver in its library — and if it finds one, it offers to download and install the new driver (as described earlier in this chapter).

If Monterey can't find a driver for your printer, you need to manually install the appropriate printer drivers before your printer will appear in the Printers list in the Printers & Scanners System Preferences pane. So go find and download the driver from the manufacturer's website, install it, and get ready to print.

One more thing: Most printer manufacturers introduce new drivers with enhanced functionality. If a CD was in the box with your printer (which is rarer and rarer these days), I'll bet the driver on it is out of date. So, ignore the CD and let Monterey take care of installing or updating your printer driver if possible. And if for some reason Monterey can't manage it (which is rare), download the most recent version from the vendor's website rather than installing the (probably outdated) version on the CD that came with the printer.

One last thing: Printer sharing

If you want to share a printer that's connected directly to your Mac (with others on your local area wired or wireless network), select it in the Printers list on the left side of the Printers & Scanners System Preferences pane, and then select the Share This Printer on the Network check box.

To fine-tune your shared printer, click the Sharing Preferences button on the right, and the Sharing System Preferences pane (which I discuss in detail in Chapter 18) replaces the Printers & Scanners pane. Make sure the check box next to Printer Sharing is enabled.

By default, printer sharing is available to everyone. If you want to limit it to specific users, click the + button below the Users section of the Sharing System Preferences pane and add them by username.

Finally, the printer is unavailable unless your Mac is up and running.

Set: Setting Up Your Document with Page Setup

After you set up your printer, the hard part is over. You should be able to print a document quickly and easily — right? Not so fast, bucko. Read here how the features in the Page Setup sheet can help you solve most basic printing problems.

Many programs have a Page Setup command on their File menu. Note that some programs use the name *Page Setup,* and others use *Print Setup.* Either way, this is the sheet where you choose your target printer, paper size, page orientation, and scale (as shown in Figure 22-2).

TIP

Become familiar with Page Setup. You might not need to use it right this second, but it's a good friend to know. Even though some apps offer some of these Page Setup settings in their Print sheets, Page Setup is the only place you find these options in many programs.

Users of network printers might see slightly different versions of the Print and Page Setup sheets. The differences should be minor enough not to matter.

Click the little question mark in the bottom-left corner of the Page Setup or Print sheets at any time for additional help. If you do, Page Setup or Printing help opens immediately in Help Center. (Okay, maybe not *immediately,* but Help Center in Monterey is faster than Help Viewer in, say, Mountain Lion or Mavericks.)

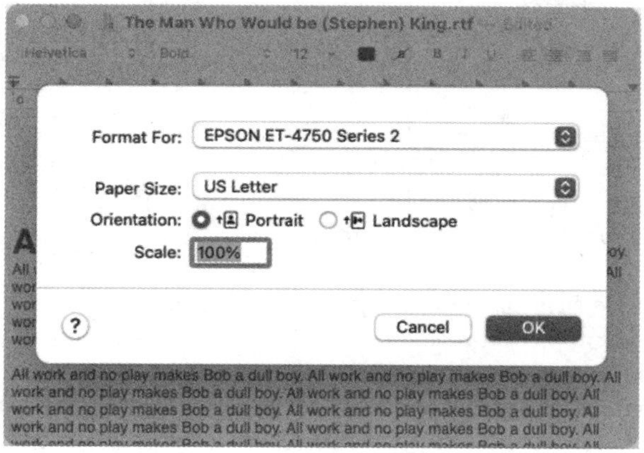

FIGURE 22-2:
The Page Setup
sheet in the
TextEdit
application.

The options in the Page Setup sheet are as follows:

>> **Format For:** In this pop-up menu, you find the name of all recognized printers. If you have several printers configured, you can choose any of them from this menu.

This menu usually defaults to Any Printer, which is the least-effective setting. Unless the printer you want to use appears here, you may not get full functionality when you print.

>> **Paper Size:** Use this pop-up menu to choose the type of paper currently in the paper tray of your printer or to choose the size of the paper that you want to feed manually. The dimensions of the paper that you can choose appear below its name.

Page Setup sheet settings (including Paper Size) remain in effect until you change them. For example, when you print an envelope, don't forget to change back to Letter before trying to print on letter-size paper again.

>> **Orientation:** Choose among options here to tell your printer whether the page you want to print should be portrait-oriented (like a letter, longer than it is wide) or landscape-oriented (sideways, wider than it is long).

>> **Scale:** To print your page at a larger or smaller size, change this option to a larger or smaller percentage.

All these options remain in effect until you choose a different option.

Some programs offer additional Page Setup choices. If your program offers them, they usually appear in the Settings pop–up menu in the Page Setup sheet. (Adobe Photoshop and Microsoft Word have them; TextEdit doesn't.)

Print: Printing with the Print Sheet

After you connect and configure your printer and set up how you want your document to print, you come to the final steps before that joyous moment when your printed page pops out of the printer. Navigating the Print sheet is the last thing standing between you and your output.

REMEMBER

Although most Print sheets that you see look like the figures I show here, others may differ slightly (or, occasionally, greatly). The features in the Print sheet are a function of the program with which you're printing. Many programs choose to use the standard-issue Apple sheet, but not all do. If I don't explain a certain feature in this chapter, chances are good that the feature is specific to the application or printer you're using (in which case, the documentation for that program or printer should offer an explanation).

Printing a document

If everything has gone well so far, the actual act of printing a document is simple. Just follow the steps here, and in a few minutes, pages should start popping out of your printer like magic. (In the sections that follow, I talk about some print options that you'll probably need someday.)

1. **Open a document that you want to print.**

2. **Choose File ⇨ Print (or press ⌘+P).**

You see the basic Print sheet, as shown in Figure 22-3.

3. **Click Print.**

4. **Wait a moment for the network to tell the printer what to do, and then walk over to your printer to get your document.**

Choosing File ⇨ Print (⌘+P) *won't* work for you if any one of the following is true for the software you're using:

» The Print command is on a different menu.

» There *is* no Print command.

» The Print keyboard shortcut is something other than ⌘+P.

If any of the preceding is true for a program you're using, you just have to wing it. Look in all the menus and check out the product's documentation to try to get a handle on the Print command for that pesky program.

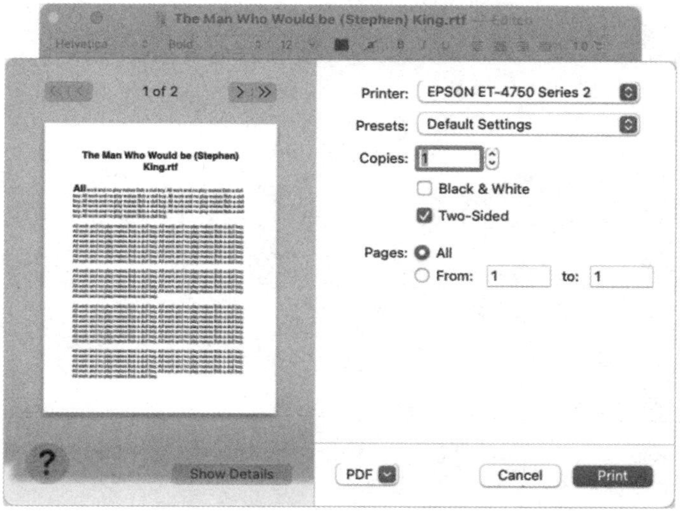

FIGURE 22-3:
Your basic
Print sheet.

Choosing among different printers

Just as you can in the Page Setup sheet, you can choose which printer you want to use from the Printer pop-up menu of the Print sheet.

REMEMBER

You can choose only among the printers you added via the Printers & Scanners System Preferences pane, as I describe earlier in this chapter in the section I lovingly call "Setting up a printer for the first time." This includes printers connected to wireless base stations and routers, as well as Wi-Fi—enabled printers. After they're set up, Macs (and other devices) within range can print to these printers wirelessly.

Choosing custom settings

By default, the Print sheet is displayed with its details hidden. As such, just four menus are available: Printer, Presets, Pages, and PDF. To reveal the rest of the Print options, click the Show Details button near the bottom of the Print sheet. An expanded Print sheet with all the details you're likely to need, as shown in Figure 22-4, replaces the more streamlined version shown previously in Figure 22-3.

TIP

Click in any of the fields and press the Tab key. Your cursor jumps to the next text field; likewise, press Shift+Tab to jump to the previous field. By the way, this shortcut works in almost any program, window, dialog, or web page that has text fields.

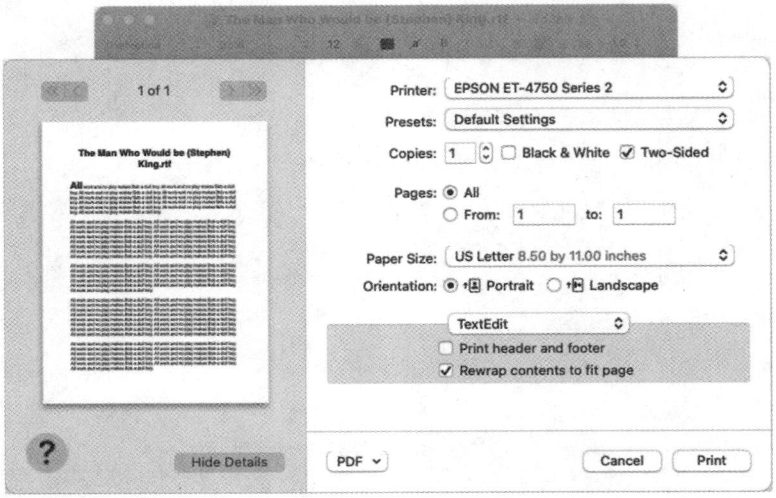

FIGURE 22-4:
Your expanded
Print sheet.

In addition to the drop-down Printer menu, your expanded Print sheet offers the following options:

» **Presets:** This menu lets you manage and save print settings, as described in the "Saving custom settings" section later in this chapter.

» **Copies:** In this text field, set how many copies you want to print. The Print sheet defaults to one copy (1) in most applications, so you probably see the numeral 1 in the Copies field when the Print sheet appears. Assuming that's the case, don't do anything if you want to print only one copy. If you want to print more than one copy of your document, highlight the 1 that appears in the Copies field and replace it, typing the number of copies you want.

» **Pages:** Here, you find two radio buttons: All and From. The default behavior is to print your entire document, so the All option is preselected. But if you want to print only a specific page or range of pages, select the From radio button and type the desired page numbers in the From and To text fields.

Suppose that you print a 10-page document and only then notice a typo on Page 2. After you correct your error, you don't have to reprint the whole document — you can reprint only the page with the correction. Reprint only Page 2 by typing **2** in both the From and To fields. You can type any valid range of pages (um, you can't print page 20 if your document is only 15 pages long) in the From and To fields.

» **Paper Size:** Use options in this pop-up menu to choose the type of paper currently in your printer's paper tray, or to choose the size of the paper that you want to feed manually. The dimensions of the paper appear below its name.

Yeah, this setting is also in Page Setup. The difference is that the settings here (in the Print sheet) apply only to *this document,* whereas the settings in Page Setup are the default for *all documents* and remain in effect until you change them in Page Setup. This can be handy when, for example, you print an envelope. If you change the paper size setting for the envelope document, you don't have to remember to change it back to Letter in Page Setup.

>> **Orientation:** Yeah (again), this setting is also in Page Setup. And once again, the choice you make in Page Setup is the default for all pages you print. Keep in mind that the setting you choose here (in the Print sheet) applies only to this document. Choose among options here to tell your printer whether the page you want to print should be portrait or landscape oriented.

The following list describes the features you can find in the unlabeled menu found in the expanded Print sheet (the one that says *TextEdit* in Figure 22–4). In addition to TextEdit, Layout, and other options I cover in a moment, your pop-up menu may offer options such as Media & Quality, Color Options, Special Effects, and Borderless Printing. (Whether you have these options depends on your printer model and its driver as well as the application from which you're printing.) Check out these options if you have 'em; they usually offer useful features:

>> **TextEdit:** The only TextEdit-specific options, as shown in Figure 22-4, are two check boxes. One governs whether to print a header and footer for this document; the other lets you choose to rewrap the contents of the document to fit the page.

You can see the results of clicking these check boxes in the proxy image of your document on the left half of the sheet.

>> **Layout:** Choose Layout to set the number of pages per printed sheet, the layout direction, and whether you prefer a border. Here are your options for Layout:

- *Pages per Sheet:* Choose preset numbers from this pop-up menu to set the number of pages that you want to print on each sheet.

  Pages appear onscreen smaller than full size if you use this option.

- *Layout Direction:* Choose one of the four icons that govern the way pages are laid out on the printed page.

- *Border:* Your choices from this pop-up menu are None, Single Hairline, Single Thin Line, Double Hairline, and Double Thin Line.

- *Two-Sided:* If your printer supports two-sided (known as *duplex*) printing, the three radio buttons allow you to specify whether you're going to use two-sided printing — and if so, whether you'll be binding (or stapling) along the long or short edge of the paper or creating a booklet.

Two check boxes — Reverse Page Orientation and Flip Horizontally — do just what they say if you enable them.

>> **Paper Handling:** Choose Paper Handling if you want to reverse the order in which your pages print or to print only the odd- or even-numbered pages. You can also specify whether the document's paper size is to be used (in which case, you might have lines that break across pages) or whether the output should be scaled to fit the chosen paper size.

>> **Cover Page:** Choose Cover Page to add a cover page.

>> **Paper Type/Quality:** Choose Paper Type/Quality to specify the type of paper in your printer and the print quality you desire. The choices are Draft, Normal, or Best when you print from TextEdit; other apps may offer other options.

>> **Supply Levels:** Choose Supply Levels to see the current ink levels for your printer.

Saving custom settings

After you customize your printer settings just the way you like them, you can save them for future use. Just click the Presets pop-up menu, choose Save Current Settings as Preset, and then provide a name for this preset. From then on, the preset name appears as an option in the Presets pop-up menu. Just choose your saved preset before you print any document, and all the individual settings associated with that preset are restored.

To manage your presets, choose Show Presets from the Print sheet's Presets pop-up menu. This nifty feature displays a list of your presets and their settings and allows you to delete, duplicate, or rename (by double-clicking their current name) your presets.

Preview and PDF Options

To see a preview of what your printed page will look like, choose Open in Preview from the PDF pop-up menu in the bottom-left corner of the expanded Print sheet. When you do so, you see the page or pages that you're about to print displayed by the Preview application.

TIP

As you probably know, Monterey can save any printable document as a PDF file. To do so, choose Save As PDF in the PDF pop-up menu in every print dialog or sheet.

If you have any doubt about the way a document will look when you print it, check out Preview first. When you're happy with the document preview, just choose File ⇨ Print, press ⌘+P, or click the Print button at the bottom of the Preview window. Or click the Cancel button to return to your application and make changes to the document.

Preview works with the Preview application. With the Preview feature, you can do cool things like these:

>> See all the pages in your document the way they'll be printed, one by one.

>> Zoom in or out to get a different perspective on what you're about to send to the printer (pretty cool!).

>> Rotate the picture 90 degrees to the left or right.

>> Insert (via drag and drop), delete, or reorder pages in Preview's sidebar.

>> Spot errors before you print something. A little up-front inspection can save paper, ink or toner, and frustration.

 Click the Show/Hide Edit Toolbar icon (shown in the margin) to reveal a small toolbar with several useful tools.

Check out the Preview program's View menu, where you'll find (among other things), four useful views: Content Only, Thumbnails, Table of Contents, and Contact Sheet, as well as the zoom commands and more.

Also check out Preview's toolbar, from which you can add or delete icons by choosing View ⇨ Customize Toolbar.

And speaking of tools, don't miss the selections in the Tools menu, which let you rotate pages, move forward or backward (through multipage documents), and unleash the awesomeness of Magnifier.

TIP

The Magnifier tool is so very darn cool that it has a rare single-key keyboard shortcut. That key is the ` (the grave accent, which shares a key with the tilde); press it to show or hide Magnifier.

One last thing: Monterey includes the capability to fax a document right from the Print sheet, but it requires a compatible device with a compatible fax modem driver. To find out whether *your* device is compatible, connect the device to your Mac and attempt to add it as a fax modem in the Printers & Scanners System Preferences pane.

6

Care and Feeding

IN THIS PART . . .

Uncover utilities you might or might not find useful (but ones you should know about just the same).

Protect your valuable data by backing it up.

Discover new Monterey features, including Universal Control and AirPlay to Mac.

Get Dr. Mac's prescription: What to do when things go wonky (which also, thankfully, doesn't happen very often).

Find the doctor's top troubleshooting tips for eliminating most wonkiness.

» **Shopping for apps with the Mac App Store**

» **Using your iPhone as a camera or scanner for your Mac**

» **Talking to your Mac**

» **Enhancing productivity by using automation**

» **Running Microsoft Windows on your Mac (really!)**

» **Controlling your Mac and iPad with one keyboard and mouse**

» **Mirroring your Mac screen to a TV or Mac wirelessly**

Chapter **23**

Features for the Way You Work

This chapter delves into some macOS Monterey features that might very well improve the ways you interact with your computer. Unlike the more mainstream applications, System Preferences panes, and utilities that I discuss in Part 1 — Desktop, Finder, Screen Saver, Appearance, Keyboard, Trackpad, Mouse, and such — the items in this chapter are a little more esoteric. In other words, you don't *have* to use any of the tools or technologies I'm about to show you. That said, many of these items can make you more productive and can make using your Mac even better. So I'd like to believe that at least some of you will *want* to use at least a few of the cool features I'm about to introduce.

I begin with three features introduced in macOS Mojave: Dark mode, a redesigned Mac App Store, and Continuity Camera, which lets you use your iDevice as a camera or scanner for your Mac.

Finally, a Dark Mode

Have you ever thought that the white background in most windows on your Mac was far too bright? Have you ever fiddled with brightness hoping to take it down a notch? I know I've gone as far as changing the background color of Finder windows to a dark shade of gray (View ⟳ Show View Options), even though it works only on windows using Icon view.

In Monterey, such machinations are a thing of the past. Now it's easy to reduce your screen's brightness by enabling Dark mode. As you can see in Figure 23-1 (top), Dark mode affects the appearance of windows, buttons, menus, and other interface elements.

To choose Dark (or Light) mode, open System Preferences and click General. The first item you see — Appearance — is where you pick your mode.

Or try Auto mode, which switches between dark and light automatically based on the time of day.

TIP

Try changing the accent and highlight colors while in Dark mode — they look slightly different than in Light mode.

And that's all there is to Dark mode. Try using it for a while. I didn't use it much in Mojave (which didn't include Automatic mode) because it was a hassle to switch back and forth manually; since Catalina introduced Dark Mode, I use Auto mode on all my Macs.

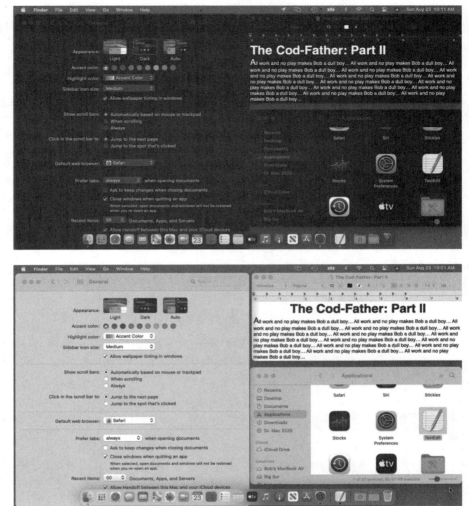

FIGURE 23-1:
Three windows, the menu bar, and the dock in Dark mode (top) and Light mode (bottom).

App Shopping, Improved

Introduced in 2011, the Mac App Store is the largest catalog of Mac software in the world. In macOS Monterey, the App Store continues to evolve, expanding on the clean look introduced in macOS Mojave.

You'll find interesting new apps and recently updated apps in the Discover tab.

The Arcade tab is home to the Apple Arcade subscription service, which offers more than 180 games with no ads and no additional purchases for $5 a month. The best part: One subscription gets you games on all your devices: iPhones, iPads, and even Apple TVs!

The Create tab is chock full of apps for video, audio, photo creation, editing, and more. The Work tab contains productivity apps galore. And in the Play tab you'll discover lots of fun and games.

If you prefer to browse by specific categories, select the Categories tab and choose from nearly two dozen top-level categories, as shown in Figure 23-2.

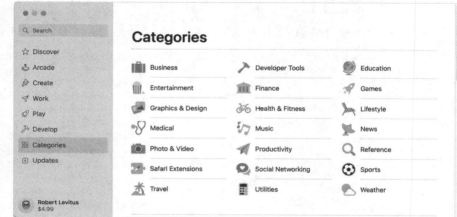

FIGURE 23-2:
The Categories tab lets you drill down from nearly two dozen categories.

When you click a category, you'll see two recommended apps at the top of the screen, followed by a pair of lists: Top Free and Top Paid. You can see only six apps at a time in each list, but when you hover your pointer over a section, Next and Previous icons appear, looking like giant greater than and less than symbols, as shown in Figure 23-3.

Finally, if any of your installed apps is in need of an update, you'll find them in the appropriately named Updates tab.

Just about everything I tell you in Chapter 19 about the iTunes Store could be said for the App Store. It works pretty much the same, and it uses the same credit card you have on file at the iTunes Store.

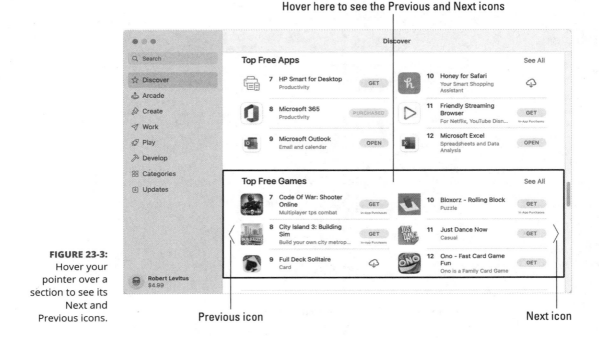

Hover here to see the Previous and Next icons

Previous icon

Next icon

FIGURE 23-3:
Hover your pointer over a section to see its Next and Previous icons.

If you see a little number on the App Store icon in your dock, it means that a number of your apps have updates available. Launch the App Store app and click the Updates tab to see the apps with updates awaiting them. Even if you don't see a little number on the App Store's dock icon, it wouldn't hurt to launch the App Store every once in a while to check for updates manually, as the little number sometimes fails to appear on the icon.

TIP

Using Your iPhone as Your Mac's Camera or Scanner

Continuity Camera is among Monterey's coolest and most useful features. It lets you use your iOS device as a camera or scanner for your Mac.

Before you try it, here are the rules:

>> Both devices (Mac and iDevice) must be logged into the same Apple ID and using two-factor authentication.

>> Both devices must be connected to the same Wi-Fi network.

>> Both devices must have Bluetooth enabled.

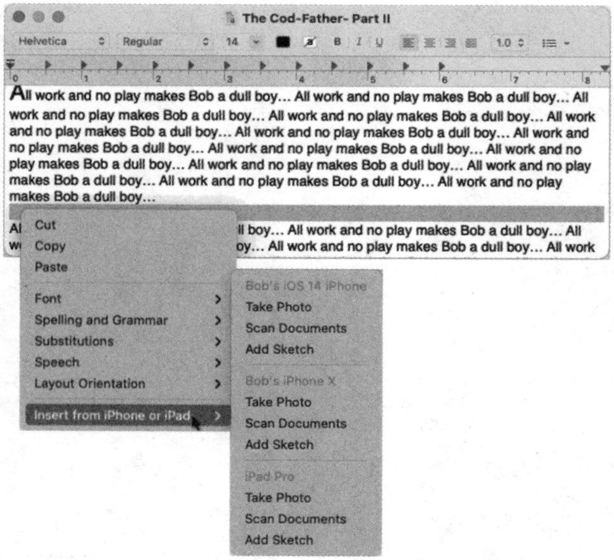

FIGURE 23-4:
If the app
supports
Continuity
Camera, the
Import from
iPhone or
iPad item will
appear in the
shortcut menu.

If you meet those criteria, you can use your iDevice as a camera or scanner and have the resulting photo or scan inserted in your document or saved to the Finder (almost) instantly.

To make the magic happen, just right- or Control-click anywhere an image or scan can be used (Notes, Stickies, TextEdit or Pages documents, and Finder, to name a few).

Not every app or document supports Continuity Camera, but if it's available when you right- or Control-click, you'll see an item called Import from iPhone or iPad in your shortcut menu, as shown in Figure 23-4.

Choose the device you want to use if you have more than one nearby. (I had three in Figure 23-4 — two iPhones and an iPad.) Choose Take Photo or Scan Documents.

If you choose Take Photo, the Camera app on your iDevice will launch automatically and you'll see one of two things on your Mac. If you right- or Control-clicked in a document, you'll see an overlay below the insertion point; if you right- or Control-clicked in Finder, you'll see a dialog instead of an overlay.

Take the photo on your iDevice by tapping the Camera app's shutter release button in the usual fashion. After you snap a shot, a preview appears offering two options: Retake or Use Photo. Tap Retake if you're dissatisfied with the image and want to try again. When you get a shot you're happy with, tap Use Photo and the shot appears in the document at the insertion point or on the desktop almost immediately.

Choosing Scan Documents is similar to taking a photo, with some minor differences. You'll still see an overlay or a dialog on your Mac, but this time it says Scan a Document rather than Take a Photo.

On your iDevice, however, the Camera app works differently. At the top-right corner is a button that toggles between Auto and Manual. In Auto mode, you move the camera up, down, and all around until the blue box contains the text you want to scan, as shown in Figure 23-5, left.

Or if you tap Auto (which switches the camera to Manual mode), you tap the shutter release button to capture text.

After you've captured a page, a preview of it appears, but in addition to the two buttons at the bottom of the screen — Retake or Keep Scan — a box appears with circles at each of its four corners, as shown in Figure 23-5, right. Drag the circles until the box contains all the text you want to scan, and then tap Keep Scan.

After you tap Keep Scan, the camera reappears with a message: *Ready for Next Scan.* If you have additional pages to scan, continue capturing them as described; when you're finished, tap Save in the lower-right corner.

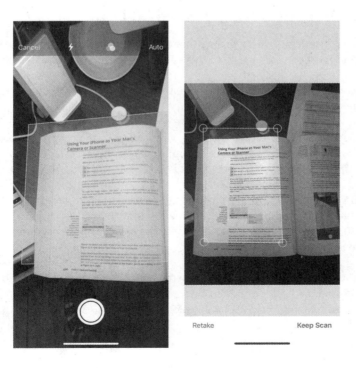

FIGURE 23-5:
Your iDevice captures the page automatically (left); drag the circles to contain the text you want to scan (right).

And that's all there is to using Continuity Camera to take pictures or scan documents with your Mac!

Talking and Listening to Your Mac

Your primary methods for interacting with your Mac are typing and reading text. But there's another way you can commune with your faithful computer: voice.

Whether you know it or not, your Mac has a lot of speech savvy up its sleeve (er . . . up its processors?) and can talk to you as well as listen. Believe it or not, it can type the words you speak and obey your spoken commands. And most of you already have a microphone built into your Mac unless your Mac happens to be a Mac mini or a Mac Pro, which require an external microphone to hear you speak.

In the following sections, you discover how to make your Mac do that and more.

Keyboard System Preferences pane: You talk and your Mac types

Some users still don't realize that dictation is available in macOS at no extra cost (and has been for years). In this section, you find out how to harness its power.

First, make sure Dictation is enabled in the Keyboard System Preferences pane's Dictation tab; if it's set to Off, click On.

TIP

Dictation requires an internet connection unless you enable Voice Control (formerly known as Speech Recognition) in the Accessibility System Preferences pane. Otherwise, when you dictate text, what you say is sent to Apple's servers for conversion to text. If you enable Voice Control, you can use Dictation without an internet connection after your Mac downloads the necessary files to your Mac. That's the good news. The bad news is that the necessary files are pretty big — a 1.2GB download that could take up to an hour or more depending on the speed of your network connection.

WARNING

Other information, such as your contacts, may also be sent to Apple over the internet to help your Mac understand what you're saying. If that makes you uncomfortable, you probably shouldn't use the Dictation feature without first enabling Voice Control.

After Dictation is enabled, with or without the Voice Control option, the feature couldn't be easier to use. First, click where you want your words to appear in a document, dialog, web form, or whatever, and then choose Edit⇨Start Dictation, or press the Fn key twice in rapid succession.

If your keyboard doesn't have an Fn key, click the Shortcut pop-up menu in the Keyboard System Preferences pane to change the shortcut to one that works with your keyboard.

When you start Dictation, a little microphone icon appears. The white filling indicates the level (relative loudness) of your voice. Try to keep the white near the middle — not too high and not too low, as shown in Figure 23-6.

FIGURE 23-6:
Volume levels for dictation (left to right): Too soft, just right, and too loud.

When you see the microphone icon, start speaking. After you dictate a few sentences, click Done and let your Mac catch up. When the words appear, you can start Dictation again. Repeat as necessary.

It might not be a bad idea to save your document after you speak a few sentences or paragraphs; if you don't, the words you dictated since your last Save will be lost if the app or your Mac crashes.

You can insert punctuation by speaking its name, such as "period" or "comma." You can also perform simple formatting by saying "new line" or "new paragraph" to add space between lines.

Here are a few more tips to help you get the best results when you dictate:

>> **Speak in a normal voice at a moderate volume level.** Try to keep the white in the microphone icon about half-full (or half-empty if you're a pessimist).

>> **Avoid background noise.** If you expect to use dictation in a noisy environment or a room with a lot of ambient echo, you should consider using a headset microphone.

>> **Be sure the microphone is not obstructed.** Check your Mac's User Guide for the location of your built-in microphone (if you have one).

>> **Be sure the input volume of an external microphone is sufficient.**
If you're using an external microphone and the white meter doesn't respond to your voice, select the microphone in the drop-down menu beneath the microphone in the Dictation tab of the Keyboard System Preferences pane.

Commanding your Mac by voice

Voice Control enables your Mac to recognize and respond to human speech. The only thing you need to use it is a microphone, which most of you have built right into your Mac (unless it's a Mac mini or Mac Pro as noted previously).

Voice Control lets you issue verbal commands such as "Get my mail!" to your Mac and have it actually get your email. You can also create AppleScripts and Automator workflows (described later in this chapter), and Finder Quick Actions (a feature I cover way back in Chapter 5) and trigger them by voice.

If you've enabled Voice Control, you can use speech commands to instruct your Mac. To see a list of commands your Mac will understand if you speak them, open the Accessibility System Preferences pane, click the Voice Control tab, and then click the Commands button. A sheet appears, in which you can enable or disable the available dictation commands, as shown in Figure 23-7.

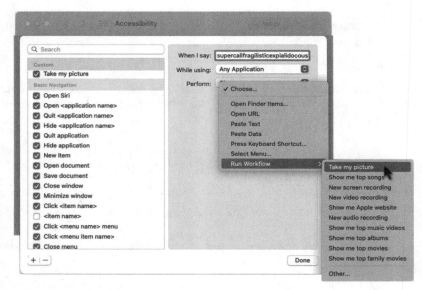

FIGURE 23-7:
The Dictation Commands sheet displaying some things your Mac will understand if you say them (properly). Usually.

TIP

If you have a laptop or an iMac, you may get better results from just about any third-party microphone or (better still) a headset with a microphone. The mic built into your Mac is okay, but it's not great. To select a third-party microphone, first connect the mic to your Mac. Then open the Sound System Preferences pane and select it from the list of sound input devices in the Input tab. Below the list is an input volume control (not available with some third-party mics) and a level meter. Adjust the Input Volume so that most of the dots in the Input Level meter darken (at least 11 out of the 15 dots).

You can also choose an external mic in the drop-down menu below the microphone in the Dictation tab of the Keyboard System Preferences pane. However, you'll need to use the Sound System Preferences pane if you want to adjust your input levels.

To give Voice Control a try, press Fn twice (or whatever shortcut you set earlier) and speak one of the items from the list of Voice Control commands, such as "Open TextEdit." If the command is recognized, it will appear in text above the microphone icon, as shown in Figure 23-8.

FIGURE 23-8:
Open TextEdit above the mic icon means your command was recognized.

This technology is clever and kind of fun, but it can also be frustrating when it doesn't recognize what you say, which occurs too often, if you ask me. And it requires a decent microphone even though the mic built into most Macs works okay. The bottom line is that I've never been able to get Voice Control to work well enough to continue using it beyond a few minutes at best. Still, it's kind of cool (and it's a freebie), and I've heard more than one user profess love for it. Which is why it's included here.

Listening to your Mac read your screen

The camera pans back. A voice tells you what you've just seen. And suddenly it all makes sense. Return with me now to those thrilling days of the off-camera narrator . . . . Wouldn't it be nice if your Mac had a narrator to provide a blow-by-blow account of what's happening on your screen?

Or your eyes are tired from a long day staring at the monitor, but you still have a lengthy document to read. Wouldn't it be sweet if you could sit back, close your eyes, and let your Mac read the document to you in a (somewhat) natural voice? Both are possible with macOS Monterey: the first scenario with VoiceOver, and the second with Text to Speech.

VoiceOver

Monterey's VoiceOver technology is designed primarily for the visually impaired, but you might find it useful even if your vision is 20/20. VoiceOver not only reads what's on the screen to you but also integrates with your keyboard so you can navigate around the screen until you *hear* the item you're looking for. When you're there, you can use Keyboard Access to select list items, select check boxes and radio buttons, move scroll bars and sliders, resize windows, and so on — all with just a simple key press or two.

To check it out, launch the System Preferences application (from Launchpad, the Applications folder, the menu, or the dock), click the Accessibility icon and then click VoiceOver or press ⌘+Fn+F5 on MacBook models and most Apple keyboards (or try ⌘+F5).

After VoiceOver is enabled, you can turn it on and off in the Accessibility System Preferences pane or by pressing ⌘+Fn+F5 or ⌘+F5.

While VoiceOver is on, your Mac talks to you about what is on your screen. For example, if you click the desktop, your Mac might say something along the lines of "Application, Finder; Column View; selected folder, Desktop, contains 8 items." It's quite slick. Here's another example: When you click a menu or an item on a menu, you hear its name spoken at once, and when you close a menu, you hear the words "Closing menu." You even hear the spoken feedback in the Print, Open, and Save (and other) dialogs.

VoiceOver is kind of cool (talking alerts are fun), but having dialogs actually produce spoken text becomes annoying fast for most folks who aren't visually impaired. (Those who are visually impaired, however, rave about VoiceOver and say it lets them do things they couldn't easily do in the past.) In any case, I urge you to check it out. You might like it and find times when you want your Mac to narrate the action onscreen for you.

Text to Speech

The second way your Mac can speak to you is via Text to Speech, which converts onscreen text to spoken words. If you've used Text to Speech in earlier versions of macOS, you'll find that it sounds slightly less robotic these days, but otherwise it's mostly unchanged.

Why might you need Text to Speech? Because sometimes hearing is better than reading. For example, I sometimes use Text to Speech to read aloud to me a column or page I've written before I submit it. If something doesn't sound quite right, I give it another polish before sending it off to my editor.

You can configure this feature in the Accessibility System Preferences pane:

1. **Open System Preferences (from Launchpad or the Applications folder, dock, or menu), click the Accessibility icon, and then click Spoken Content in the list on the left.**

2. **In the System Voice pop-up menu, choose one of the voices to set the voice your Mac uses when it reads to you.**

3. **Click the Play button to hear a sample of the voice you selected.**

4. **Use the Speaking Rate slider to speed up or slow down the voice.**

5. **Click the Play button to hear the voice at its new speed.**

   I really like Alex, who says, "Most people recognize me by my voice." My second favorite is Fred, who sounds like the Talking Moose and says, "I sure like being inside this fancy computer."

6. **(Optional) To make your Mac speak the text in alert boxes and dialogs, select the Speak Announcements check box.**

   You might hear such alerts as "The application Microsoft Word has quit unexpectedly" or "Paper out or not loaded correctly."

7. **(Optional) To make your Mac speak text you've selected in a document, select the Speak Selection check box.**

   The default keyboard shortcut for Speak Selection is Option+Esc, but you can assign any key combo you like by clicking the Options button and typing a different keyboard shortcut.

8. **(Optional) To make your Mac describe whatever is below the pointer, select the Speak Items Under Pointer check box.**

9. **(Optional) To make your Mac speak whatever you type, select the Speak Typing Feedback check box.**

10. **(Optional) To explore additional options for the previous four items, click its Options button.**

Now, to use Text to Speech to read text to you, copy the text to the Clipboard, launch any app that supports it (I usually choose TextEdit or Pages), paste the text into the empty untitled document, click where you want your Mac to begin reading to you, and then choose Edit ⇨ Speech ⇨ Start Speaking. To make it stop, choose Edit ⇨ Speech ⇨ Stop Speaking.

Another great place Text to Speech is available is in the Safari web browser. It works the same as TextEdit but you don't have to paste — just select the text you want to hear and choose Edit ⇨ Speech ⇨ Start Speaking.

TIP

If you don't care for the sound of the default voice, choose a different one in the Accessibility System Preferences pane. First click Spoken Content in the list on the left, and then choose a new voice from the System Voice drop-down menu or choose Customize to download additional voices.

Automatic Automation

macOS Monterey offers a trio of technologies — AppleScript, Automator, and Shortcuts — that make it easy to automate repetitive actions on your Mac. I mention Shortcuts in Chapter 14, but I'd be remiss if I didn't introduce you to AppleScript and Automator as well.

AppleScript is "programming for the rest of us." It can record and play back things that you do (if the application was written to allow the recording, such as Finder), such as opening an application or clicking a button. You can use it to record a script for tasks that you often perform, and then have your Mac perform those tasks for you later. You can write your own AppleScripts, use those that come with your Mac, or download still others from the web.

Automator is "programming without writing code." With Automator, you string together prefabricated activities (*actions*) to automate repetitive or scheduled tasks. How cool is that?

Automation isn't for everyone. Some users can't live without it; others could go their whole lives without ever automating anything. So the following sections are designed to help you figure out how much — or how little — you care about AppleScript and Automator.

Script Editor app: Write and edit AppleScripts

Describing AppleScript to a Mac beginner is a bit like three blind men describing an elephant. One man might describe it as the Mac's built-in automation tool. Another might describe it as an interesting but often-overlooked piece of enabling technology. The third might liken it to a cassette recorder, recording and playing back your actions at the keyboard. A fourth (if there were a fourth in the story) would assure you that it looked like computer code written in a high-level language.

They would all be correct. AppleScript, a built-in Mac automation tool, is a little-known (at least until recently) enabling technology that works like a cassette recorder for programs that support AppleScript recording. And scripts do look like computer programs. (Could that be because they *are* computer programs? Hmm . . . .)

If you're the kind of person who likes to automate as many things as possible, you might just love AppleScript because it's a simple programming language you can use to create programs that give instructions to your Mac and the applications running on your Mac. For example, you can create an AppleScript that launches Mail, checks for new messages, and then quits Mail. The script could even transfer your mail to a folder of your choice. Then there's Automator, which includes a whole lot of preprogrammed actions that make a task like the one just described even easier.

I call AppleScript a time–and–effort enhancer. If you just spend the time and effort it takes to understand it, using AppleScript can save you oodles of time and effort down the road. Therein lies the rub. This stuff is far from simple; entire books have been written on the subject. So it's far beyond the purview of *macOS Monterey For Dummies.* Still, it's worth finding out about if you'd like to script repetitive actions for future use. To get you started, here are a few quick tips:

>> **Script Editor (in the Utilities folder in the Applications folder) is the application you use to create, edit, and view AppleScripts.** Although more information on Script Editor is beyond the scope of this book, it's a lot of fun. And the cool thing is that you can create many AppleScripts without knowing a thing about programming. Just record a series of actions you want to repeat and use Script Editor to save what you recorded as a script. If you save your script as an application (by choosing Format⇨Application in the Save sheet), you can run that script by double-clicking its icon.

>> **You can put frequently used AppleScripts on the dock or on your desktop for easy access.**

>> **Many AppleScripts are designed for use on the toolbar of Finder windows, where you can drag and drop items onto them quickly and easily.**

>> **Scripts can enhance your use of many apps, including iTunes, iPhoto, and Finder, to name a few.**

>> **Apple provides a script menu extra that you can install on your menu bar in the Script Editor's Preferences window,** along with a number of free scripts to automate common tasks (in the Scripts folder in the root-level Library, or choose Open Example Scripts Folder from the Script Editor's Help menu).

>> **If the concept of scripting intrigues you, I suggest that you explore the examples in the Scripts folder (in the root-level Library or choose Open Example Scripts from the Script Editor's Help menu).** Rummage through this folder and when you find a script that looks interesting, double-click it to launch the Script Editor program, where you can examine it more closely.

Automator app: Automate almost anything

Automator does just what you'd expect: It enables you to automate many common tasks on your Mac. If it sounds a little like AppleScript to you (which I discuss in the preceding section), you're not mistaken; the two have a common goal. But this tool is a lot simpler to use, albeit somewhat less flexible, than AppleScript.

For example, in AppleScript, you can have *conditionals* ("if *this* is true, do *that*; otherwise do something else"), but Automator is purely *sequential* ("take *this*, do *that*, then do the next thing, and then . . .").

The big difference is that conditionals allow AppleScripts to take actions involving *decision-making* and *iteration* ("while *this* is true, do *these* things"); Automator workflows can't make decisions or iterate.

The upsides to Automator are that you don't have to know anything about programming, and you don't have to type any archaic code. Instead, if you understand the process you want to automate, you can just drag and drop Automator's prefab actions into place and build a *workflow* (Automator's name for a series of actions).

REMEMBER

You do need to know one thing about programming (or computers), though: *Computers are stupid!* You heard me right — even my top-of-the-line MacBook Pro is dumb as a post. Computers do only what you tell them to do even though they can do it faster and more precisely than you can. But all computers run on the GIGO principle (Garbage In, Garbage Out), so if your instructions are flawed, you're almost certain to get flawed results.

When you launch the Automator application, click the New Document button and the window and sheet shown in Figure 23-9 appear. Choose one of the starting points if you want Automator to assist you in constructing a new workflow; or, choose Workflow to start building a workflow from scratch.

I'm going to choose Quick Action for the sake of this demonstration (you'll see why in a second). When I select Quick Action and click the Choose button, I see the window shown in Figure 23-10.

The Library pane on the far left contains all the applications Automator knows about that have Actions defined for them. Select an application in the top part of the Library window, and its related actions appear below it. When you select an action, the pane at the bottom of the Library window (Text to Audio File in Figure 23-10) explains what that Action does, what input it expects, and what result it produces. Just drag Actions from the Action list into the window on the right to build your workflow.

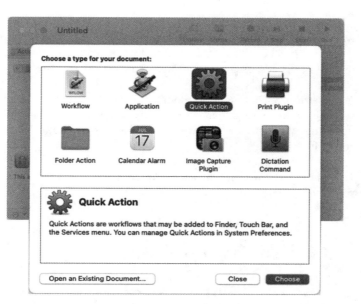

FIGURE 23-9:
Choose Workflow
if you want to
start a workflow
from scratch.

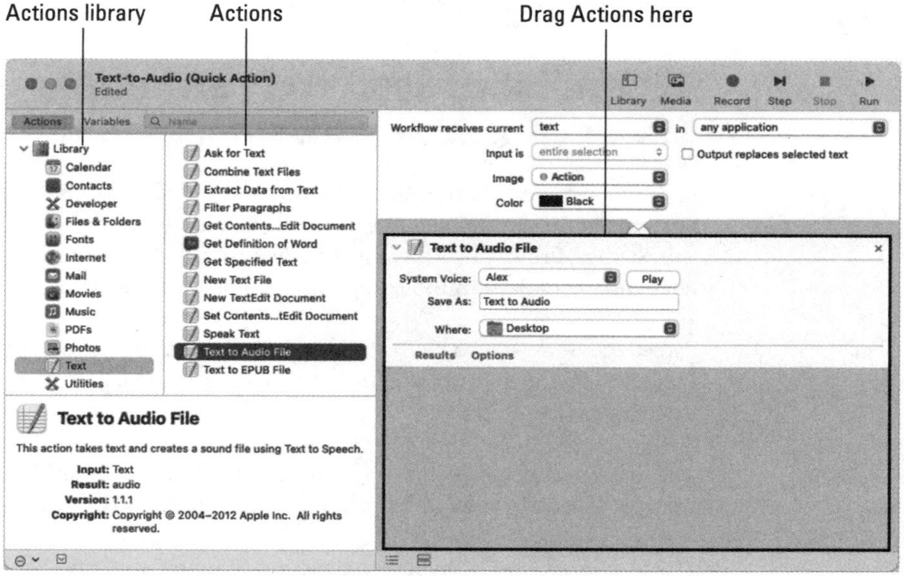

Actions library　　　Actions　　　　　　　　Drag Actions here

FIGURE 23-10:
This converts text
that I select to an
audio file.

This particular Quick Action, which took me less than five minutes of trial and error to perfect, is quite useful. First, I select text from any source — a web page, a Microsoft Word document, an email message, or whatever. Then I choose Services from the Application menu or right- or Control-click and select my newly created Text to Audio Quick Action from the Services menu. My Automator workflow then converts the selected text into an audio file and saves it to the desktop. Then I can have it read to me by the Music app at home, or on my iPhone or iPad in the car, on a plane, or just about anywhere. Sweet!

Automator is a useful addition to macOS; it's deep, powerful, and expandable, yet relatively easy to use and master. Do yourself a favor, and spend some time experimenting with ways Automator can save you time and keystrokes. You won't regret it.

TIP

For additional information about AppleScript, Automator, Services, and much more, visit www.macosxautomation.com.

A Few More Useful Goodies

Even more neat and useful technologies are built into Monterey, but I'm running out of space. So here are, at least in my humble opinion, the final handful of apps and utilities that may be useful, at least for some of you.

Accessibility System Preferences pane: Make your Mac more accessible

If you've read the chapter to this point, you got a brief glimpse of the Accessibility System Preferences pane when I discussed commanding your Mac by voice. But this System Preferences pane is mostly designed for users with disabilities or who have difficulty handling the keyboard, mouse, or trackpad.

TIP

Select the Show Accessibility Status in Menu Bar check box at the bottom of the window on the left to see the status of all Accessibility Preferences in your menu bar.

The pane has four sections listed on the left — Vision, Hearing, Motor, and General — each of which has one or more subsections.

The Vision section's Display subsection lets you alter the behavior of the screen display. For example, in the Color Filters tab you can choose Grayscale as your filter type, which will desaturate your screen into a *grayscale display* (so it looks kind of like a black-and-white TV).

Or click the Display subsection's Display tab (I know — confusing as heck) and select the check box to Invert Colors, which reverses the colors you see onscreen— an interesting if not always useful effect.

TIP

Click Display in the Vision section on the left and then click the Cursor tab at the top to enable the Shake Mouse Pointer to Locate check box. When enabled, the pointer grows much larger and becomes easier to see whenever you wiggle the mouse back and forth quickly a couple of times. Or drag the Cursor size slider to the right to enlarge the pointer at all times.

The Vision section's Zoom subsection is where you can turn on a terrific feature called *hardware zoom*, which lets you make things on your screen bigger by zooming in on them. To control it by keyboard, select the Use Keyboard Shortcuts to Zoom check box. Then you can toggle it on and off with the shortcut ⌘+Option+8 and zoom in and out using the shortcuts ⌘+Option+= (equal sign) and ⌘+Option+− (hyphen), respectively. Next, select a style — Full Screen, Split Screen, or Picture-in-Picture — from the Zoom Style pop-up menu. Enable the check box for Hover Text to display a preview rectangle under the pointer.

Finally, click the Advanced and Options button for additional options and controls.

Try this feature even if you're not disabled or challenged in any way; it's actually a great feature for everyone.

REMEMBER

You looked at the Vision section's VoiceOver subsection earlier in the chapter.

I leave it to you, gentle reader, to explore the remaining sections and subsections of the Accessibility System Preferences pane at your leisure. Until then, you might find the following useful:

>> **If you want the screen to flash whenever an alert sound occurs, choose Audio and then select the Flash the Screen When an Alert Sound Occurs check box.**

>> **To treat a *sequence* of modifier keys as a key combination, choose Keyboard and then select the Enable Sticky Keys check box.**

In other words, you don't have to simultaneously hold down ⌘ while pressing another key. For example, with Sticky Keys enabled, you can do a standard keyboard shortcut by pressing ⌘, releasing it, and then pressing the other key. You can select check boxes to tell you (with a beep and/or an onscreen display) what modifier keys have been pressed.

TIP

As useful as Sticky Keys can be, they're really awkward in applications like Adobe Photoshop, Adobe Illustrator, and other applications that toggle a tool's state when you press a modifier key. So if you're a big Photoshop user, you probably don't want Sticky Keys enabled.

>> **To adjust the delay between a keypress and its activation, choose Keyboard and then select the Slow Keys check box.**

Battery and Energy Saver System Preferences panes: For energy conservation and sleep

The Battery (notebooks) and Energy Saver (desktops) System Preferences panes are where you manage your Mac's energy-saving features.

All Macs are Energy Star–compliant (and have been for years), so the Battery and Energy Saver System Preferences panes let you do things such as turn your Mac off at a specific time or after a specified idle period.

The Battery System Preferences pane (notebooks only)

To get started, open System Preferences and click the Battery icon.

On the left you'll see a list of items specific to your Mac. Click Usage History to see your battery charge levels for the past 24 hours or past 10 days. Click Battery to control your notebook Mac's behavior when it's running on battery power (not plugged in); click Power Adapter to control its behavior when it *is* plugged in.

TIP

Turning off the display is handy if you want your Mac to keep doing what it's doing but you don't need to see its monitor. And if you're a notebook user, turning off the display will preserve your battery.

To wake up your display, merely move your mouse or press any key. Sometimes moving the mouse or a finger on the trackpad won't wake a sleeping Mac but a keystroke will. So try both (or all three) before you give up.

Below the Turn Display Off After slider in the Battery and Power Adapter panes are check boxes for other battery-related settings such as:

>> **Slightly Dim the Display While on Battery Power (Battery pane):** The display dims slightly and uses less power when running on the battery.

>> **Optimize Video Streaming While on Battery Power (Battery pane):** Reduce battery use while streaming video.

>> **Prevent Computer from Sleeping Automatically When the Display Is Off (Power Adapter pane):** Prevents sleep when the lid is closed and the display is off.

>> **Wake for Network Access (Power Adapter pane):** Enable this option if you want your Mac to wake up automatically for network access.

>> **Low Power Mode (Power Adapter and Battery panes):** This option reduces energy usage to increase battery life.

>> **Show Battery Status in the Menu Bar (Battery pane):** This option adds a little battery-status indicator icon and menu.

Finally, to start up, shut down, or put your Mac to sleep at a predetermined time, click the Schedule button and then select the appropriate check box and choose the appropriate options from the pop-up menus.

Energy Saver System Preferences pane (desktops only)

To start, open System Preferences and click the Energy Saver icon. Below the Turn Display Off After slider are check boxes for its energy-related settings:

>> **Prevent Computer from Sleeping Automatically When the Display Is Off**

>> **Put Hard Disks to Sleep When Possible**

>> **Wake for Network Access**

>> **Start Up Automatically After a Power Failure**

>> **Enable Power Nap**

>> **Prevent Computer from Sleeping Automatically When the Display Is Off**

>> **Wake for Network Access**

Bluetooth System Preferences pane: Where Bluetooth lives

Bluetooth is wireless networking for low-bandwidth peripherals, including mice, keyboards, and mobile phones. If your Mac has Bluetooth built in or is equipped with a USB Bluetooth adapter, you can synchronize wirelessly with phones and Palm devices, print wirelessly to Bluetooth printers, and use Bluetooth headsets, mice, and keyboards.

To manage your Mac's Bluetooth features, open the Bluetooth System Preferences pane by choosing ➪ System Preferences and clicking the Bluetooth icon.

Ink System Preferences pane: Visible to pen-input tablet users only

Ink is the macOS built-in handwriting-recognition engine. Sadly, it works only if a third-party drawing tablet with a stylus is connected. Even more sadly, "tablet" in this sense doesn't include your iPad (at least not so far . . .).

To write instead of type, enable Ink in this pane and you'll be able to handwrite anywhere your Mac accepts typing with the keyboard.

To manage your Mac's Ink features, open the Ink System Preferences pane by choosing System Preferences and clicking the Ink icon.

TIP

The Ink pane is one you see only if you have one of the pen-input drawing tablets that Ink supports connected to your Mac. Most of the supported drawing tablets come from Wacom (www.wacom.com), with prices starting under $100 for a small wireless stylus and drawing tablet.

Automatic Login in the Users & Groups System Preferences pane: Don't bother with the login screen

Some users don't care for the fact that macOS Monterey is a multiuser operating system and dislike having to log in when they start up their Mac. For those users, here's a way to disable the login screen:

1. **Open the Users & Groups System Preferences pane, select yourself in the list of users, and click the Login Options button below the list.**

    Click the lock and provide your password first, if necessary.

2. **Choose the account you want to be logged in to automatically from the Automatic Login pop-up menu.**

    To disable the logging-in requirement, you have to be an administrator, and you may need to unlock the Users & Groups System Preferences pane.

WARNING

When you disable logging in, you also affect all the preferences set by other people who use your Mac unless they log out of your account and log into theirs. (Yikes.) So if your desktop pattern, keyboard settings, and so forth are different from those of someone else who uses your Mac, those preferences won't be properly reflected unless each of you has a separate, individual login account. Even if you're not particularly worried about security, consider keeping logging in enabled if any other users have accounts on your machine, or if you don't want just anyone to be able to turn on your Mac and see your personal stuff.

Note that only one account is allowed to use auto-login. If another user wants to use this Mac, you need to choose ⌥ Log Out, press ⌘+Shift+Q, or have Fast User Switching enabled. And if you've disabled automatic login in the Security System Preferences pane, you can't enable it here.

Allow your Apple Watch to unlock your Mac

If you have an Apple Watch, you'll love this feature. Enable the Allow Your Apple Watch to Unlock Your Mac check box in the Security & Privacy System Preferences pane's General tab, and you can just walk up to your Mac while wearing your unlocked Apple Watch and be automatically logged into your user account without typing your password!

I use it a million times a day and it is sweet!

Boot Camp Assistant app: Run Windows on your Mac . . . really

Boot Camp is Monterey's built-in technology that allows you to run Microsoft Windows 10 and (on some Mac models) Windows 7 or 8 on Monterey–capable Macs with Intel processors. If your Mac meets the following requirements, you can run Windows on your Mac (if you so desire):

>> A Monterey–capable Mac (of course) with an Intel processor

>> A hard drive that isn't already partitioned

>> (Optional) A printer (for printing the instructions)

  It's optional 'cause you could just email them to yourself . . . .

>> A full install copy of Microsoft Windows 8 Home Premium, Professional, or Ultimate edition or Windows 10

REMEMBER

You really do need a *full retail* copy of Windows: one that was purchased in a retail box. If your copy of Windows came with your PC, you probably can't install it in Boot Camp.

To install Windows on your Mac, here are the basic steps:

1. **Launch the Boot Camp Assistant application, which is in your Utilities folder.**

   This step creates a partition on your hard drive for your Windows installation. Note that you may not find it on Macs with Apple processors (and if you did, it wouldn't work anyway as described shortly).

2. **Install Windows on the new partition.**

   From now on, you can hold down Option during startup and choose to start up from either the macOS Monterey disk partition or the new Windows partition.

TIP

If running Windows on your Mac appeals to you, you may want to check out Parallels Desktop (around $80) or VirtualBox (free). Both programs allow you to run Windows — even older versions like XP and Vista — as well as Linux on your Mac without partitioning your hard drive or restarting every time you want to use Windows. In fact, you can run Mac and Windows programs simultaneously with these products.

WARNING

In late 2020, Apple began selling Macs with custom Apple processors (known as M1 chips) instead of the Intel processors it's been using for two decades. One of the side effects of this transition is that Boot Camp will not be an option if your Mac has an Apple processor. While emulation and virtualization are both viable via third-party software such as Parallels Desktop, running Windows natively under Boot Camp just won't work.

One last thing: Apple has a special Boot Camp support page on the web at http://www.apple.com/support/bootcamp/.

AirPlay and AirPlay to Mac

NEW

AirPlay is the screen-mirroring feature that lets you stream what's on your Mac (or iDevice) screen to an Apple TV or smart TVs with built-in AirPlay. New in Monterey is AirPlay to Mac, which lets you stream photos or videos from a Mac or iDevice to a Monterey-equipped Mac.

The Mac running Monterey is also available as an AirPlay audio speaker, so you can stream music from another Mac (or iDevice) to a Monterey-equipped Mac as easily as you can stream to an Apple TV or smart TV with AirPlay.

To select a device to stream to — a Mac (running Monterey), an Apple TV, or a smart TV with Airplay — go to the Displays System Preferences pane and select the device in the Add Display pop-up menu.

Or enable the Show Mirroring Options in the Menu Bar When Available check box in the Dock & Menu Bar System Preferences pane, which adds a handy menu, shown in Figure 23-11, and lets you choose an AirPlay receiver without visiting the Displays System Preferences pane.

Screen Mirroring

Bob's M1 MacBook Air

Den

Bedroom

Display Preferences...

FIGURE 23-11:
The AirPlay menu makes life much easier for AirPlay users like me.

The bad news is that many older Macs — including my wife's eight-year-old MacBook Pro — don't support mirroring.

Handoff

The Handoff feature lets you start working on a document, an email, or a message on any Apple device and pick up where you left off on another device. To enable it, open System Preferences, click the General icon, and enable the check box to Allow Handoff between This Mac and Your iCloud Devices.

Now make sure that you're signed into iCloud with the same Apple ID on your Mac and iOS device(s) and that Bluetooth is enabled on all devices.

Handoff works with Apple apps, including Mail, Safari, Maps, Messages, Reminders, Calendar, Contacts, Pages, Numbers, and Keynote, as well as a handful of third-party apps. When another Handoff-enabled device is nearby and using one of these apps, you'll see an icon for it on the right side of the dock, as shown in Figure 23-12.

If I click that icon (note the tiny phone on it), Messages on my Mac will open and display the message or reply that's currently on my iPhone screen.

FIGURE 23-12:
My iPhone is
nearby and
using the
Messages app.

Universal Control

NEW

New in Monterey is Universal Control, which lets you control your nearby iPad with the keyboard, mouse, and trackpad from your Mac. Sadly, that's all I can tell you because this feature, like the SharePlay feature I mention in Chapter 16, wasn't available for testing when this book was printed.

The best I can do is once again invite you to visit www.dummies.com and type **macOS Monterey For Dummies Cheat Sheet** in the Search box. The cheat sheet will (soon) include articles entitled "How to Use Universal Control" and "How to Use SharePlay."

» Discovering why you should back up

» Finding out what happens to you if you don't back up

» Keeping your Mac safe from rogue viruses and malicious attacks

» Protecting your data from prying eyes

Chapter **24**

Safety First: Backups and Other Security Issues

Although Macs are generally reliable, someday your SSD (or hard drive) will die. It's not an if, it's a when—*all* disks will die someday. And if you don't back up *your* drive (or at least back up any files that you can't afford to lose) before that day comes, chances are good those files are gone forever.

In other words, you absolutely, positively, without question *must back up* your files if you don't want to risk losing them. Just as you adopt the Shut Down command and make it a habit before turning off your machine, you must remember to back up important files on your hard drive to another disk or device — and back them up often.

How often is often? That depends on you. How much work can you afford to lose? If your answer is that losing everything you did yesterday would put you out of business, you need to back up hourly or perhaps even continuously. If you would lose only a few unimportant documents if your hard drive died today, you can probably back up less frequently.

Following the comprehensive coverage of backup options, I explain the possible threat to your data from viruses and other icky things, as well as how you can protect against them.

Finally, I cover what you can do to keep other people from looking at your stuff.

WARNING

One last thing: If you turn on FileVault (described later in this chapter) and forget both your login password and your master password, your data is lost forever. Really. Not even DriveSavers (world-class data recovery experts) or Apple can recover it, so don't forget those passwords, okay?

Backing Up Is (Not) Hard to Do

You can back up your hard drive in basically three ways: the super-painless way with Monterey's excellent built-in Time Machine, the ugly way using the brute-force method, or the comprehensive way with specialized third-party backup and disk-cloning software. Read on and find out more about all three.

Backing up with Monterey's excellent Time Machine

Time Machine is an excellent backup system that has become better and more reliable since its introduction more than a decade ago. I say it's a *system* because it consists of two parts: the Time Machine System Preferences pane, shown in Figure 24-1, and the Time Machine application, shown in Figure 24-2.

To use Time Machine to back up your data automatically, the first thing you need is another disk that's larger than your startup disk. The disk can connect via USB 2, USB 3, or Thunderbolt, and can be your choice of hard drive or SSD (if you can afford to use a solid-state drive for backups).

To select a drive to use with Time Machine, open the Time Machine System Preferences pane, click the Select Backup Disk button, and then select the drive you want to use for your backups. Mine is called Time for a Backup in Figure 24-1.

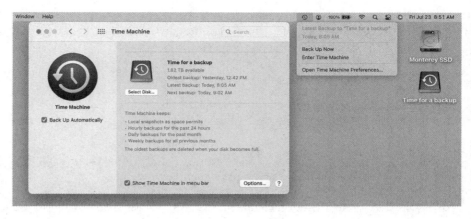

FIGURE 24-1:
The Time
Machine System
Preferences pane
and menu.

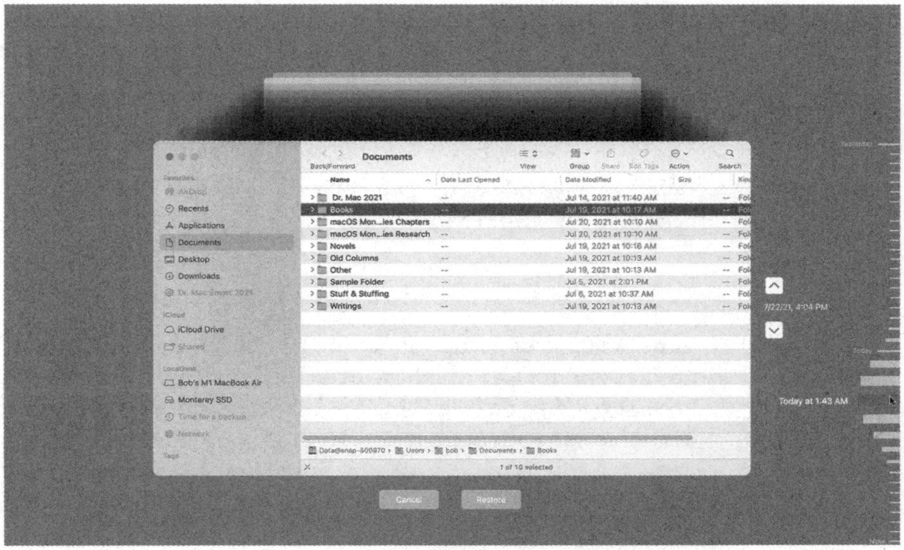

FIGURE 24-2:
The Time
Machine
application is
ready to restore a
folder in Finder.

Additional consideration

The only other consideration is this: If you have other hard drives connected to your Mac, you should click the Options button to reveal the Exclude These Items from Backups list, which tells Time Machine which volumes (disks) or folders *not* to back up. To add a volume or folder to this exclusion list, click the little + icon; to remove a volume from the list, select the volume and then click the – icon.

If your Mac is a laptop, the Options sheet also offers a check box to enable Time Machine backups when on battery power (disabled by default).

For the record, Time Machine stores your backups for the following lengths of time:

>> Hourly backups for the past 24 hours

>> Daily backups for the past month

>> Weekly backups until your backup disk is full

When your backup disk gets nearly full, Time Machine will intelligently delete the oldest backups and replace them with the newest.

TIP

That's why I recommend that you buy the biggest drive you can afford to use as your backup disk; otherwise Time Machine will be deleting backups all the time rather than archiving them for future use.

When does Time Machine run? Glad you asked! It runs approximately once per hour. If it gets stuck and forgets to run for any reason, use the Backup Now command in the Time Machine menu to get it going again.

TIP

If you enable and set up Time Machine as I just described, you'll never forget to back up your stuff, so just do it.

What does Time Machine back up?

Time Machine backs up your entire hard drive the first time it runs and then backs up files and folders that have been modified since your last backup. That's what backup systems do. But Time Machine does more — it also backs up things such as contacts in your Contacts, pictures in your Photos library, events in your calendars, and emails in your Mail, not to mention its support of versions and locking. About the only thing Time Machine doesn't back up is the content of Home folders other than your own.

Those features — sweet ones, indeed — make Time Machine unlike any other backup system.

How do I restore a file (or a contact, a photo, an event, and so on)?

To restore a file or any other information, follow these steps:

1. **Launch the program that contains the information you want to restore.**

If you want to restore a file, that program is Finder, which (as you know) is always running. So to restore an individual file, you don't need to launch anything; just switch to Finder if it's not the active application. But to restore a contact, a photo, an email message, or an event, for example, you need to launch Contacts, Photos, Mail, or Calendar, respectively.

2. **With the appropriate application running (or the appropriate Finder window open), launch the Time Machine application (refer to Figure 24-2).**

   If you selected the Show Time Machine in Menu Bar check box in the Time Machine System Preferences pane (refer to Figure 24-1), you can choose the Enter Time Machine option from the Time Machine menu (also shown in Figure 24-1).

TIP

   It will be easier to restore a file in Finder if the folder that the file is in (or was in) is the *active* folder (that is, open and frontmost) when you launch the Time Machine application. Otherwise, you have to navigate to the appropriate folder before you can perform Step 3.

3. **Click one of the bars with dates near the lower-right corner of the screen *or* click the big Forward or Back arrow on the right of the Documents window in Figure 24-2 to choose a backup to restore (Today at 1:43 AM in Figure 24-2).**

TIP

4. **Select the file, folder, Contacts contact, Photos photo, email message, or Calendar event you want to restore.**

5. **Click the Restore button below the window.**

If the file, folder, Contacts contact, Photos photo, email message, or Calendar event exists in the same location on your startup disk, Time Machine politely asks what you want to do: Replace the original, keep the original, or keep them both.

TIP

Don't forget that you can search for files or folders in Time Machine by typing a word or phrase in the Search field of the active (frontmost) window.

Backing up by using the manual, brute-force method

If you think you're too cheap to buy a big hard drive, consider this: Amazon.com has numerous 4TB external USB 3 hard drives for under $100. And if you can get by with a 2TB backup drive, prices start at around $60. By the way, these prices go down regularly, so by the time you read this they may be even cheaper.

Face it — a backup disk is a lot cheaper than data recovery (which can run hundreds if not thousands of dollars). So bite the bullet and buy the biggest backup disk you can justify.

If you're still not convinced, you should consider at least backing up important files manually.

You accomplish this by dragging said files a few at a time to another volume — usually another hard drive or solid-state drive, a USB flash drive, or a burned-to-optical media such as a DVD-R or DVD-RW. (If you use an optical disc, don't forget to actually *burn the disc*; merely dragging those files onto the optical disc icon won't do the trick.) By using this method, you're making a copy of each file that you want to protect.

WARNING

Yuck! If doing a manual backup sounds pretty awful, trust me — it is. This method can take a long, long time, you can't really tell if you've copied every file that needs to be backed up, and you can't really copy only the files that have been modified since your last backup.

Almost nobody in their right mind sticks with this method for long.

TIP

Of course, if you're careful to save files only in your Documents folder, as I suggest several times in this book, you can probably get away with backing up only that. Or if you save files in other folders within your Home folder or have any files in your Movies, Music, Pictures, or Sites folders (which often contain files you didn't specifically save in those folders, such as your Photos app pictures and Music app songs), you should probably consider backing up your entire Home folder.

As you read in the following section, backing up your Home folder is even easier if you use special backup software.

Backing up by using commercial backup software

Another way to back up your files is with a third-party backup program. Backup software automates the task of backing up, remembering what's on each backup disc (if your backup uses more than one disc), and backing up only files that have been modified since your last backup.

Furthermore, you can instruct your backup software to back up only a certain folder (Home or Documents) and to ignore the hundreds of megabytes of stuff that make up macOS, all of which you can easily reinstall from your Recovery disk or the Mac App Store.

Your first backup with commercial software might take anywhere from a few minutes to several hours and use one or more optical discs (CD-R, CD-RW, DVD-R, DVD-RW, magneto-optical disc) or non-optical media (such as another hard drive or any kind of tape). Subsequent backups, *incremental backups* in backup software parlance, should be much faster.

TIP

If you do incremental backups with optical discs, be sure to clearly label and number all the discs you use during that operation. Your backup software may prompt you with a message such as *Please insert backup disk 7*. If you haven't labeled your media clearly, you could have a problem figuring out which disc *is* disc 7 or which disc 7 belongs to that particular backup set.

One of the best things about good backup software is that you can set it up to automate your backups and perform them even if you forget. And although Time Machine is a step in the right direction and might be sufficient for your needs, it's not good enough for me. I use a total of five hard drives for backups.

Why You Need Two Sets of Backups

You're a good soldier. You listened to Dr. Mac and you back up regularly. You think you're immune to file loss or damage.

Now picture yourself in the following scenario:

>> You leave the office one day for lunch. When you return, you discover that your office has been burglarized, struck by lightning, flooded, burned to the ground, or buried in earthquake rubble — take your pick.

>> Alas, although you did have a backup, the backup disk was right next to your Mac, which means it was either stolen or destroyed along with your Mac and everything else.

This scenario is unlikely — but it *could* happen, and it does demonstrate why you need multiple backups. If you have several sets of backup disks, and don't keep them all in the same room as your Mac, chances are pretty good that one of the sets will work even if the others are lost, stolen, or destroyed.

TIP

I believe you need at least three sets of backups, with at least one of them stored offsite. I have a full backup that I update monthly in a safe deposit box at my bank. And I use a cloud-based backup service called Backblaze (`www.backblaze.com`), a second offsite backup for just $7 per month (or $70 per year), which I consider a bargain.

If you're religious about storing all your files in the Documents folder or the desktop, you can store your Desktop and Documents folders in iCloud, which counts as another offsite backup (kinda). To do that, launch System Preferences, click Apple ID, click the Options button next to iCloud Drive, and then enable the check box for Desktop & Documents Folders.

One last thing: You have the option of encrypting Time Machine backups (which isn't a bad idea if you're security conscious). Just enable the appropriate check box in the Select Disk sheet in the Time Machine System Preferences pane.

Non-Backup Security Concerns

As you probably surmised by now, backing up your files is critical unless you don't mind losing all your data someday. And although backing up is by far your most important security concern, several other things could imperil your data — things such as viruses or other types of malware, including worms, spyware, and intruder attacks. That's the bad news. The good news is that all those things are far more likely to affect Windows users than Mac users. In fact, I'd venture to say that viruses, worms, malware, spyware, and intruder attacks are rarer than hens' teeth for Mac users.

That said, here are a few precautions Mac users should consider, just in case.

About viruses and other malware

A computer *virus* is a nasty little piece of computer code that replicates and spreads from disk to disk. A virus could cause your Mac to misbehave; some viruses can destroy files or erase disks with no warning.

Malware (short for *malicious software*) is software that's hostile, intrusive, annoying, or disruptive. Malware is often designed to gain unauthorized access to your computer or collect personal data (including passwords) without your knowledge or both.

The difference between a virus and other types of malware is that malware doesn't spread by itself. It relies upon trickery, mimicry, and social engineering to induce unsuspecting users to open a malicious file or install a malicious program. So a virus is a type of malware, but not all malware is viral.

You don't hear as much about viruses on the Mac because there have been few since the dawn of the Mac operating system (so many big cats and California landmarks ago). Almost all viruses are specific to an operating system — Mac viruses won't affect Windows users, Windows viruses won't affect Mac users, and so forth. And the vast majority of known viruses affect only (you guessed it) Windows.

The one real exception here is a "gift" from the wonderful world of Microsoft Office (Word and Excel, for example) users: the dreaded *macro viruses* that are spread with Word and Excel documents containing macros written in the Microsoft VBA (Visual Basic for Applications) language. But you're safe even from those if you practice safe computing as I describe (although you can unknowingly pass them along to Windows users).

Much of the viral activity affecting the Mac operating system involved various Windows macro viruses. Sadly, a very real threat known as Flashback appeared in 2012. It exploited a security flaw in Java and stealthily installed itself on Macs. Soon after its discovery, Apple issued software updates for the Mac operating system that removed the malware and corrected the security flaw. Numerous similar instances have occurred since then, but in every case Apple has patched the operating system before many (or any) users were affected (or infected).

TIP

By default, your Mac automatically checks for software updates daily. To force it to check for updates now, just open the Software Update System Preferences pane. In my humble opinion, it's usually a good idea to install most Apple updates sooner rather than later.

Although few truly viral Mac operating system threats have been spotted in the wild so far, most malware is spread via social engineering, which is easy to protect yourself against; here's how:

>> On the Safari Preferences General tab, disable the Open Safe Files after Downloading check box.

>> If a suspicious alert or window appears on your screen whilst browsing the internet, Force Quit your web browser (⌘⇨ Force Quit or ⌘+Option+Esc) immediately.

>> If the macOS Installer launches for no apparent reason, *do not click Continue!* Don't install the software, and for heaven's sake, don't type your administrator password.

>> Don't run *any* installer — the kind built into macOS or the third-party kind — unless you're absolutely certain that it came from a trusted source.

>> Don't use credit or debit cards with unfamiliar vendors or nonsecure websites. (For example, if you don't see https instead of http, or you don't see a little lock icon in the address field of your browser, the site may not be secure.)

>> And by all means read the section on Monterey's Gatekeeper later in this chapter for details on the three different levels of protection it can offer.

REMEMBER

If you use disks that have ever been inserted into a computer you don't know and trust, you may need virus-detection software. If you download and use files from the internet, you'll be well-served by virus detection as well.

You don't have too much to worry about if

>> You download files only from commercial online services, such as CNET or MacUpdate, which are all conscientious about malware.

>> You buy software from only the App Store.

>> You use only commercial software, and never download files from websites with strange names.

You should definitely worry about malicious infection if

>> An unsavory friend told you about a website called PiratedIllegalStolenBootlegSoftware.com, and you actually visited it.

>> You swap disks or USB thumb drives with friends regularly.

>> You shuttle disks or USB thumb drives back and forth to other Macs.

>> You use your disks or USB thumb drives at public computers, photo-printing machines, or other computers likely to have had exposure to many disks.

>> You download files from various and sundry places on the internet, even ones that don't sound as questionable as PiratedIllegalStolenBootlegSoftware.com.

>> You receive email with attachments (and open them). Note that you can receive malicious software in messages that look like they're from people you know and trust. It's called *spoofing* and it's easily accomplished, so think carefully before opening an attachment and contact the sender if you have any doubt about the message's authenticity.

If you're at risk, do yourself a favor and buy a commercial antivirus program. Or try a free malware scanner such as Malwarebytes, Bitdefender, or Avira. If you think you might be at risk, scan your drive with one of the free utilities before shelling out any cash. I'm not quite ready to run antivirus software on my Mac full-time, but I do run Malwarebytes occasionally. For the record, it rarely finds anything amiss, and the few so-called malware files it caught were benign. Get it if you need it; don't if you don't.

Install recommended software updates

I mention this earlier in a short tip, but it bears repeating: By default, your Mac checks with the mothership (Apple) once a day to look for any new or updated software. If there is, your Mac informs you that a new software update is available and asks whether you'd like to install it. In almost all cases, you do. Apple issues software updates to fix newly discovered security concerns, to fix serious bugs in macOS, or to fix bugs in or add functionality to Apple applications. You should update your Apple apps and system software regularly.

You can check for application updates manually by opening the App Store app and displaying its Updates tab. If any updates are available, you'll see them here.

Open the Software Update System Preferences pane to check for system software updates, disable automatic checking, or click its Advanced button to fine-tune both automatic checking and automatic installation.

WARNING

Once in a blue moon, a software update has an unintended side effect; while fixing one problem, it introduces a different problem. This doesn't happen very often because Apple is careful, but if you want to be safe, don't install a software update until you visit Macworld (www.macworld.com), The Mac Observer (www.macobserver.com), or your favorite authoritative tech site and look at what they have to say about the update you have in mind. If there are widespread issues with a particular software update, sites like these will have the most comprehensive coverage (and possible work-arounds).

Apps need updates, too. So make a habit of launching the Mac App Store application now and then, clicking the Updates tab, and then updating any apps that require it.

Many third-party programs, including Microsoft Office and most Adobe products, use their own update-checking mechanism. Check and make sure that you have yours enabled. Many third-party apps offer a Check for Updates option in the Help (or other) menu or as a preference in their Preferences window.

One last thing: If you see a little number on the App Store or System Preferences icon in the dock, you have that many updates waiting to be installed. Launch the Mac App Store and click the Updates tab or launch System Preferences and click the Software Update icon.

Protecting Your Data from Prying Eyes

The last kind of security I look at in this chapter is protecting your files from other users on your local area network (LAN) and users with physical access to your Mac. If you don't want anyone messing with your files, check out the security measures in the following sections.

Blocking or limiting connections

The first thing you may want to do is open the Sharing System Preferences pane by launching the System Preferences application (from the Applications folder, menu, or dock) and clicking the Sharing icon. Nobody can access your Mac over the network if all the services in the Sharing pane are disabled.

Locking down files with FileVault

If you absolutely, positively don't ever want anyone to be able to access the files in your Home folder without your permission, use FileVault. This app allows you to encrypt your entire disk and protect it with the latest government-approved encryption standard: Advanced Encryption Standard with 128-bit keys (AES-128).

When you turn on FileVault, you're asked to set a master password for the computer. After you do, you or any other administrator can use that master password if you forget your regular account login password.

WARNING

I said it at the beginning of the chapter but it bears repeating: If you turn on FileVault and forget both your login password and your master password, you can't log in to your account — and your data is lost forever. Really. So don't forget these passwords, okay?

FileVault is useful primarily if you store sensitive information on your Mac. If you're logged out of your user account and other people access to your Mac, there is no way they can access your data. Period.

Because FileVault encrypts your entire hard drive, some tasks that normally access your disk might be prevented. For one thing, some backup programs (not Time Machine, of course) can choke if FileVault is enabled. Also, if you're not logged in to your user account, other users can't access your Shared folder(s).

REMEMBER

Because FileVault is always encrypting and decrypting files, it can slow older Macs a tiny bit when you add or save new files, and it can take extra time before it lets you log out, restart, or shut down. If your Mac is less than five years old, you'll probably notice little or no delay from enabling FileVault.

To turn on FileVault, follow these steps:

1. **Open the Security & Privacy System Preferences pane.**

2. **Click the FileVault tab.**

   Click the lock icon at the bottom of the pane and authenticate with your password or Touch ID.

3. **Click the Turn on FileVault button.**

To turn off FileVault, click the Turn Off FileVault button.

Setting other options for security

The General tab of the Security & Privacy System Preferences pane offers several more options that can help keep your data safe. They are as follows:

>> **Change Password:** Click this button to change the password for your user account.

>> **Require Password after Sleep or Screen Saver Begins:** Enable this option if you want your Mac to lock itself up and require a password after the screen saver kicks in or it goes to sleep. It can become a pain in the butt, having to type your password all the time. But if you have nosy co-workers, family members, or other individuals you'd like to keep from rooting around in your stuff, you should probably enable this option.

When enabled, this option offers a pop-up menu that lets you specify how long after sleep or screen saver this password protection should kick in. The options range from immediately to 8 hours.

>> **Show a Message When the Screen Is Locked:** Type the message you want on your screen when it's locked in this text entry box.

>> **Allow Apps Downloaded From:** Last, but certainly not least (at least with regard to the General tab), are two options that can help protect you from downloading and running malicious software by limiting the applications your Mac can run.

TECHNICAL STUFF

In case you were wondering, Apple calls this feature *Gatekeeper,* though that name doesn't appear in the System Preferences pane.

You have two mutually exclusive options — one is App Store and the other is App Store and Identified Developers. Select the radio button next to the level of protection you desire, and the other option is automatically deselected.

Here's what they do:

● *App Store:* This option allows you to run only apps you download from the Mac App Store. It's the safer and more restrictive setting.

● *App Store and Identified Developers:* Apple offers a Developer ID program to certified members of the Mac Developers Program. Apple gives them a unique Developer ID, which allows Gatekeeper to verify that their app is not known malware and that it hasn't been tampered with. If an app doesn't have a Developer ID associated with it, Gatekeeper can let you know before you install it.

This choice is probably the best for most users. It allows third-party apps from Apple-vetted vendors, including Microsoft, Adobe, and thousands more. It's a lot less restrictive than the Mac App Store option and a lot safer than letting you download apps from anywhere.

Finally, the Privacy tab of the Security & Privacy System Preferences pane has several potentially useful options:

>> **To Enable or Disable Location Services:** Click Location Services on the left, and you'll see a list of apps that are allowed to use your computer's current location. Select or deselect these apps to enable or disable, respectively, their use of Location Services.

>> **To Enable or Disable Other Apps Access to your Contacts, Calendars, and Reminders:** Click Contacts, Calendars, or Reminders in the list on the left and apps with access to their contents will appear on the right. Select or deselect the check box for each app to enable or disable, respectively, its permission to access Contacts, Calendars, or Reminders.

>> **To Enable or Disable Apps Allowed to Control Your Computer:** Click Accessibility in the list on the left, and apps allowed to control your computer appear on the right. Select or deselect the check box for each app to enable or disable, respectively, its permission to control your computer.

Here are some ways to protect your data:

>> Use strong passwords.

>> Don't share your passwords.

>> Don't store passwords in insecure locations (such as on sticky notes on your monitor).

>> Use a password manager (such as Keychain Access or my favorite, 1Password) to store your passwords securely.

>> Don't log in to suspicious or insecure wireless networks.

>> Don't visit suspicious websites or open suspicious emails.

>> If you have any question about authenticity, just don't click!

And that's all you really need to know about security and privacy (or at least enough to make you dangerous).

Chapter **25**

Utility Chest

macOS Monterey comes with a plethora of useful utilities that make using your computer more pleasant or make you more productive when you use your computer or both. In this chapter, I give you a peek at a handful you're likely to use that are not covered elsewhere in this book.

In the Applications and Utilities Folders

The first item, Calculator, is in your Applications folder (Go⇨Applications; keyboard shortcut: ⌘+Shift+A). All other items in this chapter are in your Utilities folder (Go⇨Utilities; keyboard shortcut: ⌘+Shift+U), which you'll find *inside* your Applications folder.

Calculator

Need to do some quick math? The Calculator application gives you a simple calculator with all the basic number-crunching functions found in a pocket calculator. To use it, you can either click the keys with the mouse or type numbers and operators (math symbols such as +, −, and =) using the number keys on your keyboard (or numeric keypad, if you have one). Calculator also offers a paper tape (Window⇨Show Paper Tape) to track your computations — and, if you want, provide a printed record. It can even speak numbers aloud (Speech⇨Speak Button Pressed and Speech⇨Speak Result).

Check out Calculator in Figure 25-1.

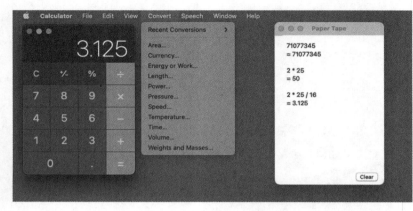

FIGURE 25-1:
Calculator (left),
Convert menu
(middle), and
Paper Tape
(right).

In my humble opinion, the most useful feature in Calculator (after Paper Tape) is the Convert menu — more specifically, the currency-conversion feature. It checks the internet for the current exchange rate before calculating the conversion for you. That's very cool.

Beyond that, Calculator has three modes: Basic, Scientific, and Programmer. Basic is the default, and you access the other two modes as follows:

>> Pressing ⌘+2 (View➪Scientific) turns the formerly anemic calculator into a powerful scientific calculator.

>> If you prefer Reverse Polish Notation (RPN), press ⌘+R.

TECHNICAL
STUFF

>> Choosing View➪Programmer (⌘+3) turns Calculator into the programmer's friend, letting you display your data in binary, octal, hexadecimal, ASCII, and Unicode. It also performs programming operations, such as shifts and byte swaps. (If you're a programmer, you know what all that means; if you aren't, it really doesn't matter.)

And that's about all you need to know to use the Calculator like a pro.

TIP

One more thing: Spotlight (and Siri) can perform many basic math calculations and conversions faster than you can launch the Calculator app.

Moving right along, the remaining applications in this section can be found in your Utilities folder (Go➪Utilities; keyboard shortcut: ⌘+Shift+U).

Activity Monitor

In Unix, the underlying operating system that powers macOS, applications and other things going on behind the scenes are called *processes*. Each application and the operating system itself can run a number of processes at the same time.

In Figure 25-2, you see 420 different processes running, most of them behind the scenes. Note that when this screenshot was taken, I had half a dozen or more programs running, including Finder, Safari, and Activity Monitor itself.

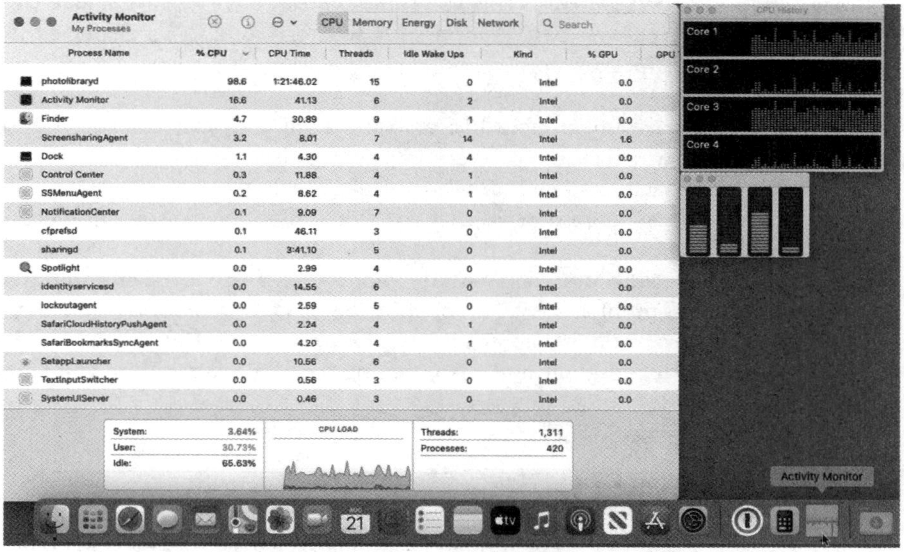

FIGURE 25-2:
The Activity
Monitor window,
two little CPU
monitors, and the
Activity Monitor
dock icon.

To display the two CPU monitor windows on the right side of the Activity Monitor window as shown in Figure 25-2, choose Window⇨CPU Usage (⌘+2) and Window⇨CPU History (⌘+3).

You also select what appears in the Activity Monitor's dock icon — CPU Usage, CPU History, Network Usage (shown in Figure 25-2), Disk Activity, or the Activity Monitor — by choosing View⇨Dock Icon. All but the Activity Monitor icon appear *live*, meaning that they update every few seconds to reflect the current state of affairs.

Note that you can't display CPU Usage or CPU History in a window and in the dock icon at the same time — those two items can be displayed on the dock or a window, but not both.

To choose how often these updates occur, choose View⇨Update Frequency.

WARNING

Setting Activity Monitor to update more frequently causes it to use more CPU cycles, which can decrease overall performance slightly.

Finally, the bottom portion of the Activity Monitor window displays information for the active tab. Select the CPU, Memory, Energy, Disk, or Network tab, and the middle and bottom portions of the Activity Monitor window change to reflect that selection.

TECHNICAL STUFF

Because all Macs that can run Monterey have at least a dual-core processor, you'll see at least two, and possibly four or more, CPUs displayed in Activity Monitor: one for each core.

Geeks and troubleshooters (and even you) can use Activity Monitor to identify what processes are running, which user owns the process, and how much CPU capacity and memory the process is using. You can even use this feature to quit or force-quit a process that you think might be causing problems for you.

WARNING

Messing around in Activity Monitor isn't a good idea for most users. If you're having problems with an application or with macOS, try quitting open applications, force-quitting applications (press ⌘+Option+Esc — the Mac three-finger salute), or logging out and then logging back in again before you start mucking around with killing processes.

Disk Utility

If you're having problems with your hard drive or need to make changes to it, Disk Utility is a good place to start. Start by clicking a disk or volume in the column on the left and then click one of the buttons on the toolbar as described in the following sections.

Volume +/−

The Volume + and Volume − buttons, introduced in Mojave, make it easier than ever to subdivide your hard or solid-state disk into virtual volumes, which look and act like separate disks but are volumes on a single disk.

If you think this sounds a lot like what we used to call *partitioning*, it is. But to understand the difference between a volume and a partition, you first have to understand the difference between APFS and HFS+ by reading the nearby sidebar.

APFS VERSUS HFS +

In the old days (before Mojave) we used the term *partitioning* to describe creating multiple virtual disks out of a single hard or solid-state drive. But with macOS High Sierra, Apple introduced a new file system called APFS (Apple File System). The old scheme (prior to High Sierra) is HFS+ (Hierarchical File System +). In other words, APFS is the modern replacement for HFS+, though HFS+ is still available in Disk Utility.

According to Apple, when you install macOS High Sierra, Mojave, Catalina, Big Sur, or Monterey on a solid-state drive (SSD) or other all-flash storage device, the volume will *automatically* be converted to APFS. However, if the drive is *not* solid-state or flash — a Fusion drive or a traditional hard disk — it will *not* be converted to APFS.

Disk Utility in Monterey can format most storage devices using either file system. If you need to manually reformat a device, consider these points made in a helpful Apple Support article:

- APFS requires macOS High Sierra or later. Earlier versions of the Mac operating system don't mount APFS-formatted volumes.

- APFS is optimized for solid-state drives (SSDs) and other all-flash storage devices.

- Disk Utility tries to detect the type of storage you're formatting, and then shows the appropriate format in the Format menu. If it can't detect the type of storage, it defaults to Mac OS Extended (aka HFS+), which works with all versions of macOS.

To make a long story short, if you have to format a solid-state drive, use APFS; for all other drive types, use HFS+.

To find out which format (file system) a device is currently using:

1. Select the device in Finder.

2. Choose File ⇨ Get Info or press ⌘+I.

3. Check the Format shown in the Get Info window as shown in the following figure.

(continued)

(continued)

Although APFS will allow you to create partitions instead of volumes, I can't think of a good reason for you to do so.

TIP

Partition button

Speaking of partitions, you can use the Partition button to create disk partitions (multiple volumes on a single disk) on disks formatted as HFS+. macOS treats each partition as a separate disk. The Partition button is enabled only when an eligible item is selected in the column on the left.

Partitioning a drive lets you create multiple volumes. A *volume* is a storage space that (from the Mac's point of view) looks and acts just like a hard drive. A *partition* is simply a designated volume on a drive, separate from all other partitions (volumes). You can create any number of partitions, but it's a good idea to limit yourself to no more than a small handful.

By the same token, it's absolutely not necessary to use partitions unless you're running Boot Camp (see Chapter 23) on an Intel-powered Mac. Many users never partition a hard drive and get along just fine. If you do choose to partition, you should probably limit the number of partitions you create. An iMac with a 1TB drive will do just fine as shipped (with a single partition); there's no need to create more.

WARNING

Be careful here. Although some adjustments can be made to partitions without loss of data, not all adjustments can. You'll be warned if what you're about to do will permanently erase your data, but I thought I'd give you fair warning first. And, of course, you should always have a backup (see Chapter 24) before mucking with your disk.

Finally, if you click the Partition button with an APFS disk selected in the sidebar, you'll see an explanation that suggests you might be happier with a volume than with a partition.

First Aid button

If you suspect that something's not quite right with your startup disk (or any other disk connected to your Mac), the First Aid button in Disk Utility should be among your first stops. Use First Aid to verify and (if necessary) repair an ailing drive. To use it, select a volume icon in the list on the left and then click the First Aid button on the Disk Utility toolbar. A dialog asks if you'd like to run First Aid on the selected disk; click Run to do it or Cancel to dismiss the sheet.

If the disk you're trying to repair is your startup disk, Disk Utility will warn you that it needs to temporarily lock the boot volume and that other apps will be unresponsive until the operation has completed, as shown in Figure 25-3. Go have a cup of coffee or something — the process takes 15-30 minutes for most disks.

When it's finished, you'll get information about any problems that the software finds.

Verifying the startup volume will cause this computer to stop responding.

This may last for several minutes or hours. To avoid this, you can run First Aid while in Recovery.

Cancel   Continue

FIGURE 25-3:
If you try to run First Aid on your startup disk, you'll see this alert before you can continue.

If First Aid doesn't find any problems, you can go on your merry way, secure in the knowledge that that disk is A-okay. If First Aid turns up a problem that it can't fix, it will advise you what to do next. In most cases, that advice is to boot from the Recovery disk (Intel processors: Hold down ⌘+R at startup on Intel-based Macs; Apple processors: Press and hold down the power button until the Recovery Options screen appears, and then click Continue) and run First Aid again.

TIP

You can't use Disk Utility First Aid to fix a CD or DVD, nor can you use it to fix most disk image (DMG) files. These types of disks are read-only and can't be altered.

Erase button

Use Erase to format (completely erase) any disk except the current startup disk.

WARNING

When you format a disk, you erase all information on it permanently. Formatting can't be undone — so unless you're *absolutely sure* this is what you want, don't do it. Unless you have no use for whatever's currently on the disk, make a complete backup of the disk before you format it. If the data is critical, you should have at least two (or even three) known-to-be-valid backup copies of that disk before you reformat.

After clicking the Erase button, a sheet drops down with a space for you to name the disk you're about to erase and you see a drop-down Format menu so you can choose the disk format.

REMEMBER

Use Mac OS Extended (Journaled) for rotational and hybrid disks, use APFS for solid-state drives.

WARNING

Don't try any of the other options (case-sensitive, encrypted, and other variations) unless you know what you're doing and have a darn good reason. Formatting a disk using many of these options can cause Mac software to misbehave. Don't do it. Only choose Mac OS Extended (Journaled) or APFS — unless you're prepared to spend time troubleshooting when your Mac doesn't work as expected.

One more thing: This warning applies only to bootable disks with macOS installed on them. If the disk isn't going to be used as a boot disk, you can format it any way you care to.

Mount/Unmount button

A drive can be connected but not available to your Mac. For example, when you eject a hard drive or SSD, it's still connected to the computer but doesn't appear in Finder. This is called an *unmounted disk.*

The Mount/Unmount button lets you dismount (eject) or mount a connected disk or partition on a disk. For reasons that should be obvious, you can't eject the disk from which you booted.

Info button

Click the Info button to see myriad technical details about the selected disk, including its size, capacity, and free and used space. One last thing: You find out more about Disk Utility (mostly how to use it for troubleshooting) in Chapter 26.

Keychain Access

A *keychain* is a way to consolidate your passwords — your Mac login password, your email password, and passwords required by any websites. Keychain Access is the application you use to manage those passwords.

Here's how it works: You use a single password to unlock your keychain (which holds your various passwords), and then you don't have to remember all your other passwords. Rest assured that your passwords are secure because only a user who has your keychain password can reach the other password-protected applications.

TIP

The Keychain Access utility is particularly cool if you have multiple email accounts and each one has a different password. Just add them all to your keychain, and you can get all your mail at the same time with one password.

A special master keychain called the Login Keychain is created automatically for every macOS Monterey user and unlocked automatically when you log into your account.

TIP

Here's how to add passwords to your login keychain:

>> **To add passwords for applications:** If the application supports the keychain, the first time you log in with your username and password, a dialog will ask if you want to add this login to the keychain. Click Yes.

How do you know which programs support the Keychain Access utility? You don't, until you're prompted to save your password in a keychain in that Open dialog, connect window, or so forth. If a program supports Keychain Access, it offers a check box for it in the user ID/password dialog or window.

If that doesn't happen the first time you provide your password, the program doesn't support macOS keychains and you're out of luck. You can add the account details manually (see the next bullet), but they won't be provided automatically when the app requests them — you'll have to open Keychain Access to look them up. The upside is that your passwords are secure as long as they're stored in a keychain.

TIP

If you select the User Names and Passwords check box on the AutoFill tab of Safari's Preferences window (Safari⇨Preferences or ⌘+, [comma]), you don't have to add sites, accounts, or passwords manually. Instead, the first time you visit a site that requires an account name and a password, Safari asks whether you would like to save your password, and then it does so.

» **To add a website (or other) password to a keychain manually:** If your login credentials aren't being filled in automatically for a website, you can add them manually using the Keychain Access application. Just click the little + (plus) at the top of the main window and type (or copy and paste) the URL of the page in the Keychain Item Name text field. Then type your username in the Account Name field and your password in the Password field, as shown in Figure 25-4. (If you're adding a password for something other than a website, type a descriptive name in the Keychain Item Name field rather than a URL.)

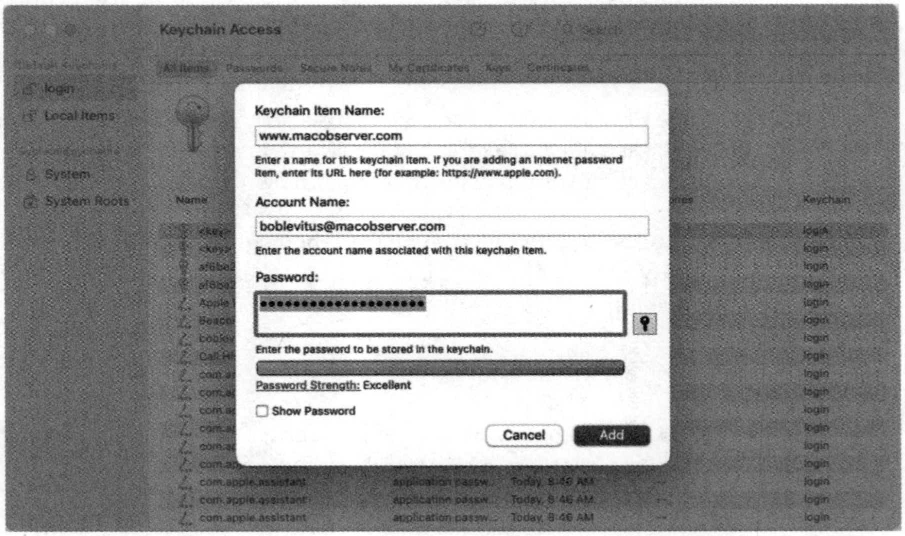

FIGURE 25-4:
Add a URL to the keychain manually by using Keychain Access.

TIP

Click the little key to the right of the password field to use the Password Assistant window, which can help you select a high-quality password.

To use the new URL password, use Safari to open the URL. If the account name and password aren't filled in for you automatically, choose Edit⇨AutoFill Form (⌘+Shift+A) and they will be.

TIP

iCloud Keychain syncing is a great feature that makes keychains even better. Turn it on (System Preferences ⇨ iCloud), and your keychain passwords will be securely synced to (and from) all your Apple devices, including iPhones and iPads.

WARNING

Just remember that this makes all your passwords available on all your devices. That's handy, but if any of your devices aren't secured with passwords or passcodes or are shared with others, all your passwords could be at risk. Just think about it before you enable iCloud Keychain.

Passwords System Preferences pane

NEW

The new Passwords System Preferences pane offers a more user-friendly interface for managing your stored passwords.

To manage a password for a website, click its name in the list on the left side of the pane. The details appear on the right in the main pane. Click the Edit button to change the username or password for this site locally (on your Mac), or click Change Password on Website to launch Safari and change your password at its source.

To copy a password to the clipboard, click the bullets (dots) in the password field and then click Copy Password. To paste the password, click in the password field and then choose Edit ⇨ Paste or press ⌘+V.

Finally, if you want your Mac to monitor and detect compromised passwords securely, enable the Detect Compromised Passwords check box.

Migration Assistant

Migration Assistant is pretty much a one-trick pony, but that pony is a prizewinner. You use Migration Assistant to transfer your account and other user information from another Mac, another volume on the current Mac, or a Time Machine backup. You need to authenticate as an administrator to use it, but it's a pretty handy way to transfer an entire account without having to re-create your preferences and other settings. When you first installed Monterey (or when you booted your nice, new Monterey–based Mac for the first time), the setup utility asked you whether you wanted to transfer your information from another Mac. If you answered in the affirmative, it ran Migration Assistant.

TIP

It's not just for new Monterey installs. You can launch this one-trick-pony anytime to transfer all or some user accounts, applications, settings, and files from another Mac, PC, or Time Machine backup to this one. You can use it also after replacing a hard drive or reinstalling macOS. Last but not least, Migration

Assistant can import user accounts, applications, settings, and files from Windows PCs as well as from Macs.

System Information

System Information (the app formerly known as System Profiler) is a little program that is launched when you click the System Report button in the About This Mac window (⌘⇨About This Mac) or double-click its icon in the Utilities folder inside your Applications folder.

It provides information about your Mac. (What a concept!) If you're curious about arcane questions such as what processor your Mac has or what devices are stashed inside it or are connected to it, give this baby a try. Click various items in the Contents list on the left side of the window, and information about the item appears on the right side of the window. Feel free to poke around this little puppy as much as you like; it's benign and can't hurt anything.

TIP

If you ever have occasion to call for technical support for your Mac, software, or peripherals, you're probably going to be asked to provide information from System Information, so don't get rid of it just because you don't care about this kind of stuff.

Terminal

macOS is based on Unix. If you need proof — or if you actually want to operate your Mac as the Unix machine that it is — Terminal is the place to start.

Because Unix is a command line–based operating system, you use Terminal to type your commands. You can issue commands that show a directory listing, copy and move files, search for filenames or contents, or establish or change passwords. In short, if you know what you're doing, you can do everything on the command line that you can do in macOS. For most folks, that's not a desirable alternative to the windows and icons of the Finder window. But take my word for it; true geeks who are also Mac lovers get all misty-eyed about the combination of a command line *and* a graphical user interface.

WARNING

You can wreak havoc upon your poor operating system with Terminal. You can harm your Monterey in many ways that just aren't possible using mere windows and icons and clicks. *Before you type a single command in Terminal, think seriously about what I just said.* And if you're not 100 percent certain about the command you just typed, don't even think about pressing Return.

Screenshot

The Screenshot app has the best screen-shooting capabilities ever in macOS, with functionality woven into the fabric of Monterey itself.

All your old favorite keyboard shortcuts for screen capture — the ones you've known and loved on the Mac since time immemorial — still work the same as always:

To capture the entire screen:

1. **Press ⌘+Shift+3.**
2. **There is no Step 2.**

To capture part of the screen:

1. **Press ⌘+Shift+4.**
2. **Move the pointer (crosshair icon) to where you want to start the screenshot.**
3. **Press the mouse or trackpad button, then drag over the area you want to capture.**
4. **Release the mouse or trackpad button to capture the selected area.**

To cancel, press Esc before you release the mouse button.

To capture a window or the menu bar:

1. **Press ⌘+Shift+4 and then press the spacebar.**
2. **Move the pointer (camera icon) over the area you wish to capture; when it is highlighted, click to capture the selected item.**

To cancel, press Esc before you click.

To capture a menu and its title:

1. **Open the menu to display the menu commands.**
2. **Press ⌘+Shift+4.**
3. **Drag the pointer (crosshair icon) over the entire menu.**

   If you want to exclude the menu's title, press ⌘+Shift+4, press the spacebar, move the pointer (camera icon) over the menu to highlight it, then click.

The best keyboard shortcut to memorize

In addition to the old, familiar screenshot shortcuts, Monterey has another relatively new keyboard shortcut that includes everything you can do using the other shortcuts and more.

This fabulous shortcut is ⌘+Shift+5, and if you're only going to memorize one shortcut for screen captures, it should be this one, which will open the floating palette of screen-shooting options shown in Figure 25-5.

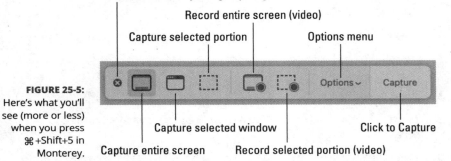

Cancel (without capturing anything)

Record entire screen (video)

Capture selected portion

Options menu

FIGURE 25-5:
Here's what you'll
see (more or less)
when you press
⌘+Shift+5 in
Monterey.

Capture entire screen

Capture selected window

Record selected portion (video)

Click to Capture

To capture your screen as a still image, first click the appropriate icon: Capture Entire Screen, Capture Selected Window, or Capture Selected Portion. When everything is the way you want it, press Enter (or Return) on your keyboard.

What happens next, before the screenshot appears on your desktop (by default), is a relatively new thing (introduced in macOS Mojave). That new thing is a floating thumbnail that appears in the lower-right corner of your screen.

If you do nothing, the floating thumbnail will disappear after a few seconds and the screenshot will appear on the desktop by default. (You learn how to save screenshots elsewhere in the next section.)

But click the floating thumbnail before it goes away and a wonderful new thing happens: A window appears with a bevy of useful tools for modifying images.

These tools are known as Markup — a systemwide set of tools for annotating PDF and image files. I mention Markup briefly in Chapter 17, but the tools aren't restricted to the Mail app — you'll also find them in the Preview app (see Chapter 20), Finder's Quick Look windows (see Chapter 10), in the Preview pane of Finder windows (if enabled), and in Finder shortcut menus. (Details on Markup appear in Chapter 5.)

These same tools also appear if you click the floating thumbnail of a screenshot before it disappears.

These powerful editing tools enable you to annotate screenshots in ways never before possible without a third-party graphics app. Now you can easily add circles, boxes, arrows, and text to your screenshots, image files, and PDFs without even launching an app.

When you've finished annotating and editing your screenshot, click Done in the upper-left corner of the window.

Monterey screen-shooting options

If you want to change the location where your screenshots are saved, click the Options menu, which is available after you press ⌘+Shift+5. The Options menu also allows you to select a timer of None (the default), 5 seconds, or 10 seconds.

Finally, the Options menu lets you enable or disable the floating thumbnail, show or hide the mouse pointer, and remember the last selection you made (for your next screenshot).

Another set of options appears when you long-press, right-click, or Control-click the floating thumbnail, as shown in Figure 25-6.

FIGURE 25-6:
Right- or Control-click the floating thumbnail and choose from these options.

Note that selecting Markup is the same as clicking the floating thumbnail — it opens the Markup window so you can annotate your screenshot.

Monterey screen recording

Screen recording — movies of your Mac (or iDevice) screens — has been around for a few years on the Mac, but it's been buried in the QuickTime Player app (see Chapter 20). I didn't discuss it in that chapter because this way is so much easier and more convenient. (If you want to make a movie of your iDevice screen, you'll still need to use QuickTime Player.)

Anyway, to make a movie of all or part of your Mac screen, begin by pressing ⌘+Shift+5. Then click either the Record Entire Screen or Record Selected Portion. If you click Record Entire Screen, the recording begins immediately; if you click Record Selected Portion, you need to drag the onscreen handles to select the area you want to record, and then click the Record icon.

To end the recording, click the Stop Recording icon in the menu bar, as shown in Figure 25-7.

Stop recording

When the floating thumbnail appears in the lower-right corner of your screen, you can right- or Control-click it for additional options, or do nothing to have the screen recording saved in your default location.

» **Dealing with the prohibitory sign**

» **Recovering from startup crashes**

» **Using Monterey's Optimize Storage**

Chapter **26**

Troubleshooting macOS

As a bleeding-edge Mac enthusiast and consultant with more than three decades of Mac troubleshooting experience, I've seen (and resolved) more than my share of Mac troubles. Over those years, I've developed an arsenal of mostly surefire tips and tricks that I believe will help you resolve many common Mac issues without a trip to the repair shop.

Alas, if your hardware is dead, then, sadly, neither you nor I can do anything about it — that's a job for your friendly Mac repairman and your fat checkbook or high-limit credit card. But if your hardware is okay, you have a darn good chance of using the suggestions in this chapter to get your machine up and running.

About Startup Disks and Booting

Although you usually see a stylish Apple logo when you turn on your computer, once in a blue moon, you may instead see a solid blue screen, a solid gray screen, a solid black screen, or something else entirely, as described in the next section.

The point is that your Mac isn't starting up as it should. When this happens, it usually indicates that something bad has happened to your Mac or your startup disk. Sometimes, a hardware component has bitten the dust; other times, macOS itself has somehow been damaged.

Rest assured that these occurrences are uncommon — many Macs and Mac users go an entire lifetime without ever having an issue. But if you ever have a Mac that won't boot, don't despair — the advice in this chapter is likely to help.

Finally, I use the term *hard disk* generically throughout the chapter to refer to hard disks (mechanical with spinning platters) or solid-state disks (electronic with no moving parts).

Finding or creating a startup disk

First things first: When I talk about *booting,* I mean using a particular disk or disk partition as your startup disk.

Monterey is available only in the Mac App Store as a download. Because you can no longer purchase a bootable installer DVD, the macOS Installer automatically creates a bootable partition named Recovery HD when you install Monterey on a disk.

I recommend that you also make a bootable Recovery disk (in addition to the one Monterey should have created) or a clone of your Mac startup disk. If not, it's something you may wish you had done when your Mac starts acting wonky.

Explaining how to create a bootable recovery disk or clone is beyond the purview of this book, but I hope you'll take it upon yourself to search the internet and figure out how to make one. Start with this Apple Support Article: `https://support.apple.com/en-us/HT201372`. And bear in mind that you can't start your Mac from a Time Machine backup.

The Recovery HD partition is a good concept, but if your hard disk dies, the Recovery HD partition generally dies with it — which is why *I strongly recommend making a bootable clone of your startup disk as soon as possible,* just in case.

I use Carbon Copy Cloner (`www.bombich.com`), a $39.99 app that lets you create a clone of your boot disk with a minimum of fuss. Or you can try SuperDuper! (shareware from `www.shirt-pocket.com`); just add a hard disk as large as or larger than your boot disk, and you'll be good to go with any of these options.

They call it a prohibitory sign for a reason

When you turn on your Mac, the first thing it does (after the hardware tests) is check for a startup disk that has a viable copy of macOS on it. If your system doesn't find such a disk on your internal hard drive, it begins looking elsewhere — on a Thunderbolt or Universal Serial Bus (USB) disk, a thumb drive, or a DVD.

At this point, your Mac usually finds the (usually internal) hard drive (or SSD), which contains your operating system, and the startup process continues on its merry way with the subtle Apple logo and all the rest. If your Mac can't find a suitable bootable disk you encounter the dreaded prohibitory sign. Think of the prohibitory sign as your Mac's way of saying, "Please provide me a startup disk."

REMEMBER

If you have more than one startup disk attached to your Mac, as many users do, you can choose which one your Mac boots from in the Startup Disk System Preferences pane or by pressing and holding down the Option key when you start up your Mac.

Rant on: If Apple can figure out a way to put a prohibitory sign on the screen, why the heck can't the software engineers find a way to put the words *I need a startup disk* on the screen as well? The curtness of such icons is one of my pet peeves about the Mac. I know — you're clever and smart (because, of course, you're smart enough to be reading *macOS Monterey For Dummies*), so now *you* know that a prohibitory sign means you should insert a startup disk. But what about everyone else?

If you encounter any of the warning signs shown in Figure 26-1, go through the steps I outline later in this chapter. Try them in the order listed, starting with Step 1. Then, if one doesn't work, move on to the next.

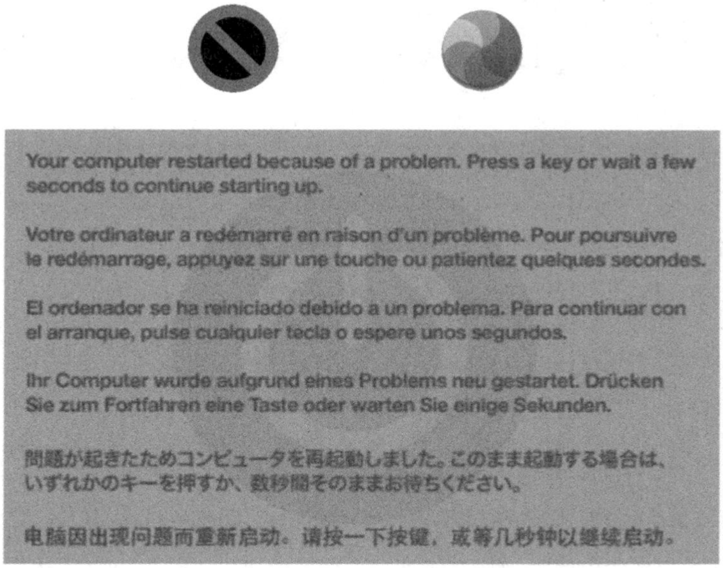

Your computer restarted because of a problem. Press a key or wait a few seconds to continue starting up.

Votre ordinateur a redémarré en raison d'un problème. Pour poursuivre le redémarrage, appuyez sur une touche ou patientez quelques secondes.

El ordenador se ha reiniciado debido a un problema. Para continuar con el arranque, pulse cualquier tecla o espere unos segundos.

Ihr Computer wurde aufgrund eines Problems neu gestartet. Drücken Sie zum Fortfahren eine Taste oder warten Sie einige Sekunden.

問題が起きたためコンピュータを再起動しました。このまま起動する場合は、いずれかのキーを押すか、数秒間そのままお待ちください。

电脑因出现问题而重新启动。请按一下按键，或等几秒钟以继续启动。

FIGURE 26-1: Any of these means it's troubleshooting time.

Recovering with Recovery HD

If you see a prohibitory sign (top left in Figure 26-1), a spinning-pinwheel-of-death (top right), or a kernel panic alert (the text in other languages that appears below the other two images) that doesn't go away when you start your Mac, the first thing to do is attempt to repair hidden damage to your hard drive with the Disk Utility program's First Aid feature.

Step 1: Run First Aid

In most cases, the first logical troubleshooting step is to use the First Aid option in the Disk Utility application.

TECHNICAL STUFF

Every drive has several strangely named components, such as B-trees, extent files, catalog files, and other creatively named invisible files. They're all involved in managing the data on your drives. Disk Utility's First Aid feature checks all those files and repairs the damaged ones.

Because your Mac isn't able to finish the boot process, you'll need to boot from the Recovery partition to perform this repair. The steps for rebooting your Mac into Recovery mode are different depending on its processor:

>> **Macs with Intel processors:** Restart while pressing ⌘+R, continuing to press them until you see the Apple logo appear. When it does, a window appears offering four buttons: Restore from Time Machine, Reinstall MacOS, Safari, and Disk Utility. Click Disk Utility to launch it.

>> **Macs with Apple M processors:** Press and hold down the power button; continue to hold it down until the Options button appears midscreen. Click the Options button, select a user and type their password, click Disk Utility, and then click Continue.

Now here's how to run First Aid using the Disk Utility app:

1. **Click the icon for your boot hard drive, to the left of the Disk Utility window.**

   Your boot drive is the one with macOS and your Home folder on it; mine is called *Monterey SSD*.

2. **Click the First Aid button in the toolbar.**

   A sheet drops down, asking if you'd like to run First Aid on that disk.

3. **Click the Run button.**

The Disk First Aid routine runs. It will take anywhere from a few minutes to an hour or more for First Aid to check and repair your disk and allow you to perform Step 6.

4. **(Optional) Click Show Details on the sheet to see (mostly unintelligible) details.**

When the routine is finished, the Done button is enabled.

If First Aid finds damage that it can't fix, a commercial disk-recovery tool, such as Prosoft's Drive Genius *may* be able to repair the damage.

TIP

5. **Click the Done button.**

6. **Quit Disk Utility.**

Choose Disk Utility⇨Quit Disk Utility, press ⌘+Q, or click the red Close Window gumdrop button.

7. **Choose 🍎le Menu ⇨ Restart to exit Recovery mode and restart your Mac.**

Make sure you're running a current version of any disk utilities you try; older versions may not be compatible with macOS Monterey (or APFS) and could make things worse.

WARNING

If everything checks out with First Aid but you still get the prohibitory sign after you restart, proceed to the next section to try a dance called booting into Safe mode.

Step 2: Safe boot into Safe mode

Booting your Mac in Safe mode may help you resolve your startup issue by not loading nonessential (and non–macOS) software at boot time. Again, the way you invoke Safe mode depends on your Mac's processor:

>> **Macs with Intel processors:** Press and hold down the Shift key during startup.

>> **Macs with Apple M processors:** Shut Down your Mac, wait 10 seconds, and then press and hold the power button on your Mac until the Startup Options window appears. Select your startup disk. Then press and hold down the Shift key, click Continue in Safe Mode, and release the Shift key.

If your Mac is set up so you don't have to log in, keep pressing the Shift key during startup until Finder loads completely. If you do log in to your Mac, type your password as usual — but before clicking the Log In button, press the Shift key again and hold it down until Finder loads completely.

You know you held the Shift key long enough if your Login Items don't load (assuming that you have Login Items; you can designate them in the Users & Groups System Preferences pane, although some programs create them for you).

Booting in Safe mode does three things to help you with troubleshooting:

>> It forces a directory check of the startup (boot) volume.

>> It loads only required kernel extensions (some of the items in /System/Library/Extensions).

>> It runs only Apple-installed essential startup items (some of the items in /Library/StartupItems and /System/Library/StartupItems). Note that the Startup Items in the Library folders are different from the Login Items in the Users & Groups System Preferences pane. Startup Items run at boot time before the login window even appears; Login Items don't run until after you log into your user account.

Taken together, these changes often work around issues caused by software or directory damage on the startup volume.

Some features may not work in Safe mode. Among them are DVD Player, capturing video (in iMovie or other video-editing software), using FaceTime or certain audio input or output devices. Use Safe mode only when you need to troubleshoot a startup issue, and reboot in normal mode as soon as possible.

Step 3: Zapping the PRAM/NVRAM

If your Mac has an Apple M processor, please ignore Step 3, which no longer applies to your Mac.

Sometimes your Mac's parameter RAM (PRAM) or non-volatile RAM (NVRAM) becomes scrambled and needs to be reset. Both of these are small pieces of memory that aren't erased or forgotten when you shut down. They keep track of things such as the following:

>> Time zone setting

>> Startup volume choice

>> Speaker volume

>> Any recent kernel panic information

>> DVD region setting

To reset (a process often called *zapping*) your PRAM/NVRAM, restart your Mac and press ⌘+Option+P+R (that's four keys — good luck; it's okay to use your nose) until your Mac restarts itself. It's kind of like a hiccup. You might see the spinning-disc pointer for a minute or two while your Mac thinks about it . . . then the icon disappears, and your Mac chimes again (unless your Mac is one of the recent models, which, sadly, are chimeless) and restarts. Most power users believe you should zap it more than once, letting it chime two, three, or even four times before releasing the keys and allowing the startup process to proceed.

Now restart your Mac without holding down any keys. If the PRAM/NVRAM zap didn't fix your Mac, move on to the section "Step 4: Reinstalling macOS."

REMEMBER

Your chosen startup disk, time zone, and sound volume may be reset to their default values when you zap your PRAM. So after zapping, open the System Preferences application to reselect your usual startup disk and time zone, and set the sound volume the way you like it if necessary.

Step 4: Reinstalling macOS

I present the procedure to reinstall the system software as a second-to-last resort when your Mac won't boot correctly because it takes the longest and is the biggest hassle. Apple has a nifty technical note on reinstallation at `https://support.apple.com/en-us/HT204904`.

Follow the instructions, taking care *not* to erase your disk before you reinstall macOS. As long as you do not erase the disk before you reinstall, you won't lose a drop of data. This procedure just installs a fresh copy of Monterey — it doesn't affect your files, settings, or anything else.

Step 5: Things to try before taking your Mac in for repair

TIP

To get your Mac up and running again, you can try one of the following:

>> **Call the tech-support hotline.** Before you drag it down to the shop, try calling 1-800-SOS-APPL, the Apple Tech Support hotline. The service representatives there may be able to suggest something else that you can try. If your Mac is still under warranty, it's even free.

>> **Ask a local user group for help.** Another thing you might consider is contacting your local Mac user group. You can find a group of Mac users near you by visiting Apple's User Group web pages at `www.apple.com/usergroups`.

If neither suggestion works for you, and you're still seeing anything you shouldn't when you start up your Mac, you have big trouble. You could have any one of the following problems:

>> Your hard drive is dead.

>> You have some other type of hardware failure.

>> All your startup disks are defective (unlikely).

The bottom line: If you still can't start up normally after trying all the cures I list in this chapter, you almost certainly need to have your Mac serviced by a qualified technician.

If Your Mac Crashes at Startup

Startup crashes are another bad thing that can happen to your Mac. These crashes can be more of a hassle to resolve than prohibitory sign problems, but they are rarely fatal.

You know that a *crash* has happened when you see a Quit Unexpectedly dialog, a frozen cursor, a frozen screen, or any other disabling event. A *startup crash* happens when your system shows a crash symptom any time between the moment you flick the power key or switch (or restarting) and the moment you have full use of the desktop.

Try all the steps in the previous sections *before* you panic. The easiest way to fix startup crashes (in most cases) is to just reinstall macOS from the Recovery partition. Again, Apple details this procedure at great length online, at https://support.apple.com/en-us/HT204904.

If you're still unsuccessful after that point, read the "Step 5: Things to try before taking your Mac in for repair" section.

Managing Storage

Managing Storage provides assistance if your startup disk gets close to being full.

Here's why it's in the troubleshooting chapter, in case you're wondering: Your Mac will slow to a crawl as your startup disk gets close to full. If your startup disk is more than 90 percent filled, you'll begin to experience slowness and jerkiness. And as the drive approaches 100 percent fullness, things grow even slower and jerkier.

Managing Storage aims to help you out as your disk fills up by scanning for duplicates, old email attachments, and downloads so you can delete them or move them to the cloud. But you should read what follows even if your disk isn't approaching fullness right now, because Optimize Storage offers several options that may keep your disk from ever getting too full.

To check it out, choose ⇨ About This Mac, click the Storage tab at the top of the window, and then click the Manage button to reveal four helpful tools, as shown in Figure 26-2:

WARNING

>> **Store in iCloud:** Store all your files in iCloud to save space, keeping only recently opened files on your Mac when storage space is needed.

This option could be convenient, but it's going to chew through your 5GB of free iCloud storage in no time. With additional iCloud storage currently selling for $0.99 a month (50GB), $3.99 a month (200GB), or $9.99 a month (2TB), it could be costly as well as convenient.

>> **Optimize Storage:** Remove from your Mac movies and TV shows you've already watched.

>> **Erase Trash Automatically:** Automatically empty files that have been in the Trash for 30 days.

>> **Reduce Clutter:** Review and delete older documents, which are broken down by category — Documents, Messages, Music, Trash, and TV — along the left side of the window.

The bottom line is that you don't want to let your startup disk come close to 100 percent full, and the Manage Storage features provide four useful ways for you to stay on top of and avert trouble before it occurs.

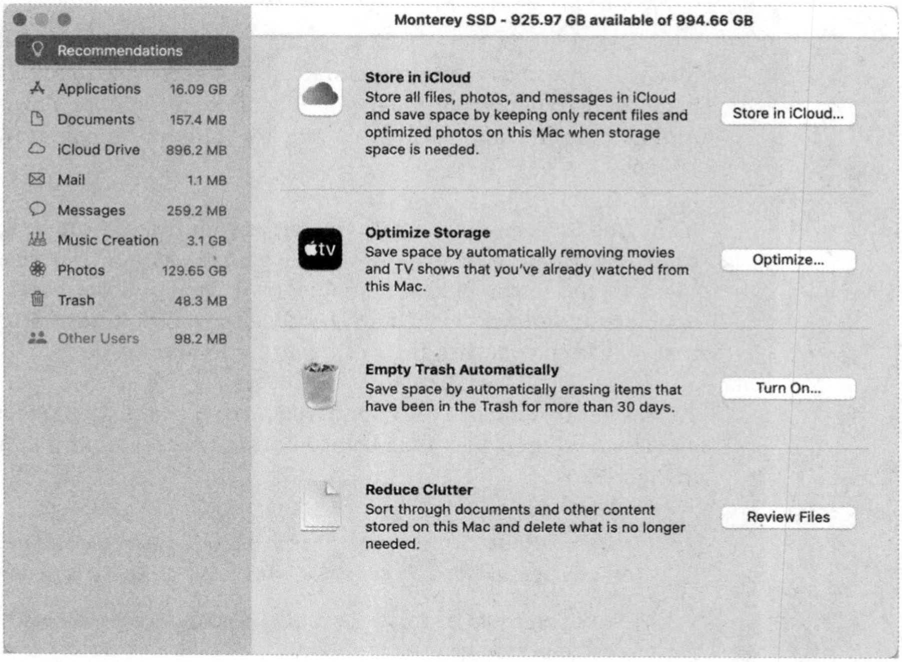

Monterey SSD - 925.97 GB available of 994.66 GB		
💡 **Recommendations**		
𝒜 Applications	16.09 GB	
🗎 Documents	157.4 MB	
☁ iCloud Drive	896.2 MB	
✉ Mail	1.1 MB	
💬 Messages	259.2 MB	
𝄞 Music Creation	3.1 GB	
✳ Photos	129.65 GB	
🗑 Trash	48.3 MB	
👥 Other Users	98.2 MB	

Store in iCloud
Store all files, photos, and messages in iCloud and save space by keeping only recent files and optimized photos on this Mac when storage space is needed.
[Store in iCloud...]

Optimize Storage
Save space by automatically removing movies and TV shows that you've already watched from this Mac.
[Optimize...]

Empty Trash Automatically
Save space by automatically erasing items that have been in the Trash for more than 30 days.
[Turn On...]

Reduce Clutter
Sort through documents and other content stored on this Mac and delete what is no longer needed.
[Review Files]

FIGURE 26-2:
If your disk is getting full, use one or more of these storage tools.

7

The Part of Tens

IN THIS PART . . .

Find ways to speed up a pokey Mac.

Get a list of awesome Mac websites worthy of your attention.

Chapter 27

Ten Ways to Speed Up Your Mac Experience

This chapter is for speed demons only. At some time in their Mac lives, most users have wished that their machines would work faster — even if their Macs have multiple cores or processors. I can't help you make your processors any faster, but here's where I cover some ways to make your Mac at least *seem* faster. Better still, at least some of these tips won't cost you one red cent.

The ten tips that follow have been finely tuned over the course of this book's many editions, often in response to suggestions by readers or editors. If you think you have a great way to speed up your Mac, please send it to me at `Monterey4 Dummies@boblevitus.com`. If it's awesome, I may include it in the next edition of this book (and give you full credit for thinking of it, of course)!

Use Those Keyboard Shortcuts

Keyboard shortcuts (see Table 27-1 for a nice little list of the most useful ones) can make navigating your Mac a much faster experience compared with constantly using the mouse, offering these benefits:

>> If you use keyboard shortcuts, your hands stay focused on the keyboard, reducing the amount of time that you remove your hand from the keyboard to fiddle with the mouse or trackpad.

>> If you memorize keyboard shortcuts with your head, your fingers will memorize them, too.

>> The more keyboard shortcuts you use, the faster you can do what you're doing.

Trust me when I say that using the keyboard shortcuts for commands you use often will save you a ton of effort and hours upon hours of time.

TIP

Make a list of keyboard shortcuts you want to memorize, and tape it to your monitor until your brain and fingers memorize them. Or photograph and print Table 27-1 and tape it to your monitor! Learn 'em once and you'll save time with them forever!

Improve Your Typing Skills

One way to make your Mac seem faster is to move your fingers faster. The quicker you finish a task, the quicker you're on to something else. Keyboard shortcuts are nifty tools, but improving your typing speed and accuracy *will* save you even more time. As a bonus, the more your typing skills improve, the less time you'll spend correcting errors. So you'll finish everything even faster!

TIP

The speed and accuracy that you gain have another bonus: When you're a touch typist, your fingers fly even faster on keyboard shortcuts, speeding them up even further. (I list a gaggle of these in Table 27-1.)

The best and easiest way I know to improve your keyboarding skills is a typing training app for your Mac such as Ten Thumbs Typing Tutor ($25.99 at www. tenthumbstypingtutor.com), any of the myriad typing-instruction apps in the Mac App Store (search for *typing*), or a free typing-instruction website such as TypingTest (free at www.typingtest.com), which also offers free typing speed tests if you're curious. For what it's worth, I type 70 words per minute with almost 100 percent accuracy.

TABLE 27-1   **Great Keyboard Shortcuts**

Keyboard Shortcut	Name	What It Does
⌘+O	Open	Opens the selected item.
⌘+. (period)	Cancel	Cancels the current operation in many programs, including Finder. The Esc key often does the same thing as Cancel.
⌘+P	Print	Brings up a dialog that enables you to print the active window's contents. (See Chapter 22 for info on printing.)
⌘+X	Cut	Cuts whatever you select and places it on the Clipboard. (I cover the Clipboard in Chapter 9.)
⌘+C	Copy	Copies whatever you select and places it on the Clipboard.
⌘+V	Paste	Pastes the contents of the Clipboard at your cursor's location.
⌘+F	Find	Displays a Searching window or tab in Finder; displays a Find dialog in most other programs.
⌘+A	Select All	Selects the entire contents of the active window in many programs, including Finder.
⌘+Z	Undo	Undoes the last thing you did in many programs, including Finder.
⌘+Shift+Z	Redo	Redoes the last thing you undid in many programs, including Finder.
⌘+Shift+?	Help	Displays the Mac Help window in Finder; usually the shortcut to summon Help in other programs.
⌘+Q	Quit	Perhaps the most useful keyboard shortcut of all. Quits the current application (but not Finder because it's always running).
⌘+Shift+Q	Log Out	Logs out the current user. The login window appears onscreen until a user logs in.
⌘+Delete	Move to Trash	Moves the selected item to the Trash.
⌘+Shift+Delete	Empty Trash	Empties the Trash.

Try a Different Keyboard

I can't quite type 70 wpm on an Apple keyboard. To type that fast or faster, I need my beloved Microsoft Natural Ergonomic Keyboard 4000 (now discontinued), my keyboard of choice for more than a decade (and I test a lot of keyboards every year.)

It's a split keyboard with bigger keys that are just right for my bigger fingers while offering just the right amount of bounce. And its integrated wrist-rest makes it super comfortable for extended sessions.

It's a USB keyboard aimed at PC users, so the Option keys have a Windows icon and the Command keys say Alt. Everything works as expected, but the weird names can be disconcerting. If you can live with those idiosyncrasies, the Microsoft Natural Ergonomic Keyboard 4000 is perhaps the best keyboard I've ever used and a bargain at around $50.

Change Your Resolution

A setting that you can change to potentially improve your Mac's performance is the resolution of your monitor. Most modern monitors and video cards (or onboard video circuitry, depending on which Mac model you use) can display multiple degrees of screen resolution. You change your monitor's display resolution in the Displays System Preferences pane. Click the Display tab, click the Scaled button, and then select a resolution to try from the list that appears.

You see many more items on the screen at native resolution, but you can make everything bigger by switching to a lower resolution, or make everything smaller (and see more of it) at a higher resolution.

How will this speed up your Mac? Well, for one thing, if you can't discern icons on toolbars and other program components, using a lower resolution may enhance your work speed. Or if you can read more lines of smaller text comfortably at a higher resolution, that will save you time, too.

REMEMBER

Choose a resolution based on what looks best and works best for you. If things on the screen are too big or too small at your current resolution, try a higher or lower resolution until you find one that feels "just right."

Finally, check out the Accessibility System Preferences pane's Zoom tab, where you can enable keyboard shortcuts to zoom in and out instantly, and Hover Text, a highly configurable mode that enlarges only what's under your pointer.

Purchase a Faster Mac

Apple keeps putting out faster and faster Macs at lower and lower prices, and all current Macs now ship with at least 8GB of RAM. Although 4GB may be enough RAM to run Monterey, if you like to keep more than one or two apps running all the time, it's not enough to run it at its best.

Check out the latest Macs with Apple's M processors — they're speedy and all are excellent values. There are currently MacBook Air, MacBook Pro, iMac, and Mac mini models, and all are rocking good computers at surprisingly reasonable prices. You might even consider a used Intel-based Mac that's still faster than yours. eBay (www.ebay.com) has hundreds of used Macs up for auction at any given time. Or try Craigslist (www.craigslist.org) if you prefer to see and touch the Mac before you commit. You might just find yourself a better, faster Mac at an outstanding price!

Another excellent option is to visit the Apple website's refurbished and clearance section. You can frequently save hundreds of dollars by purchasing a slightly used Mac that has been refurbished to factory specifications by Apple. Another advantage to Apple refurbs is that they come with an Apple warranty. If you're on a tight budget, definitely check it out (www.apple.com/shop/refurbished/).

TIP

I always buy refurbished products when I can. In fact, it's been over a decade since I bought any (major) Apple product for list price if a refurbished one was available when I needed it.

Add RAM

Your Mac can never have too much RAM, and it will run better, smoother, and faster with at least 8GB of RAM. If you have an older Mac, you may be able to add RAM at a reasonable price. You can find instructions in your User Guide booklet or on the Apple Technical Support pages (www.apple.com/support; search for *RAM upgrade* and your Mac model).

These days, most (or all) Macs are no longer user-upgradeable. These models are sometimes difficult to open, and Apple frowns upon users opening some models at all. Plus, many Macs have the RAM soldered to the motherboard or integrated with the processor, which means they can't ever be upgraded. If your Mac is upgradeable and you're uncomfortable with upgrading RAM yourself, opt for the services of an authorized, certified Mac cracker-opener.

TIP

The bottom line is that it's best to order your Mac with as much RAM as you can afford in the first place. It will cost you a little more up front, but it's worth it.

Add a Second Display

For almost as long as I've been using a Mac, I've used one with two displays. Almost all Macs today support a second monitor, and many support a third and fourth monitor. In my opinion, screen real estate is among the biggest productivity enhancers you can add — right up there with typing faster.

Screen real estate is the holy grail when working in multi-windowed or multi-paletted apps such as Photoshop, Final Cut Pro, and Logic Pro X. Two monitors are also great when you're working with two or more programs at the same time. With sufficient screen real estate, you can arrange all the windows and palettes for all programs in the way that's most expedient to the way you work.

You don't need an expensive 4K or 5K monitor. For a couple of hundred bucks, you can find a second display that will double your screen real estate. Or, if you have an iPad of recent vintage, read the next section.

Finally, in the words of my former tech editor Ryan, "Why stop at two?" Because many Macs support three or more displays, all you need are the proper cables and available ports.

Use Your iPad as a Second Display

The Sidecar feature allows you to use a late-model iPad as a second screen for your late-model Mac. You'll find the official list of supported hardware and tips for using Sidecar at: https://support.apple.com/en-us/HT210380. Or just connect your iPad to your Mac with a USB cable and then open System Preferences. If you see an icon named Sidecar, your gear is new enough; if you don't, it's not.

If you have an iPad handy, give it a try; if your Mac and iPad are up to the task, enable the Show Sidebar check box. If applicable, enable the Show TouchBar and Enable Double Tap on Apple Pencil check boxes as well. Then use the Displays System Preferences pane to arrange the iPad's position relative to your other screen (or screens) — and you're done.

Hope you enjoy all that extra screen real estate as much as I do!

Upgrade to a Solid-State Drive (SSD)

The latest and greatest storage device to appear is the solid-state drive (SSD). It uses flash memory in place of a mechanical hard drive's spinning platters, which means, among other things, that it has no moving parts. Another benefit is that an SSD performs most operations at up to twice the speed of mechanical drives.

The bad news is that an SSD is more expensive — three or more times the price per gigabyte — of a mechanical hard drive or a hybrid drive with the same capacity.

That said, most users report that it's the best money they ever spent on an upgrade. I put the biggest one I could afford (1TB) in my MacBook Pro and I'll never go back to booting from a hard disk.

My MacBook Air's internal SSD died halfway through writing a previous edition of this book. Because that's the Mac I use for screenshots, I needed the fastest and easiest fix, so I bought a 500GB external USB 3 SSD (a Samsung T5) on sale at the late, lamented Fry's Electronics for about $90.

I replaced an SSD with another SSD, but if you are still booting from a hard disk, you can speed up your Mac in a major way for under $100.

Honestly, folks, if you're only going to do one thing to make your old Mac faster, this is what you should do: Replace your hard drive with an SSD. If your Mac's SSD can't be upgraded, consider an external SSD as your boot disk (which is still what I use with my MacBook Air).

After switching to an SSD startup drive — internal or external — your old Mac will feel almost new again.

Get More Storage

Your Mac will run slower and slower as its startup disk gets fuller and fuller. If you can't afford to replace your startup disk with a bigger SSD or purchase a bigger external SSD to use as a boot disk, another option is to get a big external hard disk (much less expensive per megabyte than an SSD) and move some of your data off your startup disk and onto the external disk.

You can connect external hard disks (or SSDs) via USB or Thunderbolt. All three can be used to connect devices that require high-speed communication with your Mac — hard drives, SSDs, CD/DVD burners, scanners, camcorders, and such.

TECHNICAL STUFF

Thunderbolt, which is available on Mac models introduced since 2012, is the fastest bus around by far. That said, there are still relatively few Thunderbolt peripherals at this writing. Furthermore, the Thunderbolt devices that are out there are somewhat more expensive than their USB 3 counterparts. Although Thunderbolt shows tons of promise, at present, Thunderbolt hard drives are significantly more expensive than either FireWire or USB 3 drives.

And just to confuse things, all Macs since 2014 use USB 3 (Universal Serial Bus 3), which is many times faster than the previous generations of USB (and FireWire).

TIP

If you're buying an external USB drive, get one with USB 3. It shouldn't be much more expensive than a USB 2 drive and will be much faster. If your Mac has USB 3 ports (as all Monterey-capable Macs do), you'll be unhappy with USB 2 drive speeds.

Even if your Mac *doesn't* have USB 3 ports, you should get a USB 3 drive. It'll run at the same speed as a USB 2 drive on your current Mac — and will run a lot faster on your new Mac when you upgrade.

If you're not sure what generation of USB your Mac has, choose ➪ About This Mac, click the System Report button to launch the System Information application, and then click USB in the hardware list on the left.

The good news is that whatever connection you choose for your new disk — USB 2, USB 3, Thunderbolt, FireWire 400 or 800 — you can usually just plug it in and start using it. Unless the disk is preformatted for a PC and requires reformatting, there's nothing more you have to do!

Speaking of which, don't buy an external drive that's advertised as "for the Mac" or "formatted for the Mac." You can often save $20 or more by purchasing the generic (read: Windows) version of the disk and reformatting it as HFS+ or APFS with Disk Utility (see Chapter 25).

WARNING

Almost every Mac sold today has at least one USB-C port, which is a kind of hybrid USB/Thunderbolt port that doesn't appear on Macs prior to 2018.

To make things even more confusing, the same USB-C port also supports Thunderbolt 3 (the latest and greatest connection technology for storage and other devices requiring fast transfer speeds) and recharging.

Because the port is incompatible with every other type of USB cable ever made, you'll probably need a USB-C adapter (or USB-C hub or dock) to connect your old USB devices to your new computer's USB-C/Thunderbolt port.

Whew. Now that you know all you need to know about your new external disk, the last step is to move some data from your startup disk to the new external disk. So copy the files or folders (your large files and folders are likely contained in your Pictures, Music, and Documents folders) to the new external disk; confirm that the files have been copied properly; make sure you have a backup, just in case; and then delete the files from your startup disk.

» iMore, AppleWorld.Today, and Wirecutter

» Apple Support, Other World Computing, and the Apple Refurbished and Clearance Store

» Six Colors

Chapter **28**

Ten Great Websites for Mac Freaks

As much as I would like to believe that this book tells you everything you need to know about using your Mac, I know better. There's much more to discover about using your Mac, and new tools and products come out every day.

The best way to gather more information than you could ever possibly soak up about all things Mac is to hop onto the web. There you can find news, *freeware* and *shareware* (try-before-you-buy software) to download, troubleshooting sites, tons of news and information about your new favorite OS, and lots of places to shop.

The sites in this chapter are the best, most chock-full-o'-stuff places on the web for Mac users. By the time you finish checking out these websites, you'll know so much about your Mac and Monterey that you'll feel like your brain is in danger of exploding. On the other hand, you might just feel a whole lot smarter. Happy surfing!

The Mac Observer

www.macobserver.com

The Mac Observer gives you Apple news, views, reviews, and much more.

Disclosure: I write a weekly column called "Dr. Mac's Rants & Raves" for The Mac Observer. But I loved The Mac Observer long before I begged for a job there. TMO (as we insiders refer to it) is known for insightful opinion pieces in addition to Apple news and product reviews. In my humble opinion, the quality and depth of the writing by the TMO staff is superior to almost any other site covering the Apple beat.

Macworld

www.macworld.com

Although the print publication and exposition became extinct years ago, the Macworld site still describes itself as: "Your best source for all things Apple." And it's still true, more or less. Macworld is perhaps the best and most comprehensive source of product information for Apple products. It's especially strong for reviews of Mac, iPhone, and iPad products. For example, when you want to know which inkjet printer or digital camera is the best in its price class, Macworld can almost certainly offer guidance, feature comparison charts, and real-world test results. And you won't merely find product information here — you'll find it accompanied by expert opinions and professional editing and fact checking.

Put another way, I trust the writers and editors at Macworld more than I trust the writers and editors of many other websites. Any other sites, that is, except the others in this chapter.

TidBITS

http://tidbits.com

TidBITS is an online newsletter and website with the motto: "Thoughtful, detailed coverage of everything Apple for 30 years." With some of the richest and most insightful writing on the web, TidBITS is another must-read for me. I always look forward to reading the latest issue (which comes out every Monday) as well as articles posted regularly throughout the week.

Disclosure: I have known the proprietors of TidBITS, Adam and Tonya Engst, since the 1980s and consider them friends. That said, they've prospered and grown for 30 years because Adam, Tonya, and the contributors to TidBITS are as passionate about sharing detailed information about Apple products and services today as they were in 1990.

I recommend subscribing to the email newsletter so that you get a new issue every Monday, like I do. But even if you don't choose to subscribe, you should check out the site; TidBITS is one of my all-time faves.

iMore

`http://www.imore.com`

If you live the Apple lifestyle, iMore is your go-to website. With in-depth articles on all Apple products and operating systems, and tons of tips, hints, and tutorials as well, it's one of the sites I try to visit daily.

AppleWorld.Today

`www.appleworld.today`

For the latest in Mac news, updated every single day, check out AppleWorld.Today, which arose from the ashes of The Unofficial Apple Weblog (TUAW) after its untimely demise. With a small staff of Apple newshounds, this site keeps you on the bleeding edge of Mac news — including software updates, virus alerts, and Apple happenings. It also offers extensive and unbiased reviews of many products soon after their release.

The Wirecutter

`https://thewirecutter.com`

When I want to see what others consider the best peripherals, tech tools, and toys, I visit The Wirecutter. Now a *New York Times* company, Wirecutter has the resources to objectively evaluate many products and declare one of them "the best."

I take the reviews with a grain of salt, and typically look at the Electronics and Office sections. I've also used it to research purchases as diverse as sunscreen, an insulated water bottle, and Bluetooth headsets.

I love this site and try to visit it at least once a week, regardless of whether there's anything I need. (I know — I should get a life.)

Apple Support

`www.apple.com/support`

Do you have a technical question about any version of Mac OS or any Apple product — including Monterey? March your question right over to the Apple Support page, where you can find searchable archives of tech notes, software update information, and documentation. The Support pages are especially useful if you need info about your old Mac; Apple archives all its info here. Choose among a preset list of topics or products, and type a keyword to research. You're rewarded with a list of helpful documents. Clicking any one of these entries (they're all links) takes you right to the info you seek. The site even has tools that can help narrow your search.

The site also offers a section with user discussions of Apple-related topics. Although not officially sanctioned or monitored by Apple, it's often the best place to gain insights, especially on slightly esoteric or obscure issues not covered in other sections of the site.

Other World Computing

`www.macsales.com`

Other World Computing is the go-to place for Mac peripherals and upgrades, and my first stop when I need RAM, hard drives, SSDs, optical drives, video cards, processor upgrades, cables, discs, docks, or anything else you can think of. If it enhances your Mac, Other World Computing probably has it at a reasonable price. And, if it's memory or internal storage, you'll usually get a comprehensive illustrated installation manual and (often) an installation video as well.

Because of its inexpensive and reliable delivery and a solid guarantee on every item it sells, you can't go wrong doing business with OWC.

I buy at least half my storage devices and other peripherals and almost all RAM from OWC, and I trust them to know Apple stuff a lot more than I trust BestBuy.

Apple's Refurbished and Clearance Store

www.apple.com/shop/refurbished

I'm sure you've noticed that Apple products are rarely discounted. The price is about the same regardless of where you buy one of their devices. That's why whenever I need *any* Apple product, the first place I shop is the Apple Refurbished and Clearance page.

Apple refurbished products are "like new," with the same 1-year limited warranty as new devices. Refurbished iOS devices include a new battery and outer shell, and each device includes all appropriate accessories, cables, and operating system. Refurbished products are eligible for AppleCare and include free shipping (and returns).

If you don't see a refurbished device with the specifications you're looking for, try again later (or tomorrow) because inventory is updated throughout the day. I wanted an Apple TV 4K last month, but no refurbished ones were available. So, I used the Refurb Tracker website (https://refurb-tracker.com) to set a free alert. A few days later, an email notified me that the product was available in the refurbished store and I saved $20.

I can't remember the last time I bought a brand-new Mac or iDevice and have saved up to 30 percent by choosing Apple Certified Refurbished products whenever possible.

Six Colors

www.sixcolors.com/

Six Colors provides daily coverage of Apple, other technology companies, and the intersection of technology and culture. Its founder and editor-in-chief is Jason Snell, who was editor-in-chief of Macworld for more than a decade. Along with former Macworld writer and senior editor Dan Moren and a cast of stellar contributors, Six Colors provides timely analysis, insightful reviews, and expert commentary on all things Apple (and some things not).

This concludes our regularly scheduled programming. Thank you for your support.

Bob "Dr. Mac" LeVitus

Fall 2021

Index

Numbers

3D maps, 226

A

accessibility
  Dictation feature, 386–387
  preferences, 396–397
  Text to Speech feature, 390–392
  Voice Control feature, 388–389
  VoiceOver feature, 389–390
Action menu (Finder), 26
active windows
  overview, 30–32
  removing apps from, 57
  toolbar, 32
Activity Monitor app, 421–422
administrative users, 301
Advanced pane (System Preferences), 92–93
AirDrop
  Quick Look and, 181
  sharing files via, 296–297
AirPlay, 402–403
AirPort, 298
aliases
  of disks, 158
  Finder and, 73–76
  of folders, 160
annotating PDF files, 287, 351–352
APFS (Apple File System), 423–424
App Nap feature, 95
App Store
  dock icon, 48
  overview, 381–383
  updates on, 415
Apple Arcade, 382
Apple File System (APFS), 423–424
Apple ID, 332
Apple menu
  options in, 43–44
  overview, 13–14

Apple Music app
  listening to radio, 332–334
  overview, 48, 326–330
  playlists, 334–338
  songs
    adding, 330–332
    burning to CDs, 338–339
    filtering, 333
  view modes, 333–334
Apple Music subscription service, 326–327
Apple News app. *See* News app
Apple tech support
  hotline, 441
  website, 458
Apple TV app. *See* TV app
AppleScripts, 392–394
AppleWorld.Today website, 457
Application Support folder, 140
apps
  accessing, 194–195
  Activity Monitor, 421–422
  adding passwords to Keychain, 427–428
  App Store
    dock icon, 48
    overview, 381–383
    updates on, 415
  assigning file formats to, 154–155
  Automator, 394–396
  auto-save feature, 121, 141–143, 355
  backing-up data, 410–411
  Books
    overview, 344–348
    searching for manual, 10
  Boot Camp
    overview, 401–402
    partitioning drives and, 424
  Calculator, 419–420
  Calendar
    Contacts and, 262
    events in, 201–203
    iCloud and, 199

apps *(continued)*

    invitations, 202–203

    managing calendars, 199–201

    notifications, 203

    overview, 47

    view modes, 198–199

Carbon Copy Cloner, 436

changing menu bar, 39

choosing, 54

closing, 52, 114

Contacts

    adding contacts, 278

    FaceTime and, 269

    groups, 264–266

    importing, 263–264

    Mail and, 262, 276–278

    Maps and, 227–228

    overview, 47, 261–263

    searching in, 291

    syncing, 262, 267

    vCard format, 263, 278

CopyClip, 172

creating PDFs without, 105–106

Disk Utility

    Erase button, 426

    First Aid button, 425–426, 438–439

    Info button, 427

    Mount/Unmount button, 426–427

    Partition button, 424–425

    Volume +/- button, 422–424

in Dock

    missing, 48

    overview, 57–58

    recently used, 62

dragging files onto, 54, 154–156

FaceTime

    calling via, 268–270

    overview, 47

    starting call from Messages, 291

Finder

    Advanced pane, 92–93

    aliases, 73–76

    customizing, 90–93

    description of features, 24–25

    folder pop-up menu, 87–88

    General pane, 90–91

    Go menu, 88–89

    hiding, 86

    icons in, 71–73, 93–96

    keyboard shortcuts for, 20, 34–35

    List view, 79–81

    menu, 84–86

    navigating, 69–70

    overview, 23, 47, 66–68

    preferences, 90–93

    recently used files in, 132

    searching in, 71, 184–186

    showing folders in, 51

    sidebar, 90, 92, 120

    tagging in, 91–92

    toolbar, 26, 68–71

    version of, 84

    viewing modes, 77–82

folder location, 136

Font Book, 359–361

full-screen mode, 190

Google Chrome, 253

Home, 245

iCloud

    backing-up data to, 411

    Calendar app and, 199

    Mail and, 272

    overview, 169–170

    sharing via, 182, 287

    storing on, 326, 443

    syncing via, 262, 267, 429

icons for, 46, 72

Keychain Access, 427–429

launching options for, 121

launching upon login, 15, 51

limiting, 216

Mail

    composing, 274–276

    Contacts and, 262, 276–278

    features, 286–288

    forwarding, 273

    iCloud and, 272

    inbox, 280–282

    Mail Drop feature, 287–288

    Markup, 287

    Messages and, 292

    overview, 47, 271–272

    preferences, 278, 282

    Quick Look and, 286

replying to, 273
rules for, 284–286
setting up, 272
sharing via, 181
signatures, 283–284
smart inbox, 281–282
spam, 279
spoofing and, 414
toolbar, 272–274
using, 278
Maps
Contacts and, 227–228
determining current location, 223–224
driving directions, 230–232
favorites, 228–229
finding people and places, 224–225
flyovers, 232–233
guides, 229
Info sheet, 233–234
looking around, 233
navigating in, 225–227
overview, 47
public transportation directions, 232
recents, 230
sidebar, 228–230
traffic information, 232
walking directions, 231
Messages
communicating via, 288–292
overview, 47
sharing via, 181
Migration Assistant, 429–430
Music
adding songs, 330–332
burning music to CDs, 338–339
filtering songs, 333
listening to radio, 332–334
overview, 48, 326–330
playlists, 334–338
view modes, 333–334
News, 48, 239–241
Notes
overview, 48, 211–215
sharing via, 181
notification settings for, 207–211
opening, 52
Page Setup, 364, 370

Photo Booth, 349–351
Photos
browsing, 276
overview, 47
share menu and, 182
Podcasts, 48, 348–349
preferences, 84
Preview, 351–352, 374–375
QuickTime Player, 342–343
recently used, 43
Reminders
overview, 48, 203–207
sharing via, 182
Safari
bookmarking, 257–258
favorites, 258
Help Center, 260
links, 257
overview, 47, 253–254
Reader view, 259
Reading list, 258–259
settings for, 259
sidebar, 255–259
tabs, 256–257
toolbar, 254–255
Screen Time, 215–216
Screenshot, 431–434
Script Editor, 392–393
Shortcuts, 244–245
Stocks, 236–238
SuperDuper! 436
System Information, 430
System Preferences
Bluetooth, 127, 399
Desktop tab, 116–117
icon in, 114
Input Sources tab, 125–126
Internet connection settings, 251–252
keyboard, 122–126
microphone, 242
Mission Control, 187–189
mouse, 126–127
opening, 114
output and input options, 130
overview, 48, 113–115
passwords, 429
screen savers, 117–118

apps *(continued)*

   Shortcuts tab, 124–125

   Siri, 220–221

   sound effects, 129–130

   Text tab, 123–124

   trackpads, 127–129, 191

   UI, 118–121

  Terminal, 430

  TextEdit

   adding images, 358–359

   creating files, 354–355

   in Dock, 58

   formatting, 355–358

   printing in, 373

  Time Machine

   backing-up data with, 406–409

   overview, 16

   versions of files, 143

  Trash, 48–50

  trimming videos without, 104–105

  TV, 48, 343–344

  uninstalling, 195

  updates and security, 414–415

  updating, 382–383, 415

  Voice Memos, 241–244

  word-processing, 58

archiving email, 273

attachments

  adding to notes, 213

  in email, 276

  security concern with, 414

  in text messages, 291

audio. *See also* Music app

  blue speaker icon, 260

  books, 345–346

  changing sounds, 129–130

  enabling and disabling, 260

  messages, 291

  preferences for sounds, 129–130

  recording, 241–244

autocorrect feature, 123

Automator app, 394–396

auto-save feature, 121, 141–143, 355

B

Backblaze, 411

background, desktop, 109–110, 116–117

backing-up data

  brute-force method, 409–410

  to cloud, 411–412

  importance of, 16

  music library, 327

  overview, 405–406

  software for, 410–411

badges, 75

Baen, 347

battery-related features, 95, 398–399

blocking connections, 416

blue/black screen of death, 12

Bluetooth

  preferences, 127, 399

  sharing via, 322

bookmarking, 257–258

Books app

  computer manual in, 10

  overview, 344–348

Boot Camp

  overview, 401–402

  partitioning drives and, 424

broadband access, 251

browsers

  Firefox, 253

  Google Chrome, 253

  Safari

   bookmarking, 257–258

   favorites, 258

   Help Center, 260

   links, 257

   overview, 47, 253–254

   Reader view, 259

   Reading list, 258–259

   settings for, 259

   sidebar, 255–259

   tabs, 256–257

   toolbar, 254–255

  setting default, 120

  Spotlight and, 186–187

bulleted lists, 213

C

Calculator app, 419–420
Calendar app
  Contacts and, 262
  events in, 201–203
  invitations, 202–203
  managing calendars, 199–201
  notifications, 203
  overview, 47
  view modes, 198–199
cameras
  Continuity feature, 383–386
  creating signatures with, 104
  taking photos with, 349–350
canned signatures, 283
Carbon Copy Cloner app, 436
CDs. *See* compact discs
cellular networks, 253
check boxes, 33–34
clicking
  active/inactive windows, 30–32
  basic actions, 16–18
  double-clicking, 17
  icons, 46
  right-clicking, 17, 40
Clipboard
  contents in, 172
  copying files and folders with, 173–175
  overview, 171–173
  pasting from, 175–176
closing
  apps, 52, 114
  windows, 26–29, 31, 34–35
cloud
  backing-up data to, 411–412
  Calendar app and, 199
  Mail and, 272
  overview, 169–170
  sharing via, 182, 287
  storing on, 326, 443
  syncing via, 262, 267, 429
Cohen, Dennis R., 338
Column Browser (Music), 333–334
Column view (Finder), 77–81
commands

app-specific
  changing menu bar, 39
  News, 240–241
  Notes, 211–214
  Reminders, 204
  Stocks, 238
  Terminal, 430
  Trash, 50
basic
  closing, 35
  copying, 171–172
  creating, 147, 163–164
  duplicating, 143
  force quitting, 43–44, 413
  opening, 150–151
  pasting, 172, 175–176
  printing, 213, 370–371
  quitting, 114
  save, 142–143
  search, 76, 184–186, 224
  selections, 151
  undo, 49
bringing window to front, 38
creating aliases, 75–76
in Dock, 52–53
file-specific
  Show Inspector, 96
  stacks, 98, 100–101
  viewing modes, 82–83
menus, 26, 41–42, 51–53
navigation
  Finder tabs, 37–38
  Go menu, 88–89
screenshots, 107–108
showing/hiding UI elements
  Library subfolder, 140
  Safari toolbar, 254
  sidebar, 205
  windows, 86
smart folders, 163–164
voice
  playing songs with, 326–327
  Siri, 217–221
compact discs (CDs)
  adding songs from, 331
  backing-up data onto, 410

compact discs (CDs) *(continued)*
  copying songs to, 338–339
  icon for, 67
composing email, 274–276
compressing files, 168
Computer folder, 135
computers
  connecting remotely, 314–318
  connecting to remote computer, 314–318
  force quitting, 15
  powering on, 10–13
  purchasing faster, 450–451
  restarting, 44
  shutting down, 14–15, 44
  unlocking with devices, 401
  unplugging, 15–16
connections
  Bluetooth
    preferences, 127, 399
    sharing via, 322
  Help menu and, 20
  Internet
    calling via, 268–270
    Dictation feature and, 386
    Ethernet, 294, 298–299
    Help menu and, 20
    music files using, 331
    overview, 250–253
    settings for, 251–253
    SharePlay and, 269–270
    sharing, 321–322
    Siri and, 221
    Spotlight, 186–187
    terminology, 294–295
    Wi-Fi, 298–299
  to remote computer, 314–318
  settings for, 193
Contacts app
  adding, 278
  FaceTime and, 269
  groups, 264–266
  importing, 263–264
  Maps app and, 227–228
  overview, 47, 261–263
  searching in, 291
  sending email from, 276–278

syncing, 262, 267
  vCard format, 263, 278
contextual menus
  Action icon and, 41
  menu bar, 39–41
  right-clicking and, 17
  Services menu, 84–86
Continuity features
  cameras, 383–386
  messages, 289
Control Center, 193
Control-clicking
  overview, 17
  trackpads, 40
CopyClip app, 172
copying
  files, 68, 173–175
  folders, 173–175
  songs to CD, 338–339
crashes, troubleshooting, 442
cursors
  clicking
    active/inactive windows, 30–32
    basic actions, 16–18
    icons, 46
  double-clicking, 17
  hot corners, 189–190
  hovering, 28, 48, 162
  locating, 35
  magnifying items in Dock, 61
  preferences, 126–129
  resizing UI elements with, 28, 32, 35
  right-clicking, 17, 40
  for text, 167

D

dark mode, 380–381
dashed lists, 213
deleting
  bookmarks, 258
  desktop, 192–193
  emails, 273, 278, 281
  favorites in Maps, 229
  folders and files, 168–169
  funds in Stocks, 237

groups or smart group, 266

icons, 57–58, 64

indexes in Stocks, 237

photos, 351

songs, 335

tags, 92

users, 305–306

desktops

background

changing, 116–117

dynamic, 109–110

deleting, 192–193

folder for, 138

moving files to, 68, 351

organizing, 97–101, 190–192

overview, 24–25, 66–68

preferences, 116–117

screen savers and, 117–118

switching between, 190

windows vs., 24

devices

controlling cameras on, 383–386

networking and, 295

refurbished, 459

as second display, 452

unlocking computer with, 401

dialog windows, 32–34

Dictation feature, 386–387

directions (Map), 230–232

disabling

app icon animation, 61

audio, 260

autocorrect feature, 123

Column Browser, 333–334

dark mode, 380

FileVault, 416–417

Filter Field, 333

location services, 418

login screen, 11

routing FaceTime calls, 268

Screen Flash, 350

screen savers, 117–118

security settings, 416–418

disclosure triangles, 34, 79

discs

adding songs from, 331

backing-up data onto, 410

copying songs to, 338–339

icon for, 67

Disk Utility

Erase button, 426

First Aid button, 425–426, 438–439

Info button, 427

Mount/Unmount button, 426–427

Partition button, 424–425

Volume +/- button, 422–424

disks

display options for, 63

icons for, 47, 72–73

preferences, 62–64

sharing, 307

sorting, 63

startup, 66

troubleshooting

Erase button, 426

First Aid button, 425–426, 438–439

Info button, 427

Mount/Unmount button, 426–427

Partition button, 424–425

startup, 435–437

Volume +/- button, 422–424

viewing options for, 64

Do Not Disturb mode, 210–211

Dock

divider, 48

hiding, 61–62

icons

default, 47–48, 57

magnifying, 61

menus, 51–53

missing, 48

opening, 54–57

recently used, 62

removing, 57–58

sorting, 63

suggestions regarding, 58–59

overview, 24, 45–47

preferences, 60–64

resizing, 58

showing, 61–62

documents. See files

Documents folder, 138

double-clicking, 17

downloads folder, 48

draft email, 275

dragging

contacts to Calendar, 262

copying items by, 173–174

files, 54, 161–162, 165, 331

overview, 17

photos, 351

scroll bars, 30

selecting items by, 166–167

windows, 35

drawing tablets, 400

drivers, printer, 367

driving directions (Maps), 230–232

DRM-free e-books, 347

duplicating

guides in Maps, 229

saving vs., 148–150

dynamic desktop background, 109–110

E

e-books, 345–348

editing

events, 201

guides, 229

images, 101–103, 287

users, 305

videos, 104–105, 343

emails

composing, 274–276

deleting, 273, 278

features, 286–288

forwarding, 273

inbox, 280–282

Mail Drop feature, 287–288

Markup, 287

overview, 271–272

preferences, 278, 282

Quick Look and, 286

replying to, 273

rules for, 284–286

sending from Contacts app, 276–278

sending from Messages, 292

setting up accounts, 272

signatures, 283–284

spam, 279

spoofing and, 414

toolbar, 272–274

using, 278

emojis, 276, 292, 359

enabling

app icon animation, 61

audio, 260

autocorrect feature, 123

Column Browser, 333–334

dark mode, 380

FileVault, 416–417

Filter Field, 333

location services, 418

login screen, 11

routing FaceTime calls, 268

Screen Flash, 350

screen savers, 117–118

security settings, 416–418

encryption, 253, 412

energy saving features, 95, 399

Erase button (Disk Utility), 426

Essentials booklet, 10

Ethernet, 294, 298–299

events (Calendar), 201–203

exporting photos, 351

F

FaceTime

calling via, 268–270

overview, 47

starting call from Messages, 291

favorites, bookmarks vs., 258

features

accessibility, 396–397

AirDrop

Quick Look and, 181

sharing files via, 296–297

AirPlay, 402–403

AirPort, 298

App Nap, 95

autocorrect, 123

automation, 392–396

auto-save, 121, 141–143, 355

battery related, 95, 398–399

Bluetooth

preferences, 127, 399

sharing via, 322

Clipboard, 172, 175–176
  copying files and folders with, 173–175
  overview, 171–173
Continuity Camera, 383–386
Continuity in Messages, 289
Control Center, 193
dark mode, 380–381
Dictation, 386–387
email, 286–288
energy saving, 95, 399
Find command, 184–186
full-screen mode, 182–183
Gatekeeper, 417
Genius playlists, 337–338
Handoff, 403–404
Launchpad, 47, 194–195
Mail Drop, 287–288
Markup, 101–104, 287
Mission Control
  hot corners, 189–190
  navigating in, 192–193
  organizing windows with, 190–192
  preferences, 187–189
in Print sheets, 370
privacy report, 255
Quick Actions, 101–106
Quick Look
  as feature, 180–183
  Mail and, 286
  opening files with, 152–153
  using to open files in trash, 50
Quick Note, 215
Screen Flash, 350
Setup Assistant, 251
SharePlay, 269–270
Sidecar, 452
Siri
  calculations and, 420
  overview, 217–221
  playing songs with, 326–327
Slideshow mode, 182–183
Spotlight
  calculations and, 420
  overview, 183–187
  Siri and, 219
Sticky Keys, 397
Text to Speech, 390–392

Universal Clipboard, 175–176
Universal Control, 404
unlocking with device, 401
Voice Control, 388–389
VoiceOver, 389–390
writing, 400
Feedbooks website, 347
file formats
  assigning to apps, 154–155
  e-books, 345–348
  HEIC, 352
  JPEG, 351–352
  MP3, 339
  options for extensions, 92–93
  PDF
    annotating files, 287, 351–352
    creating without app, 105–106
  for text, 354, 357
  unsupported, 153–154
  vCard format, 263, 278
File menu (Finder), 34
files. *See also* icons
  accessing recently used, 43
  aligning, 83
  annotating, 287, 351–352
  attaching
    email, 276
    notes, 213
    security concern, 414
    text messages, 291
  auto-save feature, 121, 141–143, 355
  commands for
    Show Inspector, 96
    stacks, 98, 100–101
  compressing, 168
  containing macro viruses, 412–413
  copying, 68, 172–175
  creating, 105–106
  deleting, 124, 168–169
  dragging, 54, 161–162, 165, 331
  duplicating, 143
  in folders, 158
  grouping, 26, 70, 82
  icons for, 46, 72
  locking, 416–417
  metadata, 94–96, 154
  missing, 48

files *(continued)*
  moving, 68, 165–166
  naming, 161
  opening
    with apps, 154–156
    overview, 150–154
    without apps, 180
  organizing, 159–160
  pasting, 172, 175–176
  printing, 370–374
  renaming, 167–168
  restoring, 49–50
  saving
    duplicating vs., 148–150
    steps, 141–148
  scanning, 385–386
  searching for, 132
  selecting, 80, 151, 166–167
  sharing
    Finder icon, 70
    over network, 294–295
    via AirDrop, 181, 296–297
    via MailDrop, 287
  sorting, 70, 80, 83
  stacks, 98, 100
  storing on iCloud, 326, 443
  tagging, 70
  TextEdit, 354–355
  transferring, 291
  versions of, 143, 150
  viewing modes, 82–83
FileVault, 406, 416–417
Filter Field (Music), 333
Finder, 132
  Advanced pane, 92–93
  aliases, 73–76
  contents in, 23
  customizing, 90–93
  description of features, 24–25
  folder pop-up menu, 87–88
  folders in, 51
  General pane, 90–91
  Go menu, 88–89
  hiding, 86
  icons in, 71–73, 93–96
  keyboard shortcuts for, 20, 34–35, 86
  List view, 79–81

  menu, 84–86
  navigating, 69–70
  overview, 47, 66–68
  preferences, 90–93
  searching in, 71, 184–186
  sidebar, 90, 92, 120
  tagging in, 91–92
  toolbar, 26, 68–71
  version of, 84
  viewing modes, 77–82
Firefox, 253
FireWire port, 453–454
First Aid button (Disk Utility), 425–426, 438–439
flagging emails
  overview, 272–273
  spam, 279
flyovers (Maps), 232–233
Fn (function) key, 122
folders
  adding to sidebar, 90
  aliases, 160
  Application, 136
  Application Support, 140
  compressing, 168
  Computer, 135
  copying, 173–175
  creating, 139, 160–161
  deleting, 168–169
  Desktop, 138
  in Dock, 57–59
  Documents, 138
  downloads, 48
  files in, 158
  in Finder, 51
  Fonts, 140
  Home, 137–139, 410
  icons for, 47, 72–73
  keyboard shortcuts for
    adding to sidebar, 90
    creating, 147, 163
    displaying path, 26–27
  in Launchpad, 195
  Library, 136–140
  in Mail, 280–281
  missing, 48
  moving, 165–166
  naming, 161

navigating, 27
nested, 134–135
in Notes, 213
owner of, 308
pasting, 175–176
preferences, 62–64, 140
prohibitory sign in, 12
Public, 138, 306–307
question mark in, 12
renaming, 167–168
restoring, 49–50
selecting, 166–167
sharing over network, 306–311
smart, 162–164
sorting, 63
spring-loaded, 161–162
structure, 132–134
subfolders, 158–160
System, 137
Users folder, 133
viewing
   columns, 77–78
   lists, 79–81
   options for, 64
Font Book, 359–361
fonts, 140, 355
force quitting
  computers, 15
  keyboard shortcut, 413
  windows, 43–44
formatting text, 355–358
forwarding emails, 273
full-screen mode
  apps in, 190
  Quick Look, 182–183
function (Fn) key, 122
funds (Stocks), 237

G

Gallery view, 81–82
Gatekeeper feature, 417
General pane (System Preferences), 118–121
Genius playlists, 334–338
global Dock preferences, 60–62
Go menu (Finder), 88–89
Google Chrome, 253

Google Play, 347
graphs (Stocks), 238
gray screen of death, 12
grayscale display, 396
grouping
  contacts, 264–266
  files, 26, 70, 82
  icon for, 70
  menu for, 26
  tabs, 254, 256–257
groups
  FaceTime, 269
  networking and, 301–302
  permissions and, 308
  text messages, 290
guests, 302
guides (Maps), 229

H

Handoff, 403–404
hard-drives
  backing-up data with, 409
  icon, 67
  upgrading to SSD, 452–453
hardware
  backing-up data and, 406
  cameras
   Continuity feature, 383–386
   creating signatures with, 104
   taking photos with, 349–350
  causing startup issues, 12
  to connect to Internet, 250
  drawing tablet, 400
  external hard-drives, 409
  hard-drives
   backing-up data with, 409
   icon, 67
   upgrading to SSD, 452–453
  headsets, 221
  icons for, 67
  information about, 43
  keyboards
   ergonomic, 449–450
   Mission Control key, 188
   preferences, 122–126
  microphones, 221, 242, 387–389

hardware *(continued)*
  modems, 250, 298
  monitors, 16, 192
  mouse
    preferences, 126–127
    scrolling with, 30
    using, 16–18
  ports, 294–295, 453–454
  printers, 322, 364–368, 371
  routers, 298
  surge protectors, 15
  trackpads
    accessing Mission Control, 191
    creating signatures with, 104
    drawing and, 103
    Launchpad and, 194
    preferences, 127–129, 191
    right-clicking with, 40
    scrolling with, 30
  troubleshooting
    Erase button, 426
    First Aid button, 425–426, 438–439
    Info button, 427
    Mount/Unmount button, 426–427
    Partition button, 424–425
    Volume +/- button, 422–424
  upgrading to SSD, 452–453
  webcam, 349–350
  wireless, 127
hardware zoom, 397
headsets, 221
HEIC file format, 352
Help Center, 260
Help menu
  keyboard shortcut, 19
  overview, 18–21
HFS+ (Hierarchical File System +), 423–424
Hierarchical File System + (HFS+), 423–424
Home app, 245
Home folder, 137–139, 410
hot corners, 189–190
hovering cursors, 28, 48, 162

I

iCloud
  backing-up data to, 411
  Calendar app and, 199
  Mail and, 272
  overview, 169–170
  sharing via, 182, 287
  storing on, 326, 443
  syncing via, 262, 267, 429
icons. *See also* files
  actions, 70
  aliases, 73–76, 158, 160
  aligning, 83
  apps, 46, 72
  audio, 260
  behavior of, 66
  CDs, 67
  clicking, 46
  default, 47–48
  defined, 46
  disks, 66–67, 72–73
  dragging files onto, 54
  editing photos, 101–104
  files, 46, 72
  Finder toolbar, 26, 69–70
  folders, 72–73
  hiding, 115
  Info window for, 93–96
  magnifying, 61
  managing, 115
  menus and, 51–53
  movement, 53
  navigating, 27, 70
  opening, 54–57, 150–151
  overview, 71–73
  packages, 158
  removing, 57–58, 64
  search, 71
  sharing, 70
  sorting, 115
  suggestions regarding, 58–59

System Preferences, 114
trimming videos, 104
types of, 72–73
view mode, 79, 146
volumes, 67
images. *See also* Photos app
adding special effects to, 350
adding to TextEdit, 358–359
browsing, 276
editing, 101–104, 287
viewing in Mail, 286
iMessage
communicating with, 288–292
overview, 47
sharing via, 181
iMore, 457
importing
contacts, 263–264
PDFs to Books, 347
videos, 344
inactive windows
icons and, 46
overview, 30–32
removing app from Dock and, 57
inboxes, 280–282
incremental backups, 410–411
index sheet, 181
indicator dot, 62
Info button (Disk Utility), 427
Info window, 93–96
Input Sources tab (System Preferences), 125–126
installing
Firefox, 253
OS, 441
printers, 365–367
software updates, 414–415
uninstalling apps, 195
Internet browsers. *See* browsers
Internet connections
calling via, 268–270
Dictation feature and, 386
Ethernet, 294, 298–299
Help menu and, 20
music files using, 331
overview, 250–253
settings for, 251–253
SharePlay and, 269–270

sharing, 321–322
Siri and, 221
terminology, 294–295
Wi-Fi, 298–299
Internet Service Providers (ISPs), 251–252
invitations (Calendar), 202–203, 262
iTunes, 325–327. *See also* Music app

J

jiggling cursors, 18
JPEG file format, 351–352

K

kernel panic, 12–13
keyboard shortcuts
accessibility feature, 397
adding, 124
for aliases, 75–76
app-specific
Activity Monitor, 421
Books, 347
Calculator, 419–420
Calendar, 198–199, 201, 203
Contacts, 264–266
Disk Utility, 438–440
Finder, 20, 34–35, 86
Font Book, 360
Launchpad, 194
Mail, 272–274, 278
Maps, 224, 226
Music, 328–329, 331, 333–336
News, 240–241
Notes, 211, 213–214
Preview, 375
QuickTime Player, 343
Reminders, 204
Safari, 255–259
Screenshot, 431–434
Stocks, 238
TextEdit, 354–359
benefits of using, 447–448
commands
close all, 35
Find, 184
force quitting, 43–44, 413

keyboard shortcuts *(continued)*
    Go menu, 88–89
    Hide Others, 86
    locking screens, 44
    logging out, 44
    opening, 34, 151
    printing, 213, 370–371
    quitting applications, 114
    screenshots, 107–108
    sending item to Trash, 49
    Show Inspector, 96
    undo, 49
feature-specific
    autocorrect, 123
    Dictation feature, 387
    Mission Control, 188
    Quick Look, 50, 153, 180
    Siri, 219
    Spotlight, 186–187
    VoiceOver, 390
file-specific
    copying, 172
    deleting, 124
    duplicating, 143
    metadata, 154
    pasting, 172
    restoring, 50
    save, 142–143
    selections, 80, 151
    sorting, 83
    stacks, 98, 100
folder-specific
    adding to sidebar, 90
    creating, 147, 163
    displaying path of, 26–27
modifying, 123
navigation
    Application folder, 136
    closing windows, 35
    Computer folder, 135
    cycling through windows, 36
    exiting fullscreen mode, 28
    expanding windows, 28
    Forward and Back icons, 27, 70
    full-screen mode, 182–183
    Help menu, 19

    Home folder, 137
    Library subfolder, 140
    minimizing windows, 36
    moving between tabs, 37
    scrolling, 30
    System Preferences app, 114
overview, 44
preferences, 123–124
resetting RAM, 441
Tab key behavior, 124
text-specific
    formatting, 214
    phrases, 123
    special characters, 161
UI-specific
    Column view, 77
    Dock, 62
    Gallery view, 81
    Icon view, 78
    List view, 80
    showing/hiding sidebar, 205
    showing/hiding windows, 86
    sidebar and toolbar, 69
keyboards
    adjusting brightness, 121
    ergonomic, 449–450
    Mission Control key, 188
    preferences, 122–126
Keychain Access, 427–429

L

landscape orientation, 369, 373
Launchpad, 47, 194–195
LDIF format, 263
Library folder, 136–140
links, 257
listening
    to radio, 332–334
    to recordings, 242
lists
    in Notes, 213
    sharing, 206–207
    URLs, 258–259
    view mode, 79–81, 146
location

determining current, 223–224

menu, 252

privacy and, 418

locking

files, 416–417

screens, 44

logging in/out

features, 400–401

importance of, 314

opening files upon, 51

options for, 44

overview, 11

look arounds (Maps), 233

M

Mac App Store

dock icon, 48

overview, 381–383

updates on, 415

Mac Observer, 415, 456

macOS. *See* Monterey OS

macro viruses, 412–413

Macworld, 415, 456

Magic Trackpad 2, 128

Mail app

composing, 274–276

Contacts and, 262, 276–278

features, 286–288

forwarding, 273

inbox, 280–282

Mail Drop feature, 287–288

Markup, 287

Messages and, 292

overview, 47, 271–272

preferences, 278, 282

Quick Look and, 286

replying to, 273

rules for, 284–286

setting up, 272

sharing via, 181

signatures, 283–284

smart inbox, 281–282

spam, 279

spoofing and, 414

toolbar, 272–274

using, 278

manuals

backing-up data, 409–410

for computers, 10

for printers, 364

Maps app

Contacts and, 227–228

determining current location, 223–224

driving directions, 230–232

favorites, 228–229

finding people and places, 224–225

flyovers, 232–233

guides, 229

Info sheet, 233–234

look arounds, 233

navigating in, 225–227

overview, 47

public transportation directions, 232

recents, 230

sidebar, 228–230

traffic information, 232

walking directions, 231

Markup feature, 101–104

media

sharing remotely, 322

sharing via FaceTime, 269–270

menus

Action menu, 26

Apple menu

options in, 43–44

overview, 13–14

clicking, 18

clicking and, 17

commands in

disabled, 41–42

for selected items, 26

contextual

Action icon and, 41

in menu bar, 39–41

right-clicking and, 17

Services menu, 84–86

customizing appearance of, 119

disk preferences, 62–64

Dock, 51–53

File menu, 34

Finder menu, 84–86

Finder viewing modes, 82–84

folders and, 62–64, 87–88

menus *(continued)*

Go menu, 88–89

grouping items, 26

Help menu

keyboard shortcut, 19

overview, 18–21

Location menu, 252

opening in Dock, 51–53

overview, 25, 39

pop-up, 32–33, 87–88

pull-down, 38

search, 27

Services menu, 84–86

sharing, 27, 181–182

submenus, 42–43, 51–52

tagging, 27

Window menu, 36–38

merging calendars, 200

Messages app

communicating with, 288–292

overview, 47

sharing via, 181

metadata, 94–96

microphones, 221, 242, 387–389

Microsoft Word, 354

Migration Assistant app, 429–430

minimizing

keyboard shortcuts for, 36

windows, 28, 61

Mini-Player, 329

mirroring screens, 402–403

Mission Control

hot corners, 189–190

navigating in, 192–193

organizing windows with, 190–192

preferences, 187–189

modems, 250, 298

monitors, 16, 192

Monterey OS

benefits of using, 9

help, 18–21

kernel panic, 12–13

Library folder and, 139

overview, 8–9

packages, 158

powering on, 10–13

shutting down, 14–15

System folder and, 137

troubleshooting

Activity Monitor, 421–422

blue/black/gray screen of death, 12

booting, 435–437

crashes, 442

Essentials booklet, 10

First Aid button in Disk Utility, 425–426, 438–439

overview, 15–16

PRAM/NVRAM, 440–441

Recovery HD, 438–442

reinstalling OS, 441

Safe mode, 439–440

startup disks, 435–437

startup issues, 12–13

storage and, 442–444

updating, 414–415

version of, 13, 43

versions of, 13, 43

mounting disk, 426–427

mouse

preferences, 126–127

scrolling with, 30

using, 16–18

moving

emails, 274

folders, 165–166

UI elements, 35, 37

MP3 file format, 339

Music app

keyboard shortcuts, 328–329, 331, 333–336

listening to radio, 332–334

overview, 48, 326–330

playlists, 334–338

songs

adding, 330–332

burning to CDs, 338–339

filtering, 333

view modes, 333–334

muting emails, 274

N

naming

files and folders, 167–168

lists, 205

voice memos, 243

navigating
  Calendar, 198–199
  disclosure triangles, 34, 79
  Dock, 24
  exiting fullscreen mode, 28
  Finder, 69–70
  Launchpad, 194
  Maps app, 225–227, 229
  Mission Control, 192–193
  in Safari, 254–255
  scrolling, 30, 120
  between tabs, 37
  between windows, 27
nested folders, 134–135
networking
  blocking connections, 416
  connecting
    to Internet, 250–253
    to remote computer, 314–318
  Ethernet, 294, 298–299
  file sharing and, 294–295, 299–300
  home office, 295–297
  Migration Assistant and, 429–430
  passwords and, 318–320
  printing and, 368
  sharing and
    files, 294–295
    folders, 306–311
    Internet connectivity, 321–322
    screens, 320–321
    settings, 299–300
  unsharing and, 314
  users
    features for, 400–401
    folder for, 133
    managing, 302–306
    Migration Assistant and, 429–430
    overview, 300–302
    switching between, 401
News app, 48, 239–241
non-volatile RAM (NVRAM), 440–441
Notes app
  overview, 48, 211–215
  sharing via, 181
notifications

Calendar, 203
  muting, 290
  overview, 207–211
numbered lists, 213
NVRAM (non-volatile RAM), 440–441

O

opening
  apps, 52
  files
    with apps, 154–156
    overview, 150–154
    without apps, 180
  icons, 54–57
  keyboard shortcut for, 34, 151
  menus in Dock icons, 51–53
  System Preferences app, 114
  windows, 34–35
organizing
  desktops
    with stacks, 97–101
    windows into, 190–192
  files, 159–160
OS. *See* Monterey OS
Other World Computing website, 458–459

P

package icon, 158
pages
  options for, 369, 372–374
  printing, 364, 368–369
panes, resizing, 25, 35
Parallels software, 9, 402
parameter RAM (PRAM), 440–441
parent alias, 76
Partition button (Disk Utility), 424–425
partitioning drives, 424–425
passwords
  adding to Keychain, 427–429
  creating, 318–320
  FileVault and, 406
  screen savers and, 118
  as security measure, 417
  System Preferences and, 429

pasting
  files and folders, 175–176
  overview, 172
path bar, 68
pausing recordings, 242
PDF. *See* Portable Document Format
permissions
  overview, 308–309
  settings for, 311–314
Photo Booth app, 349–351
photos
  browsing for, 276
  managing, 351
  taking
    with other device, 383–386
    with webcam, 349–350
Photos app
  overview, 47
  Quick Look and, 182
picture-in-picture videos, 344
pinning, 292
plain text file, 357
playing
  songs, 218, 326–327
  videos, 342–344
  voice memos, 242
playlists, 334–339
plug-ins, 185
Podcasts app, 48, 348–349
pop-up menus, 32–33, 87–88, 119
Portable Document Format (PDF)
  annotating, 287
  app for viewing files, 351–352
  creating without app, 105–106
  importing to Books, 347
  options for in Preview, 374–375
  saving, 352
portrait orientation, 369, 373
ports, 294–295, 453–454
powering on
  button for, 10
  in Safe mode, 439–440
  troubleshooting, 435–437
PRAM (parameter RAM), 440–441
preferences. *See* System Preferences app
Preferences folder, 140

Preview app, 351–352, 374–375
printing
  choosing printers, 371
  directions, 231
  files, 370–374
  notes, 213
  overview, 363–364
  page setup and, 368–369
  PDF options, 374–375
  photos, 351
  saving and, 352
  setting up, 364–368
  setting up printers, 364–368
  sharing and, 368
  sharing printers, 322
  in TextEdit, 357
privacy. *See* security and privacy
processes, 421–422
programming calculator, 420
prohibitory sign, 12
Project Gutenberg, 347
protocols, 295
Public folder, 138, 306–307
public transportation directions, 232
pull-down menus, 38

Q
question mark
  in folders, 12
  in icons, 48
Quick Actions, 101–106
Quick Look
  Mail and, 286
  opening files with, 152–153
  overview, 180–183
  using to open files in trash, 50
Quick Note, 215
QuickTime Player, 342–343

R
radio, listening to, 332–334
radio buttons, 32
RAM. *See* random-access memory
random-access memory (RAM), 440–441, 450–451
recent items

accessing, 43
in Dock submenu, 52
settings for, 62
recording
audio, 241–244
screens, 108, 434
Recovery HD, 436, 438–442
reformatting disks, 426
Refurb Tracker website, 459
reinstalling OS, 441
Reminders app
overview, 48, 203–207
sharing via, 182
renaming
files and folders, 167–168
lists, 205
voice memos, 243
replying to emails, 273
reprinting, 372–373
resizing
Dock, 58
panes, 25, 35
windows, 28, 32
resolution, changing, 450
restarting computer, 44
restoring
emails, 278
files and folders, 49–50
with Time Machine, 408–409
right-clicking
overview, 17
trackpads, 40
routers, 298
rules for email, 284–286

S

Safari app
bookmarking, 257–258
favorites, 258
Help Center, 260
links, 257
overview, 47, 253–254
Reader view, 259
Reading list, 258–259
settings for, 259
sidebar, 255–259

tabs, 256–257
toolbar, 254–255
Safe mode, 439–440
saving
files
duplicating vs., 148–150
steps for, 141–148
PDFs, 352
printing and
PDFs, 352
settings, 374
scaling pages, 369
scanning
Continuity Camera and, 385–386
for viruses and malware, 414
scientific calculator, 420
Screen Flash, 350
screen savers
passwords and, 417
preferences, 117–118
Screen Time app, 215–216
screens
additional, 451–452
capturing, 107–108, 431–434
changing resolution of, 450
locking, 44
mirroring, 402–403
monitors, 16, 192
recording, 108, 434
sharing, 320–321
Script Editor, 392–394
scrolling
customizing behavior of, 120
in Finder, 29–30
in Maps, 227
overview, 27
searching
for bookmarks, 257
for contacts, 291
for files, 132
in Finder, 71
for parent alias, 76
Spotlight
calculations and, 420
overview, 183–187
Siri and, 219
for startup disk, 436

secondary-clicking
  overview, 17
  trackpads, 40
security and privacy
  blocking connections, 416
  encryption, 253, 412
  Internet connection and, 252–253
  location and, 418
  locking files with FileVault, 416–417
  malware, 412–414
  passwords
    adding to Keychain, 427–429
    creating, 318–320
    FileVault and, 406
    screen savers and, 118
    as security measure, 417
    System Preferences and, 429
  report feature, 255
  Screen Time and, 216
  settings for, 417–418
  software updates and, 414–415
  threats, 412–415
  viruses, 412–414
  VPNs, 252–253
selecting
  check boxes and, 34
  contacts, 265
  files, 80
  keyboard shortcuts, 151
  text, 355–356
sending emails, 276
Services menu, 84–86
settings. See System Preferences app
Setup Assistant app, 251
Shared folder, 307
SharePlay feature, 269–270
sharing
  calendars, 200
  disks, 307
  files, 294–295
    via AirDrop, 181, 296–297
    via MailDrop, 287
    via Quick Look, 70
  folders, 306–311
  guides in Maps, 229
  with iCloud, 182, 287

Internet connection, 321–322
  lists, 206–207
  media
    remotely, 322
    via FaceTime, 269–270
  menu for, 27, 181–182
  notes, 213
  photos, 351
  printing and, 368
  recordings, 243
  screens, 291, 320–321
  settings for, 299–300
  URLs, 255, 257
  via Bluetooth, 127, 322, 399
  videos, 343
sheets, 131, 144–145
shortcut menus
  Action icon and, 41
  in menu bar, 39–41
  right-clicking and, 17
  Services menu, 84–86
shortcuts
  app for, 244–245
  preferences, 124–125
shutting down computer, 14–15, 44
sidebars
  adding folders to, 90
  FaceTime, 269
  Finder, 27, 92, 120
  keyboard shortcuts, 69
  Maps, 228–230
  Music, 328
  News, 240
  Preview, 351–352
  recently used files and, 132
  Reminders, 205
  Safari, 255–259
  showing/hiding, 205
Sidecar feature, 452
signatures, 103–104, 283–284
Siri
  calculations and, 420
  overview, 217–221
  playing songs with, 326–327
Six Colors website, 459–460
sketching tool, 102

Sleep mode, 14, 44, 417
slideshows
    in Mail, 286
    mode, 182–183
smart functionality
    folders, 162–164
    groups, 266
    inboxes, 281–282
    playlists, 334–338
Smashwords website, 347
solid-state drives (SSD), 452–453
songs
    adding to Music, 330–332
    copying to CD, 338–339
    playing, 218, 342–343
    sharing, 269–270
sorting
    disks, 63
    files, 70, 80, 83
    folders, 63
    icons and, 70, 115
    indicator, 80
    stacks functionality, 100–101
spaces, 190–193
spam, 273, 279
spell-checker, 358
Split View, 28–29
spoofing, 414
Spotlight feature
    calculations and, 420
    overview, 183–187
    Siri and, 219
spring-loaded folders, 161–162
SSD (solid-state drives), 452–453
stacks
    defined, 45
    displaying items as, 63
    managing, 100–101
    organizing desktops with, 97–101
startup screen, 11–12
status bar, 68
Sticky Keys feature, 397
Stocks app, 236–238
storage, 442–444, 453–454
streaming music, 326

subfolders, 158–160
sub-mailboxes, 280–281
submenus, 42–43, 51–52
subscription services
    Apple Arcade, 382
    Apple Music, 326–327
subtasks, 206
SuperDuper! app, 436
surge protectors, 15
swiping gestures, 191, 194
symbols (text), 276, 359
syncing
    contacts, 262, 267
    notes, 213–214
    via iCloud, 262, 267, 429
System folder, 137
System Information app, 430
System Preferences app
    Bluetooth, 127, 399
    Desktop tab, 116–117
    icon in, 114
    Input Sources tab, 125–126
    Internet connection settings, 251–252
    keyboard, 122–126
    microphone, 242
    Mission Control and, 187–189
    mouse, 126–127
    opening, 114
    output and input options, 130
    overview, 48, 113–115
    passwords, 429
    screen savers, 117–118
    Shortcuts tab, 124–125
    Siri and, 220–221
    sound effects, 129–130
    Text tab, 123–124
    trackpads, 127–129, 191
    UI, 118–121

T

tabs
    Finder, 37–38
    grouping, 254, 256–257
    options for, 120
    overview, 32

tabs *(continued)*
  Safari, 256–257
  Screen Time, 216
  System Preferences, 116–117, 123–126
tagging
  files, 70
  menu for, 27
  notes, 214–215
  pane for, 91–92
  removing, 92
TCP/IP protocol, 295
tech-support, 441
Ten Thumbs Typing Tutor website, 448
Terminal app, 430
text
  adding to images, 103
  cursors for, 167
  emojis, 276, 292, 359
  fields for entering, 33
  file formats for, 354, 357
  formatting, 214, 276, 355–358
  keyboard shortcuts for, 123
  preferences, 123–124
  special characters, 161, 276, 292, 359
  typing using voice, 387
  wrapping, 359
text messages, 289–290
Text to Speech feature, 390–392
TextEdit app
  adding graphics to, 358–359
  creating document, 354–355
  in Dock, 58
  formatting in, 355–358
  printing in, 373
3D maps, 226
Thunderbolt port, 453–454
TidBITS website, 456–457
tiling windows, 36
Time Machine app
  backing-up data with, 406–409
  overview, 16
  versions of files, 143
toolbars
  in active window, 32
  elements in, 26
  Finder, 68–71

Mail, 272–274, 276
  Safari, 254–255
trackpads
  accessing Mission Control, 191
  creating signatures with, 104
  drawing and, 103
  Launchpad and, 194
  preferences, 127–129, 191
  right-clicking with, 40
  scrolling with, 30
traffic information (Maps), 232
transferring files, 291
Trash app, 48–50
trimming
  videos, 104–105, 343
  voice memos, 243–244
tri-state check boxes, 34
troubleshooting
  Activity Monitor, 421–422
  blue/black/gray screen of death, 12
  booting, 435–437
  crashes, 442
  Essentials booklet, 10
  First Aid button in Disk Utility, 425–426, 438–439
  overview, 15–16
  PRAM/NVRAM, 440–441
  Recovery HD, 438–442
  reinstalling OS, 441
  Safe mode, 439–440
  startup disks, 435–437
  startup issues, 12–13
  storage and, 442–444
turning on computer, 10–13
TV app, 48, 343–344
typeface, 359–361
typing, improving, 448–449

U

UI. *See* user interface
undo command, 49
unflagging emails, 273
uninstalling apps, 195
Universal Clipboard, 175–176
Universal Control, 404
universal serial bus (USB) port, 453–454

Unix operating system, 9

Unmount/Mount button (Disk Utility), 426–427

Unofficial Apple Weblog website, 457

unplugging computers, 15–16

unsubscribing from emails, 287

updating OS and apps, 414–415

USB (universal serial bus) port, 453–454

user interface (UI). *See also* cursors; desktops; Dock; menus; windows

  check boxes, 33–34

  customizing, 90–93

  dark mode, 380–381

  disclosure triangles, 34, 79

  login screen, 11

  menu bar, 39–41

  navigating, 27, 37

  preferences, 118–121

  sidebars

    adding folders to, 90

    FaceTime, 269

    in Finder, 27, 92, 120

    keyboard shortcuts, 69

    Maps, 227–230

    Music, 328

    News, 240

    Preview, 351–352

    recently used files and, 132

    Reminders, 205

    Safari, 255–259

    showing/hiding, 205

  Split View, 28–29

  tabs

    Finder, 37–38

    grouping, 254, 256–257

    options for, 120

    overview, 32

    Safari, 256–257

    Screen Time, 216

    System Preferences, 116–117, 123–126

  text-entry fields, 33

  toolbars

    in active window, 32

    elements in, 26

    Finder, 68–71

    Mail, 272–274, 276

    Safari, 254–255

users

  features for, 400–401

  folder for, 133

  managing, 302–306

  Migration Assistant and, 429–430

  overview, 300–302

  switching between, 401

V

vCard file format, 263, 278

videos

  editing, 104–105

  playing, 342–344

  sharing, 343

  trimming, 104–105, 343

viewing modes

  alphabetical, 115

  app-specific

    Calendar, 198–199

    Maps, 225–226

    Music, 329–330

    Safari, 259

  category, 115

  columns, 77–78

  dark mode, 380–381

  for folders, 64

  gallery, 81–82

  icon, 70, 79, 146

  lists, 79–81, 146

virtual assistant, 217–221

virtual private networks (VPNs), 252

VirtualBox, 402

viruses, 412–414

voice commands

  calculations and, 420

  playing songs with, 326–327

  Siri, 217–221

Voice Control feature, 388–389

Voice Memos app, 241–244

voice messages, 291

VoiceOver feature, 389–390

Volume +/- button (Disk Utility), 422–424

volumes

  defined, 68

  partitions vs., 424

VPNs (virtual private networks), 252

W

Wacom website, 400
walking directions (Maps), 231
webcams, 349–350
websites
  adding passwords for, 428
  adding to Dock, 56, 59
  Apple, 458–459
  AppleWorld.Today, 457
  bookmarking, 257
  iMore, 457
  Mac Observer, 415, 456
  Macworld, 456
  navigating, 255
  Other World Computing, 458–459
  preferences, 253–254
  Refurb Tracker, 459
  sharing, 255, 257
  Six Colors, 459–460
  Spotlight and, 186–187
  TidBITS, 456–457
  view modes, 258–259
  Wirecutter, 457–458
widgets, 209
Wi-Fi. *See* Internet connections
wiggling cursors, 18
windows
  active/inactive
    clicking on, 30–32
    icons and, 46
    removing app from Dock and, 57
  clicking icons and, 46
  closing, 26–29, 31, 34–35
  commands for, 36–38
  customizing appearance of, 120
  cycling through, 36
  desktop vs., 24
  dialog, 32–34
  drop shadow of, 32
  expanding, 26–29
  force quitting, 43–44
  keyboard shortcuts for, 36
  manipulating, 34–38
  menu for, 36–38
  merging, 37–38
  minimizing, 26–29, 61
  moving, 35
  opening, 34–35
  organizing into desktops, 190–192
  overview, 25
  panes, 25, 35
  parts of, 25–27
  resizing, 35
  scrolling, 29–30
  show list as separate, 205
  splitting, 28–29
  starting up with same, 15
  switching between, 188–190
  tabs and, 37
  tiling, 36
  title of, 26–27
  zooming, 28
Windows OS, 9, 401–402
Wirecutter website, 457–458
wireless hardware, 127
word-processing app, 58
writing features, 400

Z

zooming
  accessibility feature, 397
  on images, 103
  on maps, 227
  in text files, 357

About the Author

Bob LeVitus, often referred to as "Dr. Mac," has written or co-written more than 90 popular computer books, with millions of copies sold worldwide. In addition to co-authoring 14 editions of iPhone For Dummies, he has written versions of OS X For Dummies and macOS For Dummies covering every cat- and California locale-named operating system Apple has released since System 7 (all for John Wiley & Sons, Inc., of course).

Bob has penned the popular Dr. Mac column for the *Houston Chronicle* since 1996 and the Dr. Mac's Rants & Raves column for *The Mac Observer* for almost as long. And he's written thousands of articles, reviews, and columns for dozens of newspapers and magazines over his 30+ year career.

Bob is known for his Apple expertise, trademark humorous style, and ability to translate techie jargon into usable and fun advice for regular folks. He presented more than 100 workshops at Macworld Expos in the United States and abroad, given Macworld Expo keynote addresses in three countries, and offered his own Macintosh training seminars in many U.S. cities. (He also won the Macworld Expo MacJeopardy World Championship three times in a row before retiring.)

From 1986 to 1989 Bob served as editor-in-chief of the first desktop-published Mac magazine, The MACazine. From 1989 to 1997, he was a contributing editor and columnist for MacUser magazine, writing the Help Folder, Beating the System, Personal Best, and Game Room columns at various times.

Prior to giving his life over to computers, Bob worked in advertising at Kresser/Craig/D.I.K., a Los Angeles advertising agency and marketing consultancy, and its subsidiary, L & J Research. He holds a B.S. in marketing from California State University.

Dedication

For the ninety-second time (I counted), this book is dedicated to the only woman I'll ever love — my wife and best friend Lisa, who taught me everything I know about pretty much everything I know (except technology).

You are still the best!

And, again for the ninety-second time, this book is dedicated to my kids (now adults) Allison and Jacob, who love their Apple gadgets almost as much as I love them (my kids, of course, not my gadgets).

Author's Acknowledgments

A tip of the hat once again to my super-agent, Carole "Swifty" Jelen. She has represented me for more than 30 years and is still the world's greatest literary agent, at least in my humble opinion. That's probably why she's the only literary agent I've ever had.

Special thanks to everyone at Apple who helped me turn this book around in record time — I couldn't have done it without you. And super, extra-special super-duper thanks to Keri Walker — after almost 30 years working with Keri she's still the nicest, classiest, and hippest PR person ever.

Big-time thanks to the gang at Wiley: Steve "Is It Done Yet" Hayes; my absolutely superb editor, Susan Pink; my terrific tech editor, Guy Hart-Davis, and everyone else at Wiley who put their heart and soul into getting this book to you.

Thanks also to my family and friends for putting up with my cranky demeanor during my all-too-lengthy hibernation sessions during this book's gestation.

Super-special thanks to Interstellar BBQ, Hops & Grain's The One They Call Zoe Ale, Black's Barbecue, Torchy's Tacos, Bombay Street Food, and Saccone's Pizza for sustenance.

And last (but certainly not least), thanks to you, gentle reader, for buying my book.

Publisher's Acknowledgments

Executive Editor: Steve Hayes

Project Editor: Susan Pink

Copy Editor: Susan Pink

Technical Editor: Guy Hart-Davis

Sr. Editorial Assistant: Cherie Case

Proofreader: Debbye Butler

Production Editor: Mohammed Zafar Ali

Cover Image: © Alexander Spatari/Getty Images

Leverage the power

Dummies is the global leader in the reference category and one of the most trusted and highly regarded brands in the world. No longer just focused on books, customers now have access to the dummies content they need in the format they want. Together we'll craft a solution that engages your customers, stands out from the competition, and helps you meet your goals.

Advertising & Sponsorships

Connect with an engaged audience on a powerful multimedia site, and position your message alongside expert how-to content. Dummies.com is a one-stop shop for free, online information and know-how curated by a team of experts.

- Targeted ads
- Video
- Email Marketing
- Microsites
- Sweepstakes sponsorship

20 MILLION PAGE VIEWS EVERY SINGLE MONTH

15 MILLION UNIQUE VISITORS PER MONTH

43% OF ALL VISITORS ACCESS THE SITE VIA THEIR MOBILE DEVICES

700,000 NEWSLETTER SUBSCRIPTIONS TO THE INBOXES OF

300,000 UNIQUE INDIVIDUALS EVERY WEEK

PERSONAL ENRICHMENT

 **Staying Sharp**
9781119187790
USA $26.00
CAN $31.99
UK £19.99

 **Facebook**
Carolyn Abram
9781119179030
USA $21.99
CAN $25.99
UK £16.99

Guitar
Mark Phillips
Jon Chappell
9781119293354
USA $24.99
CAN $29.99
UK £17.99

Investing
Eric Tyson, MBA
9781119293347
USA $22.99
CAN $27.99
UK £16.99

Beekeeping
Howland Blackiston
9781119310068
USA $22.99
CAN $27.99
UK £16.99

 **Digital Photography**
Julie Adair King
9781119235606
USA $24.99
CAN $29.99
UK £17.99

 **Meditation**
Stephan Bodian
9781119251163
USA $24.99
CAN $29.99
UK £17.99

 Pregnancy
ALL-IN-ONE
6 Books in one!
9781119235491
USA $26.99
CAN $31.99
UK £19.99

 Samsung Galaxy S7
Bill Hughes
9781119279952
USA $24.99
CAN $29.99
UK £17.99

 iPhone
Edward C. Baig
Bob "Dr. Mac" LeVitus
9781119283133
USA $24.99
CAN $29.99
UK £17.99

Crocheting
Karen Manthey
Susan Brittain
9781119287117
USA $24.99
CAN $29.99
UK £16.99

 Nutrition
Carol Ann Rinzler
9781119130246
USA $22.99
CAN $27.99
UK £16.99

PROFESSIONAL DEVELOPMENT

Windows 10
Andy Rathbone
9781119311041
USA $24.99
CAN $29.99
UK £17.99

AutoCAD
Bill Fane
9781119255796
USA $39.99
CAN $47.99
UK £27.99

Excel 2016
Greg Harvey, PhD
9781119293439
USA $26.99
CAN $31.99
UK £19.99

QuickBooks 2017
9781119281467
USA $26.99
CAN $31.99
UK £19.99

macOS Sierra
Bob "Dr. Mac" LeVitus
9781119280651
USA $29.99
CAN $35.99
UK £21.99

LinkedIn
Joel Elad, MBA
9781119251132
USA $24.99
CAN $29.99
UK £17.99

Windows 10
ALL-IN-ONE
10 Books
Woody Leonhard
9781119310563
USA $34.00
CAN $41.99
UK £24.99

SharePoint 2016
Rosemarie Withee
Ken Withee
9781119181705
USA $29.99
CAN $35.99
UK £21.99

Fundamental Analysis
Matt Krantz
9781119263593
USA $26.99
CAN $31.99
UK £19.99

Networking
Doug Lowe
9781119257769
USA $29.99
CAN $35.99
UK £21.99

Office 2016
Wallace Wang
9781119293477
USA $26.99
CAN $31.99
UK £19.99

Office 365
Rosemarie Withee
Ken Withee
Jennifer Reed
9781119265313
USA $24.99
CAN $29.99
UK £17.99

Salesforce.com
Liz Kao
Jon Paz
9781119239314
USA $29.99
CAN $35.99
UK £21.99

Coding
Nikhil Abraham
9781119293323
USA $29.99
CAN $35.99
UK £21.99

dummies.com

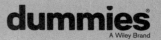
dummies
A Wiley Brand

Learning Made Easy

ACADEMIC

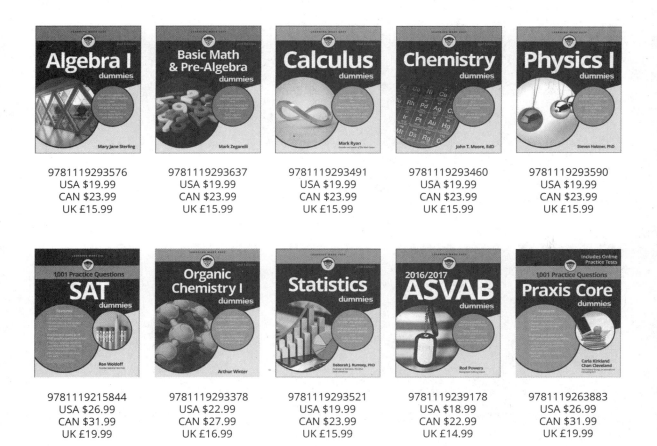

Algebra I dummies
Mary Jane Sterling
9781119293576
USA $19.99
CAN $23.99
UK £15.99

Basic Math & Pre-Algebra dummies
Mark Zegarelli
9781119293637
USA $19.99
CAN $23.99
UK £15.99

Calculus dummies
Mark Ryan
9781119293491
USA $19.99
CAN $23.99
UK £15.99

Chemistry dummies
John T. Moore, EdD
9781119293460
USA $19.99
CAN $23.99
UK £15.99

Physics I dummies
Steven Holzner, PhD
9781119293590
USA $19.99
CAN $23.99
UK £15.99

SAT dummies
1,001 Practice Questions
Ron Woldoff
9781119215844
USA $26.99
CAN $31.99
UK £19.99

Organic Chemistry I dummies
Arthur Winter
9781119293378
USA $22.99
CAN $27.99
UK £16.99

Statistics dummies
Deborah J. Rumsey, PhD
9781119293521
USA $19.99
CAN $23.99
UK £15.99

2016/2017 ASVAB dummies
Rod Powers
9781119239178
USA $18.99
CAN $22.99
UK £14.99

Praxis Core dummies
1,001 Practice Questions
Carla Kirkland
Chan Cleveland
9781119263883
USA $26.99
CAN $31.99
UK £19.99

Available Everywhere Books Are Sold

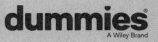

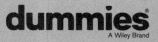